SEAGULL ONE

UNIVERSITY PRESS OF FLORIDA

Florida A&M University, Tallahassee
Florida Atlantic University, Boca Raton
Florida Gulf Coast University, Ft. Myers
Florida International University, Miami
Florida State University, Tallahassee
New College of Florida, Sarasota
University of Central Florida, Orlando
University of Florida, Gainesville
University of North Florida, Jacksonville
University of South Florida, Tampa
University of West Florida, Pensacola

SEAGULL ONE

The Amazing True Story
of Brothers to the Rescue

Lily Prellezo in collaboration with José Basulto

University Press of Florida
Gainesville · Tallahassee · Tampa · Boca Raton
Pensacola · Orlando · Miami · Jacksonville · Ft. Myers · Sarasota

Copyright 2010 by Lily Prellezo and José Basulto
Printed in the United States of America on acid-free, recycled paper
All rights reserved

15 14 13 12 11 10   6 5 4 3 2 1

Library of Congress Cataloging-in-Publication Data
Prellezo, Lily.
Seagull One : the amazing true story of Brothers to the Rescue /
Lily Prellezo in collaboration with José Basulto.
p. cm.
Includes bibliographical references and index.
ISBN 978-0-8130-3490-4 (alk. paper)
1. Brothers to the Rescue, Incorporated. 2. Basulto, José, 1940–
3. Search and rescue operations—Florida. 4. Cuba—Refugees.
I. Basulto, José, 1940– II. Title.
TL553.8.P73 2010
362.87'81097291—dc22   2010007797

Frontispiece: Painting by Roberto Cernunda

The University Press of Florida is the scholarly publishing
agency for the State University System of Florida, comprising
Florida A&M University, Florida Atlantic University, Florida
Gulf Coast University, Florida International University, Florida
State University, New College of Florida, University of Central
Florida, University of Florida, University of North Florida,
University of South Florida, and University of West Florida.

University Press of Florida
15 Northwest 15th Street
Gainesville, FL 32611-2079
http://www.upf.com

For my father, José Luis "Pepe" Fernández. He loved Cuba.

LILY PRELLEZO

*For my wife, Rita, for her patience and support at all
times, and for my children and grandchildren.*

JOSÉ BASULTO

*It is easier to lead men to combat, stirring up their passion,
than to restrain them and direct them toward the patient labors of peace.*

ANDRÉ GIDE, AUTHOR AND NOBEL LAUREATE

Contents

Preface xi

The Beginning: The Seagull and the Rafter 1

1. The Call from Billy 5

2. Gugú 8

3. The Idea 18

4. The Brotherhood 23

5. The First Rescue 33

6. The Lady Pilot 39

7. Pilots, Protocol, and Planes 44

8. The First Accident 51

9. Balseros 58

10. Acts of God 74

11. Acts of Man 84

12. Brothers to the Rescue 92

13. Close Calls 104

14. A New Home 111

15. Rafter to the Rescue 114

16. Ripples 140

17. City of Rafts 148

18. Guantánamo 158

19. Protest in Miami 166

20. Ashes 169

21. Love Is in the Air 173

22. Nonviolence 176

23. Thirteen Minutes over Havana 182

24. I Am the Change 190

25. Meet Me in Havana 199

26. Flight Plans 204

27. Shoot-Down 211

28. Havana Air Traffic Control 224

29. Brothers Down 230

30. Survivors 239

31. Memorial 247

32. We Will Fly Again 253

33. Backlash 259

34. Truth and Justice 265

35. Anniversaries 274

36. Indictment 281

37. Spies, Wasps, and the Queen of Cuba 286

38. Letting Go 292

39. Seagull One 297

40. José Basulto 301

Sources 303

Acknowledgments 315

Index 317

Preface

There was a special moment in Miami during the 1990s when the entire community came together, when people of nineteen nationalities united as one brotherhood to help another community of people suffering ninety miles away. We did it because we *are* our brother's keepers. Thousands of people stepped forward to board a plane, captain a cutter, film an event, write a check, save a life. We were all Brothers to the Rescue. It would take volumes of recorded history to mention us all by name, as we well deserve, but each and every one of our spirits has left an imprint in the few hundred pages of this book, this story, our story.

Thank you, my brother Billy, for making the call. Thank you to everyone else for answering the call. Thank you to all the pilots who risked their lives every week to save the life of someone they would rarely, if ever, meet. Special thanks to those pilots who donated their own planes, paid for their own fuel, and prayed for us through every mission. My deepest appreciation to all the observers: your pairs of eyes saved lives. Thank you to the U.S. Coast Guard for being the first to welcome so many to freedom. Thank you to the press—radio, television, newspapers, magazines—from every country in the world who testified to what was happening just ninety miles away from the freest nation on earth. Brothers to the Rescue would, literally, never have gotten off the ground without you.

Thank you to the funeral homes who gave dignity to our dead rafters. Thanks to the volunteers who welcomed those found alive, giving them food, clothing, shelter—and hope. Thank you to the writers, printers, poets, authors, publicists, technicians, and mechanics who helped us stay on task. Thank you to those who provided radios, phones, electronics, life vests, shoes, and toys that brought smiles to detained children.

All of you provided for our every financial need, from the retired elderly who gave five dollars a month, to those who sponsored fund-raisers and others who gifted us with planes. Thank you to the recording artists, the singers and songwriters, and the performers who gave of their talent to increase our treasure. Thank you to those who fed our pilots, volunteers, and rafters—from the well-known restaurants to the mothers who made *arroz con pollo*.

Thank you to every *balsero* who showed us what courage is all about. Thank you to the dissidents who bravely stayed behind to reclaim their heritage. My greatest appreciation to the lovers of nonviolence, to the believers in "I am the change," to those who put down their weapons to fight the good fight. Thank you to all the exile organizations who supported Brothers for so many years, to the elected officials who lifted our voices to the highest authorities in the land, to the attorneys and judges who stood on the side of truth and justice. My gratitude extends to the police and local government officials who protected and guarded and watched over our brotherhood.

Thank you, Lily, for telling everyone's story, for weaving together such a magical moment in time.

Thank you to the Alejandre, Costa, and de la Peña families, and to Eva Barbas, for your unwavering strength and tremendous witness to the world after losing Armando, Carlos, Mario, and Pablo. Thank you for continuing your quest for truth and justice.

Thank you to my sons, José, Felipe, and Alberto; my daughters, Ana and Monica; my brother, Alberto; and all their families, for putting up with me some of the time, but most of the time, for doing without me. Thank you, Rita, for your support, patience, steadfastness, and unconditional love.

I thank God for giving me every single one of you. We were—we still are—Brothers to the Rescue.

José Basulto

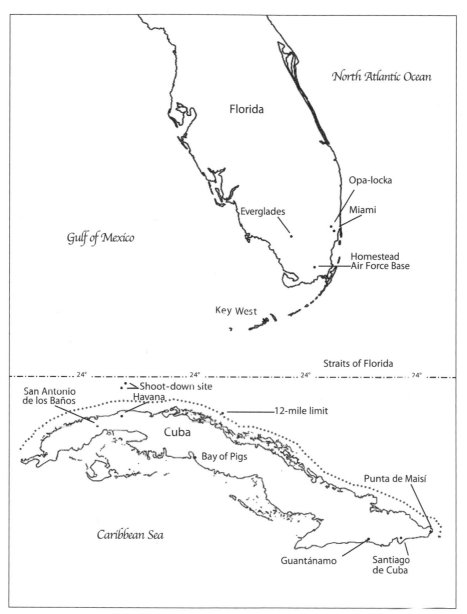

North Atlantic Ocean

Florida

Gulf of Mexico

Opa-locka

Miami

Everglades

Homestead
Air Force Base

Key West

Straits of Florida

24°   24°   24°   24°

Shoot-down site

San Antonio
de los Baños

Havana

12-mile limit

Cuba

Bay of Pigs

Punta de Maisí

Caribbean Sea

Guantánamo

Santiago
de Cuba

Map by Oscar Vidal, Eagle Lithographers, Inc.

The Beginning

The Seagull and the Rafter

History is a vast early warning system.

Norman Cousins

The seagull was the first to see him.

February in the Florida Straits carried a cool ocean breeze, but not enough to refresh his feverish body. The sun seemed to burn deliberately, and he was unable to shade his half-open eyes, his naked body lying in the fetal position with his back huddled against the side of the raft. The female gull soared overhead, stretching out her wings to their full three-foot span and flying protectively over him in circles, offering momentary relief from the sun when she made a low pass: a breath of relief, then the sun again, a breath of relief, and then the sun again.

Five long days ago, Ernesto Hernández, Gregorio Pérez Ricardo, and Gregorio's cousin, Omar Pérez, had left Cuba full of hope. Their journey began at midnight on February 15, 1990, onboard a six-foot raft carved from plastic foam and packed with dreams of reaching the United States. They would start their own business. They could send money back to Gregorio's parents, who had known nothing of his escape. Soon they would welcome the rest of the family to America.

On the third day, the bread, crackers, and water were gone, and Gregorio's cousin began hallucinating. Thinking he had reached land, the seventeen-year-old stepped out of the boat and into his death, leaving Ernesto and Gregorio grieving and holding on to life.

Drinking the blood of fish or the liquid in their eyes was a meager substitute for water, but on the second day they lost their only fishing line. Ernesto was too weak to fish with his hands, and Gregorio was fading. Gregorio's urine the night before had been dark, almost the color of blood. His kidneys were failing.

The seagull was a good sign, the bird of hope for mariners, promising a nearby shore. Upon seeing them, rafters knew the end of the journey was in sight. They offered up their prayers, crossing themselves in thanksgiving.

Gregorio desperately needed those petitions answered. He had not spoken anything that made sense in two days. Gregorio's lips remained caked half-open, without enough saliva in his mouth to wet them, let alone utter a word. His tongue protruded, heavy and dry, from his mouth, as if gasping for any moisture in the air. In his dazed state, he might have confused the seagull's wings for an angel—or *could it be the Virgin Mary?* The Virgin of Charity, Patroness of Cuba, had appeared to three fishermen four hundred years ago and saved them from the tempest. She was the protector of mariners. Was it she?

A mile away from the raft, and eight miles off the coast of Islamorada in the Florida Keys, a U.S. Coast Guard cutter was making its regular rounds that February day, patrolling a tiny part of the 1.8 million square miles of Sector 7. It was the largest Coast Guard coverage area in the United States, and within those square miles, Sector Key West was the busiest area for boat people leaving Cuba, Haiti, and the Dominican Republic. The busiest for drug trafficking, too. The task at hand was like keeping watch over a swimming pool roughly the size of Florida.

Perhaps it was the peculiar behavior of the seagull or the motion of the strange hull bobbing in the water that caught the attention of the Coast Guard. Two of the officers lowered one of their motorized Zodiacs into the ocean, climbed in, and sped over to the wayward vessel. As they approached they realized what it was: a raft constructed from a hollowed-out piece of Styrofoam and wrapped in strips of canvas.

At this point, Ernesto probably did not care who it was that approached them, even if they were Cuban officials. He just wanted someone to save his brother-in-law. He sat on the edge of the raft, steadying himself with his left hand, and waved his right arm back and forth, struggling for their attention.

The noise of the Zodiac and the activity on the water most likely triggered the seagull back to shore. As the officers neared the raft, they noticed one man waving and another man lying down. The waves made by the approaching Zodiac rocked the makeshift ark just enough to unsteady

Ernesto's exhausted body, and he fell in next to his brother-in-law. Gregorio's naked body flinched.

The Coast Guard cutter followed close behind, and one of the officers onboard took out a video camera. For many years the Coast Guard had been filming random interceptions and rescues at sea. Little did they imagine that this routine video clip would be broadcast nationwide that evening.

One officer swung his legs over the Zodiac and stepped into the raft. He struggled to understand Ernesto as he spoke to him in Spanish, gesturing wildly, pointing to his brother-in-law Gregorio. He patted Ernesto on the shoulder, a universal gesture of reassurance, and gave him a life vest.

Seeing Gregorio lying naked in the fetal position was surely unsettling. This other man was not a man at all, but a boy, maybe fifteen years old. Gregorio's eyes were neither open nor closed, but almost frozen in a stare. His lips were cracked and dry, the skin on his face taut against his cheekbones. His dehydrated skin sank into his bony limbs. The officer wrapped Gregorio's body in a white blanket. He did not give him a life vest. He attempted to give him a little water, just drops, to see if he would react, but the boy could not swallow.

The video would show the Coast Guard officer talking to Gregorio, whispering, pleading that he would be OK. He had made it to the land of freedom, if he could just hang on.

The officer cradled Gregorio's feverish, bony body close to his own. As he lifted him out of the raft, the teenager died in his arms.

Gregorio Pérez Ricardo was airlifted to Miami's Jackson Memorial Hospital and pronounced dead at 4:18 p.m. in the United States of America.

I

The Call from Billy

*The darkest places in hell are reserved for those who maintain
their neutrality in times of moral crisis.*

Attributed to Dante Alighieri

José Basulto sank into the plush sofa in the spacious family room of his
South Miami home and put his feet up on the coffee table. As he looked up
at the cathedral ceilings made of Florida pine, he let out a long sigh. It was
only Tuesday, but it had been an exhausting week already. He spent his days
as a developer of luxury homes in the pricey Cocoplum neighborhood of
Coral Gables, Florida, in the business of satisfying the needs of couples with
fewer and fewer children who needed bigger and better houses.

Basulto, fifty, was married to Rita María de Cárdenas, a forty-five-year-
old widowed mother of two daughters who had joined him and his three
young sons in 1977. His first marriage had ended in a bitter divorce and an
even uglier custody battle, in which he eventually won custody of his three
boys. The Basultos' thirteen-year marriage and their blended family had
remained loving and stable, even during the years when all five children
had been teenagers. Now all but one was out of college and on their own.
Basulto was very involved in local Cuban exile groups; Rita was a part-time
real estate agent.

He glanced down at his watch to see if it was time for the evening news
and smiled at his big gold Rolex, too flashy for his simple tastes and rarely
worn, an impulse item he bought on a dare while on vacation. He and Rita
had been vacationing in the Virgin Islands with friends, when Basulto and
his friend walked into the Little Switzerland shop in St. Thomas. The salesman behind the jewelry counter smiled at the two men and encouraged
them "just try it on." "If you buy one, I'll buy one," Basulto's friend tempted.
The two buddies slapped down their American Express cards and five min-

utes later walked away sporting gold Rolexes, giggling like two teenagers who had just bought cheap wine with a fake ID.

He forgot about the watch for a moment, and taking out a yellow legal pad and pen from the side table, started another list. He had legal pads all over the house, scattered in his office trailer at the job site, and under the car seat in his Mazda RX-7. All his lists started with the same top three items:

1. Start an exercise program.
2. Lose weight.
3. Read more.

Then the list would continue with the other items spinning in his "washing machine." That's the metaphor he used when he had a lot of things going on at once. The image was of the old Laundromat-style machines where you could see the clothes tossing about: there goes one sock, here's your pajama top, there's the beach towel, now the other sock. Constantly tossing around in a jumble, his ideas were momentarily grasped when he saw them in his mind's eye, then lost for a little while, only to return within seconds.

His thoughts turned to the plans for the coming weekend, which seemed so far away on a Tuesday evening. He and his friends were supposed to get in what his fellow flying buddies had dubbed a "$100 hamburger run" on his plane, a single-engine Cessna 172. It would cost them $100 in fuel to fly to nearby Naples or Sarasota on the west coast of Florida, just to have a hamburger. All for the love of flying, a love that began when he was eight years old.

The phone interrupted his thoughts and his list, temporarily stalled at number 3.

"Gugú, Billy's on the line," said Rita, walking into the family room. "He wants you to turn on the news." "Gugú" was his nickname, and not even his family members could recall when they started calling him that. The story went that those were his first words: "goo-goo."

William "Billy" Schuss, one of Basulto's closest friends, had just seen on the six o'clock news the images of Gregorio Pérez Ricardo, a rafter the same age as Billy's own son, dying in the arms of a Coast Guard agent. Like Basulto, Billy had three sons, and he had devoted his life to them and his wife, Maggie—a far cry from his own childhood. The son of an American father and a Cuban mother, Billy had never had a relationship with his own father because his parents had divorced when he was a baby. Watching Gregorio die in the arms of the Coast Guard agent, Billy was consumed by feelings of abandonment. He could not understand how Gregorio's father could have let him leave. Gregorio's death awakened a sense of urgency in Billy, a summons from a higher calling. So he telephoned his friend Basulto right away.

"We've got to do something, Gugú."

"You're right, Billy." Basulto could imagine Billy frowning on the other end of the line. At fifty-three, a few years older than Basulto, Billy had thick brown hair starting to go gray. His signature glower etched a permanent deep cleft between his eyebrows, piercing blue eyes on either side. It was rumored that Billy smiled—or rather, un-frowned—every so often.

Billy and Basulto had been friends since their days in the training camps of Guatemala, preparing for the Bay of Pigs invasion of Cuba in April 1961. Later, they had both worked for the CIA and served in the U.S. military.

Now the televised death of a fifteen-year-old had awakened a call to action in his friend, and he wanted Basulto's help. The rafters, the *balseros*, kept leaving Cuba, kept risking their lives in the treacherous waters of the Florida Straits.

"I'll call you back," he said.

Basulto looked up at the seven-by-nine-foot oil painting of Cuban patriot Manolín Guillot Castellano hanging in the family room at the highest point of their two-story home. A friend of Basulto's and a member of the Movimiento de Recuperación (MRR, the Revolutionary Recovery Movement, an underground movement against Castro), Guillot had hidden in the Basulto family home in Cuba after the failed Bay of Pigs invasion. He was sent before a firing squad in 1962. Artist Adelfa Cantelli was commissioned to paint his likeness for a bank opening. Years later, when the bank shut down, Basulto purchased it at an auction. It showed Guillot wrapped in a Cuban flag, bleeding from his head, his face distorted in agony.

Rita had disagreed with her husband about giving the oil canvas its present showcase in the family room. Guillot's anguished face loomed over the Basulto family day and night. Their daughters, Ana and Monica, called him "the bleeding Cuban," protesting, "Why does the bleeding Cuban have to be in the family room?" As Basulto hung up with Billy, Manolín Guillot stared down at him.

It did not look like the hamburger run was going to happen this weekend. Another project had just been tossed in Basulto's washing machine. The list on the yellow legal pad would have to wait.

2

Gugú

*Lots of times you have to pretend to join a parade in which
you're really not interested in order to get where you're going.*

Christopher Morley

José Jesús Basulto León was born on August 8, 1940, in Santiago de Cuba, on the southeastern end of the island. He was the only child of a middle-class family; his father, also named José, was a public accountant and his mother was a schoolteacher. From his earliest memory, friends and family had called him Gugú.

Young José's days were spent with his mother, Lydia. When she was not teaching the poor at the San Germán sugar plantation in Oriente Province, she devoted her days to acts of charity, activities that left an indelible mark on her young son.

The Basultos moved to Havana before José turned three, when his father was promoted to the main offices of the Punta Alegre Sugar Company. The senior Basulto stayed with the American-owned company for forty-five years, living a disciplined, routine life—something his son would never be able to emulate.

Lydia and José regularly brought food and other necessities to several poor families in Regla, a low-income neighborhood east of Havana Bay, reachable by ferry. In Regla, mother and son enjoyed long walks along the shoreline, where José would feed the seagulls. He was fascinated by the gentle creatures that would eat right out of his small hands.

Lydia died of kidney disease at the age of thirty-four, when José was only four years old. His father did not tell him until he was seven. His questions about Lydia's whereabouts always received the same answer: "she's still at the hospital." José did not believe it.

After a respectable amount of time, José's father started dating Aurora Rivero. He was not surprised when his father announced he was going to remarry. It was only then that they finally admitted to seven-year-old José that Lydia was dead. They may have been puzzled when he did not cry. How could they understand that he had been mourning in private for three years?

Four years after his father's remarriage, his half-brother, Alberto, was born. José was not happy to share his parents' attention, but the eleven-year age difference and their distinct personalities led to their being raised like two only children.

José attended the Baldor School from first grade through high school. He ignored the urgings of his parents to join team sports, although he did bowl competitively for a while. He preferred playing indoors with model toys and mechanical playthings, finding as much pleasure in taking toys apart as in putting them together.

As José grew up, his fascination turned to guns. His armory began with a .38 inherited from his grandfather. He acquired more pistols, then two .22 caliber rifles. Much later, he added a submachine gun to his arsenal. Ironically, in his entire life, José Basulto never shot a human being.

The daredevil in José came out during his teen years, when his hobbies progressed to motorcycles, fast boats, and cars. Driving his blue 1956 MGA two-seater, he entered car races without his father's permission. "Sin first, ask forgiveness later" was his motto. It was particularly easy to ask for forgiveness after he won a silver loving cup for taking second place in the Columbia Aerodrome race. Basulto senior scolded José half-heartedly. He was a doting father who did everything possible to please his son. Perhaps he felt he could not reprimand José for concealing the truth when had done the same so many years before.

During high school, José became one of the overly pampered, elite youth of Havana society enjoying Cuba in the late 1950s. He was 5'10" and slim, with an olive Mediterranean complexion, rich dark hair, engaging brown eyes, and a bright white smile.

At the same time, politics became a part of José's life through his stepmother, Aurora, whom he affectionately referred to as his "second mother." She was an activist at the University of Havana, where she worked in administration. Aurora's very Catholic ancestors had been Spanish Republicans against General Franco, yet neither were they Communists. In the late 1950s during Fidel Castro's struggle for power, José's parents were not pro-Fidel, but they *were* against President Fulgencio Batista.

After high school, José moved to Boston, joining thousands of other Cuban college students whose tradition included university studies in the United States. He took with him his MGA, which bore the word *Particular* under the license registration number. In Spanish, this meant that the car was privately owned. But it caused at least one woman in Boston to ask him, "Young man, what makes *you* so particular?" His sports car, his Latin charm, and his daring manner made his time in the United States very entertaining, and he soon discovered the difference between the American college coeds on the brink of the sexual revolution and the Cuban girls back home still being chaperoned by their grandmothers.

By 1959, in the months after Castro's triumph, José was taking his first physics courses at Boston College, after having completed a semester at Chauncey Hall Preparatory School.

But Cuba was *the* place to be. President Batista had fled the country in the early hours of that New Year's Day. The whole world was captivated by the young bearded revolutionary Fidel Castro, who swore he was not a Communist and promised a general election, soon. Revolutionary and pro-democracy groups were springing up everywhere.

José wanted to be in the middle of that, *needed* to be part of that. The political situation in Cuba made him homesick. So he left Boston College, flew to Havana, and enrolled at the University of Havana, where he befriended many of the members of the student group Agrupación Católica Universitaria (ACU), led by the young Jesuit Amando Llorente.

Most of the ACU members had attended Belén School, an elite Jesuit prep school—as had Fidel Castro himself. Some ACU members had been students with Fidel and shared his political views. Cuba needed changes in areas like agrarian reform and medical care for the poor, and some believed Fidel was the answer. José did not.

Multiple pro-democracy groups opposed to Castro sprung up in both Cuba and Miami. Concurrently, in early 1960, the CIA was coordinating a covert Cuban operation, and they recruited José Basulto as part of the ACU group. He was nineteen years old. For decades these young men would be hailed as Freedom Fighters for Cuba.

The CIA contacted various members of the mostly anti-Batista revolutionary groups in Miami and Havana, as well as some ex-members of Batista's army, then sent them to Useppa Island on the west coast of Florida, now a posh private island club. They were to be trained for an insurgency operation in Cuba to depose Castro. The group of about sixty young men— some of them in their teens—could not wait to be trained in weaponry and espionage. Up to that point, all they knew about the CIA was what they had read in spy novels or seen in movies. It was a fantasy they could not wait to play out.

What they got instead was a slew of psychological testing and mosquito bites. There were Rorschach inkblot tests, IQ tests, and associative reasoning tests. They were plied with questions on who knew who back in Cuba and the names of any Communists they had ever associated with. The CIA's goal was to ascertain the caliber of the people they had recruited, confirm that they could perform certain jobs, or predict that they would crack under pressure. They wanted to see how far these guys would go. There were about twenty Americans in the CIA group, housed in separate but equal cabanas.

It was in Useppa where Billy Schuss and Basulto became friends. Billy had originally been part of Fidel Castro's Rebel Army, but he soon saw Communism through the revolutionary rhetoric and joined the counter-revolution.

In 1961, the men from Useppa were transferred to training camps in Guatemala and Panama, joining other counterrevolutionary groups from Miami and New York. The CIA gave each man a number, starting with 2,500, in order to make their invasion force seem larger. The closer one's number to 2,500, the higher one's status. Billy's number was 2,516 and Basulto's was 2,522. When number 2,506, Carlos Rodríguez Santana, died in a military training exercise in the camps in Guatemala, one of the men suggested naming their group Brigade 2506. A patch was designed with 2506 at the top and a cross with a draped Cuban flag behind it. Brigade 2506 would forever be the identifying symbol of the fight for Cuba's freedom.

Basulto was trained for the infiltration teams in communications and radio operations, telegraphy, cryptography, intelligence, and explosives. He learned to encode, transmit, and decode messages in cryptography and Morse code. He absorbed the tradecraft of the CIA like a zealot. His handlers would warn him cautiously: "Use it for good, José, use it for good."

Between training, drills, and tests, the young men were bored. To entertain the motley group, the CIA showed old World War II movies. They made Basulto cringe, though, because the radio operator was always caught, tortured, and the first to die.

The men of Brigade 2506 were sure of victory in liberating Cuba. After all, the most powerful country in the world was their guarantor. America had never lost a war, and America was on their side.

In the early hours of April 17, 1961, fifteen hundred CIA-trained Cuban exiles landed on Girón Beach in the Bay of Pigs in the south of Cuba to raise an insurrection against Castro's forces. The original forty-eight air-strike sorties promised by the United States were reduced to eight. One hundred fifteen Brigade members died, and almost twelve hundred were captured after running out of ammunition. Some were sent directly to the firing squads.

Basulto was nowhere near the Bay of Pigs when the fighting broke out. He was with his friends Juan Marcelo Fiol, Manolito Baró, and Javier Casas at the beach in Siboney near the southeast end of the island, in Santiago de Cuba, near Guantánamo Bay. As part of the infiltration teams, he had requested ten tons of arms, to be delivered on April 19 by the Americans. The CIA, fully aware that the invasion was already doomed, sent him a coded message: "A large well-armed force has landed in South Las Villas. This is the moment for all patriots to rise and fight for a free Cuba!"

Basulto had already been apprised of Brigade 2506's debacle, so he responded: "Unable to rise up, most patriots in jail thanks to your damned invasion!" With nothing else to do while his buddies were dying on the other side of the island, Basulto and his operations team went swimming— to appear normal, to escape capture, to stay alive.

From that time on, the invasion would forever be paired with the word *failed* as part of its title. The failed Bay of Pigs invasion is revisited by historians and apologists continually, all disagreeing on the reasons for its collapse: the last-minute change in landing site, the switch from insurgency to military invasion, an eleventh-hour D-Day adjustment, the lack of communication between the CIA and the Cuban leadership, and ultimately, the Kennedy administration's broken promise of adequate air coverage—these are just a few.

For the greatest country on earth to have reneged on their promise of air support to the men they themselves had trained to liberate Cuba was unbelievable to Brigade 2506. For Basulto, it was utter betrayal.

One month later, after hiding in different safe houses, and in one case even having to threaten family members to compel them to hide him, Basulto jumped the fence into Guantánamo Naval Station. From there he traveled back to the United States for debriefing.

The Freedom Fighters did not lose hope. In late 1961, President Kennedy initiated a series of covert operations against Castro named Operation Mongoose. After a second infiltration into Cuba in November 1961 failed, a despondent Basulto broke ties with the CIA.

Many Cuban exiles, including the Basulto family, remained confident that Castro would not remain in power. The Punta Alegre Sugar Company that employed the elder Basulto continued to pay his salary. The Basultos spent the summer of 1962 at the Hotel Fontana (now nonexistent) on Miami Beach. Basulto bonded with his family that summer, swimming in the hotel pool and playing on the beach with his nine-year-old brother, Alberto.

But Fidel Castro and his revolution thrived, and when the Russian presence became evident, the whole world came to suspect what most Cubans already knew: Castro's plan included a *Communist* Cuba. Basulto felt that the United States still did not acknowledge the extent of the Russian presence only ninety miles away. He would make sure they did.

In August of 1962, he and some friends from the Directorio Estudiantil (the Student Directorate) mounted a Finnish Lathi cannon on the stern of a Bertram thirty-one-foot speedboat. On the way across the Straits, one of their extra gas tanks began to leak and they feared sparks from the cannon would blow up the boat. They continued on while the captain managed to fix it. One hundred yards from the shore on the north coast of Havana, they opened fire on the dining room of the Rosita de Hornedo Hotel, where Basulto had knowledge the Russians were living. He shot fifteen rounds from the twenty-millimeter cannon. The rest of the crew fired with everything else they had onboard.

"We would have thrown rocks at them if we'd had any," said Basulto. There was minor damage done, and none to human life. The *Miami Herald* would later refer to Basulto as "the man behind the gun."

Five days after the shelling, Manolín Guillot Castellano, whose bleeding likeness hung in Basulto's family room, was executed by firing squad.

Two months later, the October 1962 missile crisis temporarily paralyzed the world. Reconnaissance photographs taken by an American U-2 spy plane revealed that the Cubans were building nuclear ballistic missile bases. President Kennedy announced to the world that any nuclear missile launched from Cuba against any nation in the Western Hemisphere was equivalent to an attack on the United States, and would trigger a full retaliatory response against the Soviet Union. The world was on the brink of World War III. At that time, the United States had more than eight times as many bombs and missile warheads as the Soviets. For many Cubans it seemed like a golden opportunity to finally be rid of Castro.

The Kennedy-Khrushchev Accord followed. It stipulated that if the missiles were removed, the United States would never—*never*—attack Cuba. It would be years before the accord would be made public.

On December 29, 1962, President John F. Kennedy held a ceremony at the Orange Bowl stadium in Miami with some Brigade 2506 survivors. Fidel Castro agreed to exchange 1,113 prisoners for $53 million in food and medicine, all raised by private donations. Members of the brigade handed the president their standard, and he promised to return it to a free Cuba. In 1976, brigade veterans had to hire an attorney to get it back from the U.S. government. It had been kept crated in the basement of a Washington museum.

Basulto did not attend the ceremony. He was at Gésu Catholic Church in downtown Miami, marrying his first wife, Angélica. Both promises made that day were eventually broken.

On March 21, 1963, President Kennedy made Basulto a commissioned officer of the U.S. Army for what he and his friends believed would be another plan—a better, more organized plan—to invade Cuba. Their condition upon accepting these commissions was that they would be free to leave the army at any time. When news of the Kennedy-Khrushchev Accord became public, it was for Basulto like a death sentence for Cuba, and yet another betrayal. "The United States mortgaged the freedom of the Cuban people in exchange for their own security."

After Kennedy's assassination, it was obvious to Basulto and many of his enlisted friends that the United States would never invade Cuba. This triggered a mass resignation of Cuban exiles. Basulto received an honorable discharge and went into the inactive reserve system. He was never recalled to active duty.

Still, the 1960s were years of activism for the Cuban exiles, and Basulto joined many of the efforts to free his homeland. Thoughts of invading Cuba waned during the next few years as his wife, Angélica, gave birth to their three sons, José, Felipe, and Alberto. Basulto continued his education, and in 1969, graduated from the University of Miami with a degree in architectural engineering, then went on to obtain his contractor's license.

By the end of the 1960s, Basulto's troubled marriage to Angélica had deteriorated. He closed out the decade with a broken spirit and a broken marriage. It would take almost seven years and endless legal battles for him to win custody of his three sons.

After his divorce, in the early 1970s, Basulto formed Apollo Decking and Level X Contractors. The entire Basulto family worked together out of Aurora and José Basulto Sr.'s home in Coral Gables. His father took care of the accounting, and his younger brother, Alberto, moved from New York to join the family business as a civil engineer. Those special years bonded father and sons, as Aurora worked alongside and made lunch for them every day.

The 1970s would also grant Basulto's personal life a fresh start when he met a young widow at a party. A friend named Vivian had encouraged Rita María de Cárdenas to attend the party, and all Rita wanted to do was dance Cuban. "I want to dance all night!" Rita told her. And she did.

Rita was tall and shapely. She had deep, almond-shaped brown eyes under perfectly arched eyebrows, and full red lips. Basulto had to wait for a turn to dance with the very popular Rita. He invested the time in admiring her curves and watching her moves on the dance floor with her various partners. When he finally broke in, he told her, "I don't dance very well, but I'm OK with it."

She thought it was cute.

When he asked her out on their first date—flying a hamburger run—she was excited, even after protests from her friend Vivian. "Rita, do *not* go out with him; he's crazy, he's wild, and he's been like that since Cuba!" But she didn't feel right about telling him no after first saying yes, and, well, she thought he was cute. They were married a year later, and Rita's two young daughters, Ana and Monica, joined Basulto and, eventually, his three boys.

While Basulto was enjoying his new family life in the early 1980s, the situation in Nicaragua and the burgeoning Contra movement (*contra* meaning "against") captured his attention. The Contras were a counterrevolutionary organization against the Sandinistas. The Sandinistas, left-wing militants who received arms and direction from Fidel Castro, had been in power since 1979. Early on, the CIA gave the Contras financial and military assistance, and they had the support of President Ronald Reagan.

Nicaragua had been very generous to the Cubans before the Bay of Pigs. It was from their ports that the boats had been launched for the invasion, and it was from their airport that the few B-26s used in the invasion took off. Basulto wanted to help release the Nicaraguans from Cuba's influence.

This time he did not help with any plans for a military invasion; rather, he gave the Contras humanitarian support. Every day at 5:00 p.m., Basulto stationed himself at his ham radio to patch in communications from the families in Miami to the men on the front lines. He traveled to Honduras, where the Nicaraguan Democratic Force (FDN, the Fuerza Democrática Nicaragüense, one of the earliest Contra groups) was based, to help build a hospital. He witnessed amputations without adequate anesthesia, operations without gloves, and teenage boys whose faces were shot off. There he befriended former National Guard Colonel Enrique Bermúdez, who commanded the FDN, leading the Contras against the Sandinista government.

During those Contra years, Basulto reflected on the violent struggle that the Cuban exiles still craved. He often blamed himself and other Cuban exiles for fueling Castro's Communism for one simple reason: *they had left*. Change on the island had to come from within, not from Miami. This was a radical departure from the anti-Castro, pro-violence extremism of the majority of Cuban exiles.

He considered the years of trying to invade Cuba, the many failed assassination plots, the stockpiles of weapons hidden throughout the community awaiting the right time to gather arms and fight again, and the incessant cries of exiles demanding the death of Fidel—*it had all been fruitless.* Violence, which had been part of Basulto's very nature, did not elicit change in anyone or anything.

Basulto immersed himself in the chronicles of Mahatma Gandhi and the writings of Dr. Martin Luther King Jr. Later, Gene Sharp from the Albert Einstein Institute mentored Basulto on the concept of active nonviolence. It became the guiding principle for the rest of his life.

Meanwhile, Cuba had a budding dissident movement. According to author Victor Triay, certain released political prisoners like Armando Valladares and dissidents like Ricardo Bofill gave the movement a badly needed shot in the arm.

While the dissidents expanded their reach inside Cuba during the 1980s, the Nicaraguan Contra situation consumed Basulto's life and disrupted his family. When the Contra war ended in Nicaragua with the democratic election of Violeta Chamorro, the political situation seemed to stabilize. But even after the democratic election, the Sandinistas did not give back the private property they had confiscated. When Colonel Bermúdez, who had been exiled to Miami, returned for a visit to Nicaragua, he was assassinated in the parking lot of the Managua Intercontinental Hotel. His murder remains unsolved.

Basulto was devastated that the Contras had not triumphed. He felt the Americans had betrayed the Nicaraguans in the same way they had betrayed the Cubans during the Bay of Pigs. The United States had given up on Nicaragua moments before an imminent victory, just as in Cuba.

Basulto sank into a deep depression from which those closest to him thought he would never recover. The depression further alienated him from his family. There were weeks when he simply could not get out of bed. His inner struggle was analogous to the dichotomy of his outward reputations. His involvement in the Bay of Pigs honored his role as a Cuban veteran and war hero, a Freedom Fighter. He was equally an American veteran. Though patriotic to his adopted country, Basulto was openly critical of some of the actions of the U.S. government, specifically concerning Cuba. There seemed to be a polarity in his hobbies: he loved rifles but abhorred hunting. Basulto was labeled right-wing for helping the Contras in Nicaragua, and he was tagged a liberal for being a devout believer in the nonviolent movements of Gandhi and Dr. Martin Luther King Jr. He was a baptized Catholic yet he questioned organized religion and those who insisted on a set moral code. He was a man's man, yet his attorneys were women and his trusted physician was Dr. Rafael Sánchez, an ob-gyn. Basulto was called a humanitarian by those who knew him and a terrorist by governments that did not. This of a man whose middle name was Jesús, whose adult friends called him Gugú.

At the dawn of a new decade in 1990, Basulto would arise from his depression with a new conviction, a mandate, his own personal epiphany: *El cambio soy yo*, I am the change.

It would be the decade of his life.

3

The Idea

In science the credit goes to the man who convinces the world,
not to the man to whom the idea first occurs.

Sir Francis Darwin

The phenomenon of people taking to the Florida Straits spawns from the beckoning power of the Gulf Stream, born from the clockwise winds that whip around the northern Atlantic Ocean. It is strongest in the narrowest part, which passes by Havana and shoots north toward the east coast of Florida with what novelist Philip Caputo describes as "the power of a thousand Mississippis."

Gregorio Pérez Ricardo was not the first rafter to head for Florida's shores. The first Coast Guard rescue of Cuban refugees occurred on July 22, 1959, seven months after Fidel Castro's rise to power, when a group of nine was picked up in a small boat off the Dry Tortugas near Key West. During the first six years of Castro's revolution, the Coast Guard rescued almost seven thousand Cubans attempting the journey in makeshift craft.

Between 1959 and 1990 several Cuban migrations took place. Among them were the Pedro Pan operation for children in 1960–62, the Freedom Flights of 1965–1971, and migrations engineered by Fidel Castro, like the Camarioca boatlift of 1965 and the Mariel boatlift in 1980. During the intervening years, Cubans were not free to leave the island; intermittently, rafters were spotted in the Straits. The jump from 27 rafters in 1986 to 392 in 1989 coincided with the worsening economic situation in Cuba: an early warning of what was to come.

But Gregorio's attempt was different. His youth, the television coverage, and his death impacted the Miami community. He was everybody's son, and donations poured in for his funeral expenses. More than five hundred people attended a standing-room-only mass at the Virgin of Charity, a small Catholic church overlooking Biscayne Bay built forty years earlier in honor

of the Virgin Mary. Monsignor Agustín Román, a shepherd for the immi-
grants, gave a moving homily about how this unknown balsero had arrived
with no family to receive him, and yet everyone in attendance was like his
family. Leaders of the Cuban American community vied for pallbearer
positions.

Now that the rafters' plight had been spotlighted, Basulto and Billy got
to work. Basulto suggested that AVME, the Association of Veterans of Special Missions (of the Bay of Pigs invasion), could help. AVME's missions
had included the infiltration teams and other CIA-sponsored groups. The
organization was currently sponsoring the Flotilla of Brotherhood and Solidarity planned for May 20, 1990, the eighty-eighth anniversary of Cuba's
independence from Spain.

These displays of solidarity consisted of mainly Cuban exiles navigating
together in private and rented boats to the twelve-mile demarcation point,
the so-called Wall of Water that separated the Cubans over there from the
Cubans over here. Flotillas were not-so-quiet displays of external opposition to the internal problem of Cuba. They were highly organized, with
strict rules about not carrying alcohol or guns onboard. Basulto was the
head of the Information and Press Committee, so he presented the case for
the rafters to AVME.

One hundred boats were already registered to sail from Key West to a
location dubbed Punto Martí in honor of Cuba's liberator, José Martí. Punto
Martí was located at the territorial limits of Cuba's jurisdictional waters.

The seas were ten feet high on May 20, 1990, and Basulto puked his guts out
during the sixteen-hour, 158-mile round-trip of the flotilla. The bad weather
detained many boats at the dock, and only sixty of the original one hundred vessels started the voyage from Key West. Thirteen miles from their
destination, a Cuban gunboat was spotted. The flotilla was still in international waters and twenty-five miles from the coast of Cuba, but organizers
announced that they had gone far enough: it was too dangerous and the
seas were getting rougher. There were women and children onboard. The
remaining boats returned to Key West.

After stomachs settled from the flotilla experience, the rafter situation
remained on everyone's mind. The idea of organizing vessels to patrol the
Florida Straits and find rafters before they perished necessitated money,
boats, and commitment, and the last requirement would be the hardest. Basulto spoke to fishermen, to boat owners, and to various Cuban exile groups.

Everybody wanted to help; everybody had a "but." AVME even purchased a boat to help look for rafters, provoking a conflict with the U.S. Coast Guard: civilians were not allowed to search for and rescue refugees at sea, since this could be mistaken for smuggling or human trafficking.

Basulto was not enthusiastic about using boats to find the rafters because the field of vision—the horizon—was so limiting. He and Billy Schuss met with their mutual friend José Benito Clark at Basulto's house one day to discuss the difficulties of using boats. As they looked up at the painting of Manolín Guillot Castellano, the bleeding Cuban, they experienced what Basulto recalls as a defining moment, as if they were all simultaneously summoned by a Higher Power to do something about the rafters.

They determined that planes would be the best way to search for the balseros. The field of vision was greater, and the area that could be covered was more expansive. Basulto had a plane.

A few months later, a small group gathered to discuss how the idea of using planes could be implemented. In this group was Mayte Greco, a stunning, blonde-haired, green-eyed pilot in her early thirties and the mother of four small girls. Basulto was Mayte's aviation mentor, and their two families had enjoyed many hamburger runs together. She was a friend of the Basultos, and the only other woman present besides Rita, Basulto's wife.

Previous meetings had opened with the rafter problem as the main agenda item, but attendees would frequently go off-topic once the hors d'oeuvres were brought in: *pastelitos,* the little Cuban meat pies; *bocaditos,* small finger sandwiches; ham croquettes just warm from the deep fryer; cheeses; and thin slices of Spanish ham. Tangential issues of Cuba would pop up and soon everything but the rafters was being discussed. At this particular meeting, everyone was single-minded.

Before they ever did a trial run, recruited any pilots, or determined which planes would be used and who would pay for the fuel, the group tossed about names for their not-yet-born organization, names in Spanish and in English, referring to the air, the sea, the boats, the birds, their Cuban brothers. Someone mentioned the word *compañero*—"companion" or "friend"—but it was instantly rejected. Although *compañero*'s meaning ran deeper than friendship, implying a bond—something that certainly existed among Cubans—*compañero* was also part of Fidel Castro's lexicon. Castro did away with the use of Miss, Mr., and Mrs., claiming they were bourgeois terms, opting, or rather demanding, instead that names be preceded by Compañero, Comrade. No, *compañero* would not do.

"It should be a brotherhood," said Basulto, "like the Flotilla of Brotherhood and Solidarity." Then he pronounced with finality: "Brothers to the Rescue, because we are brothers, we are children of the same land."

"Brothers?" chimed in Mayte. *"Brothers?"* she repeated a little louder, as if they had not heard her the first time. *"Hellooo,* I'm here!" she said, pointing to herself.

"It's like a brother-*hood*, Mayte," said Basulto, as if the suffix "-hood" were an obvious inclusion of all things female. The other men did not even notice her protests. Basulto quickly drew up a mission statement and set up a press conference.

Once the Miami community heard about the new organization, exile leaders began arguing back and forth as to who had birthed the idea of Brothers to the Rescue. Many felt that *their* idea to save the rafters had been stolen. One of Basulto's soon-to-be ex-friends wrote him a four-page letter, more like a dissertation, reasserting that the idea was not Basulto's. He quoted Shakespeare's *Henry IV,* saying that *his* idea had been "father to the thought" of Brothers to the Rescue.

Ideas belong to no one, Basulto often replied, acknowledging that many people indeed thought like he did. When a problem, like a ball, was thrown one's way, Basulto believed there were three types of people and three types of responses: those who let the ball drop, those who caught the ball and held on to it, and those who ran with it.

The naysayers let the ball drop. Basulto was never surprised—yet always disappointed—at the power of one "no" over a group of people. A consensus could be reached, everyone full of excitement over a new project, and all it would take was one *comemierda* to say no and the rest would cave in. *Comemierda* is an all-encompassing Cuban profanity that literally means a shit-eater, but figuratively is a jerk, a snob, a know-it-all, or a fool.

Others liked to hand an idea to committees and discussions and organizations—to hold on to the idea. They enjoyed reading their quoted wisdom in the newspapers and were puffed up by the sounds of their own voices over the radio waves of Little Havana.

In the Cuban community of Miami, those who ran with an idea usually did so to be in the spotlight, the star on the local stage. The exiles dubbed it *protagonismo,* being the protagonist, a characteristic they all denied having. Protagonismo reminded Basulto of one of his favorite sermons by Dr. Martin Luther King Jr., titled "The Drum Major Instinct," where he preaches about "a desire to be out front, a desire to lead the parade, a desire to be first." In Cuban-exile Miami, the yearning to be given credit for an idea ran deep.

While other exiles claimed ownership of the idea, Billy and Basulto ran with it. Billy stepped up his flying lessons with instructor Beverly Brooks, who would later join Brothers to the Rescue. Basulto worked with graphic designers at Aida Levitán's public relations company to design the logo. It showed a silhouetted figure in black with one arm raised high in an imploring gesture, the solitary balsero riding a white raft over the blue ocean. The Cuban flag in a circle was the backdrop, with a seagull flying protectively overhead.

Within a year that symbol would be recognized not only across the United States, but more importantly, across the Straits of Florida.

4

The Brotherhood

*If you want something really important to be done, you must
not merely satisfy the reason; you must move the heart also.*

Mahatma Gandhi

A little more than a year after Billy's call, on May 13, 1991—coincidentally,
the feast day of the Virgin Mary—Brothers to the Rescue became a not-
for-profit humanitarian organization. The press conference held May 15
was broadcast on television and written up in the newspapers. Basulto and
his new board of directors did not have to wait long for the outpouring of
support—and criticism. The comemierdas with the no's were everywhere.
Fortunately, they were quickly supplanted by a wave of volunteerism from
the diverse Miami community.

Three days after incorporation, the small Brothers to the Rescue board
of directors met with Admiral Robert E. Kramer of the U.S. Coast Guard to
determine the proper protocol for search and rescue in the Florida Straits.
The feasibility studies Basulto and Mayte Greco had performed concluded
that flying at five hundred feet, the lowest altitude approved by the Federal
Aviation Administration (FAA), gave the pilots the best chances for spotting
someone in the water. They knew they would have to fly lower than that at
times—and in effect, break the rules—but Basulto reasoned that they were
operating under a much higher authority than the FAA.

The Coast Guard and Brothers agreed that when a rafter was spotted, the
coordinates would be marked and a dye marker would be thrown into the
water to aid the Coast Guard's search. The plane would then soar above two
thousand feet to radio the Brothers to the Rescue base. The operator at base
would call the Coast Guard, which would in turn dispatch a vessel to pick
up the rafters. After this several-hours-long procedure, the rescued would
be taken to Key West for processing.

That could have marked mission accomplished and allowed Brothers to fly off in search of others. But Basulto insisted that the plane stay with the balseros and fly in circles until the Coast Guard arrived, which might take up to five hours. Those long, monotonous, stifling hours of babysitting would be the hardest, but for Basulto, the most important. He could not imagine the elation of being found to be unseated by the appearance of abandonment. For those desperate souls on a makeshift raft bobbing in the water, or thrashing in the seas, the protection overhead, like the seagull, would be a comfort.

The *Miami Herald* and its Spanish counterpart, *El Nuevo Herald*, saturated the community with articles on Brothers to the Rescue. Basulto was grateful to the press for metaphorically getting Brothers to the Rescue off the ground.

One of the most influential supporters was David Lawrence Jr., publisher of the *Miami Herald*. He and his fifteen-year-old daughter Amanda flew with Basulto on one of those early missions. Lawrence remembers flying close to the territorial limits of Cuba and seeing the skyline of Havana. In the culturally polarized city of Miami, Lawrence encouraged all communities to support Brothers to the Rescue. "This strikes me as a cause, in a community of causes, about which everyone can agree."

The mother of three pilots, Susana Eckell-Lares watched the televised press conference and later read about Brothers to the Rescue in *El Nuevo Herald*. She passed on the information to her three sons: Guillermo, known as "Guille"; Adalberto, nicknamed "Beto"; and Jorge, called "Koki." They knew what they had to do.

Their father was a pilot for Eastern Airlines, and before that he had worked for Aerolíneas Argentinas in their homeland. Because flying had always been part of the Lares household, the three brothers became pilots.

The boys grew up doing everything together. Even personal choices like faith were made as a group. They had all been raised Catholic, but at thirteen, Koki broke away and joined a Baptist congregation. He reassured Susana that it was a truly Christian church, and she accepted her son's decision. Later in Miami, his brothers followed suit to worship in a nondenominational Bible-based Christian church.

Guille was 6'4", with blue eyes and dark brown hair. At twenty-five, he clearly embraced the protective—and authoritative—role of the eldest brother. Beto, twenty-three, was a little shorter than Guille, with a strong and athletic physique. Koki was only nineteen years old and still did not have his final pilot's license. His brothers gave him the nickname Koki when he was a child because they said he had a big head, like a coconut. He shared his older brothers' good looks with his brown hair, blue eyes, and a body that seemed to follow a disciplined exercise program. What set Koki apart from his brothers was his peaceful countenance, the internal goodness that radiated in his smile and in the shine of his eyes. He was the biblical David, the apple of God's eye, the son every man wanted.

Rita Basulto was answering the phones for Brothers one morning when Guille Lares called. "It's a call from a young pilot who says he and his two brothers want to volunteer, but I don't think they're Cuban, I think they're from Argentina," she said, giving the phone to Basulto.

"*Argentinos?* Three brothers?" asked Basulto. They agreed to get together.

At their first meeting at the Tamiami Airport, Basulto greeted the three brothers with a handshake and a hug.

"We want to help you save the balseros," said Guille, reporting for duty with his battalion of three.

"We have no money, and we have no planes," Beto added, "but we have our licenses and we want to help you."

Basulto was impressed with the three pilot-brother volunteers, their unity, and how they followed in their father's footsteps. At that time, Basulto's three sons had not yet expressed an interest in flying.

"If either one of us would have liked to fly, my father would have gone crazy," middle son Felipe once told a reporter. "Instead, God gave him three Argentinean sons."

The Lares brothers started flying immediately. For Basulto, the name Brothers to the Rescue would forever be interchangeable with these men who had come to his rescue. "I asked God to send me some angels," Basulto said one day to a parish priest at St. Louis Catholic Church in southwest Miami, "and He sent me the three Lares brothers from Argentina."

"Why didn't he send you some Cuban angels?" asked the priest.

"God told me He didn't have Cuban angels."

Guille, Beto, and Koki felt chosen by God to join Brothers to the Rescue. After a few missions, Guille believed it was time to bring the honor to God. "José, would it be OK if we pray as a group before each mission?" he asked.

"Sure, Guille, how would you like to do that?" Basulto responded. Basulto was a baptized Catholic, as were the majority of the people involved in Brothers. But his openness to other faiths, beliefs, races, and socioeconomic and educational backgrounds attracted a diverse group to Brothers to the Rescue.

"Well, I think it's important to dedicate every mission to God," said Guille. "He's the one that will find the balseros for us. We'll join hands in a circle and I'll pray, and maybe we can finish with an Our Father that everyone knows."

Latin men do not hold hands, except maybe in a huddle. Strange in a culture where adult sons kiss their fathers, brothers kiss brothers, and male friends greet each other with a handshake followed by an embrace. *But hold hands?*

From that moment on, the Brothers joined hands before every mission. Their prayer circle would be filmed, photographed, and publicized all over the world.

One month later, Guille Lares was named chief of pilots, responsible for interviewing and hiring volunteer pilots, as well as scheduling missions.

"Look for ones just like you, Guille," Basulto said.

Apparently Virginie Buchete Puperoux was not like Guille. Virginie was a friend of Mayte Greco's, certainly well recommended.

"I'm sorry, but we cannot take you on right now," Guille told her after the interview. A French beauty with long blonde hair and light eyes, Virginie was as tall and slender as a model. Born in Normandy, Virginie moved to the United States, studied at UCLA, and received her pilot's license in California. She was experienced, well educated, and ready to fly.

"He doesn't like me, I can tell," Virginie told Mayte. In Virginie's opinion, Guille didn't like women pilots and, like most Latin men, he was being *machista*, anti-woman.

Mayte later asked Guille why he did not give her the job—it was, after all, a volunteer position.

"I have to determine everyone's intentions, I have to make sure their background is the best, and that is the decision I made," he replied, giving no further explanation. But Mayte insisted, advocated, and pleaded for her friend.

Three months later, contrary to the machista label Virginie had applied, Guille changed his mind. The other pilots nicknamed her "La Francesa," the French girl. Virginie stayed with Brothers to the Rescue for more than three years, but La Francesa never flew with Guille Lares.

The first American pilot to join Brothers to the Rescue was Conrad Webber. Conrad had attended the press conference a few weeks earlier, when Brothers invited pilots to volunteer. Though older than most of the pilots, Conrad was young at flying and he coveted the same thing as the younger pilots: to load up his logbook without the expenses of high fuel costs or flying lessons. Saving a life was a bonus.

Right now his life afforded him a little extra time to play, so when Basulto asked him to join Brothers, Conrad impulsively said yes. Conrad Webber did not usually do things impulsively, and his decision surprised his family and friends. The latter could not understand why he was helping this new group. "Why the hell do you want to find more Cubans?" they challenged him. "Doesn't Miami have enough already?"

Conrad and his friends had been born and raised in Miami, B.C.—before Cubans. Conrad's father had been a pilot with the Canadian Royal Air Force before World War II, and had changed their German surname Weber to the more American-sounding Webber. After Pearl Harbor, when the U.S. government was interning Japanese Americans in detention camps, Conrad's father feared they would do the same with the Germans.

Conrad was in middle school when the first wave of Cubans hit Miami in 1960. His teacher announced to the class that they would be getting some new students, explaining that they were Cubans, escaping a Communist ruler named Fidel Castro. The only Spanish-speaking people these kids recognized were Mexicans or the Cuban Ricky Ricardo on *I Love Lucy*. Conrad and his classmates imagined the new kids would walk in wearing ponchos and big hats.

Conrad attended public school before Bibles were banned, so they prayed for the new students at morning prayers. When the first exile children walked into his class in January 1961, the classmates saw kids just like them, their skin color no darker than the Jewish or Italian kids. But Conrad never established friendships with them.

After living in Miami for thirty years, he would create those Hispanic friendships through Brothers to the Rescue. Flying with them would load his logbook, and saving lives wouldn't be so bad, either.

Many younger pilots, like Peruvian Carlos Gartner, joined Brothers for the flying hours. Lack of money in Peru's crumbling economy temporarily stalled Gartner's dream to become a pilot. At his mother's prodding, he called his sister in the United States, who was married to an American pilot. She sent her brother two thousand dollars. With that, he completed two hundred hours of flight instruction, earned his license, then moved to Miami. He worked two jobs while he went to school to learn English.

Gartner had worked as a bush pilot in the jungles of Peru. "Cholo," as he would be nicknamed, was adept at low passes and tricky maneuvers. The appeal of racking up hours through Brothers was soon replaced by a zeal for saving souls.

Back on the ground, the Brotherhood needed volunteers to answer phones, prepare the supply drops, and structure the organization.

The main organizer was Basulto's friend Leopoldo "Polo" Núñez. The only child of a politically active, well-to-do family in Havana, Polo attended an American school there called Ruston Academy. His heritage included generals and mayors of Havana, a vice president of Cuba, and the family tradition of an American education. Family politics also dictated taking a stand for one's beliefs. Polo's parents had been involved in the counterrevolution in Cuba and demanded, when he turned eighteen, that he get off the fence and do something. His first mission was to cover Havana neighborhoods with posters that read "Communism equals destruction." At 5'6", very fair-skinned and weighing about 125 pounds, he looked thirteen, so no one interfered with him.

But now, Polo's life was at a turning point. At forty-nine, he was about to become a first-time father. His very pregnant, thirty-eight-year-old wife did not want him risking his life with Brothers to the Rescue. In addition, the Núñezes were awfully busy. An avid writer and poet, Polo was assistant vice principal at Belén Jesuit Preparatory School in Miami, where he also taught history, chaired the Humanities Department, and managed the theater. When Basulto asked for help, Polo explained his predicament but replied,

"Of course I'll help you, Gugú." Polo became the historian for Brothers to the Rescue and the father of a baby boy.

Observers were another crucial component of Brothers to the Rescue. Their eyes would most frequently be the ones to spot the desperate souls below, the pilots being occupied with maneuvers and flying their grids. "A pair of eyes is a pair of eyes," Basulto often repeated, never judging the ability of whomever climbed in the backseat.

A tall, lanky, visually impaired thirty-five-year-old maintenance worker from the Miami-Dade Police Department came in one day to be that pair of eyes.

"I can help you," said Osvaldo Plá, brushing away thick bunches of jet black hair from his eyes. He wore his straight hair long in the back and short in the front and on the sides—a mullet cut, a style popular with country-western singers, some rockers, and a few surfers. Osvaldo was not any of these. He was also most definitely not a *yucca*, the Cubanized version of the 1990s yuppie: young up-and-coming Cuban American. Osvaldo was more like a Cuban homeboy. His clothes looked borrowed and yet seemed tailored to his lean-limbed frame. Behind his thick-lensed glasses his eyes appeared to be stinging, or chronically tired. In a few years he would be diagnosed legally blind due to macular degeneration. He had a large brown mole over his plump upper lip, which somehow harmonized with a slanted smile beneath his elongated nose. His grin, his hair, the lilt in his voice— they drew people in. Osvaldo Plá was a metaphor for not judging a book by its cover. He was not a particularly handsome man, but he was fascinating to look at.

In Cuba, Osvaldo had attended San Alejandro Vocational Arts School in Havana, where he developed a talent for portrait painting. Refusing to learn Russian and not permitted to learn English, he mastered French. Music and art were his hobbies. To earn extra money he would fashion amplifiers and speakers for the local disc jockeys.

Not wanting to leave their extended family behind, Osvaldo's parents never fled to the United States after the revolution. They existed in a world where every neighbor could be a spy and few could be trusted, so his parents kept quiet. Osvaldo did not.

One day Osvaldo was on his way to work as a disc jockey at a friend's fifteenth birthday party when there was *yet another* power outage. "The revolution is a piece of crap! Down with Fidel!" he yelled up and down the street of his neighborhood, furious at losing the small income from the job. His parents feared for his life: his rant could easily land him in jail. It was time for twenty-two-year-old Osvaldo to go. It was a good thing he was an asthmatic and could not perform his mandatory military service because that illness became his ticket out of Cuba in 1978.

When he arrived in Miami, he enrolled at Miami-Dade Community College to major in art and pursue his interest in portrait painting. Now, Osvaldo worked for Dade County, was married and raising a stepdaughter, and wanted to help Brothers to the Rescue.

He was not a pilot, but he had ideas for the Brotherhood. Some included dropping radios down to the rafters, a logical progression from shouting through a bullhorn. Others were more complicated, like installing receiving antennas that could lock on to the frequencies of radio equipment the balseros carried onboard. The ideas seemed outlandish at first, but Osvaldo's charm and passion made them commonsensical.

Basulto scrutinized this country boy from Cuba who sported a mullet haircut, was a portrait painter and self-proclaimed inventor, and spoke French. "We'd love for you to join us, Osvaldo," said Basulto, adding another dimension to his organization.

The Brotherhood continued to grow, each volunteer who joined expressing his or her own unique heartfelt reason or answering a nagging sense of unfinished business. Among the latter was Arnaldo Iglesias.

Arnaldo Iglesias was at his Miami home reading an article on Brothers to the Rescue when he put down the newspaper and blinked. He blinked again. Arnaldo had an eye condition that made it difficult to control the muscles in his eyelids, and depending on the situation, he blinked more or less, his communication style a facial version of Morse code. He looked at the headline of another story about Brothers, and he heard the voice again: "Cuba, Cuba, Cuba, when are you going to do something for Cuba?" The voice had echoed that mantra for more than thirty years: "Arnaldo, when are you going to do something for Cuba?" Arnaldo never signed on for the Bay of Pigs invasion, and thirty years later, he still felt guilty. His best friend's father, who had been a lieutenant colonel in the Cuban military under President Batista, had persuaded Arnaldo not to go. That was when the voices started.

While his compatriots were fighting against Castro's army, Arnaldo Iglesias was living in Puerto Rico on forty-five dollars a week. The first of his family to leave Cuba after Fidel took over, twenty-two-year-old Arnaldo arrived in San Juan, Puerto Rico, alone, with eleven dollars in his pocket. His job involved the computer industry. Computers were then new, an average-sized one taking up an entire office. It would be the beginning of his professional career in the industry.

But the guilt he felt over his noninvolvement in the failed Bay of Pigs invasion followed him to Puerto Rico. José Miró Cardona, who had been Castro's first prime minister in 1959 and later headed an anti-Batista democratic group in Miami, came to Puerto Rico in late 1961 to encourage the Cubans living there to join the U.S. Army and try to liberate Cuba, again. A new plan was being developed by the Americans, and this time it would work. Now, *finally*, something was going to happen. From Puerto Rico, only two men said yes; one of them was Arnaldo.

Arnaldo was inducted into the U.S. Army in 1962 and completed paratrooper basic training in South Carolina. He was puzzled when the army offered him an officer training position in Germany. "I want to be a soldier, not an officer," he said, expecting a transfer to Cuba when the fighting began. They further enticed him by offering him full U.S. citizenship. He was not even a legal resident at that point.

"All I want to do—all I enlisted to do—was to fight for my country! You're offering me a rich stepmother because my own mother is poor and infirm. *I already have a mother.*"

Arnaldo was given an honorable discharge for hardship reasons, since he was helping support his parents. Many years later, he became a U.S. citizen.

Now, the daily articles about Brothers to the Rescue tugged at his conscience. His wife, Mirta, worked with Maggie Schuss, Billy's wife, at the Cuban American National Foundation. Mirta Iglesias brought home eyewitness stories of the pilots and the volunteers, as recounted by Maggie.

Arnaldo blinked away the memories, put down the newspaper, and dialed the phone number listed in the article.

"Good morning, Brothers to the Rescue," said a young man's voice on the line. Arnaldo recognized an Argentine accent.

"Can I speak to José Basulto, please?"

The voices in his head finally stopped.

A few weeks later, Maggie Schuss summoned Arnaldo away from a relaxing beach day on Key Biscayne for his first mission as an observer. Soon, he started pilot training. Arnaldo gave up most of his weekend hours for Brothers to the Rescue. He would later computerize all the missions, and most important for the young pilots, keep an accounting of rescues.

He also handled the finances for the organization. In those early days, Basulto's American Express card kept the planes in the air. Arnaldo noticed that the majority of community donations came from older Cubans in the working-class exile neighborhoods of Little Havana and Hialeah, who donated one, five, or ten dollars a month, many adding an apologetic note wishing they could give more. Arnaldo initiated a mail campaign with monthly return envelopes, tapping the entire community. The hundreds of five- and ten-dollar donations that poured in funded Brothers' operating budget.

It was not enough. The organization needed to raise capital to buy more airplanes. They were using Basulto's single-engine plane three times a week. The others were borrowed or were rented at exorbitant costs. Maintenance checks on the aircraft were four hundred dollars each. Fuel costs ran twenty dollars an hour for a single engine, fifty dollars an hour for a twin. Some pilots even paid for their own fuel on missions.

Financially, Basulto was at a good point in his life. While they waited for donations to come in, and after maxing out his credit cards, Basulto put up money from his own savings.

They canvassed the local Cuban exile groups for larger sums, but were unsuccessful. Basulto knew plenty of influential people with money but he was not interested in working the market, or the U.S. government. Even though they were a nonprofit humanitarian organization, Brothers to the Rescue had not petitioned the United States for one cent. Basulto wanted to keep it that way. *The struggle is ours.*

5

The First Rescue

When I do good, I feel good; when I do bad, I feel bad.
That's my religion.
Abraham Lincoln

The first official mission of Brothers to the Rescue left Tamiami Airport on May 25, 1991. Tamiami serviced private and charter flights out of the southwest Kendall area of Miami. Three planes flying under the call names *Seagull One, Seagull Two,* and *Seagull Three* set out over the Florida Straits.

Seagull One was Basulto's radio call sign. With him was local television anchorwoman Lucy Pereda as observer. The copilot was René González, a thirty-year-old recent Cuban defector. René was born in the United States to Cuban parents, but his family had returned to Cuba once Castro came to power. He became a pilot and later defected from the Communist island on a fumigation plane, a Russian Antonov, and claimed asylum in Boca Chica in the Florida Keys. He left his wife and daughter behind.

Billy Schuss' call sign was *Seagull Two,* and *Seagull Three* was piloted by Guille Lares with Beto as copilot.

They found no rafters that historic day, nor on the subsequent six missions. They did spot rafts, but all were empty. Early estimates stated that only one of every four attempting the crossing made it. In the future the Coast Guard would mark the empty rafts with dye to indicate that they had been spotted.

The pilots chastised themselves: *What if we had been here yesterday? How many were lost? Who was waiting for those souls over here? How did they die?* They decided they needed to get to the rafters in the early stages of their journey. They needed to get closer to Cuba.

There is an imaginary line running east-west at the midpoint between the tip of the Florida Keys and the coast of Cuba that is charted as the 24th parallel. While the areas both north and south of this line are considered international air space and water, the United States provides air traffic control to the north of it, and Cuba to the south. Cuba's territorial limits are twelve miles off the coast.

Brothers to the Rescue needed to fly below the 24th parallel.

Basulto and his crew would be the first to fly just south of the 24th on their mission of June 2, 1991, flying east to west on an imaginary rectangular grid. Koki Lares, the youngest of the three Argentine brothers, was excited to be copilot for the first time, with his brother Guille in *Seagull Three*. Guille and Koki would stay above the 24th parallel, flying west to east.

Four hours into mission number seven, no one had found anything but empty rafts. Looking back, Guille recalled the raft he and his brother Beto had spotted on one particular mission. A glimmer of something white inside the raft encouraged them on their first low pass. When they circled down the second time, they confirmed that there *was* something in that raft, something small, white, and lacy—a baby girl's dress. But no baby girl.

Guille longed to fly south of the 24th parallel; today, he had a very good feeling. "They probably have the better area, Koki. He's always giving it to the Cuban pilots, haven't you noticed?" Guille told his brother, only half-joking. He was convinced that flying below the 24th parallel would yield better results, even though no one had had *any* results yet. Midway through the mission and against Basulto's instructions, Guille turned southwest.

There was a specific procedure used in searching for these human dots in the water, which Basulto, Billy, and Mayte had practiced in their trial runs over the Everglades. It required looking down and across. When driving a car, you keep your eyes on the road, glancing in the rearview mirror occasionally. Usually when piloting a plane, you keep your eyes ahead of you, repeatedly glancing down to check your instruments. Brothers to the Rescue pilots did not fly that way: the pilot looked left, the copilot right, and the observers, when they were not dizzy or heaving in the cramped and stifling backseats, looked out their windows toward the endless water below. On a search and rescue, no one looked straight ahead unless advised of another aircraft flying similar coordinates. That was rare; usually no aircraft except Brothers to the Rescue planes flew at or below five hundred feet.

The planes, usually three on every mission, flew out of Tamiami Airport southwest toward Key West. At that point they headed south. Each plane had a specific grid to monitor, from west to east, then back again, flying in an individual aerial rectangle. On a flat map, it would appear as one plane flying parallel above the other, marking lines like the teeth on a comb.

The Lares brothers had rerouted their rectangle and were working their way to Basulto's area—what they presumed to be the good zone—south of their own. Below, everything looked the same as it had over the previous three weeks, and there was no indication today would be different.

Rafter Rubén González had been on the water for more than eight hours by the time the planes took off from Tamiami Airport that morning, and he and his companions were calm. Rubén's four brothers had made it to Marathon Key seventeen days earlier—the day before the Brothers' inaugural flight—after four days and nights at sea. He had heard their names announced on Radio Martí, the U.S.-sponsored radio link to Havana, which had begun broadcasting to Cuba in 1985. Four of them had left Cuba, but six arrived in Miami. The González brothers came across two rafters swimming in the water after their own raft collapsed. Two others in that party had drowned. Knowing his brothers had made a successful voyage, Rubén decided to leave, too.

Before the revolution, the González family had been wealthy. Rubén's father was a surgeon who had studied in the United States, and his mother had a PhD in philosophy. Soon his father became a devout Marxist and atheist. While his father smashed the remaining religious artifacts in their home, his Catholic mother secretly baptized the eleven children. After fighting with Fidel Castro's forces, Rubén's father gave all his possessions to the campesinos, the peasants. He informed his children that the only inheritance he would leave them was his value system.

After the revolution, Raúl Castro gave Rubén's family a seven-bedroom, five-bath mansion in the formerly exclusive Nuevo Vedado neighborhood of Havana, a house that had probably been taken away from someone else's inheritance. Rubén and his siblings attended school with Raúl Castro's sons, as well as all the other children of the high-ranking military officials. It was a public school, as are all schools in Cuba, and the González children still had to undergo rationing, forced youth marches, and military service. At twenty-six, Rubén had lived a fairly sheltered life and was considered one of the privileged. The González siblings had enough to eat and adequate clothes to wear, but they had no freedom of expression.

It was not enough.

Rubén and his friends built a sturdy, wood-framed vessel with pipes bored through the hull to hold the sides together. They inserted the inner tubes from a truck tire and a tractor tire inside the frame and inflated them, snug against the sides. The bottom was wrapped with canvas to keep the sharks out, and a 10-hp Yamaha motor positioned on the stern made their boat seaworthy.

Aboard Basulto's Cessna, his friend Juan González [no relation to Rubén] was falling asleep. He had taken the day off to be an observer and his wife had not been happy about it. Juan was a door-to-door salesman of high-end cookware, and weekends and nights were his prime working hours.

"Who's going to rescue us?" his wife would protest, knowing that every day he flew was a day he earned no income.

Juan was also a member of a flying club called Fuerzas Armadas de Cuba en el Exilio (Armed Forces of Cuba in Exile, or FACE), a Cuban exile pilot group that had aligned themselves with the Brothers' cause. Juan sometimes flew missions on FACE's plane. He had been a pilot since his youth in Cuba, but the oil crisis of the 1970s prompted his career move from aviation to selling waterless cookware.

Sitting behind Basulto's captain's seat, Juan was bored, hot, and tired, and the glare of the water in the midday sun was hypnotizing. There were no headphones onboard for him, so he could not communicate with Basulto and Billy, who was copilot. The roar of the motors lulled him, and as he rested his head against the window he resolved to shut his eyes for just a moment. Basulto was focused on the patch of water to his left; Billy was frowning toward the Florida Straits on his right. They were below the 24th parallel, marking their flight plan back and forth, west to east, then back again.

Meanwhile, Guille pointed south of his rectangular grid, then headed east, intent on finding a rafter in the good zone. He told himself he would explain it all to Basulto back at the hangar; he would ask forgiveness later, after finding the first rafters. Basulto would not mind his route change if he saved some lives. Both Seagull missions were so focused on their search patterns that they did not realize they were on a collision course.

It was the roar of the motors and the turbulence caused by the wind shear of the Lares' plane that startled Juan González awake.

"¡Pero coño! [Damn it!] What are they doing here?" shouted Basulto.

Basulto, Billy, and Juan sat at attention in their seats, looking around to make sure they and the plane were OK. The three men were sharp-eyed now but still shaking, even after the plane's rattling stopped. In *Seagull Three,* the Lares knew they were going to get it from Basulto back at the hangar. They had almost caused a midair collision.

Then everything changed when Juan spotted what he remembers looked like a spider on the surface of the water. *Seagull One* was seventy miles south of Marathon when, at 12:45 p.m., Juan González spotted a raft with four souls aboard. "*¡BAALLSSA!* [Raft!]" he shouted, drawing out the word like the shout of *Goal!* at a South American soccer match. They quickly noted the coordinates, 23°49' N and 81°56' S, and did a low pass, letting the rafters below know they had been spotted. Juan took his camera out and snapped photos.

After the procedures checklist had been completed, there was a pause in the cockpit and a moment of silence, almost as if the motor had been turned off. Basulto, Billy, and Juan looked at each other and started jumping in their seats, shouting at each other. Crying. Basulto and Billy slapped each other on the shoulder; from the back, Juan happily pounded his friends.

Rubén looked up from the water and wondered who was in the plane. It was almost one o'clock and the sun was blinding him.

"It's those Brothers to the Rescue people, I heard about it on Radio Martí!" said his friend.

Seagull One could see the balseros waving a T-shirt or some rag back and forth. On the first low pass, they would later swear they saw them smiling. On their second low pass, they dropped a message inside an empty two-liter soda bottle, saying they would be calling the Coast Guard with their coordinates and to please turn off their engine. Basulto radioed the Coast Guard, who confirmed they were on their way.

At that time, the Brothers planes were not equipped with the relatively new Global Positioning System (GPS). They used either LORAN (Long-Range Navigation), or VOR (VHF Omni Directional Range). This technology required that they fly to two thousand feet to confirm their position and radio back to the base, which would alert the Coast Guard. After coming back down from two thousand feet, *Seagull One* flew protectively in circles over Rubén and his crew. But the Coast Guard took longer than expected, and Basulto had to refuel in Marathon. The Lares plane could not relay them that day, so both Brothers flights had to leave their first rafters behind, the very thing Basulto never wanted to do.

As the plane disappeared into the distance, Rubén and his crew were disheartened, wondering why they'd been abandoned. The monotony of waiting and the confusion of being left alone got to Rubén. So far the trip had been quite uneventful. It was almost a letdown. He laughed and told his friends he wanted to see some sharks. His friends were horrified, calling him insane and recounting the stories of so many they knew had not made it.

Interrupting their banter almost on cue, a black wing, longer than their twelve-foot raft, ascended from the water like a Leviathan. The slow-motion dance of the manta ray continued as it flipped over, exposing its white underbelly to the four rafters. Its movement on the flat sea rocked their raft.

"Now are you happy?" his friends yelled.

Two hours later, the Coast Guard cutter picked up the four balseros. Rubén and his group spent the night on the ship because the Coast Guard was looking for other rafters that had been spotted that day. Those were never found.

Back at the hangar after that successful mission, Guille told his brother, "You see, Koki, the Cubans got the first one."

The Lady Pilot

Women do not have to sacrifice personhood if they are mothers. They do not have to sacrifice motherhood in order to be persons. Liberation was meant to expand women's opportunities, not to limit them.

Elaine Heffner

Mayte Greco got used to the Brothers name quickly. In fact, she would have agreed to any name for the organization—just as long as she could fly.

She was born Mayte Rodríguez in Cuba and went into exile with her parents when she was one year old. Her father, Julio, had five Cuban pesos in his pocket when he landed in Miami and he used them to buy into the American dream. He worked two jobs, finished school, and became very successful.

When Julio Rodríguez Sr. bought the first family car, weekend days were for the beach and weekend evenings were for the airport. The Rodríguez family joined many others stationed along the grassy parking area along the perimeter road that circled Miami International Airport. Dubbed "submarine row," this was where young couples parked to make out after dates—or, instead of dates.

For Mayte, however, this was family time, and she fell in love with the airport, the planes, and the little blue lights. It was her favorite thing to do as a child.

Like so many Cuban refugees, Mayte had assimilated at school in English-speaking Miami, adapting to American ways, American customs. She spoke in English, thought in English; she felt American, not Cuban. Still, at home, the family kept their Cuban traditions, like eating rice and beans, celebrating the traditional Christmas Eve *nochebuena* dinners, and eating twelve grapes at midnight on New Year's Eve.

Her fascination with airplanes never faded. When most of her teenage friends at the Catholic all-girls Our Lady of Lourdes Academy High School were sneaking behind their parents' backs to meet their boyfriends, Mayte was sneaking around, too: taking flying lessons. She was a good girl, got good grades, and as far as her parents knew, she was obedient. Good Cuban girls were polite, honored their elders, and wore pearl stud earrings and thin gold bangle bracelets. Traditionally, they were chaperoned at parties, attended a college within driving distance from home, and did not leave the nest until the day of their wedding, as virgins of course. There were many traditions in Mayte's family, and Mayte had broken most of them. She didn't want to be a lady; she wanted to be a pilot.

During her first year of college at the University of Miami, while on vacation in Buenos Aires with her family, Mayte met an Argentinean named Ernie Greco. He was handsome, adventurous, four years older than she, and rich. Ernie came to visit her one month later, and they were secretly married at the courthouse in Miami. When her parents found out they were sick over it. *A decent Cuban girl like her.* The situation was remedied three months later with a big church wedding. When she gave birth to her first daughter, she remembers her mother's friends counting frantically on their fingers to ensure the proper number of months had passed since the wedding. The next three girls came one after another, but between diapers and play dates, Mayte flew.

It was a cheerleader named Monica Sosa, Basulto's stepdaughter, who first introduced Mayte to Basulto. He became her aviation mentor. When she found out about his interest in searching for rafters, she immediately wanted in.

It was Mayte and her younger brother, Julio, also a pilot, whom Basulto called for the feasibility studies and the trial runs on the airplanes: What would be the optimal flight altitude for spotting? How would they communicate back to shore? What would they do once they spotted a raft? How would they mark the raft's exact location?

Trial runs were conducted over the Everglades, the River of Grass that forms the greater part of southwestern Florida. The duo would pick a bush at random, call it a raft, and see if they could really fly over it and maintain it in sight for four to five hours at a time. The planes were small and cramped, the temperature would rise to more than one hundred degrees inside the cockpit, and the runs were tedious.

Mayte loved every minute of it.

When Mayte and Basulto advanced to the Florida Straits, they would spot what they believed to be a recreational yacht, only to fly down and realize that it was a two-thousand-passenger cruise ship. If a cruise ship looked so small from a distance, what would a raft look like? A dot. They were looking for dots on the water. They concluded that looking out at an angle was more productive than looking straight down, and that five hundred feet was the best altitude.

They practiced in Basulto's small, single-engine Cessna 172. Their list of supplies grew after each test run: cell phones, life jackets for themselves and for a rafter, and later, handheld radios, water bottles, and small packaged food items.

News of the first rescue buzzed through the community. Basulto's friend Roberto Rodríguez Tejera of cable television Channel 41 held a fund-raising telethon. Rodríguez Tejera and Basulto had been friends for years and they shared similar views on active nonviolence, an emergent movement in Cuba. The friends agreed that now more than ever there was a possibility for change from within.

The morning of the telethon Mayte Greco was scheduled to fly, and she had carpool duty. She begged another mother to cover for her in the afternoon because she would probably be late for pick-up, again. She jumped into her favorite snug-fitting jeans and a white T-shirt, brushed back her curly blonde hair, and drove the carpool rounds in her minivan. At school, she kissed her four daughters and their friends good-bye, then sped over to Tamiami Airport. She pulled into a spot on the grass in front of the hangar and greeted Basulto with a kiss on the cheek.

"You're flying with Conrad today," he told her.

Conrad Webber, the first American-born pilot to join the group, was waiting for her at the hangar, smiling, looking around at his new group of friends who were yakking back and forth about who would be flying with whom. More than a jovial smile, his grin seemed to say "I am amused." He *was* amused by his newfound friends, more like a family really, this Brothers to the Rescue organization.

"*Coño*, people, speak in English, Conrad's here!" Basulto chastised. That was how Conrad would always remember it. The Spanish-speaking pilots would be halfway through a meeting or at a dinner party, conversing in their native tongue, when someone would notice Conrad's amused smile and remember the *americano* among them. Everyone would switch to English for a while, but then someone would utter maybe just one sentence in Spanish, and like birds in flight, turning in unison in the direction of their leader, the whole flock would switch to Spanish.

Conrad's American friends thought he was crazy to work with these Cubans (lumping all Spanish-speaking people into that single ethnic background), but they did not dare say so to his face. Conrad Webber was a tough-looking guy. He was in his early forties, tall, and built like a fullback, with sandy blond hair just beginning to gray at the temples, as well as on his signature bushy mustache. His blue eyes squinted when he smiled.

Conrad Webber waited, not understanding one damn thing the Cubans were saying. Of course, they were not really all Cuban, because there were the three Argentine brothers, the French girl Virginie—he couldn't understand her *English*—the Peruvian guy Carlos Gartner, and the rest. Brothers would soon wave the nineteen national flags of the pilots represented. But for now, Conrad was the only American.

Mayte Greco was Conrad's favorite, and he was happy to be flying with her today. He loved Mayte's engaging green eyes and the gray feather tattoo she had on her back. It might not be ladylike, but it was the sexiest thing he had ever seen in his life. He was not sure how his wife would feel about that tattoo.

Conrad and Mayte had been flying together for more than two hours when they heard the good news about a rescue: the Lares brothers had spotted four men on a raft. Conrad and Mayte deviated from their search pattern to take a look, knowing it would be a while before the Coast Guard arrived. A videographer from one of the local TV stations was onboard, and he, too, was very excited to film his first rafter.

On the way there, Mayte glanced out of her window and was distracted by a dot. Or was it a floating piece of wood? Low passes confirmed what they suspected they were seeing. The first low pass must have scared the balseros because they covered their heads. On the second low pass, they looked up. On the third, the men waved.

"Another one, another one, oh—my—God—we found another one!" yelled Mayte. *Their* raft, *their* find, *their* rescue.

Conrad would later tell his friends that Mayte went "Cuban-crazy." While she screamed, Conrad saw her jerk the steering column and wrench it into her diaphragm so violently that he was certain she would be bruised the next day. They shot up from fifteen feet to two thousand in what seemed like seconds. They were on rocket power, sheer adrenaline, doing a vertical climb. Conrad feared he would have to call in a "Code Victor" for the videographer in the back. Victor meant vomit.

Mayte was so excited she could not wait to call base about the find. After soaring to two thousand, she picked up the cell phone, which in 1991 was the size of a pavement brick, and called—her mother.

"¡Maa-miii! We found a balsero!!" Then she went on to describe in Spanish the details of the rescue. Afterward, she called base and the Coast Guard, who probably had already heard the news by then.

The hangar was in party mode that afternoon. Mayte told the story over and over again, talking excitedly with her hands, gesturing, brushing her curly mane away from green eyes that kept spilling over with tears. The Lares brothers were hugging everyone, thanking God for this glorious day. Billy Schuss was actually smiling. Polo, the group historian, wrote a poem. Basulto was beaming. They had saved two groups of rafters and everyone was a hero. Channel 41 raised forty thousand dollars. Brothers ordered pizza.

Conrad Webber once again sat at the hangar, smiling, not understanding one damn thing anyone was saying, but it really didn't matter. He and Mayte had saved four lives today. No translation needed.

Later that evening, Mayte and Conrad drove three hours to Key West and met the rafters they had rescued. The father and three sons were being processed when they arrived. They were sunburned and tired, but jubilant. When they saw Mayte and Conrad, they cried, thanking them time and again.

"Why did you cover your heads at first?" Mayte asked them, curious.

"We didn't know who you were, flying around in circles. We had never heard of Brothers to the Rescue. We didn't know if you were going to shoot at us," one of them told her.

"But then you waved," Mayte said.

"Yes," answered the sunburned father. "When we saw it was a lady, we knew you would do us no harm."

7

Pilots, Protocol, and Planes

Life consists in what a man is thinking of all day.
Ralph Waldo Emerson

As the number of saved rafters increased, so did the pilots' competitive streaks. Brothers started a contest among the pilots and volunteers to see who could spot the most balseros. Upon returning from a mission, they would plaster the planes with Brothers to the Rescue stickers and record every time a raft was spotted, along with the date and the number of people rescued. The older pilots, like Conrad and Basulto, envied the Lares brothers and other young pilots like Carlos Gartner, the Peruvian bush pilot, for their excellent vision.

"Sometimes pilots in the armed forces are known for how many planes they down, or enemy they kill," Guille would explain to newcomers. "We want to be known for the people we save."

The pilots were also set apart by their new uniforms: collared polo shirts with the Brothers to the Rescue logo appliquéd on the pocket. At picnics and celebrations, the pilots held mini-initiations to present the new pilots with metal wing clips. Bumper stickers adorned their cars, and soon, the cars of people in the Miami community. Later, T-shirts and caps were ordered to hand out at fund-raisers and to throw down to the rafters.

Brothers to the Rescue saw more than just rafters in the waters of the Florida Straits. There were fishing vessels, cruise ships, and sailboats on the water. They rarely saw other air traffic, since commercial airliners flew at twenty-five thousand feet. But one day they encountered some bizarre air traffic: Cuban MiGs.

A childhood friend of Basulto's, Alfredo Sánchez, joined Brothers to the Rescue after reading about the first few missions. As teenagers in Cuba, Alfredo and Basulto had spent summers racing around on their motorcycles. Now he lived about seventy miles north of the Tamiami Airport in West Palm Beach.

Alfredo had been flying his own plane since he was seventeen. His family was in the sugar industry in Cuba, and since his father was also a pilot, they were one of the few Havana families that flew to their sugar plantation rather than take the hours-long road trip. Now Alfredo flew his own Twin Cessna Flyer 310 out of the Lantana Airport near West Palm Beach to join the other pilots in Tamiami for rescue operations.

On July 21, 1991, Alfredo's assigned grid included flying east near the Cay Sal Bank that was part of the Bahamas Islands. Guille Lares was his copilot, and there were two recently rescued rafters in the back as observers—a rare exception. Basulto did not usually allow rafters onboard to avoid conflicts of interest: some would be looking for particular family members that had set out on a raft and others had even offered to pay Brothers to find relatives in the Straits. Brothers to the Rescue never accepted any offers of money for those purposes.

Soon after takeoff, Alfredo and Guille had noticed an Aerostat balloon and made note of its location. Aerostats are basically large fabric envelopes filled with helium and they can rise up to fifteen thousand feet. The Aerostat of Cudjoe Key, sometimes called Fat Albert, is a balloon-borne radar system which looks like a Goodyear blimp, except that it is tethered by a single cable. Fat Albert was the watchdog to catch the drug traffickers in the Florida Straits.

After many hours of searching just south of the 24th parallel, the rear observer on Alfredo's plane spotted a raft with seven men onboard who appeared to be in a very fragile state. Alfredo flew up to two thousand feet and called Basulto at base and later the U.S. Coast Guard, who responded that they were at least four hours away. Alfredo and Guille notified them that they would wait. If necessary, they would run to Key West to refuel.

While Basulto was still on the phone with Alfredo, a call from the Coast Guard interrupted his conversation. A Cuban military target was rapidly approaching the Brothers plane, and they needed to leave the area immediately. They were Cuban MiGs (named after Artem Mikoyan and Mikhail

Gurevich of the Soviet design bureau), twin-engine fighter jets capable of flying at sixty thousand feet and at speeds of Mach 2.3.

Basulto told Alfredo about the MiGs, and the latter in turn consulted with Guille and the crew. Not having a GPS system, they might never be able to find the rafters again if they left. They elected to stay with the raft.

Within minutes Alfredo received a radio call specifically directed to his aircraft from a Wove 1 and Wove 2: U.S. interceptors dispatched out of Homestead Air Force Base for their protection. Flying at thirty thousand feet above Alfredo's plane, the Homestead interceptors informed Alfredo that the Cuban MiGs had returned to Cuban airspace. Wove 1 and Wove 2 would continue flying over Brothers for the remainder of their mission, while Brothers flew protectively over the rafters.

After the MiG incident, a new protocol was immediately put in place with Homestead Air Force Base. If hostile aircraft were found in international waters at the same time as Brothers to the Rescue were flying, interceptors were immediately dispatched. What normally happened was that as soon as Cuban air traffic control spotted the interceptors, the Cuban MiGs were called back.

Brothers to the Rescue also changed their standard operating procedures. Whenever a search-and-rescue mission crossed the 24th parallel, they were to contact Havana Center Air Traffic Control, informing them of their intent to fly in international waters below the 24th parallel but clear of Cuba's twelve-mile territorial limits. Those conversations were cordial on the Brothers' side and recurrently insulting from Havana Center, who sometimes used foul language and called into question the parental lineage of the pilots. Albeit through clenched teeth, the Brothers pilots responded to the name-calling in scripted responses. "Good morning, Havana, it's a beautiful day."

Rescue fever caught on and so did splinter groups. Just a few miles north of Miami, thirty-six year-old Dennis Murphy started Brothers for the Rescue of Broward County. Basulto was not happy—not because of any perceived competition, but because they had chosen the same name. Meanwhile, Dennis Murphy was upset that Basulto shunned his group.

The problem with splinter groups, Basulto told the *Ft. Lauderdale Sun-Sentinel*, is the lack of coordination and flying patterns. "We fly looking down for rafters, not looking forward." Plus, it was rare that any rafter would be found as far north as Broward County.

Brothers for the Rescue of Broward County was short-lived, but soon another rescue group cropped up in the Florida Keys. A Brothers to the Rescue volunteer spotted René González, the Cuban defector who had been with Brothers since its inception, working with another group in Marathon Key, Florida. Basulto became suspicious when his friend witnessed the pilots of that group being detained and questioned by the Drug Enforcement Agency (DEA), spread-eagled on the ground. Basulto worried the group was not a humanitarian one at all.

That one of the pilots would become involved in a drug ring, or even the mere suggestion of a connection between Brothers and drug smuggling, was Basulto's greatest fear for the organization. Brothers to the Rescue and drug dealers did, after all, fly in the same neighborhood. Rather than dropping water or radios, the drug smugglers made other kinds of drops to waiting boats below. It would be awfully tempting for anyone with that inclination to sign on for a mission as cover, then to drop off or pick up a shipment in any of the nearby Bahamas Islands.

"Clip his wings," Basulto told Guille Lares back at the hangar. "I don't know anything about that group and they may be involved in drugs." When Guille took René González off the roster, he did not protest. René Gonzalez was well liked in the Brothers group, he was *buena gente*, good people, and he continued volunteering at the hangar with other duties and participating in some of the Brothers' events.

Ongoing media coverage brought an avalanche of young pilots to the organization, and the number of missions grew. Brothers had almost twenty pilots by August 1991, flying three times a week at full capacity, but there were never enough to match the numbers of rafters floating below. Basulto needed more planes.

He learned about some Cessna FAC/0-2 airplanes that had been used in Vietnam and were now mothballed at Davis-Monthan Air Force Base in Arizona, property of the U.S. government. Basulto had committed not to ask for government money, but he reasoned that asking for unused planes was a different matter. He needed someone inside the government to petition on Brothers' behalf. He needed a connection, a sponsor, an advocate. What he got was a godmother.

Godparents, *padrinos*, are an important part of a child's life in Latin culture. Godparents do not just witness your baptism and promise to raise you in the faith. They hold prominent roles at birthdays, graduations, and marriages, maintaining a seat of honor throughout a person's life. In Spanish, the word *padrino* is also used as epithet for knowing someone with leverage, a person who can get you in touch with higher-ups. Brothers to the Rescue was about to get its own godmother: Congresswoman Ileana Ros-Lehtinen.

Ileana, as she is known to her constituents, was elected to the House of Representatives in 1989, becoming the first Hispanic woman and the first Cuban American elected to the U.S. Congress. Her husband was Vietnam veteran Dexter Lehtinen, who became the attorney for the Southern District of Florida. Ileana and her family had been acquainted with Basulto for years.

In January 1992, at Basulto's request, Ileana wrote to the Office of the Secretary of the Air Force, asking that they donate the four mothballed Cessnas to Brothers. She went into detail about the humanitarian nature of the organization, and how in only eight months they had flown 202 missions and saved 143 people.

When President George H. W. Bush did not give Basulto the answer he wanted, he petitioned the president's son Jeb Bush, who would later become governor of Florida. Mayte Greco and Guille Lares accompanied Basulto to Bush's Coral Gables office where he worked with the Codina Group of real estate developers. The meeting was positive but fruitless. Basulto would ask Ileana to try again.

Ileana was visiting the hangar one day when she told Basulto that she had been invited to fly on Air Force One with President Bush. Basulto quickly penned a letter to the president, once again requesting the mothballed airplanes. Ileana worked tirelessly to get those planes.

"Thank you," Basulto told her afterward, touched by her efforts. "By the way, I'm officially naming you Godmother of Brothers to the Rescue."

Ileana became indispensable to the organization, attending nearly every press conference and advocating for them in every situation. She petitioned everyone from the president on down for help for this humanitarian organization. She did everything in her power for Brothers—except fly.

"I'm not a good flyer, Basulto."

The letters regarding the planes continued back and forth. They were told to address the GSA (General Services Administration) and the FSPDP (Federal Surplus Property Donation Program). These agencies replied with brochures like "How to Buy Surplus Property," complete with phone numbers and contact names. Basulto phoned and contacted. The rhetoric and the runaround continued: "the DOD [Department of Defense] may help; if not contact Sales and Management at the DRMS [Defense Reutilization and Marketing Service]." Every governmental acronym was tossed their way. A new year and another administration would be ushered in before the final *no* arrived.

Yet someone always came through for Basulto, and this time, a close friend donated another plane, which they named *Ofelia*. "It's all Him," Basulto would say, pointing his finger heavenward.

As the number of missions increased, so did the learning experiences of the pilots. They practiced maneuvers and turns-about-a-point in staying above the rafters for extended hours. They fought drowsiness and boredom. The perfect eye angle for looking out their small windows, in order to lock in on the tiny dots in the water, was honed down to a science. They fought the glare, the heat, and the urge to pee (even though the guys sometimes used empty water bottles for their pressing needs, women didn't have that luxury). Like college quarterbacks, they sharpened their throwing arms by pitching water bottles and other supplies from the planes to the rafts below. Actual drops were made at ten to twenty feet above sea level, which meant that if the pilot looked away for one second, the aircraft could hit the water.

They soon realized that tossing down frozen thirty-two-ounce water bottles could easily knock out an already-weary rafter—or worse, sink the raft. Brothers started packaging water and other goods in bubble wrap, nicknaming them *pavitos*—turkeys—because the final product looked like a butterball turkey. Water bottles, T-shirts, food, and later, radios, were bundled up in bubble wrap then sealed with a Brothers to the Rescue bumper sticker across the top. Volunteers at the hangar worked assembly-line style, packaging perfect pavitos.

Billy Schuss' home became a mini Brothers to the Rescue warehouse. Someone had contacted his wife Maggie, offering to donate discarded saline solution bags from hospitals. These proved to be even better than the thirty-two-ounce soda bottles. Maggie installed a freezer in her dining room and packed it with frozen water bags that would later be enveloped in bubble wrap.

Brothers had pilots, protocol, and pavitos. They still needed more planes and more money. Little by little, Basulto dedicated more and more time to the new organization, and correspondingly less time to his paying job. As she watched their savings dwindle, Rita Basulto worried about their financial situation, she worried about her husband's employment, and she worried about his distancing himself from the children.

Basulto worried about the empty rafts.

8

The First Accident

*BE PREPARED, which means, you are always to be in a state
of readiness in mind and body to do your duty.*

Robert Baden-Powell, Boy Scouts pledge

If any of the residents in the upscale Coral Gables Cocoplum community wanted to use the clubhouse pool that morning, they would have been surprised to see a group of fully clothed young men wearing life vests taking orders from a stocky older guy sporting aviator sunglasses. Thankfully, the clubhouse pool was seldom used in this gated community, where the least expensive homes cost a million dollars. As a builder/developer of those six-thousand-plus-square-foot luxury estates, Basulto had free access to the Cocoplum clubhouse and swimming pool. The pool was a perfect place to simulate a water accident, because surely one day they would crash.

Apart from the pilots' licensing exams, logged hours, GPS seminars, and first-aid courses, Basulto held his own training sessions for the volunteers.

The young pilots may have preferred to be with their girlfriends at the beach that day, but Basulto had asked them to report for training, so there they stood, looking a little silly wearing life vests. Basulto noted their bewilderment as he arranged some plastic chairs near the edge of the pool, in groups of two and four. He led them to the chairs and they obediently sat. Then he placed a packaged inflatable life raft by each group and took out his stopwatch. He assigned roles: one would be the drowning victim, the other the rescuer, the other two observers. He saw his pilots exchange looks and raise eyebrows as they sat in their chairs. Then one by one, as hard as he could, Basulto shoved them into the pool, trying to simulate the confusion and panic they would experience if they crashed in the sea. Then he tried to drown out the laughter. BTTR Survival 101.

A few months later, Mabel Dieppa, a young Puerto Rican journalist for *¡ÉXITO!* magazine, and photographer Andrew Itkoff were loosely donning their life vests before boarding Basulto's plane. Brothers had been flying for almost a year that May 2, 1992, and *not* having someone from the media on a flight was the exception. Today's mission was number 300 and Brothers had already rescued an equal amount of rafters.

Lately their success rate had been so high that journalists participating on missions were sorely disappointed if they did not find a rafter, sometimes complaining that the day, the camera equipment, the film, and the time had all been for nothing.

Guille Lares was not keen on flying for nothing, either. He and his brothers were the most successful spotters in the organization. Other pilots felt that having one of the Lares brothers onboard almost guaranteed a balsero, as if these three pilots were human talismans in the sky. The brothers insisted that God was the pilot; He worked the miracles every day. They dedicated each mission, each rafter, to God.

The pilots also understood that flying with members of the media was more difficult than flying with trained observers. Doing so required an additional thirty minutes of safety precautions before the flight, as well as explanations on how to train the eye to look for the dots on the water. Because of the hours they kept, media reps frequently fell asleep in the backseat, something which irritated Basulto constantly. Even his friend Roberto Koltun of the *Miami Herald*, one of his favorite photographers, was guilty of the backseat snooze.

"Roberto, wake up!" Basulto would shout at him. Koltun would wake up, snap a prize-winning photo of the rafter below, and fall back into deep slumber.

"For that, Basulto never gave me my Brothers to the Rescue pin," he would complain later.

Now Mission 300 was ready to take off, so Rita and Basulto joined the pilots and crews at the hangar to send them off. Standing by his single-engine Cessna, Basulto noticed Mabel Dieppa adjusting and readjusting her life vest, nervous.

"Don't worry, Mabel. If you crash, Guille will know what to do. He's the best," he said, kidding around with the young reporter who seemed hesitant about boarding. Mabel choked out a chuckle.

Code Victors were the norm for the media reps, who usually got sick in the back of the plane as they jotted down everything they saw. Adjusting bags of camera equipment while trying to focus out of the windows required an iron stomach that most did not have. Simply moving around in the cramped space, talking through the headsets to be able to hear something—anything—above the engine roar, and sweating through a life vest in the sauna-like cockpit made getting the story a physical as well as mental struggle.

Basulto knew the media people were sometimes a nuisance for the pilots, but he was grateful to have this mouthpiece to the world. Reporters from dozens of countries had already flown with Brothers, including a representative from the Tokyo Broadcasting System, enabling thirty million Japanese viewers to see a rescue. They were raising worldwide consciousness of not only the rafter crisis, but the much older crisis on the island of Cuba.

Guille enjoyed dealing with reporters on the ground. He was a natural in front of the camera, and Basulto trusted him to be a spokesperson for the organization. His GQ looks and Argentine accent made him a favorite, especially with female reporters.

Guille called everyone together for their customary prayer circle. Carlos Tabernilla—another pilot from West Palm Beach—and his crew joined the circle; they would be flying another plane that day. Guille remembers the photographer Andrew saying he would not join in the prayer, which may have given Guille a momentary pause.

As part of the preflight plan, Guille went through the safety precautions with Mabel and Andrew, explaining what to do in case of an emergency. He used the phrase "single engine" repeatedly, and Mabel and Andrew nodded as if they understood completely what that meant. They took off at ten o'clock.

By one in the afternoon, both Mabel and Andrew seemed pretty drained, and a little bored. They had not seen a raft and the glaring sea below had them in a semi-trance. When Carlos Tabernilla called to report a raft sighting, everyone's spirits lifted. The seven rafters were fifty miles south of Key West. Mabel urged Guille to go to Tabernilla's location so they could photograph the rescue.

Forgotten were the queasy stomachs, the heat, and the boredom. Andrew shot rolls and rolls of film of the desperate souls underneath him. He captured Guille's low passes and the procedure of throwing down a pavito. Because the mission protocol was to wait for the Coast Guard, Andrew had ample time to click away during the many orbits Guille flawlessly performed. The rescue of the seven by the U.S. Coast Guard showed the heroics of the officers as they lifted the desperate rafters one by one out of the unseaworthy craft.

As they turned to leave, Carlos Tabernilla radioed Guille that he noticed some engine oil streaking red on one side of the latter's plane. Guille confirmed that he was losing oil pressure—fast—and he called Basulto on his cell phone.

Basulto and Rita were at the Virgin of Charity Church in Coconut Grove. Rita liked visiting that church to pray for the pilots, but she also wanted some time alone with her husband. She needed a neutral zone, a safe place where she could command her husband's attention to talk about their dwindling savings and the stress Brothers was exerting on their family life. But even in a neutral zone, even at church, Rita was interrupted by Brothers to the Rescue.

After explaining the situation to Basulto, Guille handed the phone to Mabel so that he could concentrate on the controls. He told his crew to prepare for a water landing.

"How are you, Mabel?" Basulto asked calmly. "You know you're flying with the best."

"*Ay*, José," she said. Over the roar of the engine, Basulto noticed the tremor in her whisper. "I forgot to tell you, but I don't know how to swim." Mabel was from Puerto Rico, and ironically many islanders, living their entire lives surrounded by water, did not know how to swim.

Basulto grimaced to Rita, who had overheard Mabel's confession. "Don't worry, you won't have to. Guille's an Olympic swimmer," he reassured her.

Mabel gave Basulto their coordinates, and he called them in to the Coast Guard.

Guille very calmly reminded his passengers of the fast-approaching landing. They immediately adjusted their life vests.

"Oh, my God . . . oh, my God . . . oh, my God . . . oh, my God." Guille turned around at the sound of Andrew's mantra.

"Oh, *now* he wants to pray," Guille thought.

The biggest danger of a water landing is that the plane might pitch forward. Basulto told Mabel and Andrew to toss out anything that could become a projectile when they hit the water. That meant that Andrew had to toss out thousands of dollars in camera equipment and all the photos he had just taken. Mabel was instructed to inform Basulto continuously of the coordinates so that he could radio them to the Coast Guard. It would also keep her mind off the descent.

"Now open the door a little, and put a shoe or something there to keep it open once you hit the water," he said. This would prevent the door from sealing shut. Mabel wedged one of her Reeboks in the door.

Finally, the motor cut off and they were gliding. Basulto asked Mabel to describe the changing color of the water and whatever else she was seeing outside the window. This would give him an idea of how near the coast they were and, once again, keep her mind off the impending crash landing.

"What color is it now?" he asked.

"Dark blue," she replied shakily.

"Anything else out there?" he continued with the seemingly mindless questions, trying to redirect her fears from the approaching collision. That, and not knowing how to swim.

"A boat," she whispered.

"Now what does the water look like?"

The colors were getting lighter and lighter, and she could even see the sand under the water. Rita took out her rosary.

"Tell me how Andrew is doing," he continued.

"Well, he's fine, and then, you know, he had to get rid. . . ."

Silence.

They had crashed.

On impact, Mabel remembers something hitting her on the side of the head and her dropping the cell phone. Within seconds, water filled the cabin.

Guille made a textbook landing about six miles south of Key West and his passengers were unhurt. His mental preparation and training for such an event paid off that day.

Guille and his crew slid out the door that had been propped open with Mabel's tennis shoe. Then Mabel remembered her purse and her notes, left behind. She sat on the wing for a few moments, like someone waiting for a bus, while Guille went back inside for them.

There was a boat in the area that belonged to the owners of the Hard Rock Café. Guille's crew was in the water less than five minutes before the fishermen picked them up. N5416K, Basulto's private single-engine plane, was visible in the crystal-clear bay waters, resting on the white sand in eleven feet of water. From Tabernilla's plane, it looked like a child's toy airplane that had been left behind at the bottom of an inflatable pool.

The fishermen took them to Key West, where they were soon joined by Rita and Basulto. The Basultos offered to fly Mabel and Andrew back to

Miami, but by that time, Mabel had already rented a car. She swore she would never fly again.

The investigation revealed that the tube that regulated the oil pressure had been severed. This seemed very strange because the plane had just received its annual inspection.

The media coverage on Guille's crash shed light on the risks these young pilots were taking every day and drew even more attention to the rafter crisis. Suddenly, every photographer that had flown with Brothers sent in pictures to the newspapers, flooding the media with the desperation in the Florida Straits.

Attorney Sofía Powell-Cosío needed one of these pictures. She worked with the law firm of Paul, Landy, Beily, and Harper in Miami.

Born in the United States to Cuban parents, Sofía and her husband, Alberto, both in their twenties, were members of a group of young Cuban Americans called Alianza de Jóvenes Cubanos (Young Cuban Alliance). The Alianza developed into a political niche for Cuban Americans in their twenties and thirties who did not see eye-to-eye with the established, older Cuban American exile groups.

In Canada, the tourist travel to Cuba was flourishing, and Alianza was involved in an ad campaign to bring attention to the realities of life in Cuba. But their budget could not cover reprint rights or a professional photographer. Alianza suggested Sofía approach Basulto.

"Sure, I have pictures, why don't you come over my house right now?" Basulto answered a surprised Sofía.

Basulto gave the young couple a warm welcome at his home. Sofía was about 5'5" and rail thin, with long brown hair, brown eyes, and sharp intelligent eyes. She wore minimal makeup, her natural look accented with big glasses. She looked thirteen.

Basulto gave her a box full of photographs of rafters. She chose one that had two men in an inner tube and used it for a billboard that would read: "As you pay to go, they die to leave." Another billboard showed a picture of a Cuban rafter family, which Sofía placed side-by-side with one of a Canadian family vacationing in Cuba, with the caption: "Your paradise, their hell." The billboards caused an uproar in Canada.

The day after her visit with Basulto, Sofía was surprised to get a call from him.

"Do you know anything about planes?" he asked her.

"I've flown in them," said Sofía.

"Can you buy me a plane?" he asked. "I need it by tomorrow at noon." Pilo Azqueta, a well-to-do Cuban American living outside Miami, had offered to buy Brothers a new plane to replace the one Guille had crashed.

"Sure." Everyone at Paul, Landy, Beily, and Harper worked round the clock to facilitate Basulto's purchase of the plane the next day. Brothers bought a twin-engine Cessna 337 Skymaster, which would be the new plane of choice for the organization. Called a "push-pull," this craft has one engine mounted on the nose and the other at the rear of the pod-style fuselage. The new plane's tail number was registered as N2506, in honor of Brigade 2506 of the Bay of Pigs invasion. It was painted sky blue, with the nose and the N2506 in bold bright yellow. It was Basulto's new baby and the signature plane of Brothers to the Rescue: *Seagull One.*

9

Balseros

. . . those who seek refuge in America will find it.

President Lyndon B. Johnson

It would be years before anyone in Cuba ever saw a televised Brothers rescue, so on an island where every bit of outside information is filtered, altered, or deleted, word-of-mouth proved the most effective means to spread the news about these saviors in the skies. Brothers to the Rescue continued to warn people through Radio Martí: "don't attempt to cross, because you will probably die." But all it took was one success story, one happy ending, to make it back to the family or the cousin of a neighbor of a sister of a friend—and there was hope. *If they made it, you could make it.*

"We don't necessarily come to live the American dream," said one rafter, "but rather, to escape the Cuban nightmare."

The Cuban nightmare escalated. The lines at the hangar were jammed with requests from family members: Please look for my uncle, he left three days ago. . . . Keep an eye out for my brother and his wife and child—they left last night. . . . My old man is out there somewhere.

Oftentimes non-Cubans reading the rafter stories could not comprehend the level of desperation that would prompt someone to take to the Straits. How bad could things really be in Cuba?

The Cuban people themselves had been led to believe that their nation was the most highly developed Latin American country, with the most advanced technology, good education, and superior medical care. It was hard for Cubans to imagine people in worse conditions than they were, but they made themselves believe it. After all, no information to the contrary was reported by the two government-owned newspapers or the two government-owned television stations.

One rafter who would not accept one more lie about the Cuban night-mare was thirty-six-year-old Nelson Alemán. Nelson had been a teacher for many years until the Cuban Revolution pulled him away from his education profession and forced him to perform manual labor on the renovation projects for the new Varadero Beach hotels. After the collapse of the Soviet Union, Cuba had welcomed foreign investors to their pristine beaches, particularly ones from Canada and Spain.

Nelson was privy to news from outside the island through his brother-in-law, who traveled with the Cuban Merchant Marine. Nelson's brother-in-law said it was all a lie, that Cuba was the *worst*, that the island had gone backward since the revolution. Cuba had *become* a third-world country.

More lies seemed to surface in 1989 during the trial of General Arnaldo T. Ochoa, Castro's highest-ranking military official and a hero of the revolution. A State Department official told the *New York Times* that there appeared to be personal problems between General Ochoa and Raúl Castro. In the span of a month he was arrested and executed for what most believed to be a fabricated charge: drug smuggling. Previous scandals over other high government officials had Cuban nationals—and the world—wondering over the apparent housecleaning the Castro brothers had implemented. It seemed like a lie to Nelson. It was.

Nelson's brother-in-law reminded him that the blockade Castro fumed about was only with the United States, not with the rest of the world. "Why don't they get what they need from other countries!"

Finally, Nelson's brother-in-law and his girlfriend jumped aboard a motorboat one day and left for Miami. Their journey, in March 1990, occurred during a severe cold front under high seas. His brother-in-law lost the tip of a finger to frostbite, and spent weeks recovering at the Krome Detention Center in southwest Miami after the couple was rescued. As soon as he was released he wrote to his family with stories of life outside Cuba. Nelson Alemán and his wife, Mercedes, thirty-four, longed for the opportunity to live that life.

The opportunity would come through Mercedes' family members, who were fishermen from Cárdenas in the northern part of the island, where the world-famous Varadero beach is located. Her family was part of the original one hundred that settled there in the 1920s. Even though he was retired, Mercedes' father still had a fishing boat, and more important, a fishing license. Without this coveted piece of paper, no one was allowed to board, let alone own, a fishing boat. Indeed, if you ever wanted to take your family out on a Sunday afternoon to see what you could catch, you would risk arrest. Children onboard any vessel were a red flag to the Border Patrol that a family may have intentions to escape.

Mercedes' father had welcomed Fidel's plan for the poor in the early days of the revolution. Education for his children was the most appealing aspect to him. His children and their children went to school and excelled in their studies. Perhaps that very education is what opened their eyes.

Mercedes was a librarian and her joy was giving her only daughter, Kalismary, the wonder of literature, even if the books had been selected by the state. But what Kalismary really wanted was a juice box, the kind that practically every preschooler in the United States drinks daily. Her friend's mother brought her own daughter a juice box every day from work; Kalismary wanted the same from Mercedes. Her friend also snacked on ham-and-cheese sandwiches, something Kalismary's family had not tasted in years.

"I work in a library," Mercedes told her, "so I bring you books. Your friend's mother works in the tourist store in the hotel. That's why she can get her daughter juice boxes."

Cuban nationals were not allowed in the tourist shops, which stocked the usual wares and gifts of most hotels worldwide. Cuban nationals were not allowed to stay in the hotels, either, no matter how much money they had. They were not even permitted to swim at the hotel beaches. That buffer kept tourists from hearing any firsthand accounts of scarcity or want on the island.

Now that they had access to a boat, the Alemán family planned their escape—because of the lies, because of General Ochoa, because of the juice box.

They began work on the *Misladys,* a twenty-one-foot boat with an outboard motor and a Bimini top. They could work in the daylight without suspicion since Mercedes' family were fishermen. It would not even draw the attention of the neighborhood police, the CDR (Committee for the Defense of the Revolution), who was privy to the most private of family affairs.

Nelson listened attentively to his father-in-law's instructions on how to handle the boat, how to navigate the seas, and how to recognize the signs of foul weather. For years they planned, because the timing had to be perfect.

Cuba was hosting the Pan American Games from August 2 to 18, 1991, so Nelson watched the Cuban Coast Guard closely to find the right opportunity. When the games ended, Nelson and his cousin decided to make their move, hoping the Coast Guard would still be preoccupied with the tourists and athletes leaving the country.

They slipped away on August 20, 1991, at about nine in the evening, from the southernmost part of the Bay of Cárdenas. They were to meet up with the rest of their friends, who had another boat, at Cayo Mono, the northernmost cay outside the bay, and from there continue on to freedom. Onboard were Mercedes and Kalismary, as well as Mercedes' sister and her daughter, a cousin, and a family of four that were friends of the Alemáns. Mercedes' parents stayed behind.

When they reached Cayo Mono they waited quietly for Nelson's cousin—as quietly as they could with the motor running. Kalismary was already feeling nauseous because of the fumes. Although she was the granddaughter of a fisherman, at thirteen, this was her first time on a boat. The group could not turn on a flashlight and they had no radio communications. There was no way to signal the other boat.

"Maybe I should turn off the engine and we might be able to listen for them," suggested Nelson.

"No!" he remembers they all said at once. "What if it doesn't turn on again?" After an agonizing wait, they decided to head out alone, convincing themselves the other boat was ahead of them.

They had packed plenty of water and nonperishables, as well as Gravinol, used for seasickness. Kalismary was the first one to need it. Their few valuables consisted of extra clothes and an antique map of Cuba from 1921 that Nelson's grandfather had given him. Made of cloth, the map was his most cherished possession, kept hidden for years.

The night was warm and calm, and once past Cayo Mono, Nelson could see the resplendence of the city of Havana and the glow of Matanzas behind him. The evening was peaceful, the motor humming reliably. Those that could find a comfortable enough space, slept.

At dawn they were awakened by giant swells, the boat riding high on the crest of the waves, then sloping down, over and over again. Mercedes helped settle everyone's stomach with a Gravinol-and-tea concoction for breakfast.

They had reached the halfway mark on the Straits of Florida when they saw *Seagull One*.

It was broiling inside the cockpit and the backs of Basulto's thighs were sticking to the seat. They had left at dawn that Wednesday morning and had already been searching for four hours. It was frustrating to think they would go back to base empty-handed, but they knew they had less than two hours of fuel left. Basulto was hopeful; he was with Guille Lares, and the Lares brothers *always* found somebody.

Guille saw some movement below. At first Basulto could not ascertain how many were in the boat because it looked like there was an onboard scuffle and attempt to hide under the tarp. They would later find out that the Alemán family and their ten passengers believed Brothers to the Rescue to be part of the Cuban Air Force.

Basulto called in the coordinates to the Coast Guard and prepared to drop a balloon. Attached to it was an empty water bottle; inside was a message of welcome to the United States. On the low pass, Guille dropped the welcoming message.

Nelson motored over and saw what looked like a birthday balloon attached to a plastic bottle. Folded inside was a sheet of yellow legal-size paper with the following handwritten message:

> Welcome to the Land of Freedom. The Coast Guard is on the way. Brothers to the Rescue.

Then the Alemáns heard a voice from the heavens calling out to them: "Are you all right? Is anyone hurt? Does anyone need emergency medical attention? Are there any small children or older people onboard?" It was Basulto, speaking through a megaphone. These were the days before walkie-talkie drops.

"No, no, no," they yelled back. They waved, laughed, clapped each other on the back, and jumped with relief and excitement.

Guille and Basulto knew they would not be able to babysit this boat for two more hours. They indicated to Alemán and his crew that they should continue to head in a northerly direction so that they would eventually meet the Coast Guard.

The arrival of the 110-foot Coast Guard cutter *Sea Hawk* dwarfed the *Misladys*. There were several officers onboard and they quickly started asking questions. Nelson and his cousin were thankful for the little English they knew. After determining that no one onboard needed immediate medical attention, the officers distributed life vests. When they were all safely aboard the cutter, the Alemán group peered over the railing at the *Misladys* bobbing lazily in the water. This vessel, their ark, which had so peacefully carried them through the still, warm, perfect night, seemed tiny and abandoned.

"Do you want to keep it?" asked one of the officers. He reminded them that they would have to pay for docking and maintenance. "Should we tow it or do we sink it?"

Their careful planning had not included what to do with the boat afterward. Nelson went back onboard the *Misladys* one final time, to retrieve his antique map and the note from Brothers to the Rescue. When he showed the map to the officers they were genuinely amazed at its age and beauty, and they passed it from one to the other. They had never seen such an impeccably conserved map, etched on cloth and drawn with such precision.

The officers climbed onboard the *Misladys* and before Mercedes could prepare herself, they took a hatchet to its beam. Mercedes let out a stifled scream, followed by unstoppable tears and sobbing.

"Is she OK?" they asked Nelson.

"Yes, yes," he replied, shrugging his shoulders, "is her father's boat, you know?"

With every thud of their hatchets, Mercedes was pierced with grief, as if the Coast Guard officers were stabbing at her heart. She ached for her parents who were left behind. She wished the *Misladys* could have brought them to freedom, too. But there was no way for the boat to make it back. For the Alemáns it was like watching someone die. They all stood silently, watching their faithful friend being claimed by the sea, a fate they had escaped.

Nelson informed the Coast Guard about the other boat, and when they radioed in, they were advised that the others had been found that morning. It had been a perfect crossing for all of them.

Within days, the men found jobs washing cars, driving trucks, and working in factories. Within a week, the two families rented a four-bedroom townhouse in Hialeah. It was then that Nelson Alemán remembered that he had left his grandfather's map on the Coast Guard cutter. He had been so nervous when he arrived for processing that he had forgotten to ask for it back. He never saw it again.

The Alemán family had made a textbook crossing, a rarity in the rafter crisis. The calls to the hangar, the radio station, and Basulto's home were unrelenting. It was heartrending to hear reports of loved ones that had left the island and had not been found. The pilots knew they were not finding all the people that were out there. Worse, they were finding many too late, coming across empty rafts.

Sometimes *raft* was too mighty a word for the empty "vessels" they came across. They had seen just about everything floating in the ocean, even a motorcycle inside a minivan. The top of the minivan had been inverted and floated on the water. Housed inside, the motorcycle's shaft fueled the propeller. There were old boats, tied-together planks, rafts with a kite for a sail, and once, a refrigerator. Its door had been removed and because of the internal insulation, it floated adequately. But apparently not well enough to keep its passengers alive. When Basulto performed low passes over the refrigerator, he noticed clothing and other items, but no people. The pilots came up with a name for the empty vessels: floating tombstones.

It was not a coincidence that at the same time Brothers to the Rescue started flying, more rafters were found. The organization did not encourage people to leave; on the contrary, every single radio show had Basulto urging people *not* to come, not to take the chance, not to risk their lives. He encouraged them to change things on the island, from within.

Cuba had already embarked on its Special Period, a term coined by Fidel Castro in the years immediately following the collapse of the Soviet Union. The only thing "special" about these years was that Cubans were asked to cinch their belts even tighter. With the end of Soviet subsidies, Cuba added an additional two hundred consumer goods to the ration list. Sundries like soap, toothpaste, and cleaning supplies were almost impossible to find. Foods of all kinds became increasingly scarce. There were gas and fuel shortages, and tractors and farm equipment were replaced by farm animals. The Cuban of the 1990s had to learn to survive, and they dubbed this new culture being "in business," which usually meant stealing from their employers then bartering the contraband goods with others. The only place where basic supplies could be purchased was at the tourist hotels, where Cuban nationals were not allowed.

Alexis García was a bartender at the new Sol Meliá, a Spanish hotel in Varadero. For every two-dollar tip he received for the communal gratuity jar, Alexis put one dollar inside his pants' pocket. He condoned his actions because the tips were never shared among his fellow bartenders, but rather collected by the hotel owners and given to government officials.

In 1992 Cuba, that one dollar represented almost forty Cuban pesos, and with the average salary being 211 pesos a month (roughly six U.S. dollars), it would go a long way for Alexis García—certainly more than Alexis' previous eight-year employment as a diving instructor.

One day the two-dollar tip came from a Spaniard who was a groundskeeper for a cemetery in Spain. Alexis was amazed that a groundskeeper could afford a two-week vacation at the new Sol Meliá in Varadero. Even if Alexis could have afforded to stay at the hotel, as a Cuban national he was banned from doing so. But Alexis had bigger plans than a stay at a hotel on Varadero beach.

After a year at his lucrative job, he was fired for stealing ninety dollars from the cash register. Even though the theft happened on his day off, Alexis was terminated. At that moment he decided he would never work for the Cuban government, which meant that he would never work at all if he remained in Cuba.

He would not remain in Cuba.

Alexis' first attempt to escape was with another family on a Zodiac raft that a lifeguard had stolen from a beach hotel. The day before departure, the family told Alexis there was no room for him, and they left him behind.

The second time, he attempted to leave with a friend who had a small boat. They planned their escape for months, splitting up the duties and scheduling the place and time of their departure. At the last moment, his friend changed his mind—and kept the boat.

The third time he decided to go it solo, on a raft he built himself over five long nights working alone in his darkened bedroom. Simply being caught with "suspicious material" like inner tubes, planks of wood, or tarp could mean a four-year prison sentence, without trial. During the construction of his one-man raft, a friend told him about a German fellow that was selling a more seaworthy craft. It deconstructed into three parts that could be easily assembled. Four people could fit into it. It was a kayak.

"It's perfect," Alexis told him. "I want it."

On the spot he gave him five hundred U.S. dollars, the equivalent of twenty thousand Cuban pesos, which represented many months of hoarding tips. For forty Cuban pesos and a bottle of rum he bought a truck tire inner tube that he planned to haul behind the kayak. The Zodiac-like raft he had built in his bedroom would be stored in the bow of the kayak for backup.

Alexis studied weather patterns and tides. He listened in secret to Radio Mambí from Miami and the Voice of America. One day he heard the voice

of a man named José Basulto who pleaded: "I am the President of Hermanos al Rescate and I urge you all in Cuba: please don't attempt to cross the
Florida Straits."

Alexis needed a partner for his journey. The friend who had connected
him to the kayak seller introduced him to a *guajiro,* a country guy, who
wanted to leave. His name was Ernesto Valladares, but everyone called him
Ñañy. He seemed like a good person to Alexis, he said he knew how to
swim, and he was ready to leave that very night if necessary. He agreed to
Alexis' most important prerequisite: that Alexis make all the decisions on
the voyage.

On Tuesday, June 16, 1992, Alexis made the rounds to say good-bye to his
family. The German guy with the kayak was scheduled to meet him at Punto
Icacos on Varadero Beach, where Ñañy and several of Alexis' friends would
help assemble the kayak. The German arrived on his motorcycle, and close
behind him, a policeman.

The group pretended to be picnicking, and were relieved to see that the
officer ignored them. Apparently he was at the beach to score some illegal
lobster from a fisherman. By the time the policeman left, it was too late to
put the kayak together.

On Wednesday, June 17, Alexis again bade farewell to his family. The
group of friends met for the second time and they started building the kayak
in the pine trees away from the beach. When it was half-assembled, they noticed the Border Patrol riding up the beach on horseback. Instinctively, the
men ran toward the sand, away from the pine trees, pretending they were
having a party, passing around a bottle of rum. Their goal was to get as close
to the water as possible, to draw attention away from the pine trees.

The group stood with their backs to the water, facing the sand and the
pine trees, where the half-assembled kayak was in full view. If the police
turned toward the trees and saw the kayak, their only journey would be to
prison. The mounted Border Patrol paused in front of the men with their
horses pointed at them, their backs to the trees.

"What are you all up to?" they asked.

"Hey, we're just enjoying the day, having some rum," they smiled, acting
a little tipsy. "Join us."

"No, we can't."

"Come on," they pleaded, "just one sip." They needed to make sure neither the guards nor their horses turned toward the pines.

"No, that's OK." And they moved on to Varadero Beach. Nervous that they would return, the group disassembled the kayak once more and stored the bags in the underbrush.

On Thursday, June 18, Alexis once again said his good-byes to his family. When his friends arrived at the pine trees, they saw the kayak was covered with what they thought was a black sheet. As they hauled the bags out, the black sheet moved. It was a shroud of mosquitoes.

Swatting and cursing, they rebuilt the kayak for the third time. The deflated Zodiac was placed in the bow, along with two cans of meat and three bottles of water. The pair finally pushed off at ten o'clock, rowing parallel to the beach, a few miles off the coast. There were lobster boats in the area so they could not go far out. It was unusual for people escaping to leave in broad daylight, but perhaps Alexis felt that the kayak would make them look like tourists playing near the shore.

They rowed quietly until just after dark, when Ñañy confessed that he did not know how to swim. Alexis was frustrated. He had painstakingly gone over the fine points with Ñañy: the sea conditions, the planning, and the monetary investment—it had taken a year of his life. Alexis had studied the tides and the weather patterns, and had buffed his body to the best physical shape of his life.

If the kayak did tip over, Alexis doubted his own ability to swim would really save him anyway. More important was that Ñañy accept his complete command over the voyage. The guajiro had agreed. Just before midnight, this particular point would be challenged.

They spotted a merchant vessel headed toward Havana, coming toward them head-on. Alexis told Ñañy to stop rowing, to avoid a collision. Ñañy got so nervous he *couldn't* stop.

As the boat got closer, Alexis had no choice but to row backward as Ñañy rowed forward, nervous and confused. The waves made by the five-hundred-foot vessel started to rock them, and Ñañy *still* would not stop. Their lives were in danger, and in a moment of desperation, Alexis reached down and unlatched the knife he had strapped to his leg.

Luckily, the merchant vessel missed them, but it left them navigating twenty-foot rolling swells head-on. Alexis put his knife away. He swore to himself that if they ever made it to Miami he would have nothing to do with this Ñañy.

At three o'clock the next morning, the sprinkle of lights off the coast of

Cuba dipped below the horizon. Just before dawn on Friday, they saw another merchant vessel lying dead in the water with all its lights turned off. It was as if it was waiting just for them, and the two men were elated.

Alexis took out his flashlight and signaled. He broke open some glow-sticks he had bought on the street in Cárdenas. The ship finally turned its reflectors on them and they were momentarily blinded, but jubilant. Alexis took out his mirror to create a brighter reflective light. Then the merchant vessel turned its lights off, its motor on, and left them. They never found out the ship's registry.

"But we were right under them!" yelled Ñañy, "They had to have seen us!" It was the lowest point of their journey, so far.

The first bad weather hit on Friday morning at about eleven o'clock, and they were pummeled by nine- to ten-foot waves. Alexis had a compass on his watch and another around his neck. They had to abandon their course to stay in front of the waves, their kayak slicing at a perpendicular angle.

During the calm, Alexis opened one of the cans of meat and they ate. They had already drunk one bottle of water and the other two had rolled to the bow of the kayak, out of Alexis' reach. Their movement was restricted so they had to urinate in their seats. When the smell was unbearable they bailed for a while. Ñañy would later swear he did not pee the entire journey, that it was all Alexis' urine in the kayak.

Friday afternoon between five and six the second bout of weather hit, forcing them to change course again. They had been rowing nonstop for thirty-nine hours. During the respite after the second storm, exhaustion overtook them and they dozed in their seats, their oars set unmoving in front of them, like black statues floating on the water. During their brief but concentrated slumber, they did not notice their kayak had changed course and was headed back to Cuba.

They awoke that night to the distant roar of a plane, but it was too high up to scream out. The water from the storm had filled the kayak waist-high, with open cans of meat and empty water bottles floating in the mixture of seawater and urine. At this point, the skin on their buttocks had started peeling, raw from sitting in water and from the friction of the back-and-forth rowing motion. If they were to try to stand up after three days of sitting, they would be unable to straighten out their legs, muscles already atrophied.

Just before midnight Friday night, they spotted a boat. It was so close they heard music playing and conversation, but even under the full moon, the revelers did not see the kayak. Alexis tried in vain to reach for the flashlight, submerged somewhere near his feet in the black stench of water. The party boat left.

When they awoke before dawn on Saturday, they corrected their position just in time for the third round of foul weather. Exhausted and disgusted by the rancid water that housed them, they started throwing overboard extra clothes, tennis shoes, and empty cans of meat. Alexis started bailing then quickly realized his mistake: anything thrown in the water would attract fish, drawn to the smells, the bits of meat still left in the cans, and other floating debris. And the smaller fish attracted larger fish. When the larger fish arrived, the guajiro started fighting them off.

"Stop!" said Alexis, a hoarse reprimand from the back of his throat. "Don't look at the water, just be still!" Motionless as the fish knocked about the bottom of the kayak, Alexis and Ñañy scrunched down in their seats, the wet stink thick below their nostrils.

At ten o'clock on Saturday morning they spotted another boat and rowed toward it. By now, the blisters on their hands ran the full length of their fingers, so full of pus that there were no breaks on the creases. Whenever they would stop rowing, the soft outer calluses would start to dry, so that when they extended their fingers to row again, a slight crackle got the liquid moving inside.

As they got closer they realized it was not a boat at all, but an island. "Listen, I don't know if that's Cuba, the Bahamas, or what," Alexis told Ñañy, "but we need to save ourselves."

Spirited by the thought of dry land, they raised the sails and headed toward the island. They were less than a mile from the island, and what they believed was their salvation, when Ñañy heard Basulto's plane.

Basulto was not looking down at the kayak, but at his watch. It was almost two o'clock and his stomach was growling. Basulto was no longer the wiry young man who had trained for the Bay of Pigs invasion, nor the dashing hero who motored over to Cuba one night and shelled a hotel. He still had his rich dark complexion and his white flashy smile, but middle age had come with a bigger appetite and a bigger waistline. Basulto loved to eat.

"Guille, I'm going in," said Basulto over the radio. All the other planes had gone back to refuel at Marathon Key and the pilots were gorging themselves at Pizza Hut. "There's nothing here today." He was copilot to Carlos Taber-nilla, a Cuban American in his early thirties who lived in West Palm Beach and kept his plane in his backyard.

"Just stay a little longer, José, until you reach Cay Sal," Guille insisted.

"No really, Guille, there's nothing, nothing," he repeated.

"Just turn a little toward Cay Sal," Guille insisted.

The Cay Sal Bank of the Bahamas is roughly thirty-three miles north of Cuba and thirty miles west of the Great Bahamas Bank. It covers more than 1,500 square miles, 99 percent of which is under water. Because of its prox-imity to Cuba, rafters would often land on the rocky islands, particularly Cay Sal, Elbow Cay, and the Dog Rocks.

Basulto was famished, but he submitted to Guille's request, steering to-ward Cay Sal.

Within moments, he saw the kayak.

"Look! Look!" he screamed at Tabernilla.

"I don't see anything."

"Yes, yes, down there!" Even though Basulto had been flying missions for more than a year, he had never been credited with a find. This was his first. He noticed the kayak was headed for Cay Sal. If it landed there, the occupants would be detained by the Bahamian authorities and be deported back to Cuba.

They were no longer using the megaphone from the plane. Osvaldo Plá, the French-speaking Cuban dissident/inventor/portrait painter who'd joined Brothers, had introduced the use of walkie-talkies.

As a ham radio operator, a *radio-aficionado,* Osvaldo was in constant contact with people in Cuba. His call sign was KB4TFF, so his radio bud-dies on the island took the last three letters of his signal and nicknamed him "Tito Fufú."

Tito Fufú convinced Basulto that dropping walkie-talkies would enable the pilots to communicate with the rafters and also get the names of the rescued back to the radio stations so family members could be alerted im-mediately. Basulto purchased hundreds of inexpensive walkie-talkie sets from Radio Shack, and Guille printed up easy instructions for the balseros to read and follow.

But on this drop to the kayak below, the walkie-talkie broke. When the nylon bag with the radio and water hit their kayak, the red dye marker burst, staining not only the water around them, but Alexis and Ñañy as well. Luckily, Basulto had included a quick note in the bag, alerting them not to land on the island.

"We're saved!" said Alexis, reaching desperately into the bag, looking for something to drink. The bottle had cracked and the water mixed with the salt water. They temporarily ignored their thirst, and in their excitement kept rowing toward Cay Sal. But overcome by dehydration, Alexis looked in the mesh bag for another water bottle. It was then he found the note:

Do not land on Cay Sal. If you do, you will be deported. The Coast Guard is on their way. Welcome to the land of liberty.

They were yards away from Cay Sal. With no time to panic, Alexis remembers feeling as if they had each been given two new sets of shoulders. On sheer adrenaline, they sped away from Cay Sal.

Content with his first find, Basulto called in a relay and returned to Marathon to refuel his plane, and his stomach.

When the Coast Guard arrived at five o'clock that afternoon, the last Brothers to the Rescue plane went home, and Alexis and Ñañy's fifty-five-hour journey ended. Alexis remembers a seven-foot-tall African American Coast Guard officer helped him and Ñañy out of their kayak. The men could barely move their legs. Alexis saw him look down at the kayak filled with water, urine, and what looked like blood. Then the officer took both men in his large hands and turned them around, lifting their arms and checking their legs. In confusion, Alexis yanked his hands away from the officer. He was surprised at his own defensiveness in the face of this huge man who towered over him, his self-protective aggressiveness probably due to dehydration. Alexis did not realize the officer was looking for wounds.

"No me toques! Don't touch me!" he said. "Water," he pleaded, in English, pointing to his mouth. It had been eighteen hours since their last drop. The officer gave them water to drink and white paper overalls to wear. When they arrived in Key West at nine o'clock at night, they were interviewed and given food and rest.

Hours later, Alexis and Ñañy still smelled like urine, sweat, and seawater. They found a hose and managed to spray themselves off a bit. After changing into orange jumpsuits, they were taken to the airport and put aboard a flight to Miami. An immigration official would meet them at the gate when they arrived in Miami and hand them over to their families. As they entered the airplane, passengers stared and moved into their seats quickly to let them pass. No one wanted to sit next to them.

After the short flight, no one greeted them at Miami International. They paced up and down the airport terminal for three hours, drawing puzzled stares as well as looks of disgust from the summer tourists. They reeked of urine, sweat, and seawater.

Two female airport personnel finally came to their aid. "Can we help you? Did you just come from Krome?"

Krome was the detention center used to house Haitian migrants. It was previously used as a processing station for rafters, but it had recently been burned in a riot and was temporarily closed. The orange jumpsuits were the prison garb of the Krome Detention Center.

"No, we didn't escape from anywhere," said Alexis, tired and frustrated, and he explained their plight. After things were cleared up a little, their families arrived and Alexis García and Ernesto Valladares were finally interviewed by Immigration.

A week later, Alexis remembers Basulto contacting him to buy his kayak to add to the collection of rafts at the hangar. They met at the Coast Guard station to retrieve it. While there, Alexis ran into the seven-foot African American agent whom he had reproached for manhandling him. The agent had words for Alexis so he asked Basulto to translate.

"You tell him that *this one time* I let him brush me aside," he said, looking squarely at Alexis, "because I had just picked him up and they were in bad shape."

"Please, tell him it wasn't personal—," Alexis started to interrupt him, remorseful over his outburst toward this man who had saved his life. The agent cut him off.

"But if he sees me on the street one day," said the Coast Guard officer, staring directly into Alexis' eyes, "he better respect me."

Respect was the first of many merits due the men and women of the U.S. Coast Guard, who worked tirelessly with Brothers to the Rescue and who gave the rafters their first taste of freedom in America. Even though it was the Brothers pilots that would spot the desperate rafters, it was the Coast Guard that would help these people out of their makeshift rafts and boats— if there were people onboard. They witnessed the floating tombstones up close when they took possession of them, looking for clues, sometimes finding one in the form of a dead body. It was the Coast Guard that sifted through clothes, empty water bottles, baby things, broken fishing lines. They answered calls no matter the weather, no matter the hour. They risked their own lives flying in helicopters, lifting people up in baskets moments before their watery deaths.

Theirs was the joy when the people were found alive. The Coast Guard gave them the necessary first aid. These men and women on the large cutters, the small Zodiacs, and the hovering helicopters tenderly cradled the babies that had been onboard; their strong arms supported the old men and women whose legs were cramped and unable to walk. They communicated in a universal language of compassion to people who were seasick, dehydrated, and dying. The Coast Guard personnel were the ones dealing with those whose kidneys were failing from drinking urine. They summoned the ambulances and the emergency vehicles. The Coast Guard struggled to make sense of those who were hallucinating, and tried to console the survivors who lost loved ones during their crossings.

Their names were rarely noted by journalists wanting the latest rescue story; their faces seldom appeared before the cameras. They were not after notoriety anyway. It was about saving lives. It was their job.

10

Acts of God

God and nature do nothing in vain.
Auctoritates Aristotelis (medieval propositions
drawn from diverse Classical and other sources)

Hurricane season begins every year on June 1. Most Miami residents had become jaded and complacent in the thirty years since the last Category 4 storm, Hurricane Donna, made a direct hit. Miami's population had more than doubled in that period. There had been many scares in the past three decades, all resulting in a few inconveniences like a missed day of school or work.

At three o'clock in the afternoon of Sunday, August 23, 1992, there were few people on the beaches of Miami, even though it was a typical ninety-plus-degree, cloudless day, with only two more weekends before Labor Day, the official end of summer. The National Hurricane Center had forecast that Hurricane Andrew, the first hurricane of the season, was heading toward Miami, and it was a monster. Rather than vying for sand space on Miami Beach that afternoon, anxious residents were waging parking wars at the supermarkets and home improvement stores. Supplies quickly ran out.

Twelve hours later, the 165-mile-an-hour winds of Hurricane Andrew cut a swath of destruction just south of Miami, slicing a direct path through the Everglades to the Gulf of Mexico before swinging northward. It was considered a dry hurricane, causing little or no flooding. The condos and hotels on the beaches and the coastal communities were spared. The city of Homestead, deep inland, was demolished. At that time it was the costliest hurricane in the history of the United States, causing $26.5 billion in damage.

The airport at Tamiami was destroyed, but not a single Brothers plane was lost or damaged. Efforts began to rent a new hangar at Opa-locka Airport in North Miami.

Hurricane Andrew was a forecaster's dream. Brian Norcross of NBC would rise to superstar fame because of his precision and calm during those horrible hours in the middle of the night during the worst storm to hit South Florida since Labor Day 1935, back when hurricanes did not have names.

It was also a golden opportunity for John Toohey Morales, who had just moved to Miami to do the weather for the Spanish-language station Univision. The only child of an Irish American father and Puerto Rican mother, John Toohey Morales was born in Schenectady, New York, then moved to Puerto Rico with his mother when his parents divorced. From his childhood, he was fascinated with space, weather, and astronomy. He graduated from the meteorology program at Cornell University, then went on to work for the National Weather Service.

There had never been a degree-holding meteorologist doing the weather on Spanish television—it was usually the job of a regular newscaster or a pretty girl. Univision asked John to drop the Toohey in his name, which was too Anglo for them, and he became John Morales. He would go on to win an Emmy in 1993 for a special hurricane preparedness segment. All thanks to Hurricane Andrew.

Another recent television transplant to Florida was WTVJ reporter Hank Tester from Las Vegas. Six weeks after his arrival in Miami, the recently divorced Tester became the principal reporter on the daily recovery efforts out of Homestead. He knew a little Spanish from growing up near the Mexican border, so he was able to conduct interviews with the Cubans that did not speak fluent English. The tall, handsome young Hank Tester became the first face to watch on the morning news, his prematurely white hair blowing in the South Florida breeze, reporting live from Homestead, the area hardest hit.

To keep their newscasters abreast of politics ninety miles away, WTVJ brought in speakers to educate their reporters. Author Andrés Openheimer promoted his book, *Castro's Final Hour;* the Cuban American National Foundation and its president, Jorge Mas Canosa, boasted of its political muscle in Washington; and other exile groups claimed prominence in helping their brothers across the Straits. When José Basulto was one of the guest speakers, Hank Tester listened.

"Finally, someone was really doing something about it," he said. He reported on many missions with Brothers to the Rescue, and he helped them develop a system whereby he could get the pilots' audio from their headphones into his tape recorder, since the plane was so noisy. Basulto and Tester became great friends and would share many special missions.

August 24, 1992, became a time stamp for Miamians. Lives were compartmentalized into what had happened "before Andrew" or "after Andrew."

The first day after Andrew, twenty-five-year-old Carlos Costa began his new job selling aircraft parts. He had graduated with honors from Embry-Riddle Aeronautical University in Daytona Beach the previous month. Like Mayte Greco, Carlos obtained his pilot's license without his parents' knowledge, yet with the ongoing financial support of Mirta and Osvaldo Costa. His mother was petrified of flying and kept questioning Carlos as to why he had to take so many pilot certifications.

"I'm studying aeronautical *science*," he explained, as if the science emphasis was a guarantee he would never leave the ground. Mirta was shocked on Carlos' graduation day when she finally realized that her son's studying aeronautical science meant he had been flying. He was *not* going to be a scientist on the ground; he was a pilot.

In Cuba in the early sixties, the Costa family had a young daughter and they wanted a better life for her, one that included private school education. Once the priests were expelled from the country and the private and parochial schools were shut down, the Costas exiled to Miami on July 8, 1962. Osvaldo Costa started working as a dishwasher in Miami, alongside lawyers and doctors in the process of revalidating their licenses. Mirta worked from home, sewing for others, then cooking for others, and finally, obtained factory work. In 1965, Mirta Costa became pregnant with Carlos but continued working until the day before delivery, on June 23, 1966. Never relaxing their Cuban work ethic, Mirta and Osvaldo worked hard to keep their children in private schools and universities. That ethic became ingrained in their son, Carlos.

At ten years of age, Carlos pulled the grass out of the backyard and planted lettuce to sell to his neighbors. On weekends, he befriended and worked with a family that had a stand in the local flea market, until he finally took it over. During his college years he worked for Sears Department

Store, until he moved to Daytona to study at Embry-Riddle Aeronautical University. Carlos was adjusting to living at home again after his years in Daytona Beach.

The Costas had not been political in Cuba, nor were they politically active in Miami. But in 1980 when the Mariel Boatlift brought 125,000 Cuban refugees to town, the Costas took in a family that had an eleven-year-old daughter. That summer she and Carlos became close friends; he was enthralled with her stories of Cuba. That, and maybe a few Three Kings Day parades in Little Havana, was the extent of Carlos' Cuban-ness. Even though his parents spoke broken English and worked in factories, and the family associated mainly with Cubans, Carlos was an all-American boy.

In 1988, long before Brothers to the Rescue was even thought of, a rafter would remind Carlos of his Cuban past. His parents were on their first vacation ever, a weekend cruise gifted to them by Carlos' sister and her husband to celebrate Mother's Day. Since Mirta and Osvaldo had never been separated from Carlos, they managed to buy him an extra ticket, and twenty-one-year old Carlos joined his parents in their stateroom.

They were at the captain's dinner when the ship's public address system alerted passengers that the ship was stopping to pick up some rafters. All the young people, many of whom were Cuban American, rushed out of the dining room for a space along the railing to witness the rescue. From somewhere deep in their Cuban DNA, these teenagers and young adults, all born in the USA, were suddenly overcome with passion, compassion, and patriotism for Cuba. The impact of that rescue stayed with Carlos: one day he was going to do something for Cuba.

Four years later, in November 1992, he was on his first mission with Brothers to the Rescue.

"Don't even say it, Mami," he countered when his mother protested on that first day. "It's the best thing I've ever done."

There was a lot of work to be done after Hurricane Andrew, and interest shifted from those stranded in the Straits to the thousands of Miamians living in hotels, with relatives, or in other cities. Thirty miles north of Miami in posh Boca Raton lived Thomas Van Hare, another recent transplant to South Florida from Washington, D.C.

In the nation's capital, Van Hare had worked under the Reagan administration managing more than 250 organizations with a budget of $3.1 billion as the gatekeeper for the grant funding of humanitarian groups. After waiting three days for FEMA to take over hurricane recovery in South Florida and seeing no action, he called his friends at the White House. He stationed himself at Opa-locka Airport and developed a field base distribution center, moving twenty tons of relief supplies a day, mainly ice, water, and diapers. A representative from the Cuban American National Foundation (CANF) sent their executive assistant, Joe García, to help. García suggested there were some Cuban groups that could benefit from Van Hare's style of management. He referred Van Hare, a pilot, to José Basulto.

Basulto was not looking for organizational structure, but then, he had not been looking for any of the volunteers that came to Brothers. "We can make this better," Van Hare told Basulto one day at Opa-locka, after having flown on a few missions as an observer. Van Hare remembers the Lares brothers were there, too; they were always there.

Basulto looked back at Van Hare, this 6'2", 170-pound americano from Washington, and anticipated that he just wanted to fly like the other pilots, so he gave his standard response. "Sure, what do you have in mind?"

Van Hare pulled out his organizational charts. "I think we all need to have titles," he began.

"We're all pilots," said Basulto.

"Yes, but we're not all the same when we're on a mission," Van Hare insisted, pulling out his job descriptions for the pilot-in-command (the pilot), mission pilot (the copilot), and mission specialist (the observer). There were flow charts and job requirements, special phrases to be used in certain situations, and call names for the pilots-in-command. Van Hare had new grids for the pilots, flying at closer intervals than before. Along with the grids were forms to be filled out by everyone onboard, a revised safety checklist, and a coding system.

He gave everyone new call names: Basulto remained Seagull One, Van Hare was Seagull Tango, Carlos Tabernilla and all the other pilots named Carlos, were Seagull Charlie. Van Hare did not have Seagull names for the Lares.

Basulto pleaded with the other pilots: "please, give him a chance." They did. They let Van Hare be an observer for the next three months.

During his months as an observer, Thomas Van Hare would not be dissuaded. While he waited for the position of pilot-in-command, a position he himself had authored, he got to work finding planes to rent.

Kemper Aviation required that a flight instructor be onboard any of their rentals. In that capacity Beverly Brooks came to join Brothers to the Rescue, first as an instructor, then as a volunteer pilot.

Beverly Brooks had been born in San Diego and raised in Seattle, Washington. She moved diagonally across the nation to make her home in Fort Lauderdale, Florida, in order to take flying lessons. She was in her early thirties, trim and fit and very petite, with wavy blonde hair and light brown eyes. Beverly had been Billy Schuss' flight instructor.

Van Hare told Beverly he wanted her to meet someone at Brothers, an Argentinean named Ivan Domanievicz. The Domanieviczes had moved to Miami from Buenos Aires, Argentina, in 1989. After college in Connecticut, Ivan decided to move to Miami to pursue his aviation career. Ivan's father had a Skymaster that had been used on one of the first missions of Brothers to the Rescue, but it had been undergoing repairs. Ivan and his father had not flown with them for more than a year.

Van Hare tried to set up Beverly and Ivan on a blind date one day, to fly a mission. Ivan had already taken off from the Tamiami hangar that day, so they missed each other on the flight. But they spoke to each other in the air.

"Would you like to go sailing?" Ivan asked Beverly. At that time, he loved sailing but did not own a sailboat.

"Sure," she said, curious to meet this new Argentinean pilot.

Beverly and Ivan finally met in person at a gathering in South Beach of Brothers to the Rescue pilots in their twenties and thirties. For Beverly and Ivan it was love at first sight. They eventually did go sailing, bought a boat, lived on it for more than a year, and crossed the Atlantic.

As Van Hare continued to play Cupid, be an observer, and develop organizational charts, he also helped Cuban American Arturo Cobo establish the Transit Center for Cuban Refugees in Key West. It was also called La Casa del Balsero, The Rafter's House.

Arturo Cobo's family had been a part of Key West since 1887, when half of the Cobo family left Spain for Cuba, the other half for Key West. Growing up in Cuba, Arturo had always felt personally insulted at the *Down with Yankee Imperialism!* slogans; after all, half of his family were Yankees.

At nineteen and against his father's wishes, the now–Cuban exile Arturo Cobo left Key West and joined the invasion forces in Guatemala and Nicaragua for the Bay of Pigs. He and many others were captured and sentenced to death by firing squad. They spent twenty months at El Príncipe Prison in Havana before finally being released under a prisoners-for-medicine agreement between President Kennedy and Fidel Castro.

For the next thirty years, Cobo alternated between his homes and businesses in Miami and Key West, always keeping close to the pulse of Cuban events.

The need for a transit center had been established more than a year before, but the local Key West government had never approved one. Cobo, who had helped process more than 100,000 Cuban refugees in 1980 during the Mariel Boatlift, noticed that this new crop of Cuban rafters would routinely be dropped off in Key West by the Coast Guard. The refugees spent anywhere from hours to several days sleeping outside the Coast Guard station under an open hut.

On the eve of Hurricane Andrew, the Coast Guard called Cobo and asked him to take care of the thirty-two rafters they were holding. Cobo called his friend and Baptist minister, Pastor Medina, who gave them shelter at his church. When the church filled to capacity, the need for a permanent structure became evident.

Thomas Van Hare's connections with the World Relief Organization in Washington and the Southern Baptist Men's Mission would help Cobo launch the center that would process thousands of rafters. Cobo put up the initial six thousand dollars of his own money to rent the structure on Stock Island. It was a small wooden building, with a kitchen, a dining area, two bedrooms with two-tiered bunk beds, and an office. A bright red Coke machine stood right outside the front door. In Cobo's office, two walls would soon be covered with more than four hundred notes from people in the United States looking for relatives they believed had left Cuba. He called it the "Wall of Sorrows."

Later, Cobo asked for help to organize a radio marathon with Tomás García-Fuste, Marta Flores, and others, and raised $200,000. When that ran out, Telemundo, the Spanish-language television station, gave him three hours on a Saturday afternoon to raise money. Cobo raised one million dollars.

The Rafter's House was like an Ellis Island for balseros. This first stop on U.S. soil would welcome the rafters and provide them medical care, clothes, food, beds, showers, a cash allowance, and for many, their first ever Coca-Cola.

Before the lights came back on in Miami after Hurricane Andrew and while there was still a citywide curfew, Brothers to the Rescue resumed their flights. They continued to provide the media access on most of their flights, and when there was no media representative aboard, the copilot or observer filmed. The heroic rescues of the U.S. Coast Guard were on the news every week. Night after night viewers in South Florida and nationwide were enthralled with the disciplined and professional men and women of the Coast Guard, who worked in tandem with the mishmash of nationalities at Brothers to the Rescue.

One day the Coast Guard took too long, though. Beto Lares and nineteen-year-old pilot Mike Murciano had spotted a raft with fourteen rafters fleeing the island. Mike Murciano had recently graduated from Christopher Columbus High School, a Catholic all-boys high school in West Dade. He worked for a dispatch company from 7:00 p.m. to 7:00 a.m. After work, he went to Brothers to the Rescue and put in another six or seven hours flying missions.

Mike's parents had come from Cuba in the early 1960s and Mike was a fourth-generation pilot. He began flying when he was fifteen years old, after school and on weekends. Mike's father was no longer flying, so he gave his son Basulto's number. He went from observer to photographer to pilot. Soon, he would be pilot-in-command.

As they waited for the Coast Guard, another ship came toward the raft—a Cuban gunboat with a machine gun on its bow.

"Son of a bitch!" cried Beto, as Mike filmed. They flew over the gunboat, watching helplessly as the Cubans forced the rafters onboard and handcuffed them to the boat. It all happened in international waters and Mike's videotape was shown nationally on the evening news. It would not be the last time.

There were other tragedies apart from the gunboat interceptions and the floating tombstones. On December 12, 1992, Guille Lares and Carlos Costa found four men on a raft. When they threw down a water bottle, one man jumped out of the raft in desperation to retrieve it. The rafter struggled to get back on but the waves pushed him away. As he battled to get back on, his friends rowed with their arms, exhausted but trying to reach their friend. They could not, and he drifted farther and farther away. From above, Guille and Carlos watched the man sink into the ocean and drown.

Christmas was approaching, and Basulto was in the Christmas spirit. There would be four planes leaving Tamiami on December 19, 1992. Three of the planes would follow the standard search-and-rescue grids, but Basulto's mission would end in Key West at the Transit House. His friend Guillermo Miranda, from Gator Industries, had donated hundreds of pairs of shoes for the arriving balseros, and Basulto was making a special delivery to Arturo Cobo. Miranda had previously donated 3,700 pairs for the Haitians in Guantánamo after the Aristide uprising.

A little before nine in the morning, Pilot-in-Command Beto Lares established radio communication with a Cubana flight on the 133.7 Havana Center frequency for a relay. Beto informed the air traffic personnel that the plane would be crossing the 24th parallel for a search-and-rescue mission in that area. Lares, copilot Carlos Costa, and observers Louis Cruz and Raúl Martínez were surprised at how cordial the air traffic controllers were that morning. Perhaps they were in the Christmas spirit, too, although Christmas had been banned in Cuba since 1969.

A cold front had just passed through the area, and they were flying in less than ideal conditions when they heard an emergency call on the frequency they were monitoring. "Seagull Flight, immediately head toward Key West International and land there. These are company orders!"

Beto asked who the company was, who was giving the orders, and who was authenticating.

"These are orders by Mr. Basulto and they must be followed at once."

Immediately all three planes headed north to land in Key West. Apparently, there were Cuban MiGs in the area and U.S. interceptors from Homestead had flown over to meet them. The Cuban MiGs backtracked to Cuba. The protocol that was established after Alfredo Sánchez's MiG encounter had been followed.

But another protocol had been severely broken. A Cuban defector named Orestes Lorenzo who resided in Florida had flown into Cuba, picked up his family, and returned to the United States.

Lorenzo, ex-Cuban military, had flown out of Cuba aboard a MiG-23 on March 12, 1991, and claimed asylum at Boca Chica Naval Air Station in the Florida Keys. Before he left Cuba he promised his wife, Victoria, he would be back for her and their two sons. On December 19, 1992, while Brothers were flying missions and Basulto was making his shoe delivery, Orestes Lorenzo kept his promise by landing a 1961 twin-engine Cessna 310 on a highway near the Varadero Beach resort, scooping up his wife and sons, and heading back to the United States.

"There's a plane full of love heading your way!" Orestes radioed to a friend in Marathon Key.

Whether the Cubans or the Americans had gotten a whiff of Orestes' plan was never known. But Cuban MiGs were in the area, American jets responded, and Brothers to the Rescue aircraft were kept out of harm's way the day of Orestes Lorenzo's reverse-defection. And protocol was respected.

II

Acts of Man

That some good can be derived from every event is a better
proposition than that everything happens for the best, which
it assuredly does not.

James Kern Feibleman

Donations dwindled a bit after Hurricane Andrew, but Brothers kept flying Tuesdays, Thursdays, and Saturdays. When Christmas Eve 1992 fell on a Saturday, Basulto knew that the pilots would not hesitate to fly on a holiday. Flying missions for Brothers was similar to working for the police, for the fire department, or in a hospital. The pilots were committed and ready for missions at any time. But Christmas Eve, with the roasted pig, the family, *nochebuena*—that was a tough one.

The Lares brothers volunteered. Beto Lares would board a Cessna 310 at the Opa-locka Airport and fly it to Tamiami to pick up his brother Guille. The plane had just undergone some minor repairs and a maintenance checkup.

The predawn sky at Opa-locka Airport in North Miami was quiet on Christmas Eve. Basulto had his eye on a hangar here, since Brothers frequently borrowed or rented planes from this airport.

Beto Lares had filed a flight plan the night before and had been given a transponder code. At the last minute, he was called to work at the Hyatt Hotel, where he was a waiter and busboy, to fill in for a sick coworker. He could certainly use the money, so he asked Koki to fly the rented Cessna to Tamiami Airport for the Christmas Eve mission. Koki was happy to replace his brother.

"What better way to spend Christmas Eve, the birth of the Lord, than looking for some poor souls lost at sea? Weren't Mary and Joseph at wits end that evening two thousand years ago, desperate for a place to lay down their head?" thought Koki. He imagined the poor rafters, alone in the Straits on such a day. The water must be very cold.

Koki Lares took off from Opa-locka at 5:50 a.m., before the tower opened. As the rented Cessna 310 took flight, early risers were turning on their house lights below him, getting ready for nochebuena, the traditional Christmas Eve dinner celebrated by Hispanics around the globe. Preparations for the *lechón,* the Christmas Eve roasted pork, usually began at daybreak. Traditionally, the pig is cooked Cuban style in a *caja China,* a "Chinese box" that resembles a square wheelbarrow and can hold a pig from sixty to one hundred pounds between two metal grills, allowing for easy turning. On top of the box sits a metal lid with two handles and a mesh grill on which the charcoal lies, following the Asian principle of cooking with the charcoal above rather than beneath the food.

The lechón is all-day affair, with family arriving at different intervals and charcoal being added every hour. Drinking can begin early in the morning, and the day ends with a dinner followed by midnight mass and the traditional toast, "El próximo año en Cuba!" [next year in Cuba!] By 1992, the toast was mostly tongue-in-cheek.

Minutes after takeoff, Koki's first engine shut down. His inner automatic pilot took over, and he went through the mental checklist. At nineteen, Koki had just acquired his pilot's license, so fortunately his training was fresh in his mind.

When the second engine shut down, he switched the fuel selectors to the auxiliary tanks. The motors came back to life, and he turned toward the closest airport, also the point of his rendezvous with Guille, Tamiami. Less than three minutes later, both engines quit for the second time. This time, he could not restart them. "Could the plane be out of fuel?"

There was only blackness below him in the Everglades, the River of Grass. Even with the landing light turned on, Koki could see nothing but a dark void. His mental checklist rolled, while a voice audible only to himself broke into his thoughts: "lower the landing gear, lower the landing gear."

Lowering the landing gear would usually cause a plane to pitch forward in a crash landing on water. A pilot *never* lowered the landing gear for a water landing. Koki ignored the voice.

"Lower the landing gear, Koki," the voice repeated. In hopes that something solid would materialize in the darkness beneath him, and in obedience to the voice, Koki lowered the landing gear.

He descended at seventy-five miles per hour toward the uninhabited Everglades. Calling a Mayday was pointless, since there was no one at the tower yet. Fifteen seconds would come and go from the time the engines shut down to the moment the rented Cessna 130 hit the murky water. Fifteen seconds to process the reasons for dual engine failure. But Koki remembers everything happening in slow motion.

On impact, the aircraft twisted, and its left engine tore away from the mounts. The top of the right wing was gashed, the tail sheared. The fuselage behind the cockpit crumpled. N6737T sank into the mud.

Koki became one with the blackness around him.

When he opened his eyes, Koki could not understand why he was so tired. And the water was so very cold, so cold that he could not feel his legs. "How long have I been asleep?" The sun was up, and he recognized that he had made it through the landing. He knew he had hit his head because it was bleeding, turning the waist-high water red.

"I have to call Guille," he said to himself. He reached back for the cell phone, which was in the luggage compartment. When he stretched his body through the small space between the pilot and copilot seats, he got stuck. He tried to push off with his legs, but the water was so cold, so very cold, he could not move. "I'll just take a little rest," he thought, and he fell asleep once more.

He woke up again and noticed the water had continued to inch up. "They'll be here soon," his muddled thoughts said. "What time is it?"

Guille Lares looked at his watch for the tenth time. At first he thought Koki must have overslept again. He had called Koki's number repeatedly, but only got the machine. Ivan Domanievicz was with Guille, and after an hour of waiting, he suggested Guille call the tower at Opa-locka.

He called the tower after seven, when it opened, but controllers could only confirm that his brother had indeed filed a flight plan and was given a transponder code, and that the plane was not there.

"*Ché*, where's Koki?" Guille called Beto at work. *Ché* was a Spanish interjection used frequently by Argentines.

"He still hasn't arrived?" Beto started to worry when he was told the airplane was no longer at the hangar.

Guille took off immediately from Tamiami aboard Domanievicz's plane, the 415 Delta.

He flew over the busy backyards of Christmas Eve day in Miami. Last-minute shoppers were parked in malls, waiting for the stores to open early on that last day before Christmas. The pigs were roasting under their first layer of charcoal.

Koki woke up again when he heard the roaring of an engine overhead. He smiled. "What took you so long, Guille? What time is it? Why am I so tired?" He knew he needed to move, the water was up to his neck and he was shivering.

Guille spotted the plane, but he did not want it to be where he now saw it: in the water. "No, not Koki; no, not him. Please let him be OK; please, God, let him be alive." The plane was submerged in the murky waters, the cockpit barely visible above the grassy lake. "Maybe he got out; maybe he's walking on the side of the road somewhere. Where? Where is the nearest road?" He kept circling over the aircraft, wanting to see something, anything.

It was when he made a very low pass that he saw the hand by the window, waving. Koki had stretched out his arm and was moving his hand back and forth so that whomever was above would know he was inside. Guille breathed a thank-you prayer. He's alive. He phoned Basulto, who was waiting at Tamiami.

"He's down there, needing my help, waving to me, and there's nothing I can do for him," he told Basulto, his voice cracking.

"If he waved to you, he's fine, Guille," Basulto reassured him, not sure himself what condition Koki might be in. "I'm calling the rescue right now."

Luis Carmona of the FAA flew to the scene of the accident in the police helicopter from Tamiami Airport. He could not tell from above what kind of shape the pilot was in, but the crash scene looked fairly clean, and he took several photos. At least this pilot was alive. Carmona was accustomed to setting aside his emotions when determining crash worthiness at an accident scene. Very few inspectors were that good. The detailed notes taken at accident sites would define safety improvements and new designs for future aircraft.

Carmona had been among the seventy investigators called to the deadliest airline crash in history on March 27, 1977, when two Boeing 747s collided in Tenerife, Canary Islands, killing 583 people. The crash at Tenerife had produced a change in communications for air traffic control, making

English the official language, and with specific verbiage. Terms like "OK" were no longer allowed.

By the time the rescue team arrived, the water was up to Koki's chin. As they took him out of the plane, he drifted in and out of consciousness.

"I'm so cold I can't even feel my legs," he repeated. They covered him with blankets. The paramedics quickly diagnosed that pilot Jorge Lares had broken his clavicle and had some damage to his leg.

"Thank God he lowered the landing gear," said one of the rescue workers. "If not he would have drowned."

Further tests at the Ryder Trauma Center of Jackson Memorial Hospital revealed paralysis from the waist down.

Koki was immobilized in a rotation bed. When Beto arrived at the hospital from his job at the Hyatt and saw Koki strapped from head to toe, he fainted.

When Koki opened his eyes for a moment and saw his brother Guille at his side, he smiled. "Ché, what took you so long?" Guille broke down and cried.

The family gathered outside Koki's room and Dr. Barth Green, head of neurosurgery at Jackson Memorial Hospital and one of the top neurosurgeons in the United States, informed them that Koki's injuries were similar to those of Cuban American singer-songwriter Gloria Estefan two years before. She had broken her back when her trailer bus crashed while on tour, and Green had inserted two titanium rods in her back.

"Except that Koki has experienced major nerve damage, also," said Dr. Green. "He may never walk again. However, there is a small possibility that surgery and intensive physical therapy *might* help."

The Lares family talked to Koki.

"Do the surgery," he said, enthusiastically. The family had no medical insurance.

Outside of Koki's hospital room, Guille and Beto cried along with their mother and sister. A steady stream of pilots from Brothers came to support them. The media arrived too, in time to get some good footage of Koki for the six o'clock news.

There were more tears when his girlfriend arrived. No one dared voice their thoughts: He'll never be able to marry, he'll never have children. Beto blamed himself: it should have been me. Guille felt an elder brother's responsibility: I should have never let him fly alone. The other pilots wondered if maybe the planes were not as safe as they had thought. Why did it have to be Koki, the youngest? He's not even Cuban.

The Basulto and Lares families spent Christmas Eve and Christmas Day at the hospital, talking to an immobilized but smiling Koki in his rotation bed. Hundreds of well-wishers from the community poured in, including Mayor Xavier Suárez, Gloria Estefan, and a rafter who claimed Koki had saved him. He, and another rafter who happened to be in the hospital at the same time, were the only two of the hundreds that Brothers had saved that came to visit.

When news got out, the community rallied around Brothers to the Rescue, but they chastised the organization as well: why was the youngest pilot of all asked to fly on Christmas Eve—alone? Why were they flying on Christmas Eve in the first place? All the major network television news shows came to film the young Argentine pilot who was paralyzed while flying on a mission to save rafters. His youth, his smile, his positive spirit wooed the masses. The international makeup of Brothers was highlighted—it's not just a Cuban thing, it's a humanitarian thing, look at that young teenage Argentinean who will never walk again.

When the mayor found out the Lares had no medical insurance, he opened a trust account at Ocean Bank in Miami to help pay for Koki's hospital bills. By December 29, only five days after the accident, they had collected more than $30,000. However, Dr. Green announced that Koki's therapy and extended hospital bills would exceed one million dollars.

At his annual New Year's Eve party, singer Willy Chirino committed to ask for donations to help Koki Lares with his one-million-dollar rehab bills.

Before the ball dropped in Times Square on New Year's Eve 1992, agent Jorge Prellezo of the National Transportation Safety Board (NTSB) confirmed that lack of fuel was not the cause of the accident. There were more than thirty gallons in the tanks. The gas valves had been installed backward by a mechanic, resulting in a total loss of engine power due to fuel starvation.

At a later trial, in an effort to recoup some money for Koki's hospital bills from the insurance company, it was revealed that the mechanic had no insurance and no assets. His only penalty was having his license suspended for thirty days.

By the end of 1992, Brothers to the Rescue had saved 374 souls in the Florida Straits. But to Guille Lares, the only soul that mattered now was his brother Koki. "We have to take care of Koki," he told Basulto. Riddled with guilt, anger, frustration, and despair, Guille and Beto explained to Basulto that they would not be flying for Brothers for right now—maybe never—they just did not know.

Basulto was devastated. The Lares brothers, *the* brothers, the men who had rescued his organization, who had rescued others, the three pilots whose names were synonymous with the organization—they would be leaving him. The brothers who brought God to their organization, the young men who had been role models to the younger pilots, who had ingrained a breath of freshness and purity and goodness in Brothers to the Rescue, were taking their leave. How could he go on without the Lares?

On January 2, 1993, the *Miami Herald* editorial board asked the community for donations, and money poured in. Brothers to the Rescue clips were shown around the world, along with Koki's smiling face from his hospital bed. Journalists from all over Europe, China, and Australia scrambled to get a seat on the next mission.

Koki Lares got a gift from the Magi on the Feast of the Epiphany, when Catholics commemorate the visit of the wise men to the Christ Child. Organizers of the 1993 Three Kings Day Parade of Little Havana proclaimed Jorge "Koki" Lares grand marshal. Koki was allowed to leave the hospital and travel in the parade in a truck, sitting in a wheelchair wearing a plastic body cast, his legs secured in iron buckles. The single-engine wreck that Guille had crashed in the Keys was hauled down Eighth Street to the cheers of the crowd. Brothers had T-shirts made that read "Miami to the Rescue of Jorge Lares." All the pilots and volunteers walked block after block of the parade, holding out cans for donations, and people gave generously. After the parade, Koki returned to Jackson Memorial Hospital for three months of intensive physical therapy.

Dr. Green and orthopedic surgeon Dr. Nathan Lebwohl were amazed at Koki's strength of character and physical endurance. They requested he do three hours of therapy a day. Koki did six. Even while at rest in his hospital bed, Koki maintained a state of perpetual physical therapy, working on his upper body and willing his legs to move. All the while he prayed and thanked God for every tiny sign of progress.

"It was God's will that it be me," he replied whenever he was asked if he was angry over what had happened. "I was chosen for this. Perhaps because it was me, the youngest, and not even Cuban, the one with the most future ahead—perhaps that is what made the community react as it did."

12

Brothers to the Rescue

It's a good thing we're not all Cuban—
we'd never get anything done.

Steve Walton, Brothers Pilot

Basulto wondered how they would start the new year and continue their successes without the Lares brothers. Everything he had previously delegated to those three men to make the organization work now required his full energy. He needed dedicated people with time to save lives.

Brothers to the Rescue was more than just the pilots; it was also all the volunteers on land. It was Maggie Schuss converting her formal dining room into a water-bottle-wrapping assembly line. It was Mirta Costa, Carlos' mother, waiting for the returning crews with steaming casseroles of arroz con pollo (chicken with rice). Brothers to the Rescue was sustained by volunteers who walked the streets of Little Havana with plastic containers, collecting spare change, and by anonymous, rich Cuban exiles like Pilo Azqueta donating planes. Brothers to the Rescue was the ninety-year-old in Little Havana who mailed in five dollars a month with a note of apology for not sending more. There were radio personalities who donated air time to plead for donations. Brothers to the Rescue were artists like Willy Chirino and Gloria Estefan, giving back with their talent during fund-raisers. Brothers to the Rescue were girlfriends who gave up Friday nights because there was a mission the next day. They were husbands who did carpools and babysitting and ballet lesson pickups because Mom was in the air, saving another mom on a raft.

Brothers to the Rescue were people like the mayor of Miami, hosting a luncheon to show film clips of rescues. It was a godmother like Congresswoman Ileana Ros-Lehtinen. There were donors, particularly the *señora de Miami Beach*, the "Lady from Miami Beach," who chose to remain anonymous and who on two different occasions donated more than $50,000.

Brothers to the Rescue were funeral homes like Caballero-Woodlawn in Miami that absorbed the costs of burial for so many rafters who lost their lives. It was American Airlines donating five thousand life vests to help keep families afloat.

Brothers to the Rescue was family. There were nice Jewish boys, good Catholic girls, Mamma's boys, and ladies' men. It was septuagenarians and teenagers and every age in between sharing pizza after saving a life. People who one day were pilots-in-command and were washing down the planes the next. Brothers to the Rescue was journalists and writers and somnolent photographers who, in the middle of a mission, had to put down their pencil or move back from their lens to acknowledge with the naked eye what they were filming for the world. A pair of eyes is a pair of eyes.

Sometimes observers could barely see at all, like Osvaldo Plá, Tito Fufú.

Tito had helped install Brothers to the Rescue's repeater station on top of a building in Marathon Key. Radio signals that could not make it to base from long distances out over the Straits would go directly to the repeater station, which would then transmit to the base at Opa-locka.

Tito went on to build an onboard antenna to find rafters on the water. He fashioned it out of an old bathroom plunger, boring wires through the wooden handle, with more wires intersecting at ninety-degree angles. This contraption he waved around the cramped space of the Cessna backseat, feeling for a signal in the air, a clairvoyant searching for a medium. Working in tandem with the plunger was a signal-measuring device with a needle that captured the intensity of a radio signal, and he hoped, that of a rafter in the water. To complete the set, Tito brought a magnifying glass to enable him to see the needle on his handheld device.

Over the Straits on a mission with Tito, a movement below would stimulate the needle. Tito would reposition the antenna, frequently poking the pilot or copilot on the back of the head. "Go north, go left, move this way," he'd say, keeping the magnifying glass over the needle marker until the signal was the strongest, shifting the antenna in small arcs around the tiny cabin. When it did not poke anyone's eye out, it worked. Thus was born "Operation Coat Hanger." The scenario of a typical mission was a half-blind man swinging around a bathroom plunger with wires sticking out in every direction inside the cramped confines of a four-seater plane, that man trying to detect radio signals on a screen he could read only with a magnifying glass.

They were successful. That was Brothers to the Rescue. Brothers to the

Rescue was everyone in the community; a testimony that it did take a village, a village of nineteen nationalities who made time to save lives.

Steve Walton had a lot of time—and some money—on his hands, and the newspaper reports about Koki and Brothers to the Rescue called him out of his comfortable lifestyle.

Steve had moved from Illinois to Florida as a teenager to attend Embry-Riddle Aeronautical University. Within two years, he was kicked out for what he would later admit was "not paying as much attention as I should have to my studies."

Now he was a captain for American Airlines, but he really wanted to fly with Brothers. He wrote Basulto a letter that went unanswered, part of Brothers' unwritten policy of dismissing the first offer of help from a pilot. Basulto felt that anyone who was serious enough would write again. Steve was so serious he not only wrote another letter—he bought himself a plane: a red-and-white Piper Apache 235. It was a four-seater, multiengine beauty.

"Listen," Steve said, when he called Brothers, "you didn't answer my letter, but I went ahead and bought an airplane. Now can I fly with you?"

Steve called his buddy Matt Blalock to join him at the North Perry Airport for Van Hare's inspection of his plane. Steve was a disciplined, rule-following pilot and Matt was a treasure-hunting, Jimmy Buffet–singing, adventure-seeking writer.

Van Hare was already inspecting the Apache when Steve and Matt arrived.

"Who's the nerd with the clipboard?" asked Matt.

When they walked over, Van Hare gave Steve a checklist of things that were not up to par on his Apache. Knowing Steve's attention to detail and the meticulous care he gave his plane, Matt felt Van Hare was personally insulting his friend, as if he had been criticizing his wife or daughter (neither of which Steve had at the time). Matt puffed up his 6'5", 265-pound frame. He was a few inches taller than Van Hare, and more than a hundred pounds heavier. Van Hare was unruffled. He invited Matt to come along for the check ride.

"Sure," he said, "even though I'm more of a boat guy." The three got in the plane and Van Hare and Steve Walton adjusted their headsets. There was none for Matt, who crammed himself into the backseats to observe the inaudible exchange of conversation between pilot and copilot.

Over the Everglades, Van Hare asked Steve to perform a power-out stall and the latter complied. Matt was caught unawares when the plane pitched forward and all he saw was alligators and grass. Matt was sure Van Hare was trying to kill them.

Returning from the test flight and after Van Hare and his clipboard left, Steve told Matt the new plans: "We're going to go fly with some Cubans."

Steve Walton did a lot of things for Brothers that made him and his shiny red plane stand out, like the signature orange utility vest layered with pockets of different sizes and depths, along with clips and hooks, which he wore over his trademark Hawaiian shirts. "Orange is the only color you're going to see out there," he said. "And if it's not attached to me when I get in the plane, it won't be attached to me when I fall in the water."

Steve showed the pilots how attaching surveyor's tape to the water bottles would make for an easier drop. By keeping a line on the bottle, they would not have to concentrate so much on making sure the water landed right next to the raft. They could also avoid accidentally hitting an already physically depleted balsero with a water bottle thrown from fifty feet in the air. Rafters would think twice about jumping out of a raft, no matter how desperately they needed water—a scene the Lares brothers had witnessed when one of their rafters drowned. Now a water bottle did not need bubble wrap or precision tossing. Attaching one hundred feet of florescent tape made close enough close enough

Steve liked to frequent a maritime supply store called Sailorman in Ft. Lauderdale. He bought a few floating smoke canisters one day, just to see what he could do with them. On a mission with Peruvian bush pilot Carlos Gartner he threw down a "smoke" in a Gatorade bottle with a note saying, "The next time you see a plane, pop the smoke."

They had found these rafters early in the day and had already called the Coast Guard, which was delayed. That meant the rafters' position would change by the time the Coast Guard arrived. The rafters were all in good shape, so the pilots decided not to stay and wait. They circled into a cloud to radio the other pilots. Coming out of the cloud, they saw smoke down below.

The rafters had followed the directions to pop a smoke the next time they saw a plane. Future instructions would have to read: "the next time you see a different plane, pop the smoke."

Smokes became a standard for the organization. Up until then dye markers had been thrown in the water to mark a raft's location. Although the dye was clearly visible from the air, it did not help the Coast Guard when a ship came to look for the rafters, because the color was on the surface of the water and could not be seen from a distance.

Along with water and radios, Walton proposed throwing down a mirror and a compass with headings. Brothers could not always babysit the rafters as Basulto wanted. If one was spotted early on in a mission, staying with one raft could mean taking half of the force out of the air for the rest of the day. There had to be a way for those rafters who were in good condition to help themselves until the Coast Guard arrived.

The pilots were well aware of the dangers of flying for the organization, and that fact was crystallized for Steve one day in Key West at the Transit Center run by Arturo Cobo. An ex-MiG pilot who had defected from Cuba was there. He had moved to Key West to perfect his English. "I'll never learn English in Hialeah," he quipped, referring to the predominantly Hispanic city just north of Miami.

"So what do you know about small aircraft?" Steve asked him, curious about his flying experience.

"Not much," replied the pilot. "There aren't too many little airplanes in Cuba."

"If you were ordered to shoot down one of these little airplanes, would you?" Steve was direct, referring to the Brothers' airplanes.

"Yes," he said proudly. "An order is an order, and you're going to execute your orders." The Cuban Air Force viewed itself as the elite branch of the Cuban armed forces, he explained. "We are equal to the world's standard."

Steve did not want to burst his bubble, but he knew full well what the world's standard was—and that Cuba was not it.

"Would you ever shoot at a Red Cross plane?"

The pilot recoiled in horror. "Never."

When Steve prodded him further, he repeated his answer: "Never."

So Steve Walton had a huge Red Cross appliqué squeegeed onto his plane's tail and right wing, and a four-foot American flag applied on the left side.

His next goal was to secure another kind of appliqué: a Brothers to the Rescue sticker pilots would earn for having spotted a rafter. Although his missions were very successful, he had still not been credited personally with a sighting. When he celebrated a find by his copilot or an observer on his aircraft, Steve referred to himself as the bridesmaid, never the bride. He wanted to be the bride.

Basulto liked to fly with all the new pilots, so he invited Steve to join him and a representative from the *St. Petersburg Times* on the N2506, *Seagull One*. Steve was not surprised when he looked back during the flight and saw the photographer asleep. Basulto's head was bobbing, too.

"Please, Steve, I just need to rest my eyes for ten minutes," Basulto said, giving Steve the controls of a plane he had never flown before. Basulto's snooze turned into Walton's find. His being the only pair of eyes open at the time, he spotted a raft with eleven people onboard. The rafters were pulling a twenty-two-foot sea anchor and had been on the water for five days.

Seagull One had to circle several times and on three occasions lost sight of the rafters. But it was a bright speck on the blue-gray water that helped Steve find them again and again. The speck turned out to be a life vest, wrapped around a little girl. It was orange.

Steve Walton got his sticker and finally knew what it felt like to be the bride.

After Guille Lares resigned, Billy Schuss took over as operations director. Carlos Costa, who had been with Brothers for almost six months, was named chief of pilots.

Carlos was borderline militant about the organization, addressing Basulto as "My General" and saluting him whenever he walked by. He poured himself into his work and strived to be at the hangar hours before every mission. His mother continued to warn him of the dangers.

"Aren't you proud of me?" Carlos would question her, seeking her approval.

"No," she would reply.

"Why?"

"Because I'm your mother, and I know the risks."

Brothers could not remain all-volunteer. They needed someone regularly in the office, now located in a small space in downtown Coral Gables.

The 1993 New Year brought them Sylvia Pascual, a Cuban lady in her late fifties who had just moved to Miami from New Jersey. She was a close friend of Maggie Schuss, Billy's wife, so she came highly recommended. Sylvia was put in charge of office work—and basically everything else.

It was Sylvia's voice that would answer the frantic calls of families begging Brothers to go out and find their loved ones who had recently left on a raft. It was Sylvia who would staff the phones and make the calls to the Coast Guard. Sylvia would reply to the love letters, those notes of appreciation and encouragement that arrived at Brothers with every mail delivery. She filed the hate mail under "Hate Mail," and thankfully that folder was small. Sylvia planned the office get-togethers; she ordered pizza in time for the arrival of the starving pilots who had been without food for up to six hours. Sylvia did payroll, Sylvia made the bank deposits, Sylvia knew where everything was. They nicknamed her SSS, a play on the universal SOS code for help, but in this case it meant *Solo Sylvia Sabe:* "only Sylvia knows."

As the organization struggled on without the Lares brothers, the local and greater communities continued to pour in donations for Koki's rehab bills.

Singer Willy Chirino committed to donating all of the earnings from his new song "Havana D.C." ("Havana Después de Castro," after Castro) to pay for an airplane for Brothers. The Cuban community in Puerto Rico donated another Cessna Super Skymaster 337, tail N108LS. On that trip, Basulto took along Alexis García, the rafter that had come over on the kayak. The new plane was christened *El Coquí*, after the native tree frog from Puerto Rico and the sound it makes: *co-quí, co-quí*. Basulto also traveled to Los Angeles for a fund-raiser held by the Brigade 2506 branch on the West Coast.

The *Miami Herald* and journalists from around the world continued to publish stories and photos of Brothers' rescue missions. Basulto would be forever grateful to the media for their coverage and promotion, and for their courage and strong stomachs on the flights. Newspaper after newspaper carried front-page pictures of the desperation of the rafters. "We could have never survived without the media," he said.

It seemed like everyone in the community wanted to be part of Brothers to the Rescue. Even a strip club in Miami Beach posted their "We Support BTTR" stickers over the exposed breasts of their pole dancer.

Good news on the Lares front came on February 26, 1993. With the help of a walker and leg braces, Koki walked for the first time in two months. Full of joy and thanksgiving, he did not sit down for another three hours.

In March 1993, Beto and Guille went back to flying for Brothers.

Two months later in a highly publicized and filmed event, Koki Lares, still in a wheelchair, joined his brothers in the prayer circle before boarding one of the planes for a mission with Brothers to the Rescue.

They saved five rafters.

Questions about the accident remained. Even after the FAA and the NTSB determined that the plane Koki crashed in the Everglades was full of fuel and that the crash was caused by the mechanic's error, criticism surrounding the safety procedures at Brothers escalated. In April 1993, Basulto and the board sent letters to all federal and state agencies, advising them of Brothers' open-door policy and urging them to perform any routine or nonroutine inspections at any time. The agencies took them up on the invitation and Brothers was plagued with visits from the FAA.

One of those FAA agents was Luis Carmona, who had been in the police helicopter the day of Koki's accident, taking pictures from the sky. Witnessing the openness of Brothers to the Rescue, he failed to understand why the relationship between this organization and the FAA was always so strained.

Carmona and Basulto soon became good friends.

Carmona was not part of the Cuban exile society in Miami, having left the island twelve years before the revolution and for nonpolitical reasons. He had lost his father when he was a boy, and he and his mother emigrated alone to the United States in 1947 for economic reasons. Though he "skipped" the revolution, Carmona's life had been full of adventure since he left Cuba as a nine-year-old.

Carmona joined the U.S. Army as a telegrapher, stationed in Frankfurt, Germany, where he was entrusted with military secrets, codes, and passwords. The army thought he was Puerto Rican, but in fact he was not a U.S. citizen. When they discovered he and forty others were not citizens, the U.S. Congress passed a law making Frankfurt, Germany, a southern district of New York, in order to naturalize forty of Carmona's group. When the naturalization ceremony was over, they waited for the officers to congratulate them. Instead they quipped, "Now we can shoot you."

Throughout his life Carmona would marry four times, fight cancer three times, crash his airplane, have a kidney removed, survive depression, join the army, and work for both the NTSB and the FAA. "I don't drink, sing, or eat fruit," he said of his picturesque life, "but what I love are the two most expensive and difficult things in existence: women and airplanes."

By their second anniversary in May 1993, Brothers to the Rescue had saved almost four hundred lives. To commemorate their two-year birthday, eight planes flew missions that day. They also witnessed another interception at sea.

Pilot Alfredo Sánchez photographed a Cuban gunboat chasing a motorized boat forty miles north of the island, in international waters. He watched the desperate balseros being forced back to their country. There was nothing he could do about it.

Basulto had stopped working as a developer and now devoted his entire workweek, as well as weekends, to Brothers to the Rescue. He dipped into personal investments and savings to pay the bills. The Basulto family income was subsidized by periodically selling off—at a fraction of their value—parcels from ten acres of industrial development land.

Basulto's children were marrying one by one and starting their own lives, but they still missed him whenever he distanced himself from family affairs. It seemed that Brothers had become his family and Brothers got all his time, attention, and money. During the absence of the Lares brothers he spent even *more* time at the hangar, as if he alone could make up for the absence of the three men who meant so much to him, like his own sons, but it was the Lares boys, not the Basulto boys, who got all his attention. When he was not at Brothers, he was visiting Koki in the hospital or trying to raise funds for his hospital bills. He was in the news, on the radio, on TV talk shows like *Good Morning America* and *Prime Time News*. To do that, he missed birthdays and family dinners and school events.

Rita and Basulto could never go anywhere in Miami without being stopped and questioned for information on the organization, on Koki, on the rafters. They called to him on the street: "You saved me. Thank you!"

Scattered throughout the community were people who did not fly nor answer phones nor welcome the rafters, yet were an integral part of the organization. These were people who gave moral support, people with time to dedicate to the people who saved the lives. For Basulto it was friends like Giles Gianelloni, an American who had grown up in Havana and was the first person Basulto flew with in Cuba when he was eight years old. It was friends like Guillermo Miranda, who listened to Basulto's disappointments and laments, and it was also a new acquaintance who would help Basulto in the coming years, an American lady with ties to the Bay of Pigs.

One afternoon it was surprisingly quiet in Little Havana. Basulto was standing before the Brigade 2506 monument located on Eighth Street near Twelfth Avenue, when his deep thoughts were interrupted by a woman with a southern accent.

"My daddy died in the invasion," she said, "and he did it for his country, because they asked him to." Basulto looked over at the thirty-something woman with blue eyes and reddish-blonde hair, standing in the middle of Little Havana. Somehow she belonged there, this *gringa* on Calle Ocho.

"I'm sorry?" he said.

"My name is Janet Ray Weininger," she said, extending her hand. "My daddy was Pete Ray, the pilot from the Alabama Air National Guard that was captured in the Bay of Pigs. Fidel shot him."

As Basulto compartmentalized this information, recalling the brave Americans who died during the failed Bay of Pigs invasion, Janet said she was interested in helping Brothers to the Rescue.

"Well thank you, Janet," said Basulto. "We need all the support we can get."

Janet Joy Ray was born in Birmingham, Alabama, the daughter of high-school sweethearts Margaret and Thomas "Pete" Ray. Married right after high school, the young couple moved to Texas, where Pete Ray would fulfill his dream of becoming a pilot. They soon had a son, and one year later, Janet was born. She always felt she was her father's favorite, a tomboy who worshiped him and was obsessed with all things military.

Pete Ray was Janet's idol, earning her admiration and commanding her respect, but the six-year-old did not hesitate to stand up to him one day when it came to getting rid of her pet dog, a mutt named Chase. "Wait 'til your father gets home," was her mother's threat.

When Pete walked in and sat on her bed, Janet rose to her full six-year-old height and met him eye-to-eye. Her father was tall, blond, blue-eyed, fit, and wearing what Janet loved most: his uniform.

"If you try to take away my dog, I will run away with him and never come back," she pronounced every word carefully. "You are *not* taking my dog."

"You're my little fighter, aren't you?" said Pete, holding back a smile. "Would you fight for me?"

"Yes," she said, holding back tears.

Janet would remember those words her entire life. She would remember the frustration of not being able to express at six years of age the honor she felt, the responsibility that she was being made worthy of having, to some-day fight for her daddy. She would have died for him.

"Yes," she repeated.

It was in Texas that Ray was first approached by the CIA to prepare for the Bay of Pigs invasion. He left for training in February 1961, and Ja-net, her mother and brother moved back to Alabama to live with Janet's grandmother.

The CIA recruited four Alabama National Guardsmen to bomb certain sites on April 19, 1961, two days after landing day. Pete Ray's plane was shot down. He was captured by Castro's troops and later shot at point-blank range. At a time when the United States was denying any involvement in the Bay of Pigs, Castro kept Ray's body in a freezer morgue as proof that the Americans had indeed been there.

The family found out about his death on May 5, 1961, when men in suits arrived at Janet's home in Alabama and the local newspaper blasted to their neighbors—some of whom she was sure did not even know where Cuba was—that *her father was a mercenary, the other three pilots, too. They had done it for money; they had gambled their lives away.* She remembers crying and crying as she crumpled the newspaper in her hands, wiping her tears with the inky sheets and smearing her face black.

At the funeral she knew it was a cover-up, even though she did not know the meaning of that word yet. She had seen a real funeral in the Negro cemetery in the woods. Real funerals had coffins, shovels, "Amazing Grace," and a body. Real funerals took place outside with preachers talking and women crying. A funeral needed a body, and there was no body here. She later found out that her father's murdered body was in a Cuban morgue, a personal prize belonging to Fidel Castro.

At fifteen, she began writing letters to Castro—more than two thousand in all—begging for the return of Pete Ray's body. The little fighter single-handedly fought the Cuban government to retrieve her father's remains. It took her eighteen years to get her father's body back home to Alabama. In 1979, her pursuit of the truth about her father's involvement in the Bay of Pigs finally ended when the CIA publicly acknowledged Thomas "Pete" Ray for his "selfless devotion to duty and dedication to the national interests of the United States." The CIA added the twenty-second star to their Book of Honor. He was awarded the Distinguished Intelligence Cross and the Ex-ceptional Service Medallion.

With financial assistance from the CIA, she later launched a campaign to rescue the remains of two other Bay of Pigs soldiers shot down over Nicaragua.

Now Janet Ray Weininger was ready to help Brothers to the Rescue. She did not know it that day, standing in Little Havana, talking to José Basulto, but a much greater pursuit for truth and justice would soon evolve over the Florida Straits.

13

Close Calls

Life's most urgent question is: what are you doing for others?
Dr. Martin Luther King Jr.

There was a sign at the hangar warning everyone about the inherent dangers, including death, of their missions. Many accidents would follow Guille's water landing in 1992; so would many close calls, as when Carlos Gartner hit a sailboat. Gartner was on a low pass over a boat that had rigged a homemade sail to its mast and he accidently clipped the masthead. The plane looked like someone had taken a small bite out of one of its wings, but no one was hurt, most importantly no one on the boat below. He immediately reported the accident to the FAA. He was still fined.

It was no secret to the FAA that Brothers frequently flew below the allowed five hundred feet—sometimes as low as ten feet to make a drop; sometimes even lower. The pilots practiced these low passes frequently, perfecting their moves with priority to protecting the lives onboard before saving those below. Only once did a masthead get in the way. On August 17, 1993, it was the water that did.

Four planes flew that day, including Steve Walton in his red Apache with the Red Cross on one wing and the American flag on the other. Aboard the *Ofelia* was José Monroy, a pilot who occasionally flew with Brothers and who wanted some flying hours. Carlos Costa reluctantly agreed to let him fly the twin-engine Cessna, the second plane donated by Pilo Azqueta, the first Cuban exile to put his money on the line for Brothers to the Rescue. Juan González, who had found the first rafters for Brothers to the Rescue more than two years earlier, would be the spotter.

On their way to Elbow Cay the *Ofelia* found some rafters. From his Apache, Steve Walton heard the news and followed Monroy. Tom Van Hare was copilot, and Matt Blalock was filming from the backseat.

The day was overcast and visibility poor. On these gray days, pilots would lose all perspective of the horizon when the overcast sky blended into the slate-colored ocean. Today the water and sky were like a solid gray curtain.

Monroy began his low passes. Juan González was happy for the close-up shots of the six rafters below, but he remembers Carlos warning him not to go so low the second time around.

The *Ofelia* was dangerously close to the water when a wind shear jolted the twin-engine craft, rattling them about. But Juan was used to that—it had happened the first time they found rafters, when Guille almost crashed head-on into Basulto. He knew something was terribly wrong when he realized he was wet.

"¡Coño! Sonofabitch, you broke the plane!" he yelled. Before Juan could finish his profanities, Carlos instinctively took control of the aircraft.

Steve Walton, Tom Van Hare, and Matt Blalock watched in disbelief as the Cessna 337 Skymaster hit the water. The greatest danger in a nosedive was that the plane would pitch forward, but what they witnessed was *Ofelia* rising from the sea in an eerie slow motion, like the sea god Poseidon. Rather than a golden trident, the Cessna had a limp propeller dangling from its broken nose.

"Feather that baby," Steve Walton called in to Carlos Costa, referring to the broken front motor. "Seagull Charlie, you're trailing smoke," he added.

But it was not smoke Carlos was trailing; it was water being forced out of the plane. There was another hole in the belly of the banged-up plane, and water was streaming from this new laceration and out the windows. Slowly but surely the water was displaced as air rushed in through the small windows and the new holes. Monroy, Carlos, and Juan were not only wet, but slick with engine oil.

Sparks danced inside the cockpit as the electronics shorted out. Carlos called in a Mayday, yelling over the sirens and alarms while wrestling with the power of the back motor and willing the *Ofelia* to take altitude.

From base, Guille Lares called in. "Tranquilo, tranquilo," he said. Take it easy, take it easy.

"I know, I know," said Costa, breathless. He would later describe to Steve Walton how his mental acuity dominated over the screeching, the Maydays, the howling of the alarms and stall warnings.

Walton flew over and under Costa's aircraft, with Blalock taking pictures and video of the bruised plane from all angles. Noticing the damaged underbelly of the *Ofelia*, Walton advised Costa not to put down the landing gear, and he called in to Marathon Airport to prepare for an emergency landing. At Walton's insistence—demands, really—they closed the airport in Marathon and had the ambulances and rescue teams in place. The media was summoned, too.

Steve Walton shepherded Carlos to Marathon, with Matt Blalock filming every move. They held their breath for the belly landing. Carlos Costa's precision was such that there was nary a wobble on touchdown and there was no further damage to the plane. It was a perfect landing.

It was a smiling Carlos Costa who stepped up to the television crews waiting for him.

"Today is my new birthday," he said.

Once again, Brothers to the Rescue needed a new plane, and once again the community would come to their rescue. Sometimes it took radio or television marathons, other times community leaders would host fund-raisers. Frequently, just holding out a bucket at a traffic light would do the job. And if that bucket-holder was Matt Blalock speaking in broken Spanish, the Cuban exile community ate it up.

Blalock bragged about the "Cuba corner" in his home, where he kept souvenirs gifted to him by Arturo Cobo of the Transit Center in Key West. In return, Blalock would speak in his broken Spanish on WQBA radio station. After listeners heard the gringo speak ("Gringo" would become Blalock's nickname), donations would pour in.

His Cuba corner contained an oar from a raft, a compass, a map of Cuba, and a picture of the first family Brothers had ever rescued. He had a case of Havana Club rum waiting to be opened the minute Fidel Castro died. Blalock kept hours of film footage and hundreds of photos of the missions. He also collected backseat stories flying with Van Hare and Steve Walton. It seemed the Americans were always together on Walton's shiny red plane.

Just as Basulto liked to fly with each new pilot, he also liked to mix up the groups. Doing so boosted camaraderie and gave everyone a chance to fly with one another. The day came when it was time for Gringo to fly with an all-Cuban crew, captained by Carlos Tabernilla. Tabernilla was flying his own plane, *El Viejo Pancho*, Old Pancho, named after the DC-3 his grandfather flew in the Cuban military. Tabernilla's grandfather had been a five-star general and head of the Armed Forces of Cuba under President Fulgencio Batista. His father had been a brigadier general and head of the Air Force. Tabernilla often retold the story of his departure from Cuba, of being awakened by his mother at two o'clock in the morning on January 1, 1959, when President Batista, his military generals, and their families fled the island. Tabernilla was eight years old and it was one of the most thrilling events of his life. Apart from it being the historic date that would usher Fidel Castro into Cuba, that early-morning flight from Havana to Palm Beach, Florida, marked the beginning of his love affair with flying. Thirty-two years later, Tabernilla was picking up another generation of people fleeing the same man.

Tabernilla lived in a private subdivision five miles west of Palm Beach, Florida, called the Wellington Aero Club, and he kept his airplane in his backyard.

He would soon be diagnosed with a cancerous tumor in his heart. Even while undergoing chemotherapy, he went on missions, his signature camouflage cap concealing his hair loss. He never talked about his condition. He just kept flying.

When the Virgin Mary started appearing at a farmhouse in Conyers, Georgia, a group from Brothers went to see the miracle, and they took Tabernilla. Soon after that visit, the tumor disappeared.

When he first met Carlos Tabernilla, Blalock quickly sized him up: he was almost his height, balding, camouflage hat, khaki pants, brown boots, serious business. Tabernilla was busy with flight preparations and did not pay much attention to Blalock.

"You're observer today," Tabernilla said, finally acknowledging Blalock, who obediently climbed in the back. Even though he was bigger and stronger than Tabernilla, Blalock felt snubbed, disregarded. He chalked it up to Tabernilla's "Cuban cockiness."

Ready for takeoff, Tabernilla and Raúl Martínez, another pilot who had just gotten his license and would be pilot-in-command that day, put on their headsets. Blalock did not get one. Then Tabernilla and Martínez started speaking Spanish to each other, oblivious to the 6'5" bull trying to arrange himself in the backseat.

Hours into the mission that day, Blalock spotted a white towel being waved back and forth frantically by a rafter down below. He tapped Pilot-in-Command Martínez on the shoulder. "Target." Martínez ignored him.

"Target. Target. Target!" he repeated, to no avail, Martínez being unable to hear him above the roaring motors. So Blalock grabbed Martínez's headset and yelled in his ear. "TAR-GET!"

"You take-a de plane!" Blalock heard Martínez say, as he let go of the controls as if they were on fire. Simultaneously Tabernilla grabbed them with an expert's embrace. Then Blalock saw Tabernilla pitch it up vertically for what seemed an eternity. He felt like the back of his head was being pulled by some magnetic force toward the rear engine. Then Tabernilla rolled on the wing as if he were drawing a question mark in the sky, but from the bottom up.

"The gringo's got something," he called into the radio. "We're going to check it out," he said, and Blalock heard "sheck" rather than "check." Then Tabernilla started spiraling, in a descending turn on the wingtip, stall alarms screeching out their warnings to *El Viejo Pancho*. For Blalock it was as if the plane were screeching to the pilot: "I don't want to fly!" The ailerons, the movable surfaces on the wings, were flapping at hummingbird speed, trying to suck in the air that they needed underneath them. The stall alarms were shrieking an incessant *eeeiiiieeee*, and Blalock watched in amazement as Tabernilla took the plane, became one with it, and at the last possible moment, rolled *El Viejo Pancho* into a perfectly level, straight flying pattern. Matt Blalock christened his move "the Tabernilla Turn."

"Good job!" said Tabernilla to Blalock, suddenly aware of him in the back, congratulating him on his find of a lone rafter on two inner tubes. He turned to Martínez and told him to throw out the dye marker. Such was the latter's precision that Martínez hit the rafter on the nose with it. Raúl Martínez was christened with a new name that day, too: "El Marcador," The Marksman.

As usual, they landed in Marathon and went to Pizza Hut. Afterward, since he was flying back to North Perry Airport, Blalock went home on Steve Walton's plane. The best part of that flight was watching the Tabernilla Turn from another aircraft.

Another day Carlos Costa flew with the Americans on *Big Red*, the nickname for Steve Walton's 235 Apache, N13BR. When flying together, these three Jewish Americans—Van Hare, Blalock, and Walton—sometimes referred to themselves as "the Yom Kippur Clipper." Today, Van Hare was pilot-in-command, Carlos would be copilot, and Matt and Steve were observers, sporting their Hawaiian shirts and singing Jimmy Buffet songs from the backseat.

Their mission area that day was over the Cay Sal Bank of the Bahamas, the westernmost and third largest of the Bahamas Banks, just thirty miles north of Cuba. Rafters had been spotted at Elbow Cay, a long, skinny, rocky island distinguished by its conical stone lighthouse, built by the British in 1839 and no longer used.

The Coast Guard had already been advised of the stranded rafters; they would now have to get the necessary permission from Bahamian authorities to pick them up. It was important that Brothers get to the rafters before the Bahamian officials. If the latter happened, the rafters were usually transferred to Nassau and detained at Carmichael Road Detention Center or, sometimes, imprisoned at Fox Hill. Both were infamous for their inhumane treatment of inmates.

Luckily for the rafters now stranded on Elbow Cay, out of the corner of his eye Matt Blalock saw the flash of a mirror, a rafter signaling to *Big Red*. There were more than a dozen people stranded on these dry rocks and it would be a while before the Coast Guard could collect them. They needed food and water. There was a toddler there, running around the rocks wearing nothing but a diaper.

Van Hare came over the island seemingly inches above the top of the fifty-foot-tall lighthouse. It was the only way to make a drop. The water bottles and radios were bundled extra thick for Cay Sal because of the rough terrain.

Matt Blalock readied for the drop. Van Hare knew the timing had to be precise, especially when throwing down a package in the vicinity of a child in diapers. A baseball thrown at ninety-five miles per hour could kill a person. He could only imagine what a two-gallon jug of water at one hundred twenty miles per hour was capable of.

As Van Hare zoomed over the lighthouse, all eyes were downcast toward the stranded rafters, focused on the drop. No one was ready for the black birds.

What seemed like five hundred birds flew up as one from inside the lighthouse, a solid black curtain blocking their view. Van Hare grabbed the controls and snapped the plane into a knife edge on a ninety-degree bank. Instinctively, the birds uniformly folded their wings, giving Van Hare a grid formation with a clean thin line to maneuver through.

"Hey, I'm like Spiderman back here!" Blalock yelled. His body was flying parallel to the island below, his two long arms pressed high against the top of the cabin, willing the plane to straighten, his legs spread-eagled, trying to engage some nonexistent brake pads that would somehow stop the plane.

Van Hare came around again. There were kids down there and the pilots were on a mission. Already rehearsed, the birds did it again, a black vertical blind blocking the sun, then opening on Van Hare's cue. He sliced through again, but they were unable to make the drop.

The only way to make a drop on Elbow Cay was to run the length of the island, but they could not risk another bird encounter. They had to fly the width, less than one hundred feet.

For Blalock, on the third try, the birds, the package he was preparing to drop, and Van Hare's knife-edge moves had him in near hysterics. Carlos Costa turned back and grabbed his arm.

"Look, Gringo," Carlos said, "God won't let us die out here. We're doing the right thing." They finally made the drop.

14

A New Home

Any old place I can hang my hat is home sweet home to me.
William Jerome

As the Brothers to the Rescue fleet grew, the planes needed a hangar. Thanks to community support, the organization was able to afford a $5,000 per month rental at the Opa-locka Airport in northwest Miami. The hangar had ten thousand square feet, enough room for ten airplanes. It was across from the Miami-Dade Police hangar and around the corner from the U.S. Customs office.

Two days before the inauguration ceremonies, Brothers was asked to perform a special mission to Cancún, Mexico. It was not to rescue a life, but rather to pick up the body of an eighteen-month-old girl named Claudia Laso Peréz who had died of dehydration when her family had escaped Cuba on a raft. Ivan Domanilevicz, one of the Argentinean pilots, went to pick up the small white coffin.

In his logbook, he wrote that they had picked up the body of a little girl whose cause of death was listed as "exposure." "And lack of freedom," he added.

On December 11, 1993, Congressman Lincoln Díaz-Balart (nephew of Fidel Castro's first wife), singer Willy Chirino, and many others inaugurated the new hangar at the Opa-locka Airport. Brothers to the Rescue christened their new home after Gregorio Peréz Ricardo, in memory of the fifteen-year-old rafter who was the catalyst of their organization.

Here the pilots would hang not only their hats, but also the nineteen flags of the nationalities that were represented by the volunteer pilots:

1. Argentina
2. Brazil

   3. Costa Rica
   4. Cuba
   5. Dominican Republic
   6. France
   7. Germany
   8. Haiti
   9. Israel
   10. Italy
   11. Jamaica
   12. Nicaragua
   13. Peru
   14. Puerto Rico
   15. Spain
   16. Switzerland
   17. Russia
   18. United States
   19. Venezuela

Here, the band of brothers and sisters would gather after missions to plaster the planes with stickers marking the mission date, the rescuers' names, and most important, the number of people saved. Mothers like Mirta Costa would bring steaming casseroles to the famished pilots returning with missions accomplished. They would savor the best Cuban coffee in the world, made by the Argentinean Koki. His secret: he never washed the coffee filter.

The day of the hangar's christening, Brothers supporter Abilio León took a picture of the more than thirty pilots then flying for Brothers. He dedicated the photo to "the most selfless heroes in the world." In the photo, Koki is standing using a walker, still doing therapy almost a year after his accident. Basulto is holding his grandson Andre, who was less than two years old, and is flanked by the five female pilots of Brothers, sometimes referred to as "Basulto's Angels."

At the new hangar, Chief of Pilots Carlos Costa would work from his new office, an area caged in with chain link on all four sides and the top as well. The nineteen national flags of Brothers to the Rescue were draped around the top. Here, Carlos would work the radios and communications, as well as schedule all the missions.

Carlos had many nicknames. Basulto called him Carlitos. His fellow pilots called him El Intenso, the intense one. Even though he had a full-time job, he worked around those hours to devote every spare moment to the organization. Carlos' peers thought highly of him and the pride he took in his work. To the other pilots it seemed that Brothers to the Rescue was his life.

The female pilots and volunteers called him "good-looking Carlos," to distinguish him from the other pilots named Carlos. Carlos Gartner was called "Cholo," a term used in his native Peru; camouflage-wearing, military-minded Carlos Tabernilla was simply Tabernilla. But youthful Carlos Costa, who was playful, cute, handsome, and *available,* was christened "good-looking Carlos."

Many remember Carlos Costa walking over to his new office that day. With pride, he sucked in his breath, pushed back his shoulders, and with a deliberate sense of purpose sauntered inside. Before entering, he looked over at Basulto, cocked his arm up to the brim of his signature "No Fear" cap, and saluted.

"Mi General," he said with respect. My General.

15

Rafter to the Rescue

Silent gratitude isn't much use to anyone.
Gladys Bronwyn Stern

Rita Basulto and Maggie Schuss were regularly on call at home. Rarely a night went by when they were not awakened at two or three in the morning by calls for help from family members in Cuba. "Please, please, my husband and son just left in a small blue boat." "My children are in a white raft, please find them." "Have you found my cousins yet?" When loved ones were found, Rita and Maggie would immediately call back the frantic and grateful family members.

As they walked or drove through Miami with their husbands, it was a rare day when someone did not call out to them: "Hey, you saved me! Thank you!" It puzzled them, though, that only a handful of rafters ever came to the hangar, or even called Brothers to express that gratitude, to say "thank you." Even when Koki was in the hospital, only two rafters paid him a visit.

At least for some rafters, it was not lack of appreciation that kept them from publicly expressing their gratitude or getting involved with Brothers to the Rescue. It was fear that loved ones left behind in Cuba most assuredly would be harassed. Others, having grown up in a world where no one could be trusted, resisted getting involved—even with the very people who had saved their lives. Others were simply too busy just trying to survive in a new country.

But there were a few rare exceptions. One day Maggie Schuss was at a Winn-Dixie supermarket when she was approached by a stock boy who halted his arrangement of canned foods to speak with her.

"You're from Brothers to the Rescue," he said.

"Yes," she replied.

"You all saved me," he said. He elaborated on his ordeal, three days at sea, and his rescue by the Lares brothers in the middle of a storm in August 1992, along with twelve others, two of them toddlers. The stock boy had written poetry about one day returning to Cuba, reiterating that what Cuba needed was love, the truth, and time. Years later, his sister would say that he was most grateful to his new country for allowing him to experience one God-given right: the right to be a human being.

"I am so thankful to Hermanos al Rescate," the stock boy told Maggie.

"Then why don't you go back and tell them?" Maggie suggested.

That balsero, Pablo Morales, took her up on the suggestion. His first volunteer job involved cleaning duties at the hangar. Later he became an observer, and finally he started studying for his pilot's license, mentored by the young pilots.

Pablo Morales was a U.S. resident waiting for his citizenship. He had left his mother and sister behind in Cuba, and eagerly awaited the day they would be reunited. He worked Monday through Friday delivering canned goods to local grocery stores, and every weekend he volunteered with Brothers. Aboard Steve Walton's plane, he practiced his English and sang Jimmy Buffet songs in the backseat along with Matt Blalock while his girlfriend, Hady, volunteered at the hangar. Pablo became an integral part of the young group of pilots who not only flew together, but partied together as friends. His experience of having spent three days on the water waiting for rescue gave him a unique perspective as an observer.

"The ocean is not blue," he would tell the pilots. "It is black."

Pablo Morales represented one end of the spectrum of rafters—one with the courage to become a member of Brothers. Perplexing to Brothers, but to some extent understandable, were the vast majority who not only did not volunteer but never came back to express their gratitude. Incomprehensible from the Miami exile perspective were those who made it to the United States but then forsook their newfound freedom to return to the island. One of those was the Triana family.

Arturo Triana's family had tasted freedom when they arrived in Miami during the 1980 Mariel Boatlift. A year later, life in the United States did not suit Mrs. Triana and she wanted to go back to Cuba. When the family returned to Havana, Triana Sr. was not allowed to stay and was deported back to Miami. The Triana brothers and their mother stayed in Cuba.

There followed the most miserable thirteen years of Arturo Triana's life. He dropped out of school, could not find a job, and yearned to leave Cuba. He remembers neighbors saying he and his brothers were trouble—not because of any deviant behavior, but because they had left like *gusanos*, worms. And they had come back only to want to leave again.

They attempted to escape in August 1992. The surf was so rough on the shore that their raft made of bamboo poles fell apart. Later they found out that the violent seas were due to Hurricane Andrew.

Dejected, Arturo Triana stayed in Cuba and fulfilled his mandatory military duty. On reviewing his file, the officers discovered the Mariel exile and re-emigration, and that he had tried to escape in 1992. He was ostracized by the group, declared ineligible for any special training, and not permitted to carry a weapon. He was, after all, a gusano. Daily, when the thirty-four soldiers in his group would file in for drills or training, he was ridiculed by his platoon commander. "There go thirty-three soldiers and one Triana!" he said, humiliating Triana further.

After his military duty, Triana and his three brothers met another pair of brothers from near their home in Camagüey who also wanted to leave Cuba. They pooled together ten thousand Cuban pesos and paid a man to build two rafts made of truck tire inner tubes wrapped in canvas.

They had no connections in Havana so they had to time their arrival in the city for the precise moment they were set to leave on the rafts. Travel between cities was not permitted unless one had family residing there or permission from the state.

In March 1993, the two sets of brothers determined to escape Cuba. They packed water and some crackers, believing the voyage would last only two days. Brothers to the Rescue was sure to spot them by then. "Timing was everything," Triana insisted. Last-minute jitters kept one of the four Trianas behind. He would eventually leave on another raft and be stranded on Cay Sal before being rescued.

They pushed off from the shore, one man rowing in the smaller raft and the other four rowing the larger one. During the four-foot seas that first night, they realized their water bottles had been tossed overboard in the frantic departure. The crackers, their only food, were soaked in seawater. Wet, cold March winds penetrated their sweaters like pinpricks. Hypothermia could not be ruled out, even in the warm waters of the Straits. There was no space to lie down, so sleep was not an option. When exhaustion overtook them, the four in the larger raft held on to one another in an effort to sleep. When that did not work, they just kept rowing.

Later that night, their raft almost tipped over when they spotted a shark. The next two evenings brought calm seas, water clear enough to see the eyes of the large fish staring up at them through the darkness. The evening clouds fashioned themselves into twisted mirages of land ahead, and one of the men began hallucinating. He ranted that he wanted to get out of the raft. His brother, sobbing, tried to console him.

By noon of the third day, the first layer of skin on their buttocks would have peeled off, the rowing motion rubbing the skin off in thin slices. The salt caking their eyes and mouth had hardened now, and the blisters on their hands and fingers, already into their third layer, were bleeding.

What was going on in their minds was worse, their brains constantly alerting their minds to thirst. A normal person in non-adverse conditions can experience reduced mental acuity once he is simply *aware* of thirst. When brain cell volume decreases because of dehydration, irritability increases, muscles twitch, and seizures become likely. As the brain shrinks, so does the capacity for rational thinking.

Arturo Triana looked up toward the heavens, wishing with all his being that something, anything, even if it were the angel of death, would come and lift him up out of his watery prison. He just wanted to be dry.

It was then that they saw the wing of the blue plane slice through the gray clouds. *Seagull One.* The pilot did not see them. Triana took out his mirror and waved it around, trying to catch any trace of sun that peeked through the dreary mass overhead. As the plane wove in and out of the clouds, the five men below waved frantically with their last bit of strength, hoarse voices beckoning the heavens.

Perhaps it was a glint off that mirror, or coincidence, or Providence that Basulto saw them. His first low pass came so close that Arturo Triana would later swear he made eye contact with Basulto. The five men cried through dry, sunken sockets. Basulto made another low pass and threw down a bottle of orange drink and a note. They rowed to it, frantic, then took turns drinking. The note said not to despair, that the Coast Guard was on its way.

They were comforted by Basulto's plane flying protectively in circles, until it disappeared. They were momentarily dejected, but within moments, another plane appeared, a red-and-white one—Steve Walton. Steve stayed with them until the Coast Guard arrived at six in the evening.

The officers helped the men out of the raft because their legs were stiff, their muscles long since atrophied, and like newborn babies they were unable to walk or steady themselves. Aboard the one-hundred-foot cutter named *Empire State* they were given paper gowns and blankets. Triana fell into the deepest and most delicious sleep of his life.

When they arrived at the Transit House in Key West, Arturo Cobo greeted them with a banquet of food. But they were unable to eat, too exhausted.

Three of the four Triana brothers had finally returned to Miami thirteen years after the Mariel Boatlift, on March 12, 1993. They did not know it then, but their timing was perfect. They arrived on the first day of the "Storm of the Century," the most intense nor'easter ever to strike the eastern United States, killing more than 250 people and cancelling a quarter of all commercial flights for two days. It caused the most damaging squall lines registered in Cuba during a winter season. More than fifty groups would call Brothers for news of their loved ones. None was ever heard from. Their names would be added to the Wall of Sorrows.

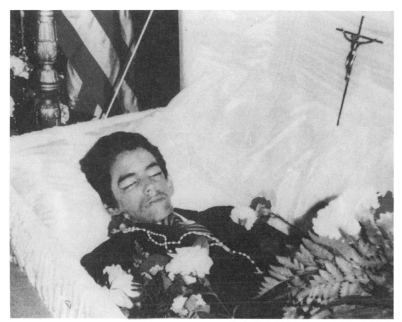

Gregorio
Pérez Ricardo,
deceased fifteen-
year-old rafter, at
Rivero Funeral
Home in Miami.
(Photo donated
to Brothers
to the Rescue
by Pedro M.
Montez.)

José Basulto at home in front of the painting of Manolín Guillot Castellano, Cuban patriot. (Photo by Roberto Koltun, *Miami Herald*.)

Brothers to the Rescue logo on *Seagull One*, the N2506. (Photo by author.)

José Basulto and William "Billy" Schuss, founders of Brothers to the Rescue. (Photo courtesy of BTTR Archives.)

Pilot Mayte Greco-Regan, flying on the twelfth anniversary of the shoot-down of the four Brothers to the Rescue pilots. (Photo by author.)

The Lares brothers: Jorge "Koki" Lares, Adalberto "Beto" Lares, and Guillermo "Guille" Lares, pilots for Brothers to the Rescue. (Photo by Lorenzo De Toro, *IDEAL* magazine.)

David Lawrence Jr., his daughter, and Brothers to the Rescue pilots after a mission. *Top row, L–R:* Billy Schuss, Carlos Tabernilla, Carlos Gartner, David Lawrence Jr. (behind propeller, wearing sunglasses), Amanda Lawrence, Guille Lares. *Second row, L–R:* Osvaldo Plá (Tito Fufú), Diego Pérez, Koki Lares, José Basulto (wearing cap), Beto Lares, Yves Houssin. (Photo courtesy of BTTR Archives.)

Steve Walton, Brothers to the Rescue pilot. (Photo courtesy of BTTR Archives.)

Crash landing of the N5416K, piloted by Guille Lares, in the water off Key West in 1992. (Photo courtesy of BTTR Archives.)

Seagull One, the N2506, signature plane of Brothers to the Rescue, which escaped Cuban MiGs on February 24, 1996. (Photo by Roberto Koltun, *Miami Herald.*)

Congresswoman Ileana Ros-Lehtinen, the godmother of Brothers to the Rescue, with José Basulto. (Photo courtesy of BTTR Archives.)

Brothers to the Rescue prayer circle before a mission. The woman with her back to the photographer is Mayte Greco. (Photo courtesy of BTTR Archives.)

Group of pilots at the inauguration of the Gregorio Pérez Ricardo hangar at Opa-locka on December 11, 1993, dedicated to "the most selfless heroes in the world." *Back row, L–R:* René González (Cuban spy), Arnaldo Iglesias, Fabio A. Vázquez, Koki Lares (using walker), Juan González, Alfredo Sánchez, Joe Husta, Guille Lares (with cap), John Toohey Morales, Javier Sosa. *Second row, standing in center of photo, L–R:* Jorge Araujo, Luis Martínez, Eduardo Domanievicz, Conrad Webber, Billy Schuss (looking to his right), Carlos Rodríguez (wearing cap), and just below him wearing cap and vest, Leopoldo "Polo" Núñez. *Third row, crouching L–R:* Juan Pablo Roque (Cuban spy), Ray Martin, Esteban Bovo Caras (looking to his left), Luis Cruz, Carlos Costa, Virginie Buchete Puperoux (looking to her right), Jennifer Torrealba (with sunglasses), Mayte Greco (with cap), Carlos Tabernilla, Steve Walton. *Bottom row, sitting, L–R:* Gilberto Pekar, Ivan Domanievicz, young son of Joe Husta, Beverly Brooks, José Basulto holding his grandson Andre Basulto. (Photo by Abilio León.)

José Basulto with Juan Pablo Roque (*standing*) and René González (*kneeling*), Brothers to the Rescue pilots who were later discovered to be spies, in front of the N2506. (Photo courtesy of BTTR Archives.)

Two rescued rafters holding a welcome letter thrown down in a plastic container by Brothers to the Rescue pilots. (Photo courtesy of BTTR Archives.)

Coast Guard rescue of rafters. (Photo courtesy of BTTR Archives.)

Steve Walton's *Big Red* with a red cross painted on the tail, spotting rafters below. (Photo courtesy of BTTR Archives.)

A Cuban gunboat intercepting Cuban rafters in order to return them to Cuba. (Photo courtesy of BTTR Archives.)

Lorenzo De Toro, editor of *IDEAL* magazine and Brothers to the Rescue supporter, at Opa-locka hangar in front of the sign warning pilots and volunteers of the danger of flying missions. (Photo by Lorenzo De Toro, *IDEAL* magazine.)

Rafters. (Photos courtesy of BTTR Archives.)

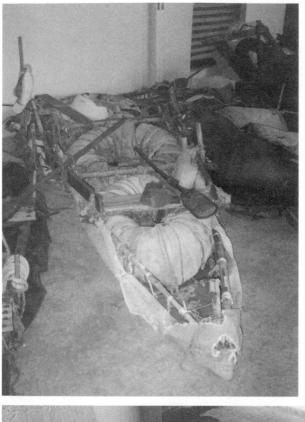

Rafts. (Photos courtesy
of BTTR Archives.)

José Basulto, president of Brothers to the Rescue; Orlando Gutiérrez-Boronat, national secretary of the Cuban Democratic Directory; Ramón Saúl Sánchez, activist and head of the Democracy Movement. (Photo by Lorenzo De Toro, *IDEAL* magazine.)

Omar López Montenegro, Cuban activist; Coretta Scott King, and José Basulto at a non-violence seminar held at the Martin Luther King Jr. Institute. (Photo courtesy of BTTR Archives.)

Above: The Lares Brothers—Guille, Koki, and Beto—with José Basulto (*top right*) and Arnaldo Iglesias (*bottom right*). (Photo by Lorenzo De Toro, *IDEAL* magazine.)

Left: Hank Tester, WTVJ anchorman who flew over Havana with Basulto, exiting *Seagull One*. (Photo courtesy of BTTR Archives.)

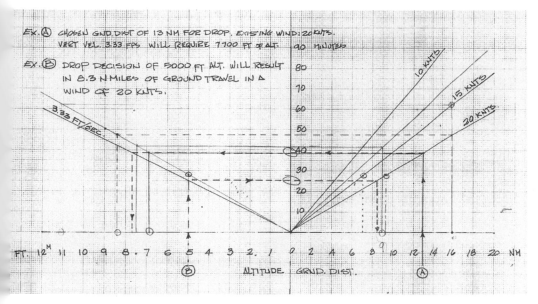

EX. Ⓐ CHOSEN GND. DIST OF 13 NM FOR DROP. EXISTING WIND: 20 KNTS.
VERT. VEL. 3.33 FPS WILL REQUIRE 7700 FT OF ALT.   90 MINUTES

EX. Ⓑ DROP DECISION OF 5000 FT ALT. WILL RESULT
IN 8.3 N MILES OF GROUND TRAVEL IN A
WIND OF 20 KNTS.

Wind studies performed by Brothers to the Rescue pilots in preparation for the leaflet drop from twelve miles off the coast of Cuba in January 1996. (Courtesy of BTTR Archives.)

Flyer reading "Comrades, No! Brothers!" blown over Havana from twelve miles off the coast of Cuba in January 1996. On the reverse were printed the thirty articles of the Declaration of Human Rights, of which Cuba is a signatory. (Courtesy of BTTR Archives.)

Armando Alejandre Jr., 45, Cuban activist shot down by Cuban MiGs on February 24, 1996. (Photo provided by Lorenzo De Toro, *IDEAL* magazine.)

Carlos Costa, 29, Brothers to the Rescue pilot shot down by Cuban MiGs on February 24, 1996. (Photo provided by Lorenzo De Toro, *IDEAL* magazine.)

Mario de la Peña, 24, Brothers
to the Rescue pilot shot down by
Cuban MiGs on February 24, 1996.
(Photo provided by Lorenzo De
Toro, *IDEAL* magazine.)

Pablo Morales, 29, Cuban rafter saved
by Brothers to the Rescue and Brothers to the Rescue pilot-in-training,
shot down by Cuban MiGs on February 24, 1996. (Photo courtesy of BTTR
Archives.)

Survivors of the February 24, 1996, shoot-down who were aboard *Seagull One*: José Basulto, president of Brothers to the Rescue; Sylvia Iriondo, president of Mothers Against Repression; Andrés Iriondo; and Arnaldo Iglesias, secretary of Brothers to the Rescue, taken on the one-year anniversary. (Photo by Roberto Koltun, *Miami Herald*.)

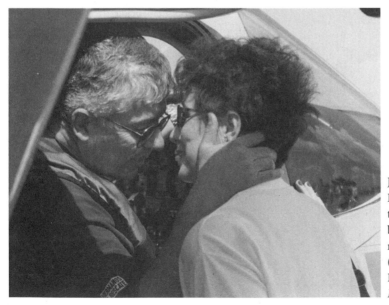

José and Rita Basulto share a tender moment before an anniversary flight. (Photo by Roberto Koltun, *Miami Herald*.)

Eva Barbas, mother of murdered
Brothers to the Rescue volunteer Pablo
Morales, with Osvaldo Plá (Tito Fufú)
and José Basulto, boarding *Seagull One*
for a memorial flight. (Photo by Lorenzo
De Toro, *IDEAL* magazine.)

Families of murdered pilots hold FBI WANTED posters at a ceremony at Florida International University. *L–R:* Mirta Costa Méndez, Osvaldo Costa, Mirta Costa, Nancy Morales, Marlene Alejandre, Maggie Khuly, Miriam de la Peña, Mario de la Peña. (Photo by Roberto Koltun, *Miami Herald*.)

Arnaldo Iglesias, holding daughter of deceased Brothers to the Rescue volunteer Luis Martínez (aka Batman), and José Basulto, before the memorial flight on the twelfth anniversary of the shoot-down. (Photo by author.)

Memorial park for slain Brothers to the Rescue pilots, with one palm tree for each man, near Opa-locka Airport. (Photo by author.)

José Basulto with seagull. (Photo by José Basulto Jr.)

16

Ripples

Once a government is committed to the principle of silencing the voice of opposition, it has only one way to go, and that is down the path of increasingly repressive measures, until it becomes a source of terror to all its citizens and creates a country where everyone lives in fear.

Harry S. Truman

On their third anniversary in February 1994, Brothers to the Rescue approached its one thousandth mission. Basulto placed the numbers from 994 to 1,000 in a hat and the pilots drew lots for the coveted number 1,000. Eduardo Domanievicz, Ivan's father, won. Missions 994 through 1,000 set out that morning and two rescues were brought about, both spotted by Carlos Costa.

At the same time, there were more than a dozen Cubans stranded on Anguilla Cay, another rocky island in the Cay Sal Bahamas Banks. The Coast Guard was unable to pick up the large group of rafters, and they were in desperate need of food and water. Knowing it would be a difficult drop, Basulto called in the Kamikaze Crew: Beverly Brooks and Ivan Domanievicz.

Whenever there was a new maneuver to try out, or a particularly (more than usually) dangerous mission, the Kamikaze Crew was summoned. This time Basulto was attempting to fly without the airplane door, making it easier to drop the bulky bundles needed at Anguilla Cay, wrapped four times bigger than the usual bubble-wrapped items.

The Cessna Skymaster cockpit door opened from the bottom up, making larger drops a nuisance. Not having the door at all would make Brothers to the Rescue deliveries easier, so they removed the door.

As Ivan flew over Anguilla Cay, Beverly passed the bundles to Basulto. The only part of Basulto's bulky frame that remained inside the door frame was his butt, firmly planted on the floor, his feet and arms dangling outside.

A harness wrapped around his belly was tethered to the backseat, since the copilot seat had been removed. Hanging out of the plane, he would have folded in half had it not been for his ever-expanding waistline.

Ivan's passes over the island got lower and lower, with Basulto's body almost parallel to the crystalline waters around the rocky cay. On the final low pass, Basulto felt such proximity to the water and the rocks that he actually scrunched up his feet, like a child riding a bike through a puddle and not wanting to wet his Sunday shoes.

"When we get back, you can shake the sand out of your shoes," said Ivan, and the three members of the Kamikaze Crew burst into laughter.

Less than a week later another group of thirty-seven Cubans was stranded at Cay Sal. Once again, the Coast Guard had not been able to pick them up, and Brothers to the Rescue got word that in the group were sick children in need of medicine. On Sunday afternoon, March 13, 1994, Basulto and Arnaldo Iglesias landed in Cay Sal and personally delivered the medicines and other supplies. They visited for a little while with the stranded balseros and took a picture of the large group that had come to wave good-bye. Many wore their new Brothers to the Rescue T-shirts.

It was a little late for takeoff, about five-thirty in the afternoon, but Basulto and Arnaldo wanted to get back home. They boarded the *Sound Machine*, the plane Gloria and Emilio Estefan had purchased for Brothers. Basulto was in the pilot's seat, his friend Arnaldo was co-pilot. As they waved good-bye to the group of balseros that had gathered to see them off, their view was unobstructed, since they were once again flying without a door. As they sped down the approximately nine hundred feet of runway—an abandoned airstrip, really—a wind shear hit them and swerved their plane into the shrubs. Arnaldo was tossed through the nonexistent door and the *Sound Machine* literally fell on top of him, fracturing his leg and bathing him in gasoline.

The rafters, who minutes before had been waving good-bye, came running to help. One of them dangled a cigarette from his mouth. "Please, buddy, put out the cigarette!" Arnaldo yelled.

The men were able to lift the plane off of Arnaldo and carry him away from the wreckage. The U.S. Coast Guard airlifted them both to a hospital in the Florida Keys. Basulto suffered a broken finger, Arnaldo a broken leg. The rafters were also eventually rescued.

After they developed the pictures they had taken with the rafters before their crash, Basulto labeled it: "The *Sound Machine*'s Final Note, March 13, 1994."

Across the Straits notes of discord were sounding. During the summer of 1994, for the first time in two decades, the Cuban people were holding anti-Castro demonstrations in the streets of Havana. Anticipating the fall of Fidel, Cubans in Miami prepared with programs such as Operation PAL (Pan, Amor y Libertad; Bread, Love and Liberty). The idea was to have prepackaged cases of food and water ready to be sent across the Straits the moment everything in Cuba changed.

Exile groups all but swore in the man they hoped would be the new president of Cuba: Jorge Mas Canosa, the most influential Cuban exile in the United States. Not only was he president of the Cuban American National Foundation (CANF, called La Fundación by locals) but he had almost single-handedly introduced legislation for the creation of TV Martí.

TV Martí was touted as the answer to getting ideas from outside Cuba into the homes of everyone on the island. It cost the U.S. government $18 million a year, and yet no one in Cuba had ever seen it, according to the U.S. Public Interests Section in Havana. (Since the United States does not have diplomatic relations with Cuba, the Special Interests Section takes the place of a consulate.) "Even if Castro jams the signal 100 percent, we will still keep the pressure on," responded Mas Canosa.

Several years later, for a lot less than $18 million—in fact, for less than $6,000—Tito Fufú and Brothers to the Rescue would broadcast a televised message from Basulto, live and in color, transmitted from *Seagull One* to the people of Cuba.

In the meantime, Tito Fufú designed a radio-transmission system aboard the N2506 in order to reach ham operators in Cuba. Basulto's announcement from international waters opened the floodgates of radio operators in Cuba:

"Good morning, Cuba! This is N2506 with José Basulto onboard, KB4-HRV—Hermanos al Rescate Volveremos (Brothers to the Rescue will return), and Tito Fufú on KB4-TTF."

The callers responding from Cuba remained anonymous for fear of arrest, but the communication between Cubans in the air and their brothers on the island continued.

One ham operator did not remain anonymous. In Cuba, Reinaldo Ló-pez Álvarez considered himself an outpost of Brothers to the Rescue. He and Tito became close friends, and Reinaldo routinely informed family members in Cuba when word of their rescued loved ones reached the radio waves.

"The people of Cuba are so grateful to Brothers," he told Tito. "You will never know the good you are doing." Reinaldo was later arrested and given a formal warning by the state. Years later, after transmitting hundreds of messages from Tito to his fellow Cubans, he was coerced into signing a document that forbade him from ever speaking to Tito Fufú again. Sign or go to prison, he was told. Reinaldo would have to wait fifteen years to be given asylum in the United States.

The month after Tito's radio announcement, eight airplanes flew out of Opa-locka Airport piloted by various Cuban pilots that had deserted from the Cuban military, sending a message of love and unity to the members of the Armed Forces of Cuba. Orestes Lorenzo, the pilot who had flown into Cuba to pick up his wife and sons, was among them, as was ex–Cuban military MiG pilot Juan Pablo Roque. Roque had come to Brothers via Brothers' attorney, Sofía Powell-Cosío, being part of her group of Puente de Jóvenes Cubanos (Bridge to Young Cubans).

Juan Pablo Roque was born in Cuba in 1955 to a family of staunch revo-lutionaries. In school, Roque was looked down on for reading muscle maga-zines, considered contraband. He dreamed of being a pilot, but in Cuba his future was determined by how he could best serve the revolution. That process included not only examining his school grades, but also his family's participation in furthering the goals of the revolution. The state kept close tabs on who attended marches and Fidel's speeches. Since Roque's mother was not active, he was ineligible for any special training programs.

A twist of fate finally landed him in pilot training, where he was derided for not being *Cuban enough*: he did not drink rum or coffee, and he did not like baseball. His cronies accused Roque of having a "European complex."

He loved flying, though, and became a MiG pilot for the Cuban Air Force. But he soon became disillusioned with the government. His story tells of a jump into Guantánamo Bay, a swim over to the U.S. naval base, and a plea for asylum. Basulto had made a similar jump in 1961.

Basulto liked Roque and welcomed him into the fold. He particularly liked that Roque had left the Cuban military and would now be flying for

Brothers to the Rescue, a great symbol for the organization. Basulto helped him find various jobs—even hiring him as his own personal trainer and recommending him to his friends, like Brothers supporter René Guerra.

The other pilots did not like Roque. Perhaps they were jealous of his movie-star looks: he was of medium height and chiseled to perfection, thanks to his devotion to bodybuilding; he had dark eyes and dark hair, a straight Roman nose, and full lips; and to top it all off, a dimple on his chin. One reporter wrote that Roque looked more like Richard Gere than Richard Gere.

Roque was clean shaven and well dressed, was careful of what he ate, and did not drink or smoke. The pilots observed how much he enjoyed posing for the camera and telling the media his story over and over again.

It annoyed them that Roque and René González, the other defector who had been with Brothers since its inception, would speak in Russian together, shunning the rest of the group. The dynamic was different from when they themselves spoke Spanish in front of Conrad: Conrad was *buena gente*, a good guy. Roque was not *simpático*, not endearing or charming or good-natured—or liked.

The pilots were wary of his closeness to Basulto. It irritated them when Roque frequently asked them, "Don't you think José needs a bodyguard?" So for the first time in Brothers' three-year history, there was some internal grumbling among the pilots, and Cuban politics became a hot topic.

The older pilots, like Billy Schuss, had changed 180 degrees from their political stances in 1960. Billy had been pro-Fidel at one time. The middle group of pilots—those in their thirties, like Carlos Tabernilla—had followed their parents' political bent. The Tabernilla family had been hard-line pro-Batista. Basulto was somewhere in between: like many Cubans, he had opposed both Fidel Castro and the corruption in the Batista government.

The Cuban American pilots who had been born in the United States, like Carlos Costa, and the new arrivals like Mario de la Peña were vehemently anti-Castro, even though their families had not been politically active in Cuba. "I'm neither for Communism nor capitalism," said twenty-two-year-old Mario de la Peña. "I'm against injustice."

What most pilots did agree on was that they did not like Juan Pablo Roque. That feeling was shared from the oldest to the youngest, nineteen-year-old Mike Murciano. And Mike was in a political hot spot of his own.

Mike Murciano's employment with Haiti Trans Air was viewed as a conflict of interest by some pilots. Haiti Trans Air did charters to Havana, and

Mike often piloted those flights. Knowing full well the reach of Castro's arm, Arnaldo Iglesias worried that Mike had placed himself in a vulnerable position. Mike explained that he did not work for Mar Azul or the other companies that were invested in hotels and such in Havana, that he simply worked for Haiti Trans Air, and Cuba was one of his routes. A typical travel day for him involved flying tourists into Havana in the morning and staying at the airport for about an hour. U.S. pilots were not permitted outside the terminal. There was usually nothing to eat, and frequently the electricity was turned off, so during the dark and hungry layovers, Mike spoke with the locals at the airport.

Mike's parents did not like his job either, but not only because of the political overtones; they feared that his last name would be recognized. As a fourth-generation pilot, Mike had a grandfather who had flown for Cubana de Aviación before the revolution. But the only attention Mike drew came from female nationals who offered him marriage—anything to get out of the country.

After the Aristide affair in Haiti in April 1994, Mike was out of a job. Mike remembers the pilots at Brothers were not disappointed, particularly not Arnaldo.

The political grumbling at Brothers was nothing compared to what was going on across the Straits, however. The pilots never imagined that the summer of 1994 would break all records for rescues at sea.

As the Special Period continued in Cuba, so did the attempts to leave. One exodus in particular would set off a chain of events that would change history.

At three o'clock in the morning on July 13, 1994, seventy-two Cuban civilians stole aboard the *13th of March* tugboat in Havana Harbor and headed north toward freedom. There were fifteen children onboard, including a five-month-old infant and several toddlers. Fourteen in the group were part of the same family, headed by patriarch Jorge García.

The seas were choppy, with four- to five-foot waves and winds blowing at about fifteen knots. Even though the boat was more than one hundred years old, the *13th of March* had been reconstructed and inspected only two months earlier. Her wooden hull was strong.

They were seven miles offshore when the first Cuban gunboat came toward them, and did not stop. "We've been compromised," cried Fidencio Ramel Hernández Prieto, 51, who was the head of operations at the Port of

Havana. Hernández had been instrumental in their months of planning the escape.

The gunboat's prow collided into the *13th of March*, shaking her seventy-two occupants. Another two Cuban boats sped toward the old vessel, one ramming the stern and the other the bow, sandwiching the tugboat. The passengers started screaming.

Then the gunboats opened their water hoses.

When the water jets hit, Hernández was one of the first to fall in the ocean. He came up out of the water, yelling at the officials in disbelief. "Hey, buddy, calm down, don't do this! Look, there are kids onboard!" he pleaded, incredulous at what was happening.

In an effort to substantiate Hernández's pleas, the mothers onboard held their children out in front of them. "*Miren*, look, there are children here!" The children were no match for the force of the hoses, the water jets shooting them clean from their mothers' embraces as they fell into the ocean, shrieking. The rest of the passengers ran belowdecks to escape the torrents. Anyone left on deck was catapulted into the water.

"Save us, *please, save us*, we have children with us!" yelled Jorge García, seeing his son, grandson, and twelve relatives in the water. "Please, my whole family is with me!" As if the hoses had been voice activated, the jets hit the García family. Beams of light searched for those still treading water, assisting the gunboat crew in their assault with the high-pressure hoses, trying to wipe clean any sign of humanity from the surface of the sea.

"Sons of bitches!" the Cubans onboard the government vessels yelled, pointing and laughing at their drowning compatriots, driving around them in circles, creating a whirlpool of death. "Counterrevolutionaries! Thieves!"

The *13th of March* sank into the dark water. Those cradled in the presumed safety of its hull went down with it. The others continued their death tread on the surface.

It was only when a Greek merchant vessel approached that the Cuban crews scurried to pull the survivors out of the water. Thirty-one adults and ten children drowned, including the captain, Fidencio Ramel Hernández Prieto.

The world curled its lips at the horror in Cuba. Pope John Paul II sent a letter of condolence to the archbishop of Havana to be passed on to the survivors and their families. Outcries from the Inter-American Commission on Human Rights of the Organization of American States, the United Nations Human Rights Commission, and Amnesty International demanded investigations.

Fidel Castro defended the actions of his border guards: "What were we going to do with those workers who did not want their boat stolen, who made a truly patriotic effort to stop them from stealing the boat?" he asked defensively. "What are we going to say to them? Let the boat be stolen, don't worry about the boat?"

Granma, the state-sponsored newspaper, claimed that the "counterrevolutionary radio stations and the nest of maggots in Miami" were responsible for the act of piracy. No one claimed responsibility for the deaths of forty-one people. Among them were all of Jorge García's family.

17

City of Rafts

We live here as if in a borrowed country.
Reinaldo Bragado

Ever since the Ladies from Havana helped George Washington fund his revolution, a unique relationship has existed between the United States and Cuba. In order that "the American mothers' sons are not born as slaves," a group of Cuban mothers sent to Virginia the equivalent of $28 million in diamonds and pearls. Historian Stephen Bonsal wrote that this amount "must be considered as the ground whereon was erected the American independence."

One hundred years after the American Revolution, the exodus of the 1860s brought Cuban tobacco growers escaping political turmoil to Tampa and Ybor City, Florida. In the nineteenth century, Cubans arriving in the United States were called émigrés. Other migrations followed, the largest one in the years after the revolution of 1959 and the failed Bay of Pigs invasion. Cubans were welcomed into the United States as exiles or political refugees. Some exiles called their existence in the United States *destierro*, which literally means unearthed, to be ripped from one's country.

When it was confirmed that what Castro had in mind for Cuba was Communism, President Johnson initiated the Freedom Flights. From 1965 to 1971, nearly a quarter million Cuban refugees landed in the United States, on 2,879 such flights. Subsequently, for twenty-two months between December 1960 and October 1962, more than fourteen thousand unaccompanied minors arrived as refugees in Miami under the sponsorship of the Catholic Welfare Bureau's program named Pedro Pan (Peter Pan flights).

It was not until 1980 and the Mariel Boatlift that the character of these migrations changed. In 1980, Fidel Castro orchestrated the moves.

It started on April Fool's Day 1980 when five Cubans crashed the gates to the Peruvian Embassy in Havana. Their numbers soon swelled to ten thousand. After a week, Fidel Castro said they were free to leave; he couldn't afford to feed them anyway. *Anyone* that wanted to leave Revolutionary Cuba was free to do so, he announced to his countrymen, his beloved compañeros. America opened its arms, and the press was all over the story. The Cubans from Miami rushed to Mariel Harbor on the north coast of Cuba in their Bertrams, their fishing boats, and their speedboats to bring back their Cuban brothers and welcome them to freedom.

But even in giving his compañeros freedom, Fidel exerted force. Fidel decided to release those in common prison, the old, the marginally sane, and the morally corrupt. When President Carter finally caught on, he told the almost two thousand vessels still in Mariel Harbor to come back home. Castro played the last card, though. No boats were allowed to leave unless they were full of Cubans, and Castro got to choose *which* Cubans could go. The ripple effect from Havana resulted in 125,000 Cuban refugees reaching Miami, many without family members to claim them. The city was unable to assimilate the sea of people, and tent cities sprang up under highway overpasses. Crime escalated, Cubans were frequently involved, and the prejudice that had seemingly disappeared after the exile immigration of the early 1960s came back.

For thirty-five years, immigration policy toward Cubans had not changed. Cubans were considered political refugees and they were always welcome in the United States. The rafter phenomenon was nothing new. Since 1959, tens of thousands of Cubans had escaped by taking to the Straits in anything that would float.

Fidel's Special Period was exacerbating the flow. And after forty-one of their countrymen had been murdered on the *13th of March* tugboat and all involved had been exonerated—even after worldwide condemnation—the Cuban people had had enough.

In August 1994 Cuba was witnessing the worst civil unrest the country had seen in decades. Castro naturally blamed it on the United States. His biographer Tad Szulc wrote that the refugee card was the only one Castro had left to play. "He has been doing this for a living for 35 years. . . . He needs breathing space and knows that the only way to get it is to force the Americans into a dialogue," wrote Szulc.

Castro was angry that the refugees, who were stealing boats from Cuba and sometimes using violence to escape, were given a warm welcome upon arriving in Florida. Although the United States did not approve of violent means of escaping the regime, Cuban exiles had always been welcomed as refugees.

This repeatedly angered the migrants from Haiti and the Dominican Republic, who played the race card that perhaps they were not white enough for a welcome to the United States. But Cuba's population now had a black majority; it would reach 70 percent in the new millennium.

Several writers called the situation the "Cuban Contradiction," and argued it was about time that U.S. policy toward Cubans be equally extended to people leaving other countries. *Miami Herald* columnist Ana Menéndez, a Cuban American herself, wrote that there should be a Haitian Adjustment Act to parallel President Johnson's Cuban Adjustment Act of 1964.

But it had been the Cubans who were abandoned at the Bay of Pigs; it was the Cubans whom President Kennedy promised that their national flag would be returned to the Brigade 2506 in a free Cuba. The Cubans were ignored once again when an opportunity presented itself during the Missile Crisis. It was Castro's government that the United States promised not to invade under the Kennedy-Khrushchev Accord and, as a consequence, Communism thrived. It was the Cubans who fled political, not economic, persecution, although now with the economic suffering under the Special Period, that last argument was being challenged. For better or worse, Cuba *was* different, and it had been so since the American Revolution. And yet the love affair that began with Washington and the Ladies from Havana was about to end.

On August 5, 1994, outraged Cuban citizens watched the government thwart another escape when they intercepted a hijacked ferry. The unrest in Cuba rippled through the country, and thousands began to prepare for what would be called the Exodus of 1994. More than thirty thousand men, women, and children headed for the Straits.

On August 7, 1994, Domingo Campo and thirteen others left aboard a boat that had a brand-new three-horsepower engine—or so they were told. The engine alone cost them five thousand Cuban pesos. They packed an extra fuel tank, to guarantee that their voyage would not last longer than three days. Unfortunately, the person who installed the motor put it in backward, and it never started. When the balseros discovered this, they were less than a mile offshore, but they decided "pa' atras ni pa' coger impulso!" [we're not going back even to get a push forward!] They dumped the engine and the fuel tank in the ocean, and rowed.

They had heard the stories of Brothers to the Rescue on Radio Martí, and how the Brothers would drop radios, water, and other supplies. Domingo's group was confident that the Coast Guard would find them within a few short days. They packed some cooked pork they had been lucky enough to find, and some water. The group of fourteen finished the pork, their only food, on the first day.

The bad weather set in on the second day. Hunger was unbearable on the third, and one of the people onboard took out a stashed bottle of honey. Domingo Campo ate some of the honey on a very empty stomach and it burned his insides.

They saw a ship one night and lit a flare. They stood up to wave at the vessel, but it passed them by. On subsequent days, they saw many other ships and boats, and even planes, the Straits busier than they anticipated. They struggled to their feet to wave, the men even setting their shirts on fire to attract more attention. The ships, the boats, and the planes ignored them.

"Where the hell are those comemierdas from Brothers to the Rescue?" they cursed.

They rationed the little bit of water they had: one sip in the morning, and one sip at night. In their cramped boat, only two people could lie down and sleep at any one time, so they took turns resting.

The traffic of planes, boats, and mercantile ships continued to ignore the thirteen men and one woman aboard Domingo Campo's boat, as if they were invisible to the multitudes on the waterway.

On the sixth day, back in Domingo's hometown a funeral was held for the fourteen people. Four other groups had left from the same town at the same time, and they had already made it to the United States. After trying to glean any information, after days of prayer, even after consulting a medium—they held a funeral for Domingo's group, displaying their photographs in lieu of coffins or bodies. His mother said it brought their community together.

By the eighth day of Domingo's journey, none of the men had shirts— they had all been burned to try to attract the attention of passing boats and planes. They had no water left and they were completely dehydrated and dejected. When they saw a mercantile ship from Croatia approaching, they decided that only one of them would wave to the ship. Maybe the passing ships did not want to take on fourteen refugees. Perhaps they would stop for one. The rest of the group tried to conserve what little energy they had left. They were exhausted. So while thirteen of them pretended to be dead, one waved down the Croatian ship. It came to their rescue.

While they waited for the U.S. Coast Guard to arrive, they retold their torturous eight-day odyssey and the ships and planes that had ignored their pleas. A Croatian who spoke Spanish explained that more than seventeen people had spotted their boat with fourteen people and radioed the information to others. But since there were thousands on the Straits of Florida at the same time, and Domingo's group appeared to be in good shape, they had gone on to rescue others. They had no idea Domingo's group had been out for eight days. Domingo's group had no idea there were thirty thousand people on the water. They did not realize that four days after their departure, Fidel Castro had ordered the Cuban Coast Guard and security forces: do *not* obstruct illegal departures. The exodus was on.

When the Coast Guard picked up the rafters and took them for processing, they were given more Gatorade and soda crackers. Domingo Campo had not eaten soda crackers in more than twenty years.

Later they were taken to the Transit Center in Key West, run by Arturo Cobo and other volunteers. "Welcome to the land of liberty!" they were greeted. Each was given new clothes and soap, razors, toothpaste, and toothbrushes—two of each item.

"Two?" asked Domingo, amazed at the generosity. When he went into the showers at the Transit Center, he noticed that those who had been there before him had left used pieces of soap, half-empty shampoo bottles, and razors. He collected them all; he had never seen such plenty. Then they were treated to a smorgasbord of foods, served hot and in abundance by the volunteers. Finally, the Transit House contacted the people of Domingo's town and told them the good news. "They made it."

After Fidel Castro's open invitation to leave, the exodus was official. Brothers to the Rescue began patrolling the Straits in anything that could fly. Thankfully, their roster of pilots was full, and they had recently welcomed onboard twenty-two-year-old Mario de la Peña.

Mario de la Peña was born on December 28, 1971, in Weehawken, New Jersey. Since he was ten years old, he had wanted to be a pilot. He was currently attending Embry-Riddle Aeronautical University while living at home with his parents, Miriam and Mario, and his younger brother.

The de la Peñas had moved to Miami around the time of the Mariel

Boatlift, so Mario's classroom was filled with children who could not speak English. He started asking questions about Cuba: "What happened in 1959? Why are these kids here now? Why can't they speak English?" The de la Peñas had never been politically active in Cuba—they had left in their early teens—so they found it hard to explain to the ever-curious Mario the complex situation ninety miles away.

He was curious about science, nature, how things grew. He spent nights gazing into the sky with his telescope, enthralled with space and the cosmos. He was creative and liked to invent and build things. His friends recalled Mario and his model rockets, one-way powerless AM radios, and slingshots. Fascinated by the ocean, he learned to scuba dive. He wanted to be in the air, so he learned to fly, enrolling at George T. Baker Aviation School concurrently during high school.

His mother, Miriam, worked for an airline, so the de la Peñas travelled extensively. Miriam remembers pointing Cuba out to them on a return flight from the Cayman Islands. "Why can't I go visit the land where my parents were born? Why? What's happening there?" Mario never stopped asking questions.

When Mario read about Brothers to the Rescue in the summer of 1994, he realized he could not only load up his flying hours, but he could also help save people from Cuba.

The coverage of the exodus of 1994 was so thorough, the pictures so agonizing, that the community longed to help. Just as during the 1980 Mariel Boatlift when anyone with a seaworthy vessel had motored to Cuba, now anyone with a pilot's license was flying over the Straits looking for balseros.

Sylvia Pascual had been managing the office for Brothers for almost two years before she went out on a mission, but listening to the constant phone calls from people on the island searching for relatives provided the catalyst she needed to brave one of the small Cessnas and fly over the Straits. A pair of eyes is a pair of eyes.

She was cramped in the back of the plane Guille Lares was flying, next to an Italian journalist filming the history-making scene below. Sylvia would describe it as "una nata humana," *nata* being the thin skin of scalded milk that solidifies when the hot liquid is cooling. A foamy layer of humans on the water is what her pair of eyes saw. Families huddled in inner tubes, young bare-chested men in rickety boats, grandfathers holding on to pieces of wood, women drowning. There were old men and women with their heads bowed, either in prayer or in anguish. Desperate mothers held up their infants to her, beseeching to be rescued first.

By six o'clock in the evening on Sylvia's first flight, Guille Lares knew they had to turn back because they were running out of fuel and daylight. They flew away from thousands still floating on the seas, like the foam on top of scalded milk. Sylvia cried all the way home.

Pablo Morales understood very well the anguish of the people below him. He had witnessed many of the 4,200 rescues that Brothers to the Rescue had made before the exodus of 1994. He was flying with Carlos Gartner, recalling his own rescue by the Lares brothers. Pablo had been praying to the Virgin Mary, holding the little statue in his hands. When he looked up and saw the plane, he had lifted the image up to the heavens.

He and Carlos Gartner had just spotted a raft with six men, two women, and a fifteen-month-old baby girl. They dropped the bubble-wrapped walkie-talkie and saw it hit the water. As the men scrambled to get the package, the mother held the baby up toward the plane. It was a scene they had witnessed before, this offering up of a child to the enveloping wings of their savior aircraft.

Below them, after reading the instructions for operating the two-way radios, rafter Alberto Martínez Tejeda identified himself and his companions. They were in a wooden boat, twenty-five miles north of Havana, and they had been adrift for several hours since their motor had broken. They had left a day and a half before from El Malecón, along with hundreds of other Cubans. It had been their fourth attempt to leave Cuba.

"We couldn't wait any longer," said a sobbing Martínez Tejeda, communicating through the radio. "But I can't believe what we've done." He was referring to the baby they had onboard. "All we want is freedom, that's all we want."

"Don't worry," Carlos Gartner assured them. "Freedom is on its way, *hermano*." Four hours later they were picked up by the Coast Guard.

For Ivan Domanievicz and Beverly Brooks those days of summer over the Florida Straits resembled a city of rafts. People meeting on the waves extended their hands to each other, bound their inner tubes together, and became family. There was nowhere you could look and not see rafts, and too many of them were empty.

It was the Coast Guard's protocol that once they found a raft and rescued those onboard, they would either mark it with an X or sink it. But the urgency now was to save people, not mark or sink rafts. There was no way of knowing whether those empty rafts represented people that had been saved or souls that had been lost. The Coast Guard could not keep up with the more than three hundred rafts a day being intercepted.

Three hundred rafts a day was too many rafts for the hangar, already overcrowded. Humberto Sánchez and Luis Martínez were the keepers of the rafts, diligently marking them with the day they had been spotted and with the number of souls aboard, or the day they had been found empty. Sometimes the empty rafts told the saddest stories, especially those containing a baby outfit, a broken oar, a split fishing line. Humberto and Luis had traveled many weekends to the Transit House in Key West to collect the rafts from Arturo Cobo. They would display them at special events as far away as the capital in Tallahassee, Florida.

Humberto and Luis always worked together, either at the hangar arranging rafts or as observers looking for more. Always a team, Luis and Humberto were nicknamed "Batman" and "Robin." Luis was a very likely Batman, with his 6'4" frame, his handsome, rugged face, blond hair, and green eyes. Humberto's only similarity to Robin was that he was shorter than Batman. Luis admired him because Humberto was involved in Cuban projects and activities, and Luis wanted to know more about the struggle in Cuba. Their friendship grew from this mentoring relationship, and Batman and Robin worked not only on the rafts, at the hangar, and as observers, but they also worked with Tito Fufú on the radio equipment, since they were both ham operators. They had been part of the Brotherhood since its earliest days.

Luis had come from Cuba on the Mariel Boatlift of 1980 when he was fourteen years old. His father paid someone to get him out on a boat called the *Lady Cracker*. The voyage in heavy seas lasted twenty-six hours. One of his most vivid memories of his arrival was when someone gave his mother a bottle of Coca-Cola. She fainted, flashing back to before the revolution.

Fourteen years later, Luis was working with Humberto and being mentored by Mario de la Peña, who was teaching him to fly. They both lived in the same neighborhood and would often bike to each other's homes.

Historically, Fidel Castro had shifted his domestic problems onto the United States. In his book *The Cuban Americans*, Miguel González-Pando wrote that Havana, not Washington, controlled Florida's coastal borders. While embroiled in the embargo issue, President Clinton was on the verge of changing U.S. policy toward Cuban refugees, a policy that had been in place for thirty-five years.

During the exodus of 1994, Florida Governor Lawton Chiles assured the people of the state that there would be no Mariel II, or any other engineered migration. He also petitioned the president. On August 19, 1994, Operation Able Vigil was put into effect by the U.S. Coast Guard in response to the uncontrolled migration from Cuba and President Clinton's new prohibition on allowing undocumented Cuban migrants into the United States.

Semantics would change immigration policy. Cubans had always been referred to as refugees, now they were labeled migrants. Clinton's new policy decreed that all migrants intercepted at sea by the Coast Guard would be detained in Guantánamo, the U.S. naval base on Cuban soil. Meanwhile, the tens of thousands bobbing in the waters of the Florida Straits had no idea that their status had been changed, that they were no longer welcome, that they would be returned to Cuba.

Nelson Alemán and his family had been in Miami for almost three years after they crossed over on the *Misladys*. Nelson never heard back from the Coast Guard about the antique map he had left on the cutter. Now he was waiting for news about his parents.

The elder Alemáns left Cuba before the policy change, but Nelson did not know if they had been rescued or sent to Guantánamo, or if they were dead. Alemán was among the hundreds calling Brothers to the Rescue every day, wondering if in that city of rafts their family had been found.

"Check the lists," Sylvia Pascual, the Brothers secretary would tell them, "keep checking the lists."

Alemán was too restless to check the lists printed daily in the newspapers or announced over the radio. On three consecutive days, he and his brothers drove from Miami to the Transit House in Key West, a three-and-a-half-hour drive each way. His parents were not on the lists.

His parents were in Islamorada, halfway between Miami and Key West. Orestes Lorenzo had been flying with Brothers to the Rescue the day before the policy changed. He had found the Alemán parents on August 18, 1994, one day before the policy change. Once again, the Alemán family had had perfect timing.

In the first week of Operation Able Vigil, the U.S. Coast Guard would interdict more than ten thousand Cubans, more than were rescued during the decade between 1983 and 1993.

For the rafters, seeing the Brothers' planes was an answer to a prayer. Seeing the Coast Guard was a dream come true. Once onboard the cutters, they were told they were going back to Cuba, to Guantánamo, to revisit their nightmare.

Mario de la Peña was in the air when Operation Able Vigil was announced. Upon his return to Opa-locka, news reporters were waiting to question the pilots about the new policy of returning the rafters. His mother remembers seeing him on television when he was notified of the policy change.

"Oh, they'll be returned?" he said, puzzled. "Then, there's no use in flying?" He was in disbelief. He wanted to ask more questions, but there were no answers for Mario at that time. He continued to fly, even though his family had strong reservations about his staying on with Brothers to the Rescue.

"I'm Cuban American," he explained. "And right now, my Cuban side's in trouble, so my American side needs to help out."

18

Guantánamo

In politics, absurdity is not a handicap.
Napoleon Bonaparte

The U.S. naval base in Guantánamo Bay, on the southeastern end of Cuba, is the oldest American base outside the continental United States, and the only one situated in a country that does not have an open political relationship with the United States. In 1902, the United States leased forty-five square miles of land and water in Guantánamo Bay for use as a coaling station. The lease agreement worked well until Castro's revolution in 1959. Since 1964, Guantánamo has been totally self-sufficient, with its own power and water sources, as well as the only McDonald's on the island of Cuba.

In 1991, the naval base's mission was expanded as some thirty-four thousand Haitian refugees escaping a violent coup stayed there. Some of them were still detained there in August and September of 1994, when intercepted Cuban rafters would raise the population to more than forty-five thousand.

Basulto stood at the end of the long conference table at the hangar, looking out at his remaining pilots. Many had decided to leave after the policy change.

"Remember everyone, we answer to a higher authority," he said, announcing that the rescue missions would continue. "We'll just need to change a few things. First of all, we can't call the Coast Guard anymore. Then, when we drop the supplies, we'll ask them on the walkie-talkies if they want assistance." Of course, if the pilots ascertained that those below were in distress then they would call the Coast Guard, even though it meant sending them to Guantánamo. At least they would keep the rafters alive.

As Guille and Beto Lares were flying on a mission one October afternoon in 1994 they realized just how much things had changed. After calling Havana Center as they passed the 24th parallel, they noticed a raft with four men and two women onboard. They looked like they were in pretty good shape, but the pilots knew that the group still had a long way to go. They did a low pass to get a better look. When they were on their second low pass, two of the men stood up.

In the past, this was the moment when the balseros would throw up their hands in an open embrace. This was the time when, if they had one onboard, a child would be lifted up toward the Brothers to the Rescue plane. Any religious relics packed for the journey would also be offered up. These were the moments when they would signal that they needed water, or that someone needed a doctor. Dramatic gestures of folded hands in prayer were pumped up into the air, a nonverbal thank-you for saving their lives.

Today was different.

The two men planted their legs firmly in the rocking boat, lifted their open palms toward them and pumped them forward. Get out of here! Their body language unmistakable: go away. If they could have, their arms would have wiped the plane out of the sky. They did not want to attract the attention of the Coast Guard, which now regularly patrolled the area looking for migrants to return and detain in Guantánamo.

The Lares brothers did not even drop a walkie-talkie. No radio communication was necessary to hear what these rafters wanted from Brothers. They wanted nothing. Guille and Beto Lares prayed for them.

By November 1994, there were thirty-three thousand Cuban detainees in Guantánamo, being held indefinitely by the United States. Twenty-four Cuban American attorneys filed a lawsuit against the unlawful detention of innocent men, women, and children who were living in the cramped, dusty tents surrounded by barbed wire. They held a press conference on the steps of the Federal Courthouse in Miami that was broadcast around the world by CNN.

Attorney José García-Pedrosa and a small group of those lawyers decided it was time to visit their clients in Guantánamo. His goal was to set up a legal clinic on the base to hear the cases of the refugees. For García-Pedrosa the trip would be thirty-four years almost to the day since he had left his native country, back in 1960. García-Pedrosa kept a journal of his visit, which he later gave to Basulto.

The day of the trip to Guantánamo, the Brothers to the Rescue hangar was buzzing with attorneys, news reporters, pilots, and former Miami Mayor Xavier Suárez, who would join them on the trip. The planes were filled to capacity with cases and cases of legal documents; some would have to be left behind. Two television cameramen zoomed in on Basulto as he instructed the attorneys to get rid of the extra weight.

Beverly Brooks, wearing khaki slacks and a dark blue polo shirt with a Brothers to the Rescue patch, would pilot García-Pedrosa. She and Ivan Domanievicz, the original Kamikaze Crew, had continued to fly with Brothers to the Rescue. The flight plan included a stop in the Exumas for refueling, then a straight path toward the eastern tip of Cuba, the Punta de Maisí. They would approach the base around the south side of the island, making a hard right into Guantánamo Bay. This route was not the shortest or most direct, but Cuban authorities would not allow them to cut across the island.

Former Mayor Suárez and attorneys Ramón Rasco and Orlando Cabrera joined the prayer group at Basulto's summons, and he dedicated the mission to God. Basulto and copilot Carlos Gartner flew aboard *Seagull One*, the N2506, with Suárez and Rasco. Ray Martin, another Brothers volunteer pilot, was Beverly's copilot, and attorneys Cabrera and García-Pedrosa were crammed into the white Cessna 337, the *Habana D.C.* (Havana After Castro).

"Welcome to the Republic of Cuba."

García-Pedrosa was overcome with emotion when he heard the words of the female air traffic controller. His journal entry described what he saw out of the small windows of the Cessna, the country he had left thirty-four years before: the green grass sloping down to meet the white sand and crystal blue waters, and in the distance, the mountain ranges. The tropical paradise he witnessed would be a sharp contrast to Guantánamo, which was nothing like the rest of Cuba, or even the rest of the Caribbean.

The U.S. naval base sits on dry and dusty, arid land, dotted by row after row of tents. GiTMO, as Guantánamo is nicknamed, is divided into two parts, with the airfield on the western side and the base on the eastern, the bay in the middle. A ferry transports employees, vehicles, and supplies every hour on the hour.

Lieutenant Colonel Harris welcomed the group and introduced them to Corporal Friend, who would be their escort for the duration of the trip.

García-Pedrosa was amazed that the corporal maintained a spotless uni-form inside the dustbowl that was Guantánamo.

The pilots were housed in bachelor officers' quarters on the leeward side of the base. The attorneys and politicians were housed in a dirty apartment consisting of six army cots and a wall-unit air conditioner. Dead cock-roaches littered the floor. The bathroom was so filthy that García-Pedrosa was embarrassed for the women who would have to share it with them. Mayor Suárez found some cleaner and paper towels to spot-clean the bath-room, and García-Pedrosa remembers Suárez walking out of the bathroom and announcing: "the bathroom is ready for inspection, sir."

The attorneys and the mayor were finally given something to eat that evening after Guarione Díaz, a friend of Suárez's and ombudsman at Gitmo, intervened.

There were twenty-three camps holding almost 24,000 Cuban detainees. Another 8,000 Cuban refugees, now called migrants, were taken to camps in Panama. At GiTMO, 3,000 were children, 92 unaccompanied. There were 250 pregnant women at the time, and many sick and elderly persons. García-Pedrosa had feared that there would be a high concentration of single males, the least favorable group of people to parole into the United States. But there were only 3,000, signifying that this migration was a migration of families. The majority of people interred had been born after Castro's government took power on January 1, 1959. Many were dissidents and political activists who had been given a choice by the Cuban government: either take their chances and leave on a raft or be incarcerated. One of those dissidents, Da-vid Buzzi, a lawyer and novelist, told García-Pedroso he had been a political prisoner three times over: under Batista, under Castro, and now under the U.S. military in Guantánamo. The greatest complaint of the detainees was that they had no idea why they were there.

García-Pedrosa noticed how thin the detainees were, even though they were given three meals a day. One of those was an MRE (Meal Ready-to-Eat) the military's freeze-dried dinner. García-Pedrosa brought one home for his children, but they would never eat it. The men, women, and chil-dren had nothing to do all day or night. The U.S. attorney general had of-fered them two choices: return to Communist Cuba or stay at Guantánamo indefinitely.

There was no running water in the camps and the refugees found themselves living in dust-filled tents on dirt floors, with sporadic bursts of electricity. All detainees were required to wear what looked like a black wristwatch with no face—a high-tech identification band.

The government required that detainees sign up to see García-Pedrosa and the attorneys. Before the proper government form was agreed upon and distributed, the detainees made up their own forms, and virtually all of them requested an audience with the attorneys. The military officials at Guantánamo picked up their petitions and kept them, to study the drafts and think things over.

Whereas the media were allowed free access to the camps and given permission to film and walk among the refugees, the attorneys were denied direct access to their clients. They were even denied the names of the designated leaders of each camp.

"Stupid," was all García-Pedrosa could respond to such bureaucracy. Another of the bureaucratic moves García-Pedrosa thought was stupid was the banning of cigarette smoking. García-Pedrosa had quit smoking years ago, so he could understand the unrest of those who wanted their smokes. The military in Guantánamo perhaps did not understand that in third-world or European countries, most adults smoked, particularly during stressful situations. After considerable pressure, the rule was relaxed to allow one cigarette per day. But if the portable toilets were not cleaned to the military's expectations, the cigarettes were taken away, indefinitely.

García-Pedrosa was not proud of the way his government was treating human beings in Guantánamo. But for the grace of God, he could have been one of the refugees holding a slop bucket in the camps.

García-Pedrosa and his team patiently explained to the few refugees they were finally allowed to see what the lawsuit was about: their freedom. They would not necessarily be welcomed to the United States, however; they might have to enter a third country. For the first time in most of their lives, it would at least, and at last, be an opportunity to be free.

Guarione Díaz, the civil liaison between the United States and Cuba, witnessed daily the misery of the detainees. He was once asked, "Should we have any hope?" He answered, "I don't know about hope, but you should have faith."

While the attorneys set up their clinic, Basulto, Beverly Brooks, Carlos Gartner, and Carlos Tabernilla had to stay on the western side of the base. They were not allowed to cross over to where the detainees were housed. They were not allowed to speak to them. One day, Basulto went to the edge of the chain-link fence that separated the U.S. naval base from the rest of the country, his country of birth, his Cuba. He crouched on his knees, stuck his arm through the barbed wire, and extended it as far as possible to grab a handful of soil. He tenderly cupped the soil from the other side of the fence and then placed it carefully in his pocket. It was Cuban soil.

Basulto and the group of attorneys said good-bye to Guantánamo on November 10, 1994. As they were rounding the eastern tip of the island, around Punta de Maisí, he banked his plane to the left and flew over Cuban land. As a bonus, he decided to drop some Brothers to the Rescue bumper stickers.

"It was just there," he said, when people questioned why he had done it. That, and he may still have been a little annoyed that he had not been allowed to speak to the detainees. The U.S. Special Interests Section in Havana would later accuse Basulto of "dropping enemy propaganda from the counterrevolutionary organization Brothers to the Rescue."

The punishment would come one month later, just in time for the holidays.

Most of the children in Guantánamo had probably never celebrated Christmas. Fidel Castro had cancelled the feast day in 1969, one reason being that it interfered with the sugar-beet harvest. It would be reinstated in 1997, just in time for Pope John Paul II's visit to the island in January 1998.

But on January 6, 1995, the children of Guantánamo would celebrate Three Kings Day, the Feast of the Epiphany. In most Spanish and Latin American countries, gift giving is celebrated on the Feast of the Epiphany, the day when the three wise men visited baby Jesus.

Maggie Schuss and others were touched by the plight of hundreds of children in Guantánamo who had never celebrated Christmas, and she wanted to send them gifts. Steve Walton and Basulto were at the hangar the day the new project was suggested. "Of course we can do it!" Basulto said, ready to tackle a new mission. Then he turned to Steve: "How can we do it, Steve?"

Within days, two thousand gifts were donated from the community and piled up high in the hangar. When a sergeant major at Guantánamo told Steve that the gifts had to be wrapped, Maggie Schuss put out a plea on the radio stations. "Everyone in Miami showed up at the hangar with wrapping paper and scissors," Maggie remembers. The two thousand gifts were wrapped.

Steve Walton had to find a plane big enough to take the toys to the good little boys and girls of Guantánamo: a *Little Engine That Could* fly. A friend connected Steve to Valiant Air Command in Titusville, Florida, a nonprofit organization dedicated to finding and restoring historic aircraft. They had a C47 named the *Tico Belle*, which had flown in the Normandy Invasion during World War II. If Steve Walton would provide fuel, oil, and a maintenance allowance, as well as room and board overnight in Miami for the pilots, the C47 would transport the toys.

On January 5, 1995, the *Tico Belle* pilots took off on their mission. No one from Brothers to the Rescue was allowed to go with the plane to deliver the toys. It was an unconfirmed but obvious chastisement for Basulto's flyover of the Punta de Maisí on the previous flight to Guantánamo.

Once again, Cuba did not allow an overflight. What most people think of as a ninety-mile flight from the United States to Cuba turned into more than six hundred miles and four hours of flight time each way.

Moved by the World War II transport plane landing at their base, the GiTMO men welled-up with pride knowing the *Tico Belle* had flown in Normandy. "You guys have guts," said the naval aviator that did the walk-around of the aircraft. The marines treated the pilots like heroes.

None of the pilots of the *Tico Belle* were allowed to cross the bay when the toys were ferried across to the children. But every good little boy and girl in Guantánamo received at least two gifts from the Magi that Epiphany Day in 1995.

The flight made the cover of *Paralelo 24*, the new Brothers to the Rescue magazine designed, written, and edited by Arnaldo Iglesias.

The conditions in Guantánamo deteriorated to such an extent that one thousand detainees asked to go back to Cuba. But doing so was not as easy as simply walking through the gates, or even jumping the fence as Basulto had done in 1961 or swimming the bay as Juan Pablo Roque had done thirty years later. Charter companies were hired to fly people out—companies like Miami Air, where Mike Murciano now worked.

The irony could not be missed. On one day, Mike Murciano could conceivably fly his charter to Homestead to pick up Cuban rafters who had been intercepted by the Coast Guard and drop them off in Guantánamo. That same charter could then pick up a group of detainees at the camp who wanted to return to Cuba, and fly them back to Havana. There, Mike saw them whisked away on yellow buses with curtains blocking the windows. Mike never found out where they went from there.

It was confusing and emotional for the young pilot, since he was still flying missions for Brothers to the Rescue. It was not far-fetched to imagine that the same rafter he may have spotted on a previous weekend, and perhaps even dropped a radio or a water bottle to, had been intercepted by the Coast Guard and held in Homestead. That same man, woman, or child could then have been placed on Mike's flight back to Guantánamo, to be detained in his own country. Mike's only consolation was that at least Guantánamo was American soil.

Picking up the detainees in Guantánamo bothered him the most. "How can you want to return to Cuba?" he would sometimes ask his passengers. After risking death on the Florida Straits to escape the tyranny of Cuba, some still preferred to go back to Castro's Communism rather than endure the deplorable conditions in Guantánamo. And Mike was the one taking them back.

19

Protest in Miami

AUSCHWITZ, TREBLINKA, GUANTÁNAMO
BTTR placard protesting detention camp at Guantánamo

On September 10, 1994, President William Jefferson Clinton made an agreement with Cuba to increase legal migration. This would aid the thirty-three thousand detained in Guantánamo to gain entry into either the United States or other countries. The following day, Fidel Castro issued directives to his security forces to prevent further illegal departures.

Basulto confronted the media daily on the rafter crisis. He wanted the world to hear the truth of how Castro once again had manipulated U.S. policy on Cuban refugees. Basulto was steadfast in bringing the issue to the forefront. He and Brothers to the Rescue were on television, in the newspapers, on the radio waves. They were also stationed alongside the 836 expressway.

There was no avoiding the daily gridlock of the 836 expressway that took thousands of commuters from downtown Miami to the suburbs of southwest Dade County. One of the most congested sections ran between Miami International Airport on the north side and the Blue Lagoon office park on the south, named after the artificial lake surrounded by industrial park buildings.

Humberto Sánchez, the raft collector, aka Robin, sat in the middle of Blue Lagoon in one of the rafts from his vast assortment. There were usually jet skis or small motorboats playing in Blue Lagoon, certainly not a lone man sitting on a raft. The homebound, weary commuters of Miami would probably not even have noticed Humberto, if it were not for the sign he was holding:

AUSCHWITZ, TREBLINKA, GUANTÁNAMO

Humberto shielded his eyes, looking rather bored, while some commuters honked in support. Others gave him the finger. Most just rubbernecked for a few seconds then looked away and continued their dreary ride home.

The intention of Brothers to the Rescue was to point out that Guantánamo was a detention camp, like the two German camps. Of course, the Jews' stays in the detention camps had ended in their extermination. Nothing of the sort would happen to the detainees at Guantánamo.

The Jewish community was outraged. How could Brothers to the Rescue compare Guantánamo with its thirty-three thousand inhabitants to the extermination sites of so many millions?

Others in the community sensed that Brothers to the Rescue had become another Cuban-exile political organization. When lives were being saved on individual missions, the humanitarianism showed clearly. But when a few hundred Cubans a year turned into more than thirty thousand one summer, that was too much humanitarianism for one exhausted community to support. The Mariel Boatlift of fourteen years ago seemed to have happened yesterday.

But the Cubans kept fleeing their Communist island and there were others ready to step in. Much like the *coyotes* taking Mexicans across the border for twenty thousand pesos—the equivalent of a year's wages—a new crop of Miami entrepreneurs would soon set up shop in the human trafficking business. A pickup point would be determined and the refugees would be smuggled from there into Miami on powerboats. As soon as their dry feet touched U.S. soil and monies were exchanged—usually from Miami relatives—they were abandoned. Within ten years, 85 percent of Cubans coming into the United States were doing so by crossing the Mexican border, paying the new Cuban traffickers ten thousand dollars a head, ransoms paid by Miami relatives. Allegedly, half of the money stayed on the island, to pay the Cuban police to look the other way.

Fishermen from Miami would also spot the random rafter from time to time. The Good Samaritans would hoist the rafters onboard their vessels and give them water, clean clothes, and a fishing rod. That way it would all seem normal if they were stopped by the U.S. Coast Guard. When the group returned to the dock with their catch, no one would keep track of how many went out and how many came back.

Others fleeing Cuba continued their roulette with the Florida Straits. History will never know how many died, some estimates are that only one out of five survived.

Many pilots decided to leave Brothers to the Rescue, claiming there was no reason to go out and look for balseros that could not be saved. Gone were the days when the desperate souls on their sinking vessels would shout, wave, and risk their lives to be seen by one of their planes. Now, knowing that if their coordinates were given to the Coast Guard they would be returned to Guantánamo, the rafters would wave the planes away. After dropping water bottles and occasionally compass readings guiding the rafters to shore, the pilots returned to Opa-locka.

Money was becoming an issue, too. Brothers' donations in 1993 and 1994 had topped $1.1 million. By 1995 the figure was closer to $300,000.

For Basulto, the biggest issue remaining was guiding people within Cuba on the path to change. Since 1991, when the Coalición Democrática Cubana (Cuban Democratic Coalition) held their first significant street protest demanding the release of political prisoners, Cuba's dissidents had been organizing. The arrest, beating, and imprisonment of renowned poet María Elena Cruz Varela that year received international condemnation for Cuba's human rights violations. Cruz Varela was finally released in 1994 and moved to Spain.

In Miami, Basulto spread his message of active nonviolence and the internal dissident movement with his entire spirit. To help those struggling inside Cuba, Basulto pleaded for more fund-raising drives, telethons, and collections. They were met with derision. *Miami Herald* writer Carol Rosenberg called the new mission "less sexy" than rescuing rafters. Miami Commissioner Tomás Regalado told him that donors weren't interested in educating Cubans about peaceful paths to ending Communist rule. He told Basulto he could not do a radio marathon for that.

"The people say, 'Castro! You have to kill the son of a bitch!'"

20

Ashes

*I always felt that the great high privilege, relief and comfort of
friendship was that one had to explain nothing.*

Katherine Mansfield

There were dead people in the Brothers to the Rescue hangar. Shelved away
amongst the walkie-talkies, the flares, and the water-bottle turkeys, at any
particular time there could be several small heavy boxes, about twelve inches
square, containing the remains of Cuban exiles.

Many exiles dreamed of being buried in Cuba one day. In fact, many
funeral homes had prepaid plans in place, so that the moment it was fea-
sible, perhaps when the Castros were ousted, remains could be exhumed,
transported, and reburied in Cuba. Even though the once family-owned
mausoleums were currently in shambles in the previously well manicured
cemeteries of Cuba, it was still important to be buried *there.* Rather than pay
for a burial of ashes, only to have to disburse more money to have them exhumed later, some people chose to give their ashes to Brothers to the Rescue
for safekeeping. Perhaps they hoped the organization would involve itself in
burial procedures after the fall of Fidel.

Once the moratorium on cremation for Catholics was lifted in 1963, the
Church still required proper Christian burial. If ashes were not to be buried
in the ground, but rather at sea, the Church preferred they be dropped in a
container, not scattered. Specific prayers were to be read.

So housed among the rafts, radio equipment, and airplanes, there were
dead people at the hangar. Those not adhering to strict Catholic code sometimes asked the pilots please to scatter their ashes on their next mission, accepting the Florida Straits as close enough to Cuba to count as being buried
over Cuban soil.

Basulto's friend Félix Rodríguez needed some ashes laid to rest, ashes of a mutual friend from their CIA days. For this person's remains, close enough was not good enough.

Félix Rodríguez had been in the infiltration teams with Basulto for the Bay of Pigs. On two separate occasions after the failed invasion, the CIA assisted Félix with weapons and plans to assassinate Fidel Castro.

Félix left the CIA for a while and joined the army in 1963 along with Basulto. But the Agency wanted him back, and he worked for them for more than two decades. During the Vietnam War, Félix flew more than three hundred helicopter missions and was shot down five times.

In 1967, the CIA needed someone to head a team in Bolivia to hunt down Ernesto Ché Guevara, the leftist guerrilla leader and accomplice of Fidel Castro's revolution. The CIA had interviewed dozens for this job, drilling the candidates on their loyalty and readiness to aid the U.S. government. When asked how much time they would need to prepare, some candidates needed a day, others asked for a week or ten days, and the rest needed as much time as possible to get ready. Félix's reply got him the job.

"If there's time, I'll go home and say good-bye to my wife, get some clothes, and then leave. If there's no time, I'll call her from here and say I had to leave. If there's even less time, let's go, now. I'll give you the number and *you* call her," Félix said.

It was Félix Rodríguez who received the order from the Bolivian high command that Guevara was to be killed. He was the last person to see Ché Guevara alive except for the Bolivian soldier who shot him dead.

During the 1980s he was in nearly every Central American country fighting Communism. He was involved with the Nicaraguan Contras, his name linked to Oliver North's in the Arms-for-Hostages debacle of that decade. He was later accused of accepting ten million dollars in drug money. In 1986, his closed congressional hearing was presided over by future presidential hopeful Senator John Kerry, a man Félix highly disregarded. Félix was ultimately acquitted of all charges.

In 1989, Félix Rodríguez wrote a CIA tell-all called *Shadow Warrior*. Several years later, Mike Wallace did a special *60 Minutes* segment on the life of Félix Rodríguez, highlighting his involvement with the Contras in Nicaragua and his close ties to the first President Bush.

Félix maintained many friendships, and enemies, in most of the governments of developed and many of the underdeveloped countries of the world. Right now he needed a favor from his friend Basulto. Félix needed his help in keeping a promise he had made to another friend, a promise about spreading ashes over Cuban soil. Basulto would help him keep that promise.

On the morning of March 7, 1995, Basulto prepared two flight plans for a search-and-rescue mission. Félix climbed in the back of *Seagull One,* the N2506, with a video camera. Flying copilot was Jorge Luis Borges, holding his father's ashes in a small cardboard box. His father, Segundo Borges, had worked with the resistance inside Cuba, showing counterrevolutionary soldiers how to receive air drops and perform maritime pickups. After the failed invasion, Borges hid in Santa Clara, southeast of Havana, until a maid from one of the safe houses identified him and he was arrested. He escaped from prison by boring a hole through the cement wall with an iron rod from the cell's bedpost. Borges had recently died of cancer. Before his death he had asked his friend Félix to spread his ashes over Cuban soil.

Two planes headed south toward Cárdenas, where Varadero Beach was located on the northern coast of the province of Las Villas. The plane above the N2506 would be a decoy on the radar screen. When Basulto crossed the 24th parallel he shut off his transponder. He did not radio Havana Center.

As they neared the coast of Cuba, the N2506 began her descent. The other plane stayed at altitude so that if Cuban radar picked up a signal, it would be the higher plane, not Basulto's. If Basulto's plane was picked up on any screen, it would appear to be a ship or a boat on the horizon, for he was flying only three feet above the water. One cough, one twitch, one sneeze, and the plane would pitch into the water. The occupants' view was the same as if they were on a pleasure boat.

No one said a word, irrationally fearing their voices— rather than the noise of the motors—would give them away. Jorge Luis tenderly held his father's remains while Basulto and Félix kept their eyes riveted on the water. They were barely breathing, communicating telepathically, waiting for the right moment to let Segundo Borges rest in peace.

Approaching the coast, they saw a Cuban tanker leaving port, but it paid no attention to the blue object almost hydroplaning above the water. As soon as they were over some cays that they recognized as Cuban soil, Jorge Luis gently placed the box carrying his father's ashes at the rim of the copilot's window and tipped it over, allowing his father's remains to fly back home. The three men remained silent. It was not yet time for a sigh of relief.

Suddenly, Basulto snapped on the radio and called the Havana Tower, the loud click breaking the silence. They were still over Cuban soil at 11:05 a.m. when he announced his short eulogy: "At this moment, may he rest in peace: a Cuban patriot, Segundo Borges." Then he turned it off again.

It did not matter to Basulto if the tower personnel had heard him or not. They probably would not recognize his voice, whom he was speaking of, or what it was all about. It was better that way. This act was not under the umbrella of active nonviolence or civil disobedience. There would be no press awaiting them at the hangar or accusations by the FAA. This was a private matter of honor between friends.

Félix, Basulto, and Jorge Luis continued their flight back home in silence. They never revealed publicly that they had flown over Cuban territory to scatter Borges' ashes.

21

Love Is in the Air

*Alas! The love of women! It is known
To be a lovely and a fearful thing!*
Lord Byron, *Don Juan*

In the January 2, 1995, issue of *People* magazine, José Basulto was named one of the "Twenty-Five Most Intriguing People of the Year," alongside former President Jimmy Carter and Princess Di. Even though South Floridians may still have been intrigued by José Basulto, the love affair between Miami and Brothers to the Rescue was losing steam after the 1994 exodus. But at the hangar, there was still plenty of love to go around.

The greatest love story of Brothers to the Rescue belonged to Ivan Domanievicz and Beverly Brooks, who had been an item since their first flight almost two years before. They met at Brothers and courted before, after, and some would rumor, during missions. It would be several years before they married, but right now Ivan and Beverly were preparing to buy a sailboat and complete their first Atlantic crossing.

Back on dry ground, there were love stories as well. Both Carlos Costa and Pablo Morales were seriously involved with their girlfriends, but neither had popped the question yet. Pablo had finally started his piloting courses and was busy working, volunteering, and studying.

Mayte Greco had divorced her Argentinean husband, and she would later marry Paul Regan. Regan also had five children so the Greco-Regans took on the adventure of being newlyweds with ten teenagers.

Koki Lares was getting ready to wed the Panamanian girlfriend who had remained faithful to him after his crippling accident. They had waited two and a half years after the accident to make sure they were ready to live the rest of their lives with the challenges of his spinal cord injury. Many years later, on the seventh anniversary of his accident, Christmas Eve 1999, their first son was born.

Guille Lares would soon be marrying his fiancée, Paula. But before that, he would be best man for Juan Pablo Roque, the Cuban defector who was a volunteer pilot for Brothers to the Rescue. Even though the other pilots did not really mesh with Roque, they would be there for his wedding, scheduled for April 1, 1995. April Fool's jokes were plentiful.

Roque had met his fiancée, Ana Margarita Martínez, in Bible study at University Baptist Church in Coral Gables almost three years before. Ana Margarita laughed off the jokes about her selected wedding date and said she was not superstitious at all. It was during her children's spring break, so the date was convenient.

Ana Margarita was a Cuban exile who had come to Miami on a freedom flight in 1966. Now at age thirty-five, after two failed marriages and with two children entering their teens, she felt she had finally met the man of her dreams. She knew that Juan Pablo Roque, "J. P." to her, loved her children, and they saw in him the father they both craved. In fact, Roque desperately wanted another child with Ana Margarita—and he wanted her pregnant before his upcoming fortieth birthday. Every time he brought the subject up, she evaded him. He still had a son in Cuba, and now he would also be responsible for Sasha and Omar, Ana Margarita's children.

Many of the pilots and volunteers from Brothers attended the wedding at University Baptist Church and the reception at the home of some friends. Ana Margarita and Roque were a beautiful couple. She wore a white gown with a full skirt, tulle around the décolletage, her dark hair in a becoming up-do with ringlets cascading along her cheeks, a crown of diamonds clasping her veil. Roque made the most of his movie-star looks dressed in a black tuxedo and white tie. It was a fairy-tale wedding.

As a gift to the groom, Guille Lares flew the newlyweds to a honeymoon retreat at Andros Island in the Bahamas, and picked them up four days later.

As Roque's fortieth birthday approached in October, Ana Margarita continued to skirt the issue of having a child together. Instead, she gave him a surprise party, at the home of the same friends who had hosted their wedding reception, Luis and Matilde Alexander.

Roque was summoned to what he thought was a business meeting at the Alexanders' home. When one hundred well-wishers shouted "Happy

Birthday!" Ana Margarita was moved by her husband's expression of absolute happiness, something he had not experienced in his forty years. J. P. seldom spoke to her about his childhood in Cuba, and he did not get along with his brothers or sister. His own brother had counseled Ana Margarita not to marry him.

But on his fortieth birthday his closest friends, including those from Brothers, joined him in dancing, drinking, eating, and of course, a birthday cake. Ana Margarita had the cake made in the shape of an airplane. After the crowd sang "Happy Birthday" and he blew out his candles, Roque picked up the knife and cut the cake, in half.

In addition to working at Tamiami Airport, being a personal trainer, and doing any other odd jobs that came his way, Roque was also writing a book. He titled it *Desertor* (Deserter), not because he had deserted the Cuban Air Force and come to the United States, but because that is what they used to call him in school for repeatedly skipping classes. *Desertor*'s publication in November 1995 was made possible by CANF, and a small group celebrated at Le Festival Restaurant in Coral Gables.

During the event, Roque spoke from a podium and thanked an endless list of people who had helped him. Ana Margarita was glad that her face was hidden behind a video camera, as she filmed him during this special moment, because he failed to mention her name. She had helped him tirelessly in the editing of the book. She was his wife. She had appeared in several photos in the book, but her name was never included in the captions. She felt humiliated in front of his closest friends.

"It's a highly political book, Anita," he told her later. "I don't want your name involved in any of that, okay?"

22

Nonviolence

*Cowardice asks the question, "Is it safe?" Expediency asks
the question, "Is it politic?" Vanity asks the question, "Is it
popular?" But, conscience asks the question, "Is it right?"
And there comes a time when one must take a position that
is neither safe, nor politic, nor popular but one must take it
because one's conscience tells one that it is right.*

Dr. Martin Luther King Jr.

On May 2, 1995, President Clinton officially ended the open-door policy for
Cubans. He repealed President Johnson's Cuban Adjustment Act of 1966,
put new restrictions on travel to Cuba, prohibited sending money to family
members on the island, and legalized the return of Cubans intercepted at
sea.

The 33,000 in Guantánamo would eventually all make it to the United
States or other host countries. But for those still taking to the Straits, a new
"Wet-Feet/Dry-Feet" policy would apply. Under that law any Cuban migrant arriving by sea who made it to dry land—had "dry feet"—before being
intercepted would be granted an Immigration and Naturalization Service
(INS) interview and the opportunity to stay. Any rafter intercepted at sea—
with "wet feet"—would be immediately repatriated to Cuba.

The group whose image suffered the most through this change in policy
was the Coast Guard. Previously seen as the heroic saviors of desperate
rafters, now the Coast Guard was seen as the enemy. Like lurking police
cruisers on interstate highways, the U.S. Coast Guard became the legal Le-
viathans of the sea. Previous footage showing Coasties risking their lives
to lift children from sinking rafts onto rescue helicopters and cutters were
replaced with images of choppers creating tidal pools that prevented the
rafters from swimming to shore. The arms of the agents that before had welcomed the sunburned and dehydrated were now filmed pummeling those
struggling onto the sands of Miami's beaches, with tourists gawking and

snapping pictures. They were following orders, obeying the new law, doing their job.

Fidel Castro coerced the United States into admitting twenty thousand Cubans per year on a lottery system. Castro continued to blame the United States for encouraging the rafters to flee, for defending the hijackings of Cuban boats that led to the riots, and eventually for the mass migration itself. As soon as he was reassured that twenty thousand would be able to leave his country every year, Castro made immigration from Cuba illegal once again.

Even though the number of rafters drastically diminished, Brothers continued to fly, albeit much fewer missions.

Brothers sponsored a civil disobedience seminar at Florida International University in Miami, and invited the community to attend. Gene Sharp from the Albert Einstein Institution and representatives from the Dr. Martin Luther King Jr. Center were among the panelists.

Two days after President Clinton's announcement of the Wet-Feet/Dry-Feet policy, Brothers to the Rescue and other groups, such as the Comisión Nacional Cubana (National Cuban Commission) led by Ramón Saúl Sánchez, implemented their first group act of civil disobedience by closing down the Port of Miami.

Yearly, more than four million cruise ships cross under the bridge that leads to the Port of Miami, as do nine million tons of cargo. Both businesses support more than 90,000 jobs and have an economic impact on Miami-Dade of more than $12 billion. The "Cargo Gateway of the Americas" was about to be brought to its knees by a 120-pound pregnant attorney.

On May 4, 1995, Sofía Powell-Cosío noticed a lull in the traffic going over the causeway to the Port of Miami, so she walked over to the middle lane and sat down. She was almost seven months pregnant and carrying her older daughter, ten-month-old Daniela, in her arms. A horrified police officer came running up to her.

"Give me your daughter!" he demanded. "This is child endangerment."

"Fine," she said, and she held out a bewildered but still content Daniela. "Although this is a peaceful protest." Then Sofía informed the police officer that she was an attorney. "You can take her, but be aware that I will sue the city, because you have no reason to take my daughter away from me in a peaceful protest. But here, please, take her."

The police officer gave Daniela back to Sofía, who remained sitting on the asphalt. "Man! You're crazy!"

Arnaldo Iglesias gave Basulto's attorney a new nickname that day: Cagafuego, which literally means one who shits fire. Arnaldo and Basulto had stood their ground with Sofía, too, and were carted off to jail for a few hours. But they were most proud of Cagafuego.

A few days later, the *Miami Herald* wrote about the young, svelte, twenty-nine-year-old, seven-months-pregnant attorney carrying her baby daughter. Sofía looked down at her growing belly, flattered that they had called her "svelte."

They practiced another round of nonviolent protest a few weeks later. On May 16, they asked all businesses to halt operations at two o'clock in the afternoon and walk out to protest the Clinton policy change. For the most part Hispanic businesses did just that. In ninety-five-degree heat, more than seven thousand people walked down the streets in Little Havana.

In Havana, Cuba, there had been similar protests over the policy change, as well as the so-called trial of Francisco Chaviano. The former mathematics professor had been keeping his own figures on the numbers of people leaving Cuba "illegally" and dying on the Straits of Florida. He himself had tried to leave in 1989, but was caught and imprisoned. In prison, he founded the Cuban Rafters Council, an organization of people imprisoned for having tried to exercise their right to leave the country by their own means. The United Nations Universal Declaration of Human Rights, to which Cuba was a signatory, stated that all people had the right to leave and return to their own country.

Chaviano persisted in condemning Cuba's human rights violations. Government officials broke into his home, beat him, and arrested him. Amnesty International denounced the incident and requested that he be freed. During his trial in Cuba, Basulto coordinated an effort with Orlando Gutiérrez-Boronat of the Cuban Democratic Directory to provide an attorney for Chaviano. Brothers to the Rescue pilots flew near the coast of Havana, back and forth, up and down, with journalists and attorneys onboard ready to defend Chaviano. Naturally, they were never granted permission to land. Chaviano was finally released, *thirteen years later.*

Still fresh in the minds of the Cuban exile groups was the sinking of the *13th of March* tugboat and the forty-one people that had been murdered by Cuban gunboats. Those souls needed to be honored, so a commemorative flotilla was planned for July 13, 1995, to mark the one-year anniversary of the tugboat sinking.

This time the flotilla would be spearheaded by Ramón Saúl Sánchez, head of the National Cuban Commission. Sánchez, known in the community as Ramoncito or Saúl, was a leader in the civil disobedience movement among exiles and sometimes referred to as the Gandhi of the Cuban diaspora. He and Basulto had become good friends.

The idea of toppling a Communist military dictator through nonviolence was a hard sell to replace the military aspirations of most Cuban exile groups. But Ramón had thought it out very carefully during the four and one-half years he spent in federal prison, years of reorganizing his beliefs and putting into practice what he was well known for: hunger strikes. His most recent fast occurred in response to Clinton's Wet-Feet/Dry-Feet policy, and the ACLU successfully secured a permit for him to conduct his hunger strike on federal property.

All Ramón really wanted was to return to Cuba and walk the streets of Havana. This right was guaranteed under the Universal Declaration of Human Rights, and Ramón wanted to go back.

Ramón was a country boy from Matanzas, Cuba. When he was ten years old, in 1967, his father sent him and his younger brother to the United States aboard one of the Freedom Flights. His mother stayed behind to take care of his grandmother. Neither was ever granted an exit visa, and Ramón never saw them again.

When he was fifteen, Ramón joined Alpha 66, a group of sixty-six mainly businessmen and professionals that had organized in Puerto Rico with the intention of making commando-type attacks on Cuba to maintain the fighting spirit of the Cuban people after the failure of the Bay of Pigs invasion. It was the beginning of Ramón's involvement in the struggle for Cuba's democracy.

In 1982, a federal grand jury in New York put him in prison for refusing to testify against a group that was accused of an assassination attempt against Fidel Castro. After a year in prison, he began his first hunger strike. On the twenty-fifth day, he lost consciousness. The government obtained an order to force-feed him, and they had to strap him down to do so. While he was belted down, Ramón remembers the captain of the guards kicking him in the groin. Other beatings would follow.

After Cubans started protesting around the prison in New York, he was sent to Springfield, Missouri, where Ramón experienced a cold he never dreamed possible. They placed him in a bare cell, stripped him down to his underwear, and left. The freezing air around him, seeping through the cracked windows of his cell in that Springfield winter, resulted in frostbite on one ear.

He remained on his hunger strike until they forced in another feeding tube and this time, left it in. It was in prison that he made a commitment to promote to the Cuban exile community and to the Cubans on the island the philosophy of nonviolent protest for the freedom of Cuba.

When he returned to Miami he began attending various meetings of the many established exile groups. When he addressed Brigade 2506, he met Basulto. The two men began a friendship that brought them closer together than brothers.

Ramón was tall and thin, sported a signature mustache, and had jet-black hair. Basulto was of medium height and stocky, definitely unaccustomed to hunger strikes. Yet, so often were they seen together that on many occasions one was confused for the other.

Basulto and Ramón were on similar journeys toward nonviolence. Ramón proposed that Brothers to the Rescue join the flotilla of what would later be called the Democracy Movement, named after the boat Ramón had purchased: *Democracia*.

"I'll do whatever you want, Ramón," Basulto told him. "Just don't ask me to give up food."

It was while eating lunch one day that Basulto, Guille Lares, and others realized that the day of the flotilla would be a perfect venue for an act of peaceful civil disobedience, an opportunity to connect with their Cuban brothers on the island. The *Democracia* planned to go inside the twelve-mile limit of Cuban waters to lay red roses at the exact spot the Cuban gunboats had rammed the *13th of March* and murdered forty-one people. Brothers wanted to drop another kind of message from their Cessnas: bumper stickers that read *Compañeros No! Hermanos!* (Comrades No! Brothers!)

After lunch, Basulto purchased three bulletproof vests.

The FAA wanted a sit-down with Basulto, and they sent Mike Thomas from the Miami Flight Standards District Office to deal with him. The topic was the pilots' accompaniment of the upcoming flotilla and their plans to cross into Cuban waters.

Thomas had met many times with Basulto. Luis Carmona Sr. also attended. Carmona, who had investigated Koki's Christmas Eve crash, was a supervisor in Thomas' office and a friend of Basulto's. Thomas wanted to make sure that Basulto understood that rules were in place for their safety. Basulto wanted Thomas to understand that rules were sometimes made to be broken.

After the meeting, Basulto and Billy Schuss spoke to several pilots at Brothers and told them there was a chance they would be flying into Cuban waters and that doing so was against the law—and dangerous.

"Mario, I'm only going to mention this once, and then it will never be discussed again," Billy Schuss explained to Mario de la Peña over the phone. "I will not judge you no matter what your answer is—so pay close attention," he went on. "This is serious." Billy explained there was a possibility that they would fly over Cuban territorial waters on the day of the flotilla, and outlined the dangers involved. He wanted to make sure no pilot on that day felt pressured or compelled to accompany the flotilla, which was becoming more confrontational every day.

"And if the Cubans ask us to land, we will refuse. They will not force us," he said to Mario. "We could die, and it has to be your choice." Billy remembers the twenty-two-year-old pilot did not wait for him to finish.

"I'll take my chances," Mario told him.

23

Thirteen Minutes over Havana

*There are many causes that I am prepared to die for, but no
causes that I am prepared to kill for.*

Mahatma Gandhi

The afternoon before the planned flotilla, after stopping at the Virgin of
Charity Church on Biscayne Bay for a special blessing given by Father Santana, the *Democracia* made its way from Miami to Key West. Father Santana
was the pastor of the little church on the bay, the spiritual home of so many
refugees.

Mario Castellanos, another Brothers volunteer, was onboard. Mario was
anxious to reach Key West, where Tito Fufú and others would be joining
him. Tito had installed the same navigation system that was used on the
planes on the *Democracia* so that they could stay connected at all times. He
had also installed a VHF antenna to transmit back to the Brothers to the
Rescue hangar. On the day of the flotilla, Carlos Costa would work out of
his caged office.

Mario Castellanos was a little puzzled when he boarded the *Democracia*
and saw the stacked cases of water bottles, snacks, and other food supplies.
"What?" he thought, "Are they planning some kind of picnic?" For once, Mario, who weighed more than three hundred pounds, was not thinking about
food. He was thinking about whether or not they would all be arrested.

On the way down to Key West, the Coast Guard intercepted the *Democracia,* boarded the vessel, and searched for weapons. They found none.

The next morning, just before sailing, Mario Castellanos felt a little
uncomfortable over the number of people onboard, more than thirty of
them, including one woman. Captain Mirabal would sail the boat, and Carlos Harrison from Channel 6 would film the historic event. Miami–Dade
County Commissioner Pedro Reboredo was also onboard. Channel 6 had a

chopper in the air, and their anchorman, Hank Tester, was aboard Basulto's plane. The *Democracia* and about a dozen other boats left before daylight on Thursday, July 13, 1995, on a mission to throw red roses on the very spot, six miles from the Cuban coast, where forty-one of their brothers and sisters had been murdered exactly one year before. Thankfully, the seas were calm on that hot and sunny, typical Caribbean day.

As Guille, Hank Tester, and Basulto boarded *Seagull One* at Opa-locka Airport, Basulto passed out the bulletproof vests. "Just sit on them," he said. Guille and Hank were a little puzzled, but they did as they were told. "Listen, if they shoot at us, it will be from below," said Basulto. "Let's keep our asses covered."

All the Brothers' planes had media reps onboard. After all, they were deliberately going to fly over Cuban territorial waters that day, and the media wanted to capture that moment. Billy Schuss was flying *El Coquí*, the plane donated by the Puerto Rican branch of CANF, with Mario de la Peña as copilot and ex-political prisoner Cary Roque in the back.

There was no Intracoastal Waterway marker signaling the twelve-mile limit of Cuban territorial waters, or for that matter, the exact place where the *13th of March* sank. But what the thirteen approaching vessels saw on the horizon confirmed that they were on the edge of Cuban waters: Cuban gunboats in formation, with a secondary line of smaller boats. There was a Cuban helicopter and a twin-engine Antonov 23 hovering above them. Two MiGs zoomed overhead.

The *Democracia* moved on, with its twelve companion boats. As soon as it crossed the imaginary line marking the twelve-mile territorial limit, the gunboats sprinted toward the flotilla in what looked like a pincer formation, their steel bulk a slow-motion version of greyhounds being let loose from their starting gates.

From about fifty feet above, the Brothers to the Rescue planes watched them advance. So did the news helicopters and the other planes that were flying that day. Wanting a closer look, the Brothers planes flew lower and the Channel 6 helicopter hovered protectively over the *Democracia*. The *Gaviota* (which means seagull and is one of the two government-owned aircraft companies) helicopter from Cuba did likewise over the gunboats. As the Cuban boats advanced toward the *Democracia*, they shouted through their bullhorns that the boats were now in Cuba's jurisdictional waters, and that they—the Cubans—were not responsible for whatever happened. Ramón

Saúl Sánchez sat confidently on the bow pulpit, his legs dangling over the water. His crew yelled back at the gunboats. They took pictures.

The *Democracia* sailed on, its pilgrimage not complete until they reached the hallowed waters where forty-one Cuban brothers died one year before.

Mario Castellanos was holding a red rose, as were most of the men, waiting to toss them at the spot of the tugboat massacre. A passing cruise ship might have questioned the scene: a boatful of burly adult males holding satiny red roses yelling at military boats in formation.

Tito Fufú was communicating with the Brothers planes that were flying overhead, Carlos Harrison from Channel 6 was talking to his news crew, and photographer Rudy Marshall filmed the approaching Cuban boats. No one expected the collision that sent the thirty-plus crew tumbling into each other like bowling pins.

"They're hitting us! They're hitting us," cried Tito Fufú over the radio, confirming to Basulto and Billy what they were witnessing from above.

Mario Castellanos' three hundred pounds slammed inside the pass-through between the wheelhouse and the deck of the boat. Mario radioed Carlos Costa back at base. "They're ramming us! They're ramming us!"

Grunts and shouts of surprise and shock erupted at once. None of them had braced themselves for what they had seen coming right at them, perhaps willing the Cubans to stop with the sheer force of their disbelief. Commissioner Reboredo, his foot too close to the railing, would end up losing a toe.

"They're hitting us!" Tito repeated, picking himself up from the floor, his arm a bloodied mess. "Call the Pentagon!"

"Call the Pentagon? Tito must be really nervous," thought Mario, heaving himself up from the deck. He noticed Tito's bloodied arm and went over to help his friend. At the same time, someone yelled to him to go down below to see if they were taking in water. Mario Castellanos remembered that the *Democracia* had five bilge pumps, so he was confident they would be OK. But over the ramming of the gunboats, the thwacking of the helicopter blades, and the zooming in and out of the Brothers' planes, there was one noise Mario couldn't hear: the engines. Captain Mirabal, up on the bridge, had mentioned to him that the only problem with the *Democracia* was that the engine could not be started from up top. They were dead in the water, being repeatedly sandwiched by the Cuban gunboats. Mario ran to the controls to start up the engines.

As he descended to the engine room, Mario noticed that he was still holding on to the red rose. "A rose, a little red rose," he thought, imagining just how ridiculous he must look right now. "What the hell am I going to do with this damn rose?" He wished they *had* carried weapons onboard. He threw the rose overboard in disgust, went down below, and turned on the motors.

Aboard *Seagull One*, Basulto was witnessing and hearing the commotion below. *Call the Pentagon?* Basulto had heard scores of off-the-wall comments from his good friend Tito Fufú, but *call the Pentagon?* He flew lower and lower, below some of the masts of the boats that were quickly leaving the *Democracia* behind. There were television helicopters in the foray as well, and airplanes from other groups flying in solidarity.

"It's the damndest thing I've ever seen!" said Hank Tester, filming the scene from above. He channeled his energy into maintaining a steady camera, breathing only when absolutely necessary. It was like a combat video from World War II, with a sea battle in process, minus the firing. Cuban gunboats (albeit with their guns loosely wrapped in canvas) were ramming the *Democracia* on both sides, with a second line of military vessels close behind. Hank's network, WTVJ, also had a helicopter hovering over the *Democracia*, with their chief photographer, Mike Zimmer, onboard.

"Now what?" asked Billy over the radio. Basulto and Guille looked at each other and without uttering a word knew what they had to do. They pointed south.

"A La Habana," said Basulto. To Havana.

Their goal now was to divert the gunboats from the *Democracia* and direct the attention of the Cuban military toward their planes. Billy and Mario de la Peña followed Basulto toward Cuba.

Like a scene in a horror movie where the hero tries to distract the monster away from the victim about to be eaten, when the gunboats saw the Brothers' planes going south they turned away from the *Democracia*.

Aboard *Seagull One*, it did not really matter that they were sitting on bulletproof vests. If any one of those gunboats uncovered their weapons and fired, it would not be their asses they would have to worry about. Hank concentrated on the camera. He wanted to get over Havana as soon as possible; the Cubans would be less likely to shoot at them over the city. They would not endanger their own citizens. At least Hank didn't think so.

Photographer Rudy Marshall from WTVJ was struggling to steady himself as he wrapped up the filming onboard the *Democracia*. He needed to get his footage back to the station.

From thirty feet up, chief photographer Mike Zimmer opened the WTVJ helicopter door and lay on his stomach, his upper torso hanging over the edge. He lowered a basket down to the *Democracia* for Marshall to drop in his video, but it did not reach the photographer below. The helicopter flew a little lower. Tight rings of waves made by the helicopter's propellers bobbed the *Democracia* up and down, and the outriggers slapped against the belly of the chopper. Finally, Marshall was able to drop the video in, and Zimmer hauled it up and hustled back to Florida for a breaking news report. They did not realize that at that very moment their colleague Hank Tester was on his way to Havana.

Hank's lens filled with the city of Havana. It was only later, when they watched the taped footage over and over again, that they would recall the buildings they had flown not over, but between. Hank sat behind Guille, the copilot, so he never saw the people waving from Morro Castle, but they were there, to the left of the plane. The crew flew around El Malecón, Havana's famed seaside walkway, and then completed another, tighter circle over the city. All the time, Guille was tossing bumper stickers out the window, a constant stream of Comrades No! Brothers! to those below. He also threw down some religious medals donated by an elderly woman at the Virgin of Charity Church. Time seemed to stretch out before them as they soaked up the Cuban capital below, but their actual time over the city was thirteen minutes. Basulto yelled over his right shoulder to Hank.

"Quieres más? Quieres más?" Do you want more?

Without thinking, Hank answered in Spanish: "No! No más, por favor!" Simultaneously, Basulto and Guille turned around to laugh at Hank, who had put down the video. Hank quickly picked up his camera and captured the two pilots in that nervous moment of comic relief. Hank never imagined that photo would later be used in court, out of context and against his friends.

Behind them, Mario de la Peña was relieved of his copilot position in order to take photograph after photograph of Havana's rapidly approaching skyline, using Luis Martínez's (aka Batman's) camera. He had forgotten that he had only the one roll of film in the camera, and when he saw the famous Morro Castle, he looked at the counter to see how many shots he had left.

It read twenty-five, meaning the roll of twenty-four exposures was done. He chastised himself for not having saved a few shots for what is the very symbol of Havana, the Morro Castle, much like what the Statue of Liberty is to New York, or the White House to Washington. He snapped it anyway, and just in time, for they were already headed back, following Basulto.

It took ten minutes to get back into international airspace. Ten minutes of exposure to the Cuban gunboats below and the Cuban MiGs that had circled the flotilla earlier. Ten minutes of vulnerability in the sovereign waters of Cuba. Ten minutes passed before they saw the U.S. Coast Guard sailing protectively under them. For the pilots and copilots, they were ten minutes of the most focused flying of their lives. For Hank Tester, the longest ten minutes of his life.

Mario de la Peña and Batman went to the one-hour lab at Eckerd Drugs that very evening. The twenty-fifth picture on the roll was there: the Morro Castle perfectly framed and detailed.

To most Cuban Americans in Miami, Billy and Basulto were instant heroes. On a television show called *Miami Ahora* (Miami Now), host Manuel Reboso called Basulto's flyover one of the most heroic acts of any exile. Others accused Brothers to the Rescue of political activism.

Hank Tester knew he could never go back to Cuba as long as Fidel Castro was alive. "Now they know who I am," he would tell others. His live shots on the five o'clock news from Key West, and then further coverage at eleven o'clock the evening of the flyover, boosted his career. Others in the media questioned his decision-making process. Hank stayed out of all the grilling by the Feds. After all, he was a news reporter, he was not the pilot. Hank had not broken any U.S. laws, but he had almost shattered his nerves.

He was still a little shaky the next evening when he arrived at Centro Vasco Restaurant, at that time the benchmark of Miami Cuban cuisine, to celebrate the birthday of another WTVJ photographer, Carlos Rigau. Hank definitely needed a drink and he got one, then another, along with bantering and kidding around, accompanied by slaps on the back and talk about bravado and manhood.

Then he saw Luly.

María de Lourdes González Piñeiro, nicknamed Luly, worked with Rigau's wife, who had encouraged a reluctant Luly to come to the party. Like

Hank, Luly was recently divorced, and she had two children. Hank thought Luly was the cutest thing he had ever seen in his life.

For both it was love at first sight, and they were married less than two years later. But the date inscribed in his wedding ring would read July 14, 1995, the day they met, the day after Hank Tester had flown thirteen minutes over Havana.

On Saturday, two days after the flotilla, the ailing *Democracia* returned to Miami, greeted by supporters waving Cuban and American flags. According to Cuban-style estimates, a crowd of three thousand held a rally at José Martí Park. The Miami Police Department's estimate was nine hundred.

A few weeks later, the Cuban Democratic Directory invited Mario de la Peña to speak on their radio program. The main aims of the organization were many. They included identifying Cubans who were advocating change, supporting them and studying their growth, seeking international support, monitoring political prisoners, and supporting the nonviolence campaign. It was this last point that had sealed the friendship between Orlando Gutiérrez-Boronat and Basulto.

Orlando was head of the Directory and a good friend of Mario de la Peña's. Billy Schuss and Mario had been right behind Basulto in the overflight of Havana, and Orlando wanted more details of that historic flight to be heard on a radio program that would be broadcast in Cuba.

The Directory's structure allowed them to seek U.S. grants and petition U.S. foundations. Basulto wished that the Directory could operate without government involvement. "The struggle is ours," he would repeat. He would abide by his promise never to petition the U.S. government for monetary assistance for Brothers.

The night of the show, Orlando was sure they would have a heavy listenership in Cuba. "What would you tell a Cuban pilot who's listening now?" he asked Mario. "What would you tell him if he's ordered to shoot you down?" Orlando was expecting Mario to say, "Don't do it; we're brothers, and we're on the same side." But Mario was quiet for a moment.

"I would tell him to shoot," Mario said. "Shoot, because you're not a free man, you're enslaved. I know why I am here and I know what I'm fighting for.

"I'm a Christian," he added. "So I would forgive you."

On September 1, 1995, the FAA wrote Basulto a solemn letter suspending his commercial pilot's license for 120 days for violating FAR 91.703, operating a U.S.-registered aircraft within a foreign country in noncompliance with the regulations of that country, and FAR 91.13, operating an aircraft in a careless or reckless manner so as to endanger the life or property of another.

On September 2, Basulto flew on another mission.

24

I Am the Change

*Now I'm a soldier that bears no arms. When I was young, my
hero was John Wayne. Now I like Luke Skywalker. I believe
The Force is with us.*

José Basulto

Carlos Costa and Mario de la Peña stood on the bike path of the highest
of the three bridges on the Rickenbacker Causeway linking Miami to the
Village of Key Biscayne. It was a sunny December day, and the winds were
blowing between ten and fifteen knots. Sailboats glided across the bay, their
white puffed mainsheets and swollen jibs billowing over the aqua blues and
greens of Biscayne Bay.

Tourists on their way to the beaches at Crandon Park may have wondered why these men were littering off the bridge. Carlos and Mario were
throwing little papers into the wind, watching them fall, and taking notes.
Carlos Costa, "good-looking Carlos," had fashioned a plumb line to the edge
of the water by hanging his tennis shoe from a long strip of surveyor's tape.
The leaflets fluttered in the wind, some taking air and flying higher than the
seventy-eight-foot elevation of the bridge. With a stopwatch they noted the
drop rate as the two-by-six-inch papers gently landed.

When the Brothers to the Rescue "physicists" returned to the hangar
from their wind studies off the bridge, they drew up diagrams with the wind
direction, speed, and rate of fall. Carlos gave his general the information he
needed for his new project: floating leaflets over Havana. They concluded
that if their planes flew at twelve thousand feet and maintained their position twelve miles off the coast of Havana and out of Cuban airspace, the
leaflets would make it over the capital under perfect wind conditions.

"It's gonna work," said Basulto, happy with the experiment's results. Later,
WTVJ anchorman Hank Tester interviewed Dr. K. Y. Fung, a physics professor at the University of Miami, who confirmed Basulto's drawings and

estimates. It was not the first time a drop like this had been made. The Chinese Communists had received similar protests from the opposition in the 1950s. On the local news, Tester performed his own test from the roof of the Channel 6 station, three stories high. With winds of about eight to ten knots, the flyers landed half a mile away.

Brothers to the Rescue printed half a million flyers to float over Havana. One side of the leaflets had messages printed in bold blue and red that said: I AM THE CHANGE, COMRADES NO! BROTHERS!, and THE STREETS BELONG TO THE PEOPLE. On the other side, Orlando Gutiérrez-Boronat of the Directory suggested that each leaflet list one of the thirty Articles of the UN Declaration of Human Rights, of which Cuba was a signer.

The only thing Brothers needed for a successful mission was perfect wind conditions, and John Morales, the weatherman at Channel 23, would be on call to forecast those conditions.

John Morales' popularity had skyrocketed after his coverage of Hurricane Andrew in August 1992. He had been flying with Brothers since they had moved to the Opa-locka Airport. He could finally afford to get his multiengine license and had received his rating in 1993. He and Guille Lares became very close friends, and his knowledge of the weather came in handy for planning missions. Morales' skills at forecasting were elevated to the level of prognostications by the Brothers to the Rescue pilots. Because he could "predict" the weather, they christened the straitlaced and serious John Morales with the nickname "Walter Mercado," after a flamboyant television astrologer whose trademarks were wildly colored capes, designer suits, heavy makeup, and a sharp wit. Mercado's shows consisted of dramatic revelations and predictions of the zodiac.

The only similarity between John Morales and Walter Mercado was a link to Puerto Rico, where both their mothers were born. But since they were both Puerto Rican and in the predicting business, and protocol determined everyone had to have a nickname, John Morales was referred to as Walter Mercado.

Morales had stopped flying with Brothers after the 1994 exodus and the subsequent change in the law. Though he was not Cuban, he could appreciate Basulto's passion for the nonviolent struggle and support for the internal dissidents, but to Morales it was all about rescuing rafters, and that was no longer allowed by U.S. immigration policy. Basulto was unable to convince him that even more lives could be saved through the internal dissident groups. His friendship with Basulto and the organization continued, and by forecasting weather conditions he was helping them more than he would ever know.

But Morales could not help Brothers to the Rescue without the cooperation of Mother Nature—and the FAA. The first attempt to float the flyers had to be scrapped because of an FAA inspection that grounded the mission. Basulto felt the unannounced inspection was very strange and too coincidental. The public did not know of Brothers' plans for the flyers, and only a select few of the pilots had been informed. For the first time, Basulto suspected that inside the Brothers organization there lurked an informant.

Basulto welcomed the cool, windy days of the 1996 New Year. Brothers was planning what could be its most dangerous mission of all: dropping half a million leaflets to float over Havana. This was different from the stickers released during the July 1995 flotilla, when Basulto, Guille Lares, and Hank Tester had flown thirteen minutes over Havana. That flyover had not been planned. The stickers he carried that day were meant for the Cuban gunboats; their message: ¡Compañeros No! ¡Hermanos! (Comrades, No! Brothers!) What Brothers to the Rescue was preparing to do was more than rescue a single rafter on the high seas, and more daring than a thirteen-minute act of civil disobedience. Brothers to the Rescue wanted the entire population of Cuba to take ownership of their basic civil rights. It would be their greatest show of active nonviolence and they named their mission Operation Dr. Martin Luther King Jr.

"This is the week," John Morales told Basulto during the first week of January 1996. He called Basulto from the weather station. "The winds are perfect."

January 9, 1996, was a solemn day at the hangar. The usual group would not be there to pray with them in a circle. The customary ribbing and laughing would not precede this flight. Koki would not be making Cuban coffee with the dirty filter. Four pilots—Basulto, Billy Schuss, Arnaldo Iglesias, and Juan Pablo Roque, the Cuban defector—arrived at the hangar for what everyone except Roque knew was going to be a very special mission. Basulto had not told Roque that today would be the day of the leaflet drop. When Roque arrived, they informed him of the seriousness of that day's mission.

As customary, they prepared a flight plan and sent it off.

Then Billy, Basulto, Arnaldo, and Roque suited up and Basulto mounted a video camera on a pedestal. Basulto explained to the pilots that they were about to fly near the territorial limit of Cuba, twelve miles from shore, and that while remaining in international airspace, they would drop leaflets that they hoped would reach Havana.

"Today's mission is very different from the others," Basulto said into the camera, in an even and serious tone. "We want to send the people of Cuba a message. We are all Cubans here, Cubans for Cubans. We want our presence to be respected. We will not be flying over Cuban territory."

He continued with a message to his family and others left behind. "If we are forced to land and perhaps appear on a televised broadcast, and if you hear us saying anything in contrast to our opinions in the past, you know we will be saying those things under pressure."

Arnaldo, wearing a heavy jacket and a black ski cap, spoke into the camera and reminded everyone of his signature blinking. "If we are forced to land, and if I am forced to say something on camera, I will try my very, very hardest not to blink. That means that what I am saying is under force," he said.

Billy said the opposite—that he would blink continuously as a sign that he was being coerced.

"We are on a nonviolent mission," said Roque into the camera. He was wearing a well-cut black jacket that accented his movie-star looks. "If we are forced to land, I ask that the officers that knew me from before will give me a chance to speak. Please, listen to me, and let me defend myself. And please let my son, Alejandro Roque Trevilla, know where I am."

Roque would not blink or perform any kind of physical cue to let people in Miami—like his wife Ana Margarita—know if he was lying or being coerced. In fact, he did not mention her or his stepchildren in his farewell. His supplication was addressed to his old Cuban military buddies. It seemed like a passionate plea for a mercy he was doubtful of receiving.

They left before dawn. The jackets and hats came in handy, because at twelve thousand feet the air temperature inside the cockpit was below forty degrees, a far cry from the usual one hundred degrees at five hundred feet.

When they reached the twelve-mile limit, they opened the airplane door, which had been secured with a cable so that it would not swing up. The papers had been packed in pillowcases, and as soon as Arnaldo hoisted them out of the door, the suction from the air pressure and the wind speed made the bags collapse, sealing in their contents. They tried several times, but it was extremely difficult to release the messages, and only a few actually made it out of the bags.

Bitterly disappointed, they returned to the hangar with most of the leaflets still in the bags, their mission aborted. Morales and his divination rod were put on standby.

The wind conditions remained favorable all week. They decided to try again on Friday, January 13, and this time, Carlos Costa and Mario de la Peña joined Arnaldo and Basulto, flying in two separate planes. Roberto Rodríguez Tejera, Basulto's friend and one of his main collaborators in the nonviolence movement, video-taped new messages for each of the pilots to leave behind for their loved ones. Carlos Costa made a particularly impassioned speech complete with a farewell to his family "in case anything happened."

This time they put the leaflets in ten standard cardboard file boxes. They removed the backseats of the two planes to accommodate them.

At the twelve-mile limit, Arnaldo once again cracked the door open, then threw the flyers out, one box at a time. The moment he stuck his arm out the door, the papers and then the boxes were violently sucked out, like in airplane horror movies. He worked furiously, throwing out box after box from the back section of the plane. Basulto, too, threw fistfuls from his pilot's window.

It was cold inside the cockpit, and the thin air made breathing difficult and gave Basulto a nosebleed. Basulto and Arnaldo worked at adrenaline-pumping high speed. When they were finished, Basulto turned to look at his friend, who was leaning against the back wall of the cockpit, gasping for breath. The messages of hope to the Cuban people were flying around him inside the plane, like oversized confetti at a celebration, with a non-blinking Arnaldo the lone exhausted reveler.

"How are you doing, hermano?"

Arnaldo just nodded, still trying to catch his breath, lying back on a featherbed of flyers.

In Cuba, Yamilet Chen López was walking in her Havana neighborhood that morning when what she thought was money came floating down from heaven.

"Dinero! Money!" she cried out to her neighbors, and soon it was a madhouse. Even when they realized it was not money, the crowd kept getting bigger, and everyone started collecting and reading the little papers. In other neighborhoods, the militia was called and reporters filmed them snatching the papers out of people's hands.

Leaving their office at Havana Press, Rafael Solano and Julio San Francisco Martínez García decided to take a walk. One year earlier Solano had founded Havana Press, a small agency of independent journalists who worked out of his home in San Miguel del Padrón, near Havana. They had worked for years for Castro's government-run press until their disappointment with the revolution reached its peak and they broke off on their own. Solano and San Francisco had been promoting Concilio Cubano, the Cuban Council, whose 130-member group of dissidents was scheduled to have an unprecedented meeting on February 24, 1996.

Concilio's first seeds were planted by a card-carrying, loyal member of the Communist Party, a pro-revolution, pro-Fidel, Ché Guevara–loving, Afro-Cuban eco-pacifist named Leonel Morejón Almagro. Appalled at the proliferation of nuclear weapons and the universal stockpiling of arms, he wrote a letter to Ronald Reagan that culminated in the formation of Naturpaz (Nature Peace). He collected thousands of signatures until he was stopped with the severe warning that only Fidel Castro could speak on the ecology, the environment, and nuclear weapons. "If you want, you can go camping and take pictures, experience nature that way," he was told. When he persisted he was branded an agent of the CIA.

"I have never even seen an American in my entire life!" he said. Morejón's heart's desire was to become an attorney, so he signed on the dotted line that he would not pursue Naturpaz. "That day, I became a dissident," he said. After graduating from law school at the University of Havana, he defended political prisoners and dissidents. In taking up their cause, he noted the polarizing divisions among all the dissident groups. To bring them all together, he formed Concilio Cubano. The Afro-Cuban dissident would ultimately be nominated for the Nobel Peace Prize.

The Council was probably not on Solano's mind when he saw his neighbors running back and forth, snatching what looked like money from the sky. When Solano and San Francisco saw what they were and read what was printed on them, they knew they had a choice: ignore them or let the news out. At that point they did not even know who had thrown the leaflets, but they were sure that whomever it was had probably been shot out of the sky.

They debated what the odds of a public revolt would be if they announced the incident on the airwaves. If the people took to the streets, Solano and San Francisco would probably be taken to the firing squad.

They collected about eight flyers, went back to their office at Solano's home, and called the Miami radio stations. Basulto and the others had not yet landed in Opa-locka when thousands of listeners in Miami heard some unnamed person on the radio read what was printed on the flyers. For once, the news in Cuba was advising listeners in Miami of something they did not know.

The chief of Cuban State Security heard it too, and he informed his generals that if there were a riot, the leaders of Havana Press were to be shot before dawn in front of their offices. For now, they were to be arrested immediately.

Upon his return, Basulto was told of the Havana Press communication, so that evening he called Solano and San Francisco. The journalists were relieved to hear his voice, thankful they had not been shot down. The *Miami Herald* later wrote that Cuba's military at that time was unable to maintain tight security because of economic problems and a fuel shortage.

By the next morning in Cuba, the police had managed to collect thousands of leaflets, tearing them out of people's hands, and arresting those who would not turn them over. But many residents in Havana managed to hide their leaflets as if they were more valuable than gold.

"There was no butter to spread that Sunday morning, but there were leaflets to cover your hard piece of government-rationed bread," Solano would write. That morning, Havana Press received numerous calls from radio stations, in particular Radio Martí in Miami. By Sunday afternoon, Solano and San Francisco had been picked up by the police for questioning, along with other Cuban dissidents.

Dropping dollar bills would not have had a greater impact than the flyers, although money would certainly have been appreciated. The message was getting through: *you have basic human rights—exercise them!* It was Brothers' hope that perhaps the leaflets and the timing of the Cuban Council would stir more to action and greater internal opposition.

After half a million leaflets with the Declaration of Human Rights fell from the heavens that day, Basulto was accused of flying over Havana. In Miami,

Basulto was severely chastised by the local press, and the FAA suspended his license again.

"They [the U.S. government] enticed me before to go drop bombs on Cuba," Basulto responded to the *Miami Herald*. "Why should the government bother me now if I go drop leaflets, especially about human rights?

"Let us act," he continued, pleading for the U.S. government to stay out of it. "Your help in the past has not been successful." He was of course referring to the failed Bay of Pigs invasion and the subsequent betrayals. *The struggle is ours.*

Exile groups were divided over Basulto's actions. The majority would not believe that he had not flown over Havana; they could not accept that those leaflets flew for twelve miles. Some felt he was grandstanding, a bit of the *protagonismo* he disavowed. Others hailed him as a leader of the internal dissident movement.

Either way, most had a hard time accepting the change in this man. He had been trained by the CIA to use bombs on Cuba; now he was dropping leaflets. He had been part of a U.S.-backed plan to fight his own countrymen, but in the past four years he had saved more than four thousand of them from drowning in the Florida Straits. Some pro-Castro governments labeled him a terrorist. The espionage trainings he had attended when he was twenty years old had been replaced by weekend retreats on nonviolence and civil disobedience. The world wanted to divide José Basulto into all the parts they knew him to be. They did not want to see or hear what he so dramatically professed: "I am the change."

A week after the drop, an independent reporter from Miami visited Havana and asked Yamilet Chen López what she was going to do with her flyer.

"Oh, I have it hidden in my house," she said in the filmed interview. "If they find it I'll be fined fifteen hundred pesos, or even put in jail." There had been police on every block in every neighborhood, searching at random, even asking children for the leaflets.

"What would you like to tell the exiles in Miami?" the reporter asked.

She looked directly at the video camera. "Send medicine, please, and food, but especially medicine."

"But isn't health care in Cuba free? Aren't there enough doctors for everyone?" the reporter asked.

"Not if you don't take him coffee or cigarettes," said Yamilet, very matter-of-factly. "They won't treat you nice unless you take them coffee or cigarettes."

"Tell them, our brothers in Miami, to send medicines to the homes, *not to the doctors*, especially medicines for lice. Everybody has really bad lice." She looked directly at the camera once more. "Help us, we're dying."

Alberto Alfonso Fernández, another Havana resident, felt the same way. "Listen, the people are very happy here with the leaflets, but help us with food and medicine." He looked to the left of the camera at someone else that was in the room but not on camera. He looked again to whomever was there, and that person apparently gave him the go-ahead. "And send arms, we can't do it alone, and we have no borders. We are ready to fight, but we have no leader. Send us arms."

Back at home, Basulto was repeatedly criticized for ignoring the risks and for provoking Castro. They could not believe those flyers had flown twelve miles. The media and even close friends charged him with being too political, too confrontational. "The difference is, we confront without weapons," he defended.

25

Meet Me in Havana

They deem him their worst enemy who tells them the truth.
Plato

On January 19, 1996, Brothers to the Rescue issued a press release citing the success of Operation Dr. Martin Luther King Jr. The following week Basulto wrote Dexter Scott King requesting the use of the Dr. Martin Luther King Jr. Center facilities in Havana for the Cuban Council meeting on February 24. It was estimated that more than five thousand people would be part of the Concilio. Over the ensuing weeks, dozens of letters from various organizations echoed Basulto's request for a meeting venue in the capital, but the permission was never granted.

In Cuba, Leonel Morejón Almagro, who had been elected by Concilio as one of its organizers, went directly to the Dr. Martin Luther King Jr. Center in Havana. The pastor there told him he could not use the facilities, that Concilio was too political, and he called State Security to hound Morejón. They were relentless, persecuting him, his extended family, and his wife daily. She eventually miscarried when her blood pressure skyrocketed. Finally on February 13, 1996, Morejón was imprisoned.

On February 22, Brothers to the Rescue secretary Sylvia Pascual released another press announcement that four planes would fly on February 24, 1996, the 101st anniversary of the rallying cry of José Martí that began the War of Independence in 1895. Called El Grito de Baire (the Shout of Baire), the War for Independence began simultaneously in four towns in Cuba on that date, one of them being the town of Baire. On February 24, two planes would go out on a humanitarian mission over the Florida Straits and two planes would fly to the Bahamas to deliver much-needed supplies to the 230 Cubans still detained there.

At the same time, Havana would be hosting an unprecedented meeting of the 130 dissident groups called the Cuban Council. They still did not have a venue, but there was much excitement over the gathering.

"*Oye,* Basulto, what's going on with the Council?!" Armando Alejandre Jr.'s booming voice broke into Basulto's concentration as he prepared for the up-coming press conference at the hangar. Armando had come to give Basulto moral support.

Armando, age forty-five, had been coming to the hangar to help with the Cuban refugees detained in the Bahamas. An activist for Cuban causes, Armando had never been on a rescue mission, mainly because of his size. He stood 6'7" and weighed about 250 pounds. He could not sit in a cramped plane for hours on end for a mission, but he was steadfast in making trips to the Bahamas, a shorter, one-hour commute from Miami.

Born in Cuba, Armando came to the United States in 1960 when he was ten years old. He was the fourth child and long-awaited son of Armando and Margarita Alejandre. His mother would often say that if he had not come after his three sisters, her husband would have kept trying for a son even after ten daughters. Armando was coddled and pampered by his parents and sisters, and he responded not as an overindulged child, but with affection and loyalty.

His parents were surprised by his passion for Cuba. Armando turned eleven on April 16, 1961, the day before the Bay of Pigs invasion. When the news first broke in Miami about the fighting on Girón Beach, he responded with enthusiasm and cries of "Fidel is leaving! Fidel is leaving! We can go back home!"

When they did not go back home, he claimed the United States as his own, and at eighteen, the day after his graduation from La Salle High School in Miami, he enlisted in the Marines. He was not yet an American citizen, but Armando felt an urgency to repay the United States for everything the country had done for the Cubans. After training in Camp LeJeune, North Carolina, he spent nine months in Vietnam.

Armando loved to write, and while on his tour of duty, he wrote his mother every day. He studied creative writing in college and his personal goal was to become the Cuban Hemingway.

Years later, Armando married Marlene. The couple now had an eighteen-year-old daughter, Marlene, attending the University of Florida. Marlene was her daddy's girl; at six feet tall, she had inherited her father's height.

It was Armando who chauffeured Marlene and her friends to basketball practice. It was Armando who counseled her on colleges, and in a move far removed from the typically overprotective Cuban father, he encouraged his only daughter to go away to school rather than remain close to home.

This was a particularly unusual move since all the Alejandres had remained close to home. In fact, they all lived on the same block. In the early 1970s, Alejandre Sr., a contractor, purchased several properties in South Miami and subsequently built homes for his three daughters and son and their respective families. All the backyards connected the growing families.

Armando Jr. was famous for his one-man anti-Castro demonstrations. At one protest, he jumped over the wall of the Cuban Interests Section in Washington and broke his leg. Another time, when Cuba joined other Latin American and Caribbean countries at the Ibero-American Summit—called Cumbre de Cartagena—Armando went home and packed his clothes and a Cuban flag. He asked his sister for cab fare, told his wife he was leaving, and then boarded a plane to Cartagena, Colombia, to heckle the crowd. Alone.

When Fidel Castro was in New York in 1994, he joined fellow activist and friend Sylvia Iriondo, head of Mothers Against Repression, to take a stand against Fidel's speech in Harlem. Sylvia was also involved with Brothers to the Rescue and their flights to the Bahamas. It was in New York where Sylvia and Armando's friendship strengthened. It was not unusual for them to speak on the phone five times a day. On the same visit to New York they also protested in front of the Cuban Mission. On the walk over, Sylvia noticed Armando kept stooping down to pick something up from the streets of New York. When questioned, he replied that he was picking up horse manure to throw at the door of the mission.

Armando's current passion was helping the internal dissident movement in Cuba through the Cuban Council. As part of the organizing group in Miami, Armando was working on obtaining a venue for the unprecedented meeting in Havana. In Cuba, the Cuban Council had filed for a permit to assemble, citing Articles 54 and 63 of Cuba's present constitution, allowing peaceful assembly. Their goals included engaging in a dialogue within and outside of Cuba in order to progress toward a nonviolent transition to democracy. The Council's platform called for unconditional amnesty for political prisoners and a guarantee of human rights for every Cuban. The Brothers to the Rescue flyers had just reminded everyone of that.

Brothers to the Rescue sent the Council two thousand dollars in aid. It never reached Leonel Morejón Almagro.

Several meetings were held around Miami in the weeks preceding the Cuban Council. Mirta Costa, Carlos' mother, attended one hosted by CANF. Mirta greatly admired President Jorge Mas Canosa, and she had become an active member. Several pilots from Brothers to the Rescue were there, too. She had not seen any of them since the leaflet drop, an event Mirta had criticized in no uncertain terms to her son Carlos, who had been part of the now highly controversial mission.

Mirta had done everything a mother could possibly do to dissuade her son from flying with Brothers to the Rescue. She was concerned about his intense dedication. He went to the hangar every day before work to dispatch the flight plans and send off the missions. If there was food to be delivered to the Bahamas, Carlos would make sure it was still warm when the plane landed. He organized the flights, flew the missions when he was not at his day job, and then cleaned the planes and the hangar. He was losing his hair prematurely and was always sporting his "No Fear" cap. Mirta was worried. She wanted her son on the ground.

Mirta ran into Arnaldo Iglesias at the CANF meeting. Still seething over the leaflet drop, which she considered a direct provocation to Fidel Castro, she approached him with a stern message. "Listen, Arnaldo," she said. "I don't want any heroes."

Meanwhile in Havana, Leonel Morejón Almagro was arrested February 13, 1996, followed by 140 other activists days later, and the Cuban government forbade the Council to meet. Basulto believed there was a possibility of rafters taking to the Straits on February 24, to protest the cancellation of the Cuban Council meeting. He also hoped that some of the remaining dissidents, and the public in general, would stage some sort of peaceful civil disobedience. He decided Brothers would fly that day in solidarity with their Cuban brothers.

Unbeknownst to Brothers to the Rescue, Congressman Bill Richardson was invited by the Cuban government to visit Havana, where he met with Fidel Castro and top government officials on January 17, 1996, just four days after the leaflets floated into Havana. The Brothers' overflights came up at the meeting. Then in February, the week before the arrests of the 140 dissidents, Retired Admiral Eugene Carroll and a group of retired U.S. military officers were visiting Havana. Meetings like these that included members from other U.S. government agencies were not uncommon at a time when

President Clinton was trying to improve relations with Cuba. The retired admiral sat across the conference table talking with Cuban military authorities in Havana, discussing a myriad of topics. One of those topics was the leaflet drop. Cuba maintained that the planes had flown over Havana, invading Cuba's sovereignty, yet they had no radar proof of any incursions.

It was during one of these meetings with retired U.S. generals when Cuban Air Force General Arnaldo Tamayo turned to Admiral Carroll and asked him a very pointed question.

"What would be the U.S. reaction if we authorized a shoot-down of the Brothers to the Rescue planes?"

26

Flight Plans

*We ourselves feel that what we are doing is just a drop in the
ocean. But if that drop was not in the ocean, I think the ocean
would be less because of that missing drop. I do not agree with
the big way of doing things.*

Mother Teresa

Expectations were high for the upcoming Cuban Council meeting in Havana, even though the government had cancelled the meeting and jailed several dissidents. As Basulto prepared his flight plans to support his Cuban brothers, other people made plans of their own.

Juan Pablo Roque—Miami

At three o'clock in the morning on Friday, February 23, Ana Margarita Roque was awakened with a tender good-bye kiss from her husband, J. P. His early-morning departure was in order to transport a boat to Key West, a job that would pay him two thousand dollars. Ana Margarita was not happy about the separation—they had only been married ten months—but they certainly needed the money. She reminded him to take his cell phone battery charger.

She did not know much about the job that day, but she had noticed her husband was jumpy lately. The day before he had been at Basulto's house, grumbling about a donation Brothers had made to the Cuban Council. Ana Margarita did not involve herself too much in politics or in her husband's odd jobs. Because of those jobs, he had been able to buy himself a Jeep Cherokee and a Rolex, both of which he treasured. Ana Margarita was happy in her marriage and her children loved their stepfather. She went back to sleep, content.

When she woke up the next morning, she noticed that Roque had forgotten his battery charger. She started calling him as soon as she got to work, but his phone was turned off. By the time she left work at five in the afternoon, she still had not heard from her husband, and she was worried. She went to pick up his paycheck, and then later, to retrieve his Jeep Cherokee from the parking garage where her mother lived. Roque loved his Jeep and liked to keep in the covered garage at his mother-in-law's.

Ana Margarita's mother tried to calm her daughter's fears, reminding her that the boat trip would last until Sunday. After all, there was a possibility Roque had no reception. But when she got home, Ana Margarita's apprehension heightened. In her husband's closet she discovered that he had left behind his wallet and all his credit cards. All of his clothes, however, were gone.

The Brothers to the Rescue Hangar—Opa-locka

Mayte Greco was not exactly working the camera like a runway model. She was a mother, she was a pilot, she was a tomboy. But she was also a natural beauty, so no matter how she posed, she looked stunning. Carolyn Russo, a photographer for the National Air and Space Museum, had come to Miami to photograph the Brothers to the Rescue aviatrix for an upcoming book and museum exhibit called *Women and Flight*, featuring thirty-six female aviators.

Mayte had already been featured in a 1995 video called *The Sky's the Limit*, where she had asserted that it was harder to be a mother than a pilot. "The plane is always the same," she said. Her comment was corroborated this Friday morning, when Mayte arrived late for the photo shoot because she had spent the night in the hospital with her three-year-old son (adopted after the four girls were born) who had a high fever. Mayte was dressed in her signature work clothes: jeans and a white T-shirt. She posed inside one of the blue-and-white Cessnas that would be flying on Saturday's mission. Mayte would not be going on the mission because of the photo shoot. Russo wanted pictures of Mayte with her five children, and these would have to wait until Saturday when they would be off from school.

Russo snapped Mayte leaning her arm across the top of the open Vietnam window of one of the planes. This window, named for the specific design used during the war, was a Plexiglas square carved into the door, making it easier to look down and spot rafters.

The hangar was full of airplanes, rafts, memorabilia, and supplies for Cuban detainees being held in the Bahamas. Sylvia Iriondo, from Mothers Against Repression, and Armando Alejandre had been visiting the Cubans detained in the Bahamas almost weekly, taking them food and provisions. Mayte stood for a shot next to a pile of rafts. She lovingly pointed out Basulto's baby, the N2506, *Seagull One*, to Russo. "He doesn't like anyone touching it," Mayte warned.

The Brothers to the Rescue Pilots—Miami

On Friday afternoon, Chief of Pilots Carlos Costa was having a hard time scheduling pilots for Saturday's mission. The flights were to have included three planes to the Bahamas and three planes on a search-and-rescue mission, but just minutes earlier, the Bahamians had cancelled the flights because a Cuban delegation was going to be there. Their reason for not allowing Brothers to bring supplies to the detainees: they didn't want any trouble.

When Carlos informed Basulto late Friday afternoon about the cancelled trip to the Bahamas, the latter told him to change the flight plans to search-and-rescue missions only. It was crunch time and Carlos needed to fill three planes: Mayte was doing a photo shoot for two days, Guille and Beto Lares had not flown in months, Koki would be at the base, and Alfredo Sánchez had to go to a family wedding. Carlos was feeling a cold coming on, so he called Bert McNaughton, an American pilot volunteer, and asked him to take his place.

By late Friday evening, Carlos had three planes and pilots: Mario de la Peña would fly the *Habana, D.C.*; Basulto would fly the N2506 with Arnaldo Iglesias; and Carlos would fly the third plane, the *Spirit of Miami*. He was feeling much better and he was satisfied with his roster, so he called McNaughton and told him that he did not need him to fly after all. Pablo Morales, the rafter that Guille Lares had saved two years before, would be his observer.

The Pilots' Mothers—Miami

Mirta Costa, Carlos' mother, was not happy that her son was feeling better and would be flying on a search-and-rescue mission—the first one in months. She was not happy that Carlos would be flying at all. She had never told her son of the nightmare she had had a few weeks before.

Her nightmare began with her arrival at work, where she noticed the desks were arranged differently and people were out of focus. Her supervisor approached her and in a very calculated voice announced, "Carlos Costa died."

Upon awakening, Mirta was in such a state of shock that she immediately picked up the phone and dialed her neighbor in a panic. Mirta did not realize it was five o'clock in the morning.

When she told her husband, Osvaldo, about the dream, he reminded her that a colleague at Mirta's workplace had a sister who was dying of cancer. The Monday after Mirta's nightmare, when she arrived at work, the staff was told that their coworker's sister had indeed died during the weekend.

"Are you over the scare?" Osvaldo had teased Mirta when she came home.

"Listen, Comemierda . . ." Mirta began, upset by his ridicule. But then she let it go.

Later that Friday evening, Miriam de la Peña heard Mario walking down the hall, snapping his fingers. He was flying tomorrow, she thought to herself, recognizing Mario's signature reaction every time he got the call from Carlos Costa.

He had gotten home late that Friday night to have dinner with his parents. Settling in for a relaxing evening, he was watching television with his father when he went to his room to answer Carlos' call, which set off the finger-snapping.

"I'm flying tomorrow, I'm fly-ing to-mo-row," chanted the twenty-four-year-old, snapping his fingers and strutting into the living room. Mario had just started an internship at American Airlines in Miami. He had been offered one in Dallas, American's home office, but he refused it in order to finish his last semester at Embry-Riddle, stay in Miami, live at home, and fly with Brothers to the Rescue.

Miriam was not as excited as her son. There had been so much controversy over the leaflets that had been thrown in January, and Basulto was still fighting allegations that he had flown over Havana. Mario had been part of that. They all adamantly denied flying over Cuban territory the day of the leaflet drop.

There had been plenty of proof and witnesses the day of the actual fly-over, on July 13, 1995, when Mario had flown over Havana with Billy Schuss. Miriam was still upset about that one, and the entire de la Peña family had chastised Mario. Miriam's only comfort was that her son was not pilot-in-command that day. He had been taking photographs. Mario later confessed to his parents that he had been eager to see the country where his family had been born.

What most bothered Miriam about that overflight was that one of the consequences had been that Brothers to the Rescue was denied permission to fly to the Bahamas at Christmastime to bring presents to the little children detained in the camps. Today, Brothers to the Rescue had been denied access once again, this time because of a visiting Cuban delegation.

Tomorrow's mission was a standard search-and-rescue, Mario reassured his parents. He would be nowhere near the coast of Cuba.

Washington, D.C.

Upon his return to the United States from his visit with the Cuban generals in mid-February, Admiral Eugene Carroll informed the Center for Defense Information of Cuba's change in policy toward Brothers to the Rescue. He repeated the Cubans' question: "What would happen if we shot down one of the Brothers to the Rescue planes?" Carroll had responded that it would be a public relations disaster.

On Friday, February 23, government officials were worried that Brothers would attempt a flyover of Havana the next day in solidarity with the Cuban Council, even though dissidents had been jailed and the unprecedented meeting would not take place after all. A State Department officer had reported that "Cuba was in a rough mood" and less likely to show restraint.

Friday afternoon, Defense Intelligence Agency Senior Analyst Ana Belén Montes met with Admiral Carroll and representatives of various federal agencies to hear about their experience at the meetings in January. Montes was considered the nation's senior intelligence expert on the Cuban military. For sixteen years, she had basically called the shots regarding U.S. policy toward Cuba.

Late Friday evening in Washington, it was past Richard Nuccio's bedtime but he could not sleep. Nuccio was President Clinton's Cuba advisor, and he was worried about a possible shoot-down tomorrow. He had e-mailed his concerns at 6:44 p.m. to National Security Deputy Samuel "Sandy" Berger, the number-two person at the White House. He told Berger he felt that "this may finally tip the Cubans toward an attempt to shoot down or force down the planes." American intelligence had reported that Cuba had been practicing confronting slow-flying aircraft just weeks earlier. Nuccio then called his friend Jean Kirkpatrick, President Reagan's former UN Ambassador, and told her he was convinced something dreadful was going to happen to the Brothers to the Rescue planes. When Kirkpatrick asked him how he knew that, he did not respond.

Nuccio never heard back from Sandy Berger, and he never contacted Brothers to the Rescue with his concerns. He would later defend that he did "all that we legally could to discourage Mr. Basulto's reckless behavior and to deter the use of force by Cuba." Except pick up the phone.

A U.S. official whose name was withheld from the press would later defend Nuccio's inaction by saying that Basulto went ballistic every time they threatened him about not flying.

"I listen to warnings," Basulto would respond. "I won't listen to threats."

Richard Nuccio spent the night tossing and turning.

The Federal Aviation Administration

After Brothers to the Rescue had issued their press release announcing that they would be flying on February 24, the FAA put its own flight plan into effect. They asked Tyndall Air Force Base in Panama City, Florida, to send up a special B-94 radar balloon to monitor the Brothers' flight that day.

They also contacted March Air Force Base in Riverside, California, where they regularly supervised radar scopes covering the waters of the Caribbean. The base employed defense-trained specialists in contact with all major military radar systems around the country that provided constant surveillance of U.S. borders, primarily for catching drug smugglers. The FAA asked radar specialist Jeffrey Houlihan of the U.S. Customs Agency to track the flights, make computerized prints of them from the radar scopes, then immediately forward them to Washington. Houlihan had heard quite a bit about the Brothers to the Rescue organization, but he had never been asked to log a Brothers flight. The FAA told him that Brothers was going to make a political statement against the Communist government of Cuba.

Nobody from Tyndall Air Force Base, March Air Force Base, or the FAA ever contacted Basulto or any member of his organization to let them know that they would be documenting their flights on Saturday, February 24.

The Cuban Council Meeting—Miami

The Hyatt Hotel in Coral Gables was crowded with representatives from dozens of Cuban exile groups gathered to discuss the Cuban Council. More than ninety different groups had voiced their support for the Cuban Council. Even though hundreds of activists had been arrested and jailed in Cuba, and the Council meeting had been cancelled, the exiles in Miami felt that demonstrations would be held in Cuba the next day, February 24, 1996. The publicity over the Council had been constant for the past two months, particularly after the leaflets had flown into Havana on January 9 and 13.

Sylvia Iriondo from Mothers Against Repression took Armando Alejandre Jr. with her to speak with Basulto. Basulto relayed Carlos Costa's recent message informing them that their mission to the Bahamas had been cancelled because of a Cuban delegation visit. Sylvia and Armando were disappointed that their resupply mission was cancelled, but when they found out Basulto was going to fly his humanitarian missions anyway, Sylvia asked if she and her husband could join him. Carlos Costa needed more observers, so Basulto agreed to let them come along.

Sylvia remembers Armando pleading with her to advocate for him to Basulto so that he could join them also. Armando wrote Basulto a note expressing his heart's desire to go on a mission. He gave it to Sylvia and she put it in her purse. When Sylvia spoke to Basulto about Armando's request, Basulto would not give her a definitive answer. It was one thing to fly Armando and his 6'7", 250-pound bulk to the Bahamas, a relatively quick one-hour trip. It was another thing entirely to do a five-hour mission over the Florida Straits. If Carlos had already scheduled other observers, Armando would not fit in the cramped Cessnas.

"Just be at the hangar by seven, and we'll see," Basulto told him.

27

Shoot-Down

There is nothing in Cuba that threatens U.S. security.
Retired Admiral Eugene Carroll

Mission-in-Command Pilots Mario de la Peña and Carlos Costa left their respective homes before seven o'clock on Saturday morning, February 24, 1996. It was so early that neither one woke up his mother to say good-bye.

Armando Alejandre Jr. also left his house before dawn. He was in such a rush to get to the hangar that he never kissed his wife good-bye, even though Marlene called out to him from the front door of their house.

Carlos Costa was not satisfied with the roster for that morning's missions, so he went to Juan González's house to plead once more. González had spotted the first rafter five years ago, he was an excellent observer, and they needed him today. It was just daylight when he arrived at the González home, and Carmen González opened the door.

"Who's going to rescue us, Carlitos?" said Carmen, standing in the door frame of their modest home in Miami Lakes. She was only half-joking. "You know that Saturdays are his most important days," she went on. "He really can't go."

Carmen was a volunteer at Brothers to the Rescue and supported their cause, but her own family needed rescuing right now—financial rescuing. The waterless cookware business her husband represented was not as lucrative today as twenty years before. Young couples cooked less at home, and newlyweds did not really care whether a copper-clad aluminum pot was going to last forever. Most of their marriages would not.

Behind his wife Juan shrugged his shoulders in a sign of surrender, his arms bent with his palms facing up. "What can I do?"

Once at the hangar, a little after seven in the morning, Carlos Costa called in six flight plans for a departure of 10:15 a.m., and he included Carlos Tabernilla's and Alfredo Sánchez's planes, even though he knew by then that they would not be flying.

"Let me ask you a question," said Ivonne Grate of the Miami Automated International Flight Service Station, "is this, ah, different from what you guys normally do?"

"No, it's not," replied Carlos.

The pilots and crews started arriving at the Brothers to the Rescue hangar: Basulto, Arnaldo, Carlos, Mario, Pablo, and Armando. Koki Lares was there, too; he would be monitoring the radios that day—and probably making Cuban coffee with the dirty filter.

Sylvia and Andrés Iriondo had overslept and they were on their way.

It was just as well since Basulto had been informed that Elio Díaz, the mechanic that worked on the Brothers' planes, had been detained in Cuba for several days and had just arrived the night before. They all wanted to hear what it was all about, so they decided to leave a little later.

"Qué pasa, Elio?" Basulto greeted Elio as he arrived at the hangar. Elio was buena gente, good people, and the pilots liked him. He was in his early thirties, more than six feet tall, and had an ample belly. He had dark hair, brown eyes, and a bushy mustache. When he smiled, his round cheeks puffed out, making his eyes squint cheerfully.

Elio Díaz had left Cuba when he was ten years old in 1971, onboard one of the last Freedom Flights. He and his family were guajiros, country people. They grew their own food in Cuba and had pretty much supported themselves. Elio would always say, to the chagrin of some, that the revolution did not really affect him: it had neither given him anything nor taken anything away.

Elio had been flying back from Honduras to deliver a new plane to a client when they suddenly experienced engine trouble and had to make an emergency landing in Pinar del Rio, Cuba. Because the pilot was a Colombian and Elio was an exiled Cuban, the pair may have seemed suspicious to the Cubans, and they were held for questioning. They were detained and interrogated until five o'clock in the morning of the next day. From there they were taken to the notorious prison at Villa Marista in Havana, infamous for its detention of political prisoners and now headquarters of State Security. They were also forced to pay the cab fare.

"Let me tell you a funny story," said Elio, his cheeks puffing up. "I had taken these Brothers to the Rescue T-shirts you guys had given me, because I knew I was going to be doing a lot of work on the planes. Well, I had two, and one of the Hondurans asked if he could have one, so I gave it to him. The last day, I was wearing the other one, and it was all sweaty and dirty, full of grease, but he asked me for that one too, for his friend. He said he didn't mind it was dirty so I took it off and gave it to him. Well, while they were interrogating us in one room, they were searching our luggage. Can you imagine what they would have done to me if they had found those T-shirts?"

The mechanic had been questioned over and over again by Cuban officials, together with the Colombian pilot and then separately, asking what they were doing in Honduras and what had happened to the plane. Their stories coincided: they were not hiding anything—except the relationship that Elio had with Brothers to the Rescue. He denied everything, over and over again, saying he did not know Basulto at all, did not work on the Brothers' planes, had nothing to do with them.

While Basulto, Arnaldo, Carlos, and Mario spoke with Elio, the Iriondos arrived and joined Armando Alejandre Jr. nearby in some folding chairs. Sylvia remembered she needed to make copies of a letter to Attorney General Janet Reno, asking her not to extradite political activist Elizabeth Pis. She, Arnaldo, and Basulto had been at a rally in front of the Justice Department in downtown Miami the previous afternoon, protesting on behalf of Pis. She asked Pablo Morales to show her how to use the copy machine.

Sylvia made small talk with Pablo, and he recounted his rescue story. "I promised that if I was saved, I would do for other Cubans what Brothers did for me," he said. "And you should hear my mother talk about me in Cuba!" he went on. "She's not afraid of anyone. She tells everyone that I volunteer at Brothers to the Rescue and that I'm getting my pilot's license."

Sylvia was touched by the way he spoke about his mother, Eva Barbas. Eva was a tough little woman, barely five feet tall and ninety pounds, yet she would laugh in the face of Communist interrogators in Cuba. Sylvia was also stirred by Pablo's dedication to and appreciation for Brothers to the Rescue. Who better than Pablo could understand the plight of rafters, having been one himself?

While Elio was telling his stories that morning, Cuban MiG fighter jets were spotted in the Florida Straits in the same area where the Brothers to the

Rescue planes would have been flying as indicated in the flight plans Carlos Costa had filed that morning. Homestead Air Force Base sent out two interceptors to meet the MiGs, in accordance with set protocol. No activity was reported and all planes went back to their respective stations.

By the time Elio finished his story, it was almost eleven—early enough to leave but too close to lunch, and Basulto's stomach was growling. Carlos wanted to leave early because he had plans to meet friends at the beach for a barbecue. His bag was packed and ready in the trunk of his car. But the group decided to eat first, so Carlos cancelled three of the six flight plans and scheduled three planes for a 1:00 p.m. departure. The same grids would be followed today as usual, with Basulto's plane flying closest to the twelve-mile limit off the coast of Havana.

Mario de la Peña decided to call his mother and tell her that he would not be home until much later than expected. When he rang her at eleven fifteen that morning, Miriam thought he had already returned from his mission.

"Are you back already?" she asked, and looked out the kitchen window to check on the weather.

"No," he said. "They're talking to some guy here. I don't know what's going on." Those would be the last words Miriam would ever hear from her son.

When he finished his call, Mario went and bought Burger King for the group.

The group of eight going out on the day's mission gathered near the three planes for their prayer circle. Mayte Greco was there, too, to finish her photo shoot with Carolyn Russo. When they finished, Koki wished them a safe flight.

After the prayer, Andrés Iriondo told his wife, Sylvia, that they should fly together. "That way if something happens, we'll be together." Sylvia remembers looking at him in disbelief, his comment a classic men-are-from-Mars statement.

"That's exactly it, Andrés," she replied, remembering her not-yet-teenage son back home. "If something happens," Sylvia said, thinking of a possible engine failure or crash into the ocean, "one of us should survive." But as sometimes happens in Cuban marriages, the man won the argument and they both boarded Basulto's plane, with Arnaldo Iglesias as copilot.

Sylvia and Andrés were given headphones so that they could hear the conversations not only of Basulto and Arnaldo, but also of the other two planes. That way, all eight of them would be able to communicate throughout their mission.

Just past one o'clock, the three planes were lined up for takeoff. Sylvia nervously glanced across the runway to Mario de la Peña's plane, a blue-and-white Cessna with a red stripe, the *Habana D.C.* Armando flashed her the V for victory sign, his face beaming from the copilot's window. Mario smiled and waved from his pilot's seat.

Behind them were Carlos Costa and Pablo Morales, flying in the blue-and-white *Spirit of Miami,* the plane used in Mayte's photo shoot the previous afternoon.

At 1:11 p.m., the three Cessna 337s took off from Opa-locka Airport on a humanitarian mission to search for rafters. It was a beautiful February afternoon, a crisp Miami winter's day. The seas were flat and visibility was clear, not a cloud in the sky. In military jargon, CAVU: ceiling and visibility unlimited.

At 1:55 p.m., Senior Detection Systems Specialist Jeffrey Houlihan at March Air Force Base in Riverside, California, had radio confirmation of the three Brothers aircraft flying south toward the 24th parallel. As instructed by the FAA, Houlihan was logging the Brothers' flights in case the pilots were going to make some kind of statement in Cuba.

At 2:55 p.m., a Cuban MiG-29 and a MiG-23 took off from San Antonio de los Baños Air Force Base, located less than thirty miles southwest of Havana. Officials at the North American Air Defense Command (NORAD), based in Colorado Springs, Colorado, began tracking them. The NORAD controllers alerted the Florida Air National Guard's 125th fighter wing at Homestead Air Force Base in Florida. By 3:00 p.m., two F-15 tactical fighters were placed on high alert as the MiGs continued their trajectory north. Homestead had already run through this drill in the morning, when Cuban MiGs had been spotted heading toward the 24th parallel. Pilots boarded the fighters and taxied out to the runway, motors running, waiting at battle stations.

At the same time the MiGs were spotted by Houlihan, the three Brothers aircraft sighted a U.S. Navy P-3 Orion flying in the opposite direction as they proceeded west along the 24th parallel, just before turning south. Later, U.S.

reports would stipulate that the Orion was on another mission, in no way connected to the flight of the Brothers aircraft.

As they approached the 24th parallel, Mario and Carlos called in to Havana Center and gave them their registration numbers and codes: *Habana D.C.*, N5485S, squawking 1224, and *Spirit of Miami*, N2456S, squawking 1223. When he was fifty nautical miles north of the twelve-mile limit of Cuba's territorial waters, Basulto radioed Havana with his transponder code, 1222. "Brothers to the Rescue and myself, president of the organization, José Basulto, send you warm greetings," he said.

"OK, OK, received, sir; we inform you that the area north of Havana is activated. You are taking a risk by flying south of the 24th." It was their standard response.

"We know that we are in danger each time that we fly into the area south of 24, but we are ready to do so as free Cubans," was Basulto's response. He was, after all, in international waters. Basulto looked down and saw a cruise ship, the *Majesty of the Seas*, as well as a fishing vessel, the *Tri-Liner*.

Carlos Costa also saw the boats and he informed *Seagull One*. Mario was a little higher north on his grid; he radioed Basulto and asked if he should wait there.

"Sure, why not?" Basulto said, thinking the three planes would later realign themselves to fly in their usual grids, spaced three miles apart.

Shortly before 3:00 p.m. all three Cessnas had crossed the 24th parallel, and Mario de la Peña and Carlos Costa broke off into their grids while Basulto headed south, near the twelve-mile limit of Cuba.

"Bárbaro!" (Spectacular!) Sylvia Iriondo said into the headphones, as Basulto hugged the coastal limit. She was mesmerized by the skyline of the country she had left when she was fifteen. Inspired, she took out a small piece of paper and wrote down a thought that burned in her heart, yet contradicted the very beauty around her: "The sea that bathes my country brings us messages of death," she wrote. She tucked the paper inside her purse.

Basulto thought Havana Center should know just how beautiful the city looked at that moment, so he called them again. "We're reporting twelve miles off the north of Havana, on our search-and-rescue mission towards the east," he said. "It's a beautiful day and Havana looks wonderful from here. A very warm hello to you and the entire people of Cuba from Brothers to the Rescue."

"Havana, received," said the Cuban air traffic controller.

Basulto continued his parallel route east while Arnaldo Iglesias filmed the skyline. Air Force radar would later indicate that *Seagull One* dipped a mile or so inside Cuba's twelve-mile territorial limit for a few minutes.

It was an amazingly beautiful day, not a cloud in the sky, and the sea was flat, reflective as a mirror. The turquoise waters met Havana's elegant skyline, which was framed much farther away by the steep rise of mountains. Any Cuban exile witnessing the beauty these four passengers were experiencing could have been transported to the Havana they remembered. Basulto's crew may have been lulled by the hum of the engines, the clarity of the air, the explosion of colors before them: the emerald and turquoise waters, the green earthy mountains, white slivers of sandy beaches, the zigzag of downtown Havana's buildings. Havana was resplendent, yet contained within that splendor were nineteenth-century prisons detaining hundreds of dissidents.

If any one of Basulto's passengers was momentarily suspended in thought by these contrasts, the flash of gray that streaked across the windshield of the N2506 was an ominous reminder to snap out of it. It was a Cuban MiG.

"One, Mike," said Mario de la Peña, calling Basulto. Mario's call name was Seagull Mike and Carlos' was Seagull Charlie.

"Give me the camera," said Basulto to Arnaldo, "and you take the plane. They're going to shoot at us," he said calmly. "Look, they just shot out a flare. OK, we have MiGs around us," and then he let out a nervous "hee-hee."

"They're going to shoot at us?" said Sylvia, incredulous at the words and at Basulto's dispassionate remarks.

"They're going to shoot at us," Basulto said, matter-of-factly and unaffectedly, his voice a monotone. "Look, they just dropped a flare to mark us," as if he were pointing out a routine procedure or a change in the weather pattern. "OK, we've got MiGs around us," he said into the radio, now more sedate, addressing the other pilots.

The message would sound daunting to any passenger, yet Brothers to the Rescue had seen this scenario play out before, so none of the pilots lost composure. The three pilots flying that day concentrated on their roles as pilots-in-command, and their most important duty was to safeguard their passengers. Procedures were in place for different emergencies, and Brothers to the Rescue would follow those protocols.

The Cuban MiGs had a protocol to follow if an aircraft was in jurisdictional waters (which the Brothers planes were not) without previous authorization. International air-interception codes required an intercepting aircraft to make certain visual signals. First, it was required to make itself visible, as well as put out a call on the emergency radio frequency 121.5. Then the intercepting aircraft, the MiG in this case, would be required to rock its wings, first in a position in front and to the left of the aircraft invading the sovereign zone, and then in front and to the right of the aircraft. This signaled that the invading aircraft needed to leave the area it had no authority to be in. According to protocol, the intercepted aircraft would then respond by rocking its own wings in acknowledgment and would be required to follow the interceptors out of the area. Once out of the area, the interceptor would make an abrupt upward breakaway of ninety degrees or more as a sign indicating you are free to proceed. In other words, *get the hell out of here.* The last resort would be to circle the aircraft, lead it back to an airport, and force it to land.

The Cuban MiGs did none of these.

"Seagull Charlie, Seagull One," Basulto called Carlos.

"Seagull One," answered Carlos, "there's a MiG in the air. Bogey in the air. Where are you?"

"The MiG is to the north of us and they just dropped a flare, apparently to use as a reference," Basulto said. At that moment, Carlos was twenty-nine miles from Cuba and Mario was thirty-one miles away. They were both in international airspace. The only plane that, according to U.S. radar, dipped into Cuba's twelve-mile limit for a minute or two was Basulto's.

Mario broke in to their conversation. "Seagull Charlie, Seagull Mike . . . Charlie, Mike." Carlos didn't respond to Mario's call, so Mario radioed Basulto to see if he had heard from Carlos Costa. Mario gave Basulto his coordinates and Arnaldo read off their own coordinates. He then wrote the numbers on his hand: latitude 23'25", longitude 82'20".

"Negative," said Basulto, and he continued to call Carlos. "CHARLIE," he said a little louder this time, "Seagull One."

"Mike is with you," said Mario.

"SEAGULL CHARLIE, are you with us?" Basulto insisted. "SEAGULL CHARLIE, SEAGULL ONE . . . SEAGULL CHARLIE, SEAGULL ONE . . . SEAGULL CHARLIE . . ."

Koki Lares broke into the conversation from base, and Basulto told him he had lost radio contact with Carlos.

"CHARLIE, BASE . . . CHARLIE, BASE," called Koki. But Carlos did not answer.

"Do you want me to—well, never mind," said Mario, not finishing his question. At that point, radar graphs would show Mario breaking away from his grid and entering an orbiting pattern, apparently trying to find his friend Carlos.

"Did you see the smoke, the MiG?" Basulto asked Mario. Basulto started his trajectory north.

"I didn't see the MiG, but I saw smoke and a flare," said Mario. They continued to try to radio Carlos, but Seagull Charlie did not respond. Basulto and Mario talked back and forth about the smoke, about the MiG, and about the flare.

"OK, now I see another flare, another ball of smoke," said Basulto. "CHARLIE, is that you? SEAGULL MIKE, SEAGULL ONE . . . SEAGULL MIKE, SEAGULL ONE," repeated Basulto. "OK, Arnaldo, you try, try and get through to Carlitos." Arnaldo repeated his call to Carlos, and then to Mario, over and over again: "SEAGULL CHARLIE, SEAGULL MIKE . . ."

Something had gone terribly wrong, Basulto thought. It was one thing to lose radio contact with one plane, but to have lost contact with both of them? Perhaps on one plane the radio could have shorted, or there had been an emergency water landing or some other onboard crisis. But both planes? The absence of the customary chatter and banter among the pilots was unnerving.

It was too quiet.

"Let's go towards that boat," said Basulto, pointing to the *Majesty of the Seas* cruise ship below. His mental washing machine was on overdrive, but the momentary silence had allowed an awful thought to be thrown in. The nagging thought that Carlos and Mario could have been shot down was unacceptable, overwhelming, inconceivable. Carlos' last words to him had been: "where are you?" Mario's last communication: "I didn't see the MiG." Basulto could not see the MiGs right now either. His concern was that he could not hear his friends. "Where were they? Where were the MiGs?" At the same time, Basulto knew he had to do something. He flew over toward the *Majesty of the Seas*, reasoning that the MiGs would not shoot a heat-seeking missile at him if he was over a passenger vessel.

"We gotta get the hell out of here."

After attempting once again to call their friends, Arnaldo saw Basulto turn off his transponder.

"We're next," said Basulto.

The *Majesty of the Seas*, a Norwegian-flagged 268-meter passenger vessel, was returning to Miami after its weekly excursion to the Caribbean. It was twenty-five nautical miles off the coast of Havana when at approximately 3:23 p.m. First Officer Bjorn Johansen saw an explosion five hundred feet above the bridge of the cruise ship. He noticed the *Tri-Liner* fishing vessel maneuvering near some other wreckage. Since there was no distress call, the officer of the watch ignored it, thinking it was some kind of military exercise.

Crewmember Sean Patrick Gearhart was on the deck of the *Tri-Liner*, a white-hulled, forty-eight-foot fishing vessel. Things had been pretty quiet and the boat captain was napping. Looking out at the clear sky, Gearhart saw what looked to him like an American F-15 fighter jet flying overhead and another aircraft fuselage on fire. He ran inside and woke up the captain, and they both saw the aircraft tumbling into the water, about three hundred yards astern. As they neared the crash site, they noticed very little wreckage, only an oil slick and a 1½-foot-square orange floating device, with green dye or antifreeze bleeding into the water around it. They looked up again and just north of them they saw what they thought was another F-15 fire a missile at another small aircraft and a wide body of fire fell in the water. They noticed the *Majesty of the Seas* in the area. Thinking they were witnessing U.S. Navy maneuvers, they did not report anything.

In Miami, Ana Margarita Roque wanted to talk to her husband and she could not reach him on his cell phone. Ever since Roque had left at 3:00 a.m. on Friday, she had not spoken to him. She called René Guerra's home. Guerra was a friend of Basulto's and a volunteer pilot. Roque was Guerra's personal trainer, too. Marta Guerra, his wife, could hear the panic in Ana Margarita's voice and tried to reassure her. Later, Marta called Rita Basulto to see if she knew whether Roque was flying that day. Rita told Marta she did not know anything about Roque's whereabouts except that he had been to their house the previous day.

"Ana Margarita said that all his good clothes are gone, but he left his cell phone charger, wallet, and credit cards," Marta told Rita.

"Ese se fue para Cuba!" Rita heard René Guerra, Marta's husband, bellow over the phone, insisting that Roque had gone to Cuba. *Cuba? Roque?*

"I really don't know anything about it," said Rita.

On Jeffrey Houlihan's radar screen at March Air Force Base the three Brothers to the Rescue planes appeared as orange squares. The MiGs came up as white Xs. Houlihan had seen the white Xs heading toward the orange squares. At 3:15 p.m., he immediately called the control room at Tyndall Air Force Base in Panama City, Florida, which is responsible for the air defense of the southeastern United States. Houlihan called in what would later be documented as a 911 call.

"Do you see that primary aircraft, 500-knot primary?" asked Houlihan. Houlihan knew the standard operating procedure to deploy interceptors every time Cuban MiGs headed north toward the United States, crossing their own twelve-mile territorial limit. Houlihan nicknamed this designated area "the Southeast Air Defense Cone of Paranoia."

"Yes, we've been briefed," the on-duty officer told him.

"Well, it looks to me like a MiG-23 heading directly towards the United States," Houlihan responded.

"Yeah, we're taking care of it," they responded.

Six minutes later, Houlihan saw one of the orange squares disappear. This happened sometimes when the Brothers to the Rescue planes flew too low and radar could not pick them up so close to the water, but the square with the transponder code 1223, Carlos Costa's plane, never came back up. When seven minutes later another orange square disappeared, Jeffrey Houlihan knew something was terribly wrong.

"We're next." Sylvia Iriondo mentally repeated what she had heard Basulto say. "You've got to be kidding, they're going to *shoot* at us?" She took out a yellow pad from the pocket of the seat in front of her and wrote down what she had just witnessed: that at about 3:30 p.m. they had seen smoke to the north of their aircraft, which they thought was a flare. They lost contact with Carlos and Pablo. Three minutes later they saw a larger patch of smoke to the north and lost contact with Mario and Armando. Then she wrote down that Basulto had said there were MiGs in the air and that they were going to shoot at them.

More eerie than Basulto's words was the deafening silence. Gone was the chatter among the three pilots, the intermittent conversations overheard from other aircraft in the area, the scratchiness every time someone's voice fed into the speakers. It was the silence that made Sylvia believe they were dead. "This is what death is like: first the absence of noise, then the flashes of your life." Her mind scrolled through her life and she saw her children and her mother; she said good-bye to them all. She took out her round metal thumb rosary and started praying, and with her free hand found comfort in her husband's. She hadn't even finished a decade of Hail Marys before Basulto turned the transponders back on and she heard him calling "Mayday, Mayday," and she realized that they were not dead. Basulto had simply turned off their headsets.

Now the comforting noise was back, the desperate calls to the hangar, Basulto giving Koki instructions to call the families, the rhythmic crackle of air conversation. Miami Center was telling Basulto to land in Key West, and Basulto tried to relay the events that he had seen but still could not piece together—or accept. Sylvia, Andrés, and Arnaldo remained still and silent, in a deafening silence, the kind of silence that makes noise in your soul. Sylvia continued to pray.

Basulto looked back at the Iriondos. "Why are we going to land in Key West if our base is at Opa-locka?" he said, almost as if he were asking their permission to change routes. Then he swerved the plane north and raced for Opa-locka.

Out of nowhere in that pristine CAVU-blue sky there suddenly appeared one solitary cloud, the size of a small house, a safe haven for *Seagull One* on its race northeast. Basulto believed the MiGs would not be able to spot him on their radar, that they needed a visual lock-in, so he weaved around as much as possible, his puffy habitat of condensation and dust seemingly moving with him. He did not realize that the first set of MiGs was on their way back to Cuba, and a second set was chasing him. Radar times and taped communications would later corroborate that the Cuban MiGs had traveled well past the 24th parallel, to within three minutes of the coast of the United States.

Basulto called Rita at home and told her that something had happened and to meet him at Opa-locka. Even though she persisted in asking him what, he would not tell her. He called the base and explained to Koki that he had lost contact with the other two planes, and that Koki should phone all the family members and tell them to go to the hangar. Suspecting foul play, he also called his attorney, Sofía Powell-Cosío.

From the time the first set of MiGs was spotted to the moment the second set of MiGs began their retreat to Cuba, fifty-three minutes would elapse.

Seven minutes ticked down between the first shoot-down and the second. At Homestead Air Force Base in Florida, the F-15s had been waiting with their engines running since 3:00 p.m. They could have been off the ground in two minutes and in the area within ten. But for those fifty-three minutes, while Jeffrey Houlihan watched white Xs obliterate orange squares and heard Tyndall confirm that they were taking care of the situation, while the aerostat radar balloon tracked the chase over the Florida Straits, while NORAD, SEADS (Southeast Air Defense Sector), CARIBROC (Caribbean Regional Operations Center), and Miami Air Traffic Control sorted out conflicting information on the events transpiring, and while the United States taped the cockpit conversations of the Cuban MiG pilots, the orders to the men on the F-15s were clear: stand down battle stations.

28

Havana Air Traffic Control

A belief in the supernatural source of evil is not necessary;
men alone are quite capable of every wickedness.

Joseph Conrad

Across the globe, air traffic control is partitioned into numerous zones monitored by different countries. Each zone is then divided into "corridors" handled by specific air traffic controllers. Air traffic control rules around the world are fairly standard, and the main responsibility of the controller is to separate aircraft to prevent collisions. In most countries, the territorial limits are twelve miles off the coast.

In the United States, the FAA oversees air traffic control; in Cuba, the controllers are supervised by the military, usually ex-pilots, which would oftentimes prove very frustrating to the controllers. The Cuban controllers were trained in the computerized systems and they spoke English, whereas the military personnel frequently did not. The so-called supervisors normally wore their military uniforms. However, when visitors were expected, they wore the uniform of Cubana de Aviación, as if they were civilians employed by the government-owned and government-controlled airline.

Whenever Brothers to the Rescue, or any flight originating from Miami, crossed south of the 24th parallel, they entered the Havana Center sector. Havana ATC always received Brothers' flight plans ahead of time, so they knew when to expect them and how long to monitor them. Miami Center would call Havana Center and hand over the flight. Since Brothers usually flew their missions at or below five hundred feet under Visual Flight Rules (VFR), their flights would constantly appear and reappear on the air traffic control screens, dipping in and out of radar.

Flyovers of Havana are strictly prohibited. For any flight to cross over other parts of Cuban land, the airline needs previous government approval and a fee has to be paid in advance.

Everything that happens in ATC offices worldwide is taped: the audio between the controllers and the flights; the visual on the radar screens; the conversations between different aircraft. Havana ATC would later report that on February 24, 1996, the computers were down.

The day before the shoot-down, Ana Miriam Ávila was scheduled to work at Havana ATC, but her supervisor called her and said that Ana's team, which they termed a *brigada* (brigade), was being switched with two other controllers, named Ricardo and Ramón. Ana had worked at Havana ATC for six years. It was a high-pressure job and she was not upset to have the Saturday off. She did not give much thought to the switch until the following afternoon, when the events of February 24 began to unfold.

She believes it was either Ricardo or Ramón who informed the Brothers to the Rescue pilots that the area south of the 24th parallel was activated. The ATC operators at Havana Center had a list of set responses prepared specifically for the Brothers pilots. They were always to indicate that the area was activated, they were not to engage in cordiality or friendships, and they were not to discuss their personal lives. Ricardo and Ramón had consistently followed those rules.

What Ricardo and Ramón witnessed on Saturday, February 24, 1996, is not public knowledge. That day, they were in the role of what their fellow workers dubbed the "controllable controllers."

On the afternoon of February 24, 1996, two brothers, Francisco and Lorenzo Pérez Pérez, both lieutenant colonels, put on their jumpsuits and helmets and boarded a MiG-29. Major Emilio Palacios boarded a MiG-23. The two fighter jets departed from the San Antonio de los Baños Air Force Base, located about thirty miles southwest of Havana, and headed north.

At about three o'clock in the afternoon, the MiGs spotted the *Majesty of the Seas* cruise ship and the *Tri-Liner*. The gray flash that Basulto and his crew had seen across their windshield was on its way to Carlos Costa's blue-and-white Cessna.

At 3:18 p.m., the MiGs had the *Spirit of Miami* locked into their radar. Ground control wanted the registration number but all the Pérez Pérez brothers could confirm was that the plane was a blue-and-white Cessna 337.

At Havana ATC, Ricardo and Ramón would remain silent. They would not have been concerned if they knew the United States was taping their conversations, because they said next to nothing after the Brothers to the Rescue planes crossed the 24th parallel. Ground Control Chief Rubén Martínez Puente was guiding the MiGs toward the two Cessnas that were more than twenty miles away from the coast of Cuba.

"Authorize us, cojones! We have it," said Palacios on the MiG-23, excited that he had found the first plane. It was important for them to make a visual on the Cessnas. The missiles were heat-seeking, and they did not want them diverted to other aircraft, or worse, to the cruise ship below.

"Give me instructions," Pérez Pérez said. "Instructions!" he demanded. "Give us the order to destroy!"

At 3:20 p.m. the order was given to destroy the Brothers to the Rescue Cessna 337 piloted by Carlos Costa, whose last recorded words to Basulto, his general, were: "Where are you?" Onboard was aspiring pilot and ex-rafter Pablo Morales, looking for Cuban balseros just like him.

One minute later, the Pérez Pérez brothers pushed a button and a 9½-foot R-73 air-to-air missile carrying a 16.3 pound warhead hit the *Spirit of Miami* from behind. The rocket's length was one-third the overall length of the thirty-foot push-pull aircraft. Carlos and Pablo never knew what hit them.

In California, the orange square that Jeffrey Houlihan watched disappear from his screen contained two young men in their twenties with their whole lives ahead of them. Carlos had a mother whom he had not said good-bye to that morning, a mother who did not want him to fly, a mother whose nightmare had foretold his death. Carlos left behind his father, his sister, and her family. He had a good job at Miami International Airport and he was militant about his work with Brothers to the Rescue. Good-looking Carlos, the intense one. Carlitos was gone.

Pablo had a girlfriend he was ready to marry. He was learning to be a pilot so that he could save others as he himself had been saved. He had a mother and sister in Cuba that he wanted to bring to the United States. It would take his death to accomplish that.

"WE HIT THEM! WE—HIT—THEM—COJONES!" The Pérez Pérez brothers celebrated. "He's out of commission! This one won't fuck around anymore!"

"Congratulations!" said ground control in Havana, and told them to mark the spot.

"There's a boat nearby. The debris fell there," the MiG pilots informed the controller. "The boat is moving towards it." The *Majesty of the Seas* was steering toward the wreckage. From the top deck, tourist Barbara Lamonica took out her video camera and filmed the line of smoke on the horizon. Her video would be the only footage of the murders.

While the *Majesty of the Seas* and the *Tri-Liner* were heading toward the remains of the first plane shot down, Basulto noticed the smoke and the flare. So did Mario de la Peña. He did not realize it was Carlos' and Pablo's ashes. Mario started to ask Basulto if he should do something, but he never finished his question. He reaffirmed that he saw smoke and a flare. Those would be the last words the world would ever hear from Mario de la Peña. Radar would indicate that Mario started flying in circles, probably looking for his friend Carlitos. That's when the MiG-23 must have spotted him.

"We have another plane," said Major Palacios.

"Don't lose him," said the Pérez Pérez brothers. They must have noticed Mario was flying toward the area of the first shoot-down, so the brothers maneuvered toward the *Habana D.C.*

"We're on top of him, we're on top of him," they said excitedly. "Are we authorized to destroy?"

"Authorized," was the response from Havana.

"We copy, we copy, now let us work, let us work," said the MiG-29.

"Be calm," encouraged the MiG-23.

At 3:28 p.m., the Pérez Pérez brothers fired at Mario and Armando.

In California, Jeffrey Houlihan saw another orange square disappear. That little mark on his screen was Vietnam veteran Armando Alejandre Jr., the one-man human-rights activist who aspired to be the Cuban Hemingway. Armando had recently started law school. He left behind a daughter in college and his wife of twenty-two years, whom he had not kissed good-bye that morning because he was too excited about flying with Brothers to the Rescue. He would never see his parents again or his adoring sisters. His last gesture to his good friend Sylvia Iriondo was to flash the V for victory sign.

Another section of that orange square represented the youngest pilot to die that day, twenty-four-year-old Mario de la Peña, whose finger-snapping had forewarned his parents that he would be flying that day. Mario had stayed in Miami to start his internship with American Airlines because he wanted to remain close to his parents and his younger brother, as well as his other brothers at Brothers to the Rescue. Mario, who never stopped asking questions, never received an answer to the last question of his life: where was Carlos? Mario was gone from Houlihan's radar screen, the same Mario who, with heartfelt sincerity, had affirmed over the radio waves that he would forgive the pilot who had just blown him to bits.

"DESTROYED! We destroyed the other one! Patria o muerte, cojones!" (Fatherland or Death!) The Pérez Pérez brothers celebrated once more, their voices escalating to a raspy breathiness.

After Mario and Armando were shot down, the *Tri-Liner* fishing boat moved toward their wreckage and found nothing but an orange float and a green slick.

Ground control in Cuba was watching the fishing boat's movements. "Be careful," warned ground control. "There's a fishing boat there."

Before the jubilant crews of the MiG-23 and MiG-29 returned to Cuba, another set of MiGs took off from San Antonio de los Baños. They knew there was another plane out there, and they had to finish the job. They passed over the *Majesty of the Seas* and the *Tri-Liner*. By 3:34 p.m., they had a visual on *Seagull One*, carrying Basulto, Arnaldo, and the Iriondos.

"I think it's on my right. No it's five degrees off to my right. I'm on top of it. No I can't see it," the pilot said, finding and then losing Basulto, who at this point had found the safe haven of a single cloud.

"Can you identify it?" asked ground control.

"It's a Cessna 337, light blue," said the pilot. "Now I lost it, I passed it."

"It's at twelve o'clock, give me the registration," demanded ground control at San Antonio de los Baños.

"No, I lost it again," said the MiG.

Basulto would later say that he thought the MiG pilot made a conscious choice not to fire at him, that perhaps some goodness deep inside him kept him from discharging the missile. Another explanation could be that the MiG had already crossed the 24th parallel and did not want to risk going farther north, fearing the interceptors that had been out that very morning. Maybe it was the cloud.

Or God.

The chase went on until 3:53 p.m., when new orders came in from the ground to the Cuban pilots. "You're too high up. Abort." What ground control meant by "high up" would be debated for years. The highest Basulto flew that day was not quite six thousand feet, so they could not have been referring to altitude if they had a visual on him. Basulto and others would argue that too high up meant too far north of the 24th parallel.

For fifty-three minutes on February 24, 1996, two different sets of Cuban MiGs chased three Brothers to the Rescue planes in international airspace. Two were shot down, killing four young men. For fifty-three minutes the F-15s remained on battle stations in Homestead Air Force Base, the pilots eager to take action with a five-minute response time. Had they been released as soon as the Cuban MiGs crossed the 24th parallel, all three planes would have survived. Takeoff after the first shoot-down would probably have saved Mario and Armando. Had they been authorized after the first two shoot-downs, the MiGs chasing Basulto might have returned to Cuba immediately. For fifty-three minutes, U.S. Customs and Air Force radars watched orange squares disappear from their radar screens, replaced by white Xs. A 911 call was made and "handled." For fifty-three minutes, Tyndall Air Force Base in Florida and March in California witnessed the assassination of three American citizens and one legal resident.

Tape recordings would later confirm that at the precise moment when Basulto decided to forgo the orders to land in Key West and take a sharp right turn and head toward Opa-locka, he was thirty miles southwest of Key West. The Cuban MiGs were within three minutes of the coast of the United States of America.

29

Brothers Down

*The only mistake the Cuban government made February 24
was that they missed one plane.*

Letter to the editor, *Florida Keys Keynoter*, March 13, 1996

"Doctor, State Security is here to get you," a fellow prisoner told Leonel Morejón Almagro, leader of the Cuban Council. Morejón remembers being led out of the prison by soldiers carrying AK-47s into a waiting van loaded with attack dogs. Other militia covered the roofs of the prison, machine guns cocked. Rumors that the Americans were coming to attack Cuba roared down the halls of Valle Grande Prison in Havana. American planes had been shot down, and the prison was in an uproar. Morejón did not yet know the planes belonged to Brothers to the Rescue, but he did know why they had been shot down: because of the Cuban Council.

Basulto kept flying to his home base at Opa-locka. He planned to go directly to the hangar, but Air Traffic Control Specialist María Ramírez radioed him, demanding he land and present himself immediately to the U.S. Customs trailer, which was located adjacent to the Brothers to the Rescue hangar.

"We did not do any foreign stoppage," Basulto told her.

"You are to report to the Customs trailer, period."

It didn't sound good to Basulto, but he was going to follow instructions and go to Customs. His mind was reeling with what had happened a little more than an hour before. He mentally replayed the sighting of the MiGs, the cruise ship below, the flares, the smoke, and finally, the silence. The silence from Seagull Charlie and Seagull Mike could only mean one unfathomable thing: Cuba had actually shot down the two planes and his friends were dead. *No, it couldn't be.*

After Basulto made his calls from *Seagull One*, Arnaldo Iglesias called his wife, Mirta. She asked him what he was doing.

"I'm flying," he said, trying to keep his voice calm.

"Do you know what time it is?" she asked, upset. She reminded Arnaldo of the commitment they had that evening, and asked if he had forgotten about it. "Are you going to be home on time? You always do the same thing!"

"Mirta," he said quietly. "Two of our planes were shot down."

When Guille Lares called Ana Margarita Roque so that she could tell her husband to come down to the hangar, she remembers Guille's voice shaking with rage as he explained the cold-blooded murder that had just taken place over the Florida Straits. Ana Margarita told Guille that she had not heard from J. P. since early Friday morning. She recounted to Guille the little she knew about Roque's boat trip.

For Ana Margarita, the next two days would be filled with an incessant rush of callers asking for Roque. "No, he wasn't on the planes," she told concerned friends and family. "No, thank God, no." What she could not confess to the worried callers were her rising fears: that he had disappeared, or worse, that he had returned to Cuba.

Maggie Schuss was having trouble reaching Carlos Costa's parents, so she drove to their home. When they did not answer the door, she asked their neighbors please to tell them to go immediately to the hangar. As the news and rumors spread across Miami that Saturday afternoon, hundreds worked their way over to the hangar at Opa locka.

Roberto Rodríguez Tejera was the first person to arrive, having been summoned by Basulto from *Seagull One*. Rodríguez Tejera worked for La Cubanísima radio station, and had been one of the few friends to encourage and support Basulto in the nonviolence movement. On January 13, 1996, he had filmed Carlos Costa's impassioned farewell to his parents. It would be the last time he saw Carlos.

A stunned Koki Lares was waiting for Rodríguez Tejera at the hangar. Rita Basulto arrived, too, and minutes later, a despondent Billy Schuss. With Billy's arrival, the floodgates of people and media and government officials descended on the Brothers to the Rescue hangar.

Guille and Tito Fufú stood guard at the door of the hangar. Every time the door swung open to let in another pilot, volunteer, family member, or journalist, the cacophony of shouts from outside reverberated against the aluminum walls of the hangar: "Down with Fidel Castro! Murderer! Kill Castro!" Then the door would close on the ten thousand square feet of muffled sobs and mournful questions.

Before each member of the press or television corps came in, they automatically placed their station's microphone on the conference table that was set up just outside the hangar, where an agitated crowd was assembling on the other side of the chain-link fence.

Mayte Greco rushed in with Carolyn Russo, the photographer, who had still been interviewing her on Saturday afternoon when the call came in. Russo would later write that the hangar seemed strangely empty to her on Saturday night, even though it was full of people. It was then she realized that the blue-and-white Cessna she had photographed Mayte in was missing. It had been shot down.

Lined up against one wall of the hangar were dozens of rafts, boats, and planks of wood that the balseros had used as transportation to navigate the Florida Straits. When Mario de la Peña's parents walked in, they remember feeling a little disoriented as to whom to approach or what to ask. Basulto had not arrived, so they sat on one of the rafts and bowed their heads, perhaps in prayer, or agony, or mourning.

Pablo Morales' girlfriend was there, too. Maggie Schuss remembers her petite frame shaking uncontrollably.

René González, the Cuban defector, arrived at the mob-like scene and approached Billy. Later, no one remembered calling him. "Did you hear?" he asked Billy, who was flanked by reporters and cameras. "Roque's been gone since yesterday."

"No, I didn't know," said Billy, not giving a second thought to González's statement, and he quickly turned away to tackle yet another unanswerable question.

When Basulto's attorney Sofía Powell-Cosío arrived with Polo Núñez, U.S. Customs still had Basulto, Arnaldo Iglesias, and the Iriondos detained. They would not let Sofía and Polo inside.

"My name is Sofía Powell-Cosío and I am Basulto's counsel and I want access to my client," she said in an even, precise tone.

"I'm sorry, ma'am, but my instructions are not to let anyone inside," the officer said, seeming almost irritated by her request.

"Why?" asked Sofía.

"He's being debriefed right now, ma'am, and so—"

"Well, if he's being debriefed, and I'm his counsel, all the more reason to let me in," insisted Sofía. "He has called me and asked for me to be here. Everyone is entitled to representation."

Sofía felt the officer gaze down at her. Polo Núñez stood beside her quietly, knowing Cagafuego certainly had something up her sleeve.

"I can't let you in, ma'am. We're very sorry."

"Mr. Basulto is my client; he has made it known to you that I was on the way to see him. He is expecting me, and I demand to see my client." Sofía had a very exacting way of expressing herself in direct, complete sentences, never leaving a doubt as to precisely what she wanted to get across.

"We can't let you in," he said. He seemed a little tired of the verbal ping-pong at this point.

Sofía looked across the tarmac toward the hangar. Dozens of local and national radio, television, and newspaper journalists were there; every member of the press was armed with a tape recorder, a notepad, and a camera. And it seemed like every Cuban American exile was holding a placard with a death threat toward Fidel Castro.

"OK," said Sofía, looking back at him, and perhaps for a split second the officer may have been relieved. "Look over there," she said, pointing to the mob. "This is your choice."

Sofía got his attention once again.

"You can either let me in, or—you see that zoo over there? I'm going to go over there and tell all those press people and all those television stations—who by the way, are *dying* for a juicy story which no one has any details on right now—I will go over there and tell them I'm here. I'll tell every one of them that I am Mr. Basulto's attorney, that I'm knocking on the door to see my client, and that *you* won't let me in."

She paused to make sure the message had sunk in.

"I'll be right back." Sofía started walking toward the mob.

"No, no, no," he said. "You can come in."

Had Sofía carried out her threat and walked toward the mob, she might have seen in the dimming evening light what appeared to be a lone figure on the tarmac, just yards away from the hangar. It was really two people: Maggie and Billy Schuss, holding on to each other in a tight embrace, their tears spilling, taking a moment alone as they waited for Basulto.

Maggie would remember over and over again her words to Pablo Morales at the Winn Dixie supermarket almost four years ago: "well, why don't you go and help?" He had listened to her and it had cost him his life.

Inside the Coast Guard trailer, more men in suits were fighting with Basulto over the cockpit tape he had from the flight aboard *Seagull One*. Basulto routinely taped his own recordings by running a wire from the earphone of his headset into the tape recorder, which he placed in one of the pockets of his utility vest. Whenever a rafter was found, Basulto would hold the tape recorder next to the walkie-talkie to record the names of the balseros. That was more efficient than having to write everything down.

But on this tape were his recorded conversations with Mario and Carlos, as well as the exchange with Havana Center Air Traffic Control. The officials were trying to persuade him to give it up with a promise that they would make him a copy.

"No, I'll make a copy for *you*," Basulto told Mike Molinari. Right now, the tape was all he had. Basulto did not trust them, afraid they would alter the recording. He managed a crooked smile when Sofía walked in with Polo.

"That's OK, we'll take care of it," Molinari offered, a little edgier this time, and he reached out to take the tiny cassette from Basulto. Basulto was quicker. The voices escalated as Sofía walked over and stood next to her client.

"What's going on, José?" she asked him directly, ignoring the others. She was Sofía the mother, acting as if she were separating squabbling siblings who were blaming each other for having started it. Basulto explained quickly that the FBI wanted the original tape from the recorder, that he had offered to make them a copy, right here, right now, but the FBI didn't have recording equipment there. They wanted him to give up the tape, and he didn't want to give it to them. As he spoke, the FBI agents kept interjecting on Basulto's explanations.

"What's the matter?" asked another officer. "Don't you trust the U.S. government?"

Basulto jerked his head and faced the man squarely. "No, sir, I don't."

"José, just give me the tape," Sofía said, a little exasperated with the bickering men. He quickly gave her the tape.

Sofía looked at the uniformed and suited men around her: the FBI and CIA agents, the Customs officers, and the police. "You want this tape?" she said. "You can come and get it."

She cupped the cassette inside the palm of her hand, then put it inside her shirt, tucking it safely inside her bra. "But I strongly suggest you don't do that."

Sixty miles north of Opa-locka, Basulto's childhood friend Alfredo Sánchez was at a wedding reception when his grandson's babysitter called him about the Brothers to the Rescue tragedy. When the babysitter's call came in, and Alfredo informed his wife, Ritín, she gasped in horror.

"I know, I know," was all Alfredo could tell her. He walked home, changed out of his suit, drove over to the airport in Lantana, and boarded his plane. As soon as he took off, he realized he had not removed his new contact lenses, which were burning his eyes. But the stinging did not redirect what was going on in his mind: "I was supposed to have flown today." Less than twenty-four hours ago, Carlos Costa had called him, counting on him, since Alfredo always flew on Saturdays. But Ritín had intercepted the phone call and told Carlos that they could not miss today's wedding, since it was their daughter's best friend.

When Alfredo arrived in Opa-locka, there were press people everywhere, and family and friends. He noticed Mario de la Peña's parents, Miriam and Mario, sitting off to the side on top of a raft, in a state of complete bewilderment. Mirta and Osvaldo Costa, Carlos' parents, were there, too, badly shaken. A family member had given Mirta a sedative to calm her nerves. Armando Alejandre Jr.'s parents soon arrived, as did Armando's sister, Cristina. Brothers' volunteers were congested in the huge hangar and overflowing outside of it. Police finally roped off the area, pushing back the crowd who had trespassed beyond the chain-link fence, holding signs threatening death to Fidel Castro.

Word reached the mourners inside the hangar that Alfredo had just arrived, and friends in the crowd turned toward the door, hoping he could provide an answer to the confusion that was all around them. As soon as he walked inside, Alfredo was blinded by the lights. He shielded his eyes, wishing once again that he had had time to remove his new contact lenses. It was then that he heard a spine-tingling shriek from Mirta Costa, who was walking toward him.

"Alfredo, oh my God, Alfredo, did you find him, did you find him? Please, please, tell me that you found him!" Mirta Costa assumed that Alfredo had come from a search-and-rescue effort. She knew how close Alfredo and Carlos were, she knew Alfredo was supposed to have flown today. "Please, God, tell me you found Carlitos!"

Alfredo saw her through the parting crowd and squeezed the corners of his eyes, his contacts burning.

"Oh my God, oh my God, oh my God, noooooo!" Mirta screamed. She must have assumed that Alfredo dabbing his eyes was a sign that her only son was gone. Alfredo and the crowd watched her as she walked over to one of the planes and started pummeling it with her fist.

Alfredo was distraught over the death of his young friends and felt a twinge of survivor's guilt. At the same time, he felt a strange assurance that the murder of these four would bring about the end of Fidel Castro. There would be war. The Americans would go in and finish what they started in 1961. They would never allow four innocent, unarmed civilians to be shot out of the sky in international waters. Just like the prisoners at Villa Grande in Havana, Alfredo believed retaliation was a sure thing.

At last Basulto and the others were allowed to go to the hangar, where microphones had been readied for him to explain to the community and to the world what he did not have words to explain. When he got there, he saw Billy. Before he approached the waiting microphones, he and Billy and the family members took a moment to huddle in a corner of the hangar, to weep, to embrace.

"They shot them down, they shot them down . . . I saw MiGs . . . we lost communication . . . then it was quiet." Basulto extracted himself from the group, then trod over to the cameras, his hair disheveled, his face marked with streams of tears, his body that of a much older man than he had been that morning.

Rita was there along with Basulto's youngest son, Albert. Albert would be his father's bodyguard for the next several days, never leaving his side. Basulto's younger brother, Al, also came to his aid by being his personal driver. He would chauffeur his older brother to a myriad of meetings, press conferences, and services that awaited.

While Basulto and Sylvia Iriondo dealt with the press, Arnaldo Iglesias put on his sunglasses and disappeared into the background. He was still shaken up, in disbelief. The only thing he was blinking back today was tears. When the cameras moved in toward Arnaldo, he stepped back. He did not want to speak; he did not have any answers. Later he would wonder about all the survivors, the pilots that were supposed to have flown that day and did not. What would have been the U.S. response if one of the shot-down pilots had been named McNaughton? If an American named Bert McNaughton had been in danger, rather than Americans named Carlos Costa and Mario de la Peña, would the F-15s have been released from their battle stations?

Would an American Vietnam veteran with a more Anglo surname than Alejandre have encouraged the Clinton administration to retaliate?

Arnaldo was torn by the anguish of the grieving mothers. Mirta Costa would soon remind him: "I told you I didn't want any heroes."

Sylvia Iriondo would handle the press. She was an expert, well versed, and striking in appearance. Sylvia was in her early fifties, but her hair was completely white, kept short in a layered youthful style, and she had piercing blue eyes. She was very well respected in the Miami community as the president of Mothers Against Repression and for her involvement in Cuban issues from the time she was exiled to the United States at fifteen years of age. Sylvia had always been comfortable with the cameras, so she forced herself to regain composure immediately.

"What message has Fidel Castro given the world today?" she was asked. She replied that it was the message Castro was giving his own citizens that was the most powerful—and the most threatening. Sylvia spoke directly and deliberately into the cameras, something she was accustomed to doing.

"If I, Fidel Castro, can destroy, in plain light of day, unarmed planes with *American citizens* onboard, on a humanitarian mission in international waters; if I can kill them with premeditation and in cold blood," Sylvia paused for emphasis, "*what can I not do to you?*"

It was almost midnight in France when Virginie Buchete Puperoux, La Francesa, saw the news on television. She was overseas visiting her family. She sat there stunned, soaking in the gravity of the news report. Her father phoned her and made her promise never again to fly with Brothers to the Rescue.

Before closing up the hangar that evening, Maggie Schuss had Pablo Morales' Jeep driven inside the hangar for safekeeping. As they were locking the doors, an employee from Miami International Airport approached Maggie and Billy. "Here," he said, handing an open box to Maggie. "It's from Carlos' desk drawer." Maggie looked inside and saw on the top a little figure of a plane, a toy actually. She thought it was strange that someone from Carlos Costa's office would have emptied out his drawer. But stranger things had happened that day.

"Give it to the parents," Billy told her, but Maggie felt that now was not the right time. They put the box in the trunk of their car and forgot about it for several days. They never got the name of the man who brought it.

Earlier in the afternoon, before Basulto had touched down in Opa-locka, news reports in Costa Rica announced the shoot-down of the planes *over Cuban waters*. Miami-Dade Commissioner Pedro Reboredo was visiting there with his wife. Reboredo remembers hearing the news announcement between three o'clock and three-thirty in the afternoon, just minutes after Mario de la Peña and Pablo Morales were murdered. The Costa Rican news added that a survivor had been found.

Cuban news reports would later release his name: Juan Pablo Roque.

30

Survivors

Let your tears come.
Let them water your soul.
Eileen Mayhew

Survivor's guilt was first diagnosed in the 1960s when several therapists recognized similar conditions among Holocaust survivors. Feelings of not having done enough to save those who had died, or of being unworthy of survival, resulted in a deep sense of guilt. José Basulto dispelled concerns about any survivor guilt he may have had. "God chose the one to live who could point to the truth of what happened here," he said.

Early in the morning of the shoot-down, observer Louis Cruz was already dressed in his Brothers to the Rescue T-shirt, shorts, and sneakers, ready to walk out of his house to go meet the pilots at the hangar. He turned on his ham radio at home, and heard his friends Carlos Costa, Tito Fufú, and some other guys chatting. He identified himself on the radio, but no one copied him. Carlos had not called him to fly today, but since Louis usually flew on Saturdays, he decided to go see if he was needed.

But the grass stopped him. When Louis opened his front door, it was as if every blade were standing at attention crying out to him: "cut me." Louis also thought of the cries he would get from his wife if he did not mow the lawn. He stayed home and cut the grass. After he finished, his neighbor invited him out on his new boat, so Louis Cruz would spend the afternoon on the water. He was still enjoying his neighbor's boat when his beeper went off, with a call from the hangar. "Come in *now*," Koki had said. "We're missing two planes."

Luis Martínez, Batman, had told Carlos that he could fly on Saturday, but Friday night his boss changed his schedule and called him in to work. Batman spent a very boring Saturday morning at work. By eleven, no one had come in to buy asphalt, so he finally persuaded his boss to let him go. He drove to the hangar, hoping to catch the guys on their return from their scheduled early-morning mission.

Batman was two blocks away from the hangar, at the four-way stop that leads to the Opa-locka Airport, when he changed his mind. Carlos Costa and several friends were having a barbecue at Batman's house that evening, and he was in charge of buying the meat. "They're probably not back yet," he thought, "let me go buy the meat for the party." It was twelve-thirty when Batman made that decision and pulled a U-turn at the four-way stop. At that moment, the eight people going out on the mission were arguing about who was flying with whom. Batman was about one hundred yards away from them. He would have ended up on Carlos' plane.

At five-thirty on Saturday afternoon, Batman was back at the same four-way stop, having been summoned to the hangar. There would be no U-turn this time.

He had his ham radio turned on in the car, and he remembers hearing Carlos Costa's voice. "Don't worry, Batman, we'll see each other at the hangar."

He was so relieved to hear his friend's voice! Elated! When he walked into the hangar and saw the despair and agony on Mirta Costa's face, he rushed to comfort her. "Don't worry," he told her. "I just spoke to him on the radio. He's fine."

However, Carlos Costa's mother was not fine, and whether it was the agony or the tranquilizers, she never remembered Batman telling her this. But later, Luis Martínez felt very guilty, not from survivor's guilt, but about having given a mother hope. "I heard his voice," he would recount later with unwavering certainty, at the same time acknowledging that it happened three hours after the shoot-down. "I heard his voice."

The twenty-one-year-old Batman outlived his friend Carlos by only twelve years. He was diagnosed with leukemia in 2007 and died the following year, two days before the twelfth anniversary of the Brothers to the Rescue shoot-down, leaving behind his wife, his stepson, and his three-year-old little daughter.

Billy Schuss had not flown that day because it was the final day of the harvest at Talisman Sugar Corporation, where he worked. It was considered the most important day of *la zafra* (the harvest) because it would determine the quantity of that year's crops.

There had been another kind of harvest over the Florida Straits that day, a gleaning of the best Brothers to the Rescue had to offer. In a twisted turn of events the grim reaper was Fidel Castro, his scythe an R-73 missile, and his yield the cold-blooded murder of the first fruits of Brothers: Armando, Carlos, Mario, and Pablo. Curiously, that day all the people flying had been Cuban-born or of Cuban ancestry, something that rarely happened in an organization comprised of nineteen nationalities.

Leonel Morejón Almagro, who would remain in a Cuban prison for fifteen months, noted the cross-section of Cuban men that were murdered that day. Armando had been born in Cuba and had come to the United States at ten years old, yet he had expressed his love of his adopted country from his first moments of exile. He was a one-man Cuban human-rights activist, yet he was also a faithful and proud American Vietnam veteran, a Cuban who grew up in America. Carlos and Mario were American-born of Cuban descent. Neither family had ever been political about Cuba. Yet something in Carlos' and Mario's Cuban hearts had pulled them toward alleviating the suffering of a people whose language they struggled with, even while they lived as all-American boys. They were the true Cuban Americans, their "American side helping out the Cuban side," as Mario would say. Pablo was a product of the revolution, Castro's "new man," yet even new men cannot bear living without freedom. Pablo left his country of birth and risked his life on the Florida Straits to be free. As a free man, his own life was taken away as he worked to help the new men still struggling in Cuba.

In the hope of finding survivors, the U.S. Coast Guard launched a search-and-rescue effort, using Key West as a refueling station. A C-130 plane covered more than 330 square miles of the Florida Straits, the pilots wearing their night vision goggles throughout Saturday evening. The F-15s from Homestead were not to be detained on battle stations should anything come up. The Coast Guard cutters *Nantucket* and *Paw Paw* skimmed over the ocean, and an H-65 Dolphin Helo helicopter buzzed close to the waters, scrutinizing any floating debris. They would work tirelessly until Sunday night.

They would find nothing but two oil slicks.

Basulto gave another press conference at the hangar on Sunday. He and the other pilots and volunteers wore their Brothers to the Rescue polo shirts with a black tape across the organization's insignia. He urged the people of Cuba to respond, to take action, to change from within.

The only ones that took action in Cuba were the military, who arrested more dissidents. The Cuban government stubbornly maintained that all three aircraft had violated their sovereignty and that the two planes were shot down in Cuban waters.

The same morning, a press briefing by Secretary of State Warren Christopher revealed to the world that Retired Admiral Eugene Carroll and other Washington officials had met in Havana with Cuban military authorities from February 5 to 9, just weeks before the shoot-down. At that time they had been pointedly asked what the U.S. reaction would be if the Cubans authorized a shoot-down of the Brothers planes.

CNN interviewed Carroll. He looked squarely into the camera and acknowledged that he had told the pertinent authorities in Washington about Cuba's threat of a shoot-down. He would suffer no character assassinations.

"But what about the position that they were unarmed civilian planes?" asked anchorwoman Catherine Callaway.

"I'll give you an analogy," said Carroll. "Suppose we had planes flying over San Diego from Mexico, dropping leaflets and inciting Governor Wilson (the governor at that time). How long would we tolerate these overflights after we had warned them against it?"

Apparently Carroll was under the assumption, as was much of the world, that the two leaflet drops in January 1996 involved overflights of Cuban airspace. He also must have been under the impression that Armando, Carlos, Mario, and Pablo were in Cuban jurisdictional waters when they were shot down, when in fact, Carlos Costa was twenty-one miles, and Mario de la Peña was twenty-two miles, away from Cuba's coast. Perhaps during all his meetings in Havana, Carroll had come to accept what the Cuban military had told him: that Brothers to the Rescue were flying over Havana and it had to stop. The only times Brothers to the Rescue had flown over Cuba were when Basulto rounded the Punta de Maisí on the trip to Guantánamo in November 1994, and on July 13, 1995, when he had flown thirteen minutes over Havana.

Maybe the analogy of Mexican civilian planes dropping leaflets over San Diego and getting blown out of the sky by the U.S. Air Force was not such a good comparison. The United States would never shoot down unarmed civilian planes.

The shoot-down coverage in Cuba was a little different, although just as confusing. Cuban officials had lined up a story they were not able to use: that all three planes were shot down and Juan Pablo Roque was the lone survivor. The hole in that story was that *Seagull One* and her occupants were alive and Basulto's cockpit audio recording was intact.

What had mysteriously been erased were all the recordings and radar information at Havana Center Air Traffic Control. Ricardo and Ramón, working Sector C, the corridor where the shoot-down took place, blamed the computer equipment.

But there was another tape recording, also intact, with the recorded voices of the Cuban MiG pilots chasing the two planes, shooting them down with exclamations of glee and profanity. It was brought to light at a special meeting of the UN Security Council held Sunday night, headed by UN Ambassador Madeleine Albright.

"Cojones!" the pilots screamed when Carlos and Pablo were pulverized. "Fatherland or Death!" they shrieked when Mario and Armando were blown to bits. The UN Security Council listened to the U.S. tape recording and heard the sinister satisfaction in the voices of the Pérez Pérez brothers, noting the profound absence of humanity in their celebrations. Madame Albright also heard the second set of MiG pilots and the electrifying chase after *Seagull One*. The inhuman, raw, evil cries of euphoria from the Pérez Pérez brothers repulsed the free nations of the world.

"Frankly, this is not cojones," Ambassador Albright said to the world on Monday morning. "This is cowardice."

Cuba's Minister of Foreign Affairs Roberto Robaina had a rebuttal to Albright's comment. "On her first point, we've always had more than enough," he said, "and as to cowardice, we have had no experience."

Albright ordered the Council of the International Civil Aviation Organization (ICAO) to investigate the shoot-down, but months would pass before Basulto and the rest of the world heard those voices. The first traitor they heard from was Juan Pablo Roque.

The Cuban delegation that was supposedly in the Bahamas on Saturday, the same delegation that prevented Brothers from visiting the detainees there, was none other than Juan Pablo Roque, who had been ex-filtrated from the United States by the Cuban government the Friday before the shoot-down. But Roque was not only spying on Brothers for the Cuban government, he was also spying on them for the FBI.

Footage showed him descending the steps of a Cubana de Aviación aircraft, much the same way a dignitary or head of state would be filmed upon arrival. He was still wearing his Rolex and his wedding band.

Sunday night Roque was interviewed by reporter Fabiola López Roque (no relation) on Cuban television. Reverse-defection seemed to have affected his style. He was wearing a frumpy blue-and-white checked long-sleeved shirt and dark gray pants. His wedding band was gone.

His initial story was that he regretted leaving the military and escaping Cuba through Guantánamo. But if that were true, would not the Cuban Armed Forces have arrested him at the airport? He later told the Cuban press about his work with the FBI and that Brothers had plans to introduce weapons into Cuba to attack various targets. He never expanded on what those weapons were, where they were stashed, and which targets were under scrutiny.

Roque also emphasized that the U.S. government knew about the shoot-down, that they had told him personally.

"The FBI, what is it? Is it a travel agency?" he responded sarcastically to the reporter. "It is the government. FBI Agent Oscar Montoto told me on February 21: 'Don't go on that mission because they're gonna knock you out of the sky.' The U.S. government knew they were going to be shot down," Roque claimed.

The FBI had paid Roque $6,720.42 for his misinformation on Brothers to the Rescue. They still owed him $1,500.00, but Special Agent Paul Philip, in charge of the Miami office, said they would not send him his final wages.

Rumors would abound for years about just how well Roque survived in Cuba after the shoot-down. Some claimed he was under house arrest. Other rumors alleged he was in a wheelchair after a botched attempt on his life. One newspaper photo showed him standing in a long line, waiting to get inside a Havana dollar store (a store where items not normally available in Cuba could be purchased with U.S. dollars, not an American-type dollar store).

Reporters plied Roque with questions about his abandoned wife in Miami, but he refused to talk about her. He was asked what he missed most about the United States.

"My Jeep Cherokee," he replied.

On Monday morning after the shoot-down, the FBI visited Ana Margarita Roque and roped off her home. She called Rita Basulto in hysterics.

"Rita, he used me, he used me! What am I going to do? I loved him." Ana Margarita would lose her job and suffer from depression after her husband's betrayal. Her children would miss J. P. terribly, the stepfather they loved so much. She was gawked at all over Miami, referred to as "the spy's wife."

Later, Ana Margarita would sue the Cuban government for sexual battery. She would claim that all sexual relations between her and Roque, posing as her husband while he was a spy for the Cuban government and an informant for the FBI, had been tantamount to rape. She received a final judgment of annulment on October 15, 1996. She was given title to the Jeep Cherokee.

The entire world responded with outrage. The European Union, so many journalists from which had flown with Brothers, strongly condemned the shoot-down. Press conferences were held almost daily and statements were issued as more information was disclosed. Some media commentators looked for a reason to blame Brothers to the Rescue.

"The issue isn't whether they were in Cuban territorial waters or not. You cannot shoot down unarmed civilian aircraft, period," said Richard Nuccio, the presidential advisor on Cuba, masking his own survivor's guilt. Nuccio's premonition the night before the shoot-down had materialized. He defended Brothers' right to be where they were, but several years later, Nuccio would lay part of the blame on José Basulto.

In Washington, President Clinton declared a national emergency and authorized the secretary of transportation to make and issue regulations to prevent unauthorized U.S. vessels from entering Cuban territorial waters. No regulations were issued for Cubans entering the territorial waters of the United States.

At a White House press briefing two days after the shoot-down, White House Press Secretary Mike McCurry announced that "the measures the president has defined will make Cuba pay the price, and more importantly, make Cuba adhere to international norms of civilized behavior."

When the president addressed the nation, he said that what had happened was "wrong and the United States will not tolerate it." He requested that Congress suspend all charter air travel from the United States to Cuba, he implemented further travel restrictions on visits by Cuban officials to the United States (not on visits from the United States to Cuba), he asked Radio Martí to expand its reach, and he solicited Congress to take money from Cuba's frozen assets in order to compensate the families of the four deceased men.

"They're going to turn the families against you," Janet Ray Weininger told Basulto. She believed that by throwing money at the situation, the government was going to twist things around and make him the culprit.

Basulto countered that, on the contrary, all that had happened would make them stronger. He told his good friend Lorenzo De Toro of *IDEAL* magazine, "God wanted me to survive this and I will dedicate my life to find out why."

A few weeks later, a select group of journalists for *Time* magazine interviewed Fidel Castro. Reginald K. I. Brach Jr., Joelle Attinger, and Cathy Booth titled their article, "Fidel's Defense." They asked him if he had ever thought of calling President Clinton. The Maximum Leader was stunned and seemed to be at a loss for words in an unaccustomed pause.

"I have never talked to any president of the United States. The exiles would murder Clinton if they found out he was talking to me."

The National Union Fire Insurance Company of Pittsburgh, Pennsylvania, never paid the insurance compensation for the shot-down planes. They claimed that there was a provision for an "act of war—whether a war is declared or not."

31

Memorial

If you devote your life to seeking revenge, first dig two graves.
Confucius

Carnaval—the Latin American version of Mardi Gras—was cancelled.
"You can't party while in mourning," said Leslie Pantín, organizer of the
yearly event that since 1978 had included parties, street fairs, and an eight-
kilometer run on Calle Ocho—Eighth Street—in Little Havana. In 1988, a
119,986-person conga line made it into the Guinness Book of World Records. The festival raised thousands each year for the Kiwanis Club scholar-
ship program.

But this year, there would be no conga lines or dominoes tournaments.
It was a time for mourning and remembrance. And for calming down the
Cuban Americans.

The US government was well aware that scattered throughout Miami
were mini-arsenals in the garages and spare bedrooms of well-to-do and not
so well-to-do Cuban exiles. Some Americans feared that the exiles would
attack Cuba. Fidel Castro had deliberately shot out of the sky three unarmed
American citizens and one legal resident who were performing a humanitarian mission over international waters. It was an act of war, and in many
minds retaliation was warranted, yet the United States was doing nothing
about it. Maybe the Cuban Americans would.

A few days after the shoot-down, Basulto, his friend Julio Estorino, Father
Francisco Santana from the Virgin of Charity Church, and some members
of CANF, visited the State Department in Washington, D.C., to discuss the
murders. On the return flight, Father Santana suggested to Basulto that
Brothers to the Rescue do a memorial flight to the exact point where the
men were shot down. It would be referred to as Punto de Mártires, Martyrs'
Point.

That suggestion would cost Captain Anthony "Tony" Tangeman of the U.S. Coast Guard the longest week of his life. Captain Tangeman was chief of law enforcement for the Coast Guard, stationed at Coast Guard Head-quarters in Washington, D.C., and he worked with the State Department, the Justice Department, the INS, the FAA, the Department of Defense, and the National Security Council. He was well acquainted with the Democracy Movement of Ramón Saúl Sánchez. His first month on the job encompassed the day the *Democracia* got rammed, the day that Basulto and Billy Schuss flew over Havana. Tangeman had attended the National Security Council meetings regarding the flyover of Havana. He sensed that Brothers to the Rescue was asking for trouble.

Yet Tangeman vehemently denied the rumors that the U.S. government was partially responsible for the shoot-down. "Not only no, but hell no!" he responded. He believed that if the U.S. government had had any indication that something would happen, they would have used any legal means, for whatever reason, to keep Brothers to the Rescue from flying down there and losing their lives, as well as avert an international incident.

Basulto disagreed. He believed that the U.S. government was expecting a confrontation. Richard Nuccio had felt it in his core; indeed, thoughts of a shoot-down kept him awake the night before. Basulto felt the government had undertaken gargantuan efforts before the shoot-down to document the demise of Brothers to the Rescue.

Captain Tangeman remembers the days leading up to the memorial ser-vice as a continuum of meetings. The memorial was planned to include both a flyover of aircraft and a flotilla of private vessels. For the Coast Guard, the State Department, the Department of Defense, and many other govern-ment agencies, there were not only daily meetings, but multiple daily meet-ings and innumerable phone calls that week. The U.S. government wanted to make sure that Brothers to the Rescue and the Democracy Movement complied with all rules and regulations, especially safety standards, while exercising their legal right to do what they felt they had to do.

Upon returning from Washington, Basulto was apprised that Sylvia Iri-ondo's group, Mothers Against Repression, and dozens of other commu-nity organizations were also planning a memorial service at the Orange Bowl football stadium. President Kennedy had addressed Brigade 2506 at the Orange Bowl in 1962, honoring the returned prisoners from the failed Bay of Pigs invasion and promising to end Castro's regime. On Saturday, March 2, 1996, one week after the shoot-down, the Orange Bowl would host a funeral.

"We're going to fly there Saturday," said Basulto to the group of remaining pilots at the hangar, "because that's what the guys would have done. I understand, completely and without any kind of judgment and pressure, that some of you may not want to fly anymore."

Eighteen planes quickly filled with pilots and copilots volunteering to follow Basulto to Martyrs' Point. As usual, almost every plane would carry a member of the media.

On February 29, two days before the memorial, President Clinton issued an Emergency Cease and Desist Order detailing strict punishments to anyone making an unauthorized entry into Cuban waters. The penalty would include immediate license revocation, which was the maximum civil penalty, and seizure of the aircraft.

Neither the order nor the possibility of another shoot-down would deter Basulto. "If we're shot down at the memorial, I hope other pilots go out again the following week," he said. "And if they get shot down too, then I hope more go out the next week."

Hundreds of supporters gathered at the hangar on Saturday, March 2, 1996, to wish the Brothers a tearful farewell. Among them was Ana Margarita Roque.

The Rafters Rescue Legion and the Cuban American Pilots Association joined Brothers to the Rescue. Mayte Greco was the only female pilot. Father Francisco Santana, who would perform the prayer service, flew with Basulto, along with Orlando Gutiérrez-Boronat, head of the Cuban Democratic Directory and one of Mario de la Peña's closest friends. Orlando had been in Mexico when he found out about the shoot-down. His first thoughts were of the radio program where Mario had said that if he were ever shot down by the Cuban military, he would forgive the pilot.

Brothers to the Rescue's departure was delayed due to rain. For many, it seemed like the heavens were in mourning. Finally, when there was a break in the weather, a C-130 Coast Guard plane accompanied the small aircraft out of Opa-locka.

When they reached latitude 23'33" and longitude 82'17", Father Santana recounted over the radio how one week ago the men were assassinated, and that their mortal remains rested in the same waters where so many had lost their lives. "Bless our Cuban brothers, the people on the island, so near and yet so far," he said. "Give us the liberty we want." Then he prayed an Our Father and recited Psalm 23.

Below them, the pilots could see that today, the United States had their back. Under President Clinton's orders, and under the leadership of Captain Tangeman, the U.S. Coast Guard's armada included two HH60 Jayhawk helicopters, which hovered around the Brothers planes flying over Martyrs' Point. The U.S. Navy employed three vessels, one of them the USS *John L. Hall*, a guided missile frigate; another was the 378-foot cutter *Gallatin*, carrying an MIC-75 76 mm Oto Maler anti-aircraft gun. In all, there were eleven cutters, six helicopters, and one C-130. No doubt some pilots were thinking, "Where were they last Saturday?"

During the memorial service over international waters, Havana Air Traffic Control continuously monitored its corridors. The sector was pretty empty; the only other flight in the area was a plane from Cubana de Aviación doing a test flight. When Basulto reached the spot where the pilots had perished, the Havana air traffic controllers heard Father Santana's prayer and Basulto's airborne eulogy. Basulto ended with his wish that one day we would all be able to return to a free Cuba.

The pilot on Cubana de Aviación also heard Basulto.

"Yeah, and when you return, I hope they fucking blow your ass out of here too!" the air traffic controllers heard the pilot say.

Ana Miriam Ávila, the Havana air traffic controller who was taken off duty the day of the shoot-down, was stunned by the pilot's gross comment. She noticed that even the military personnel were shocked by the gratuitous cruelty. They looked at each other, said nothing, and then went back to their screens. The computers were working that day.

More than sixty thousand people carrying American and Cuban flags filed into the Orange Bowl to honor the four fallen souls that had been shot down the previous week. U.S. Ambassador to the United Nations Madeleine Albright was invited to address the crowd at the ceremonies. Like many in the crowd, she knew what it meant to be in exile. The Czech-born Albright was twice forced to flee her native land with her parents, to escape first the Nazis and later the Communists. When she addressed the crowd, she did not use the derogatory word the MiG pilots had triumphantly bellowed, the profanity that would forever be Albright's referential trademark in the Cuban exile community. But because she had used it, she was already one of them. Albright later recalled the ride from Miami International Airport to the Orange Bowl, when people yelled "Madame Cojones" from their cars. Albright had also universally denounced the MiG pilots' actions. She understood what Communism was all about. The crowd gave her a standing ovation and shouts of welcome, lending the funeral an almost celebratory air.

Famous for wearing brooches on her lapel, Madame Albright (who would later write *Read My Pins*) wore an antique pin of a bluebird with diamonds encrusting the head and wings. "I wore it head-down in honor of the fallen pilots," she said.

Most of the crowd did not know that there was going to be an overflight of the stadium that day. Fighter jets had frequently overflown the Orange Bowl as part of patriotic celebrations and big-name football games. There would be no fighter jets at the memorial, just as there had been no fighter jets seven long days before. On their way back from Martyrs' Point, *Seagull One* and another Brothers to the Rescue plane flew over the stadium to the thundering applause of the people below. At full throttle *Seagull One* could barely reach 150 mph, but today she was in no hurry. Today there were no MiGs in the air. She took her time from end zone to end zone, so that every single mourner would get a chance to look up and see her, flying at a low rumble. Every heart would have an opportunity to pause and grasp the meaning of what the men and women on those planes had done today, what the men on the other planes had done one week earlier.

Today, Brothers to the Rescue was giving the world an object lesson in what nonviolence was all about. They were exercising their freedom as citizens of the freest country on earth to give dignity, respect, and honor to four of their fallen. It was something they were willing to die for.

The planes returned to Opa-locka, then the pilots headed to the Orange Bowl to join Madeleine Albright and the grieving. The patriotic crowd offered up the Cuban and American national anthems. A Marine Corps band played taps for Vietnam veteran Armando Alejandre Jr. After several invited guests addressed the crowd, Basulto got behind the microphone and called out the men's names, one by one.

"Armando!"

"Presente!" the crowd yelled, indicating that in spirit Armando Alejandre Jr. was present with them, and would be forever. Basulto continued with each pilot's name, his voice cracking from time to time, tears in his eyes.

"Pablo!"

"Presente!"

"Carlos!"

"Presente!"

"Mario!"

"Presente!"

The same weekend, officials from the Cuban military were invited to New York City to compare notes on what had happened on February 24, 1996. Cuba claimed to have solid evidence that the planes were shot down over their territorial waters. In order to call Cuba's bluff, Washington invited a delegation over, and paid all their expenses. The six Cuban military intelligence officers picked up their visas in Mexico, arrived in New York City, and were shown the classified CIA files of February 24, 1996. The United States showed Cuba its proof; Cuba never showed the United States anything.

There was talk of a briefcase with aviation charts that had been picked up by search and rescue, but they preferred not to show its contents to the world. That aviation charts could have remained unscathed after the missile attack seemed preposterous, yet the Cuban officers insisted they had the briefcase and charts. Havana Center could have easily set any doubts to rest by showing their radar graphs proving that Mario's and Carlos' planes were in their jurisdictional waters. Their rebuttal: let the United States prove that the planes were *not* there.

U.S. intelligence agencies would later reveal that Cuban MiGs had been spotted test firing air-to-air missiles at slow-moving aircraft one week before the shoot-down.

When he found out about the New York City meeting, Basulto compared it to a gathering of revisionist historians. He believed that what took place in the Big Apple while the world was mourning for the four men was the United States and Cuba agreeing on a common story as to what exactly took place, making sure there were no overtones that could imply any complicity on the part of the United States.

Ultimately, such an agreement would probably never happen. Since 1959, it had been difficult for Cuba and the United States to agree on anything.

On April 17, 1996, the anniversary of the failed Bay of Pigs invasion, the names of Armando Alejandre Jr., Carlos Costa, Mario de la Peña, and Pablo Morales were added to those who had died trying to liberate Cuba for the past thirty-five years.

32

We Will Fly Again

He who sees a need and waits to be asked for help is as
unkind as if he had refused it.

Dante Alighieri

Koki was operating a forklift at the hangar when Aurelio Hurtado de Mendoza, Basulto's old friend and former flight instructor, walked in. Although Basulto had been flying since his teens in Cuba, it was Aurelio who had signed him off for his pilot's license in Miami back on August 8, 1971, Basulto's thirty-first birthday. He and Aurelio had remained friends over the years.

"I'm ready to fly," he told Koki. Basulto and Guille Lares were out on a mission aboard *Seagull One*, so Koki called them.

"Tell him to wait for me," Basulto said.

Aurelio had always yearned to fly with Brothers, but he could never afford the revalidation of his own license.

The day of the shoot-down Aurelio came home shaken, and he pulled out his old logbooks. His wife left him alone with his grief, and Aurelio was silent for a long time.

"I'm going to do it," he told his wife. "I'm taking out our savings and I'm getting all my licenses." He had not flown a plane since 1987. Although they lived on a fixed income, his wife would not dissuade Aurelio. He had endured years of needling from other pilots who questioned why he did not fly with Brothers.

In seven days, Aurelio did it: he got his single-engine, multiengine, and flight instructor's licenses. It cost him his life savings of three thousand dollars. Basulto was moved by what his friend had done.

"I'm sorry I wasn't here before, hermano, but I'm here now," Aurelio said.

Many pilots had left the organization, so Basulto was happy to add one more to his roster. Basulto was even happier when he found out that Aurelio had his instructor's license.

"Why do you need a flight instructor?" he asked Basulto. "All these pilots have their licenses."

"Yes, but they need refresher courses every two or three months," Basulto explained. "They always need to be prepared for emergency procedures. And now more than ever, we need a flight instructor."

"Who was doing it?" Aurelio asked.

"Mario."

The community was divided in its support for Brothers to the Rescue. Once lauded as a humanitarian organization of nineteen nationalities, Brothers to the Rescue was now often referred to as an "anti-Castro Cuban-exile organization."

Many in the community mourned along with the families and the pilots, but others blamed Basulto, accusatory fingers wagging *you asked for it.* The hero's welcome for the daring July 1995 overflight of Havana morphed into an accusation of breaking international law. The floating of half a million leaflets into Havana turned like a chameleon from a fantastic act of non-violent civil disobedience into a personal vendetta from Basulto to Castro, daring him to come to the mat. Basulto would never be able to dispel the rumor that on the days of the leaflet drops Brothers had flown over Cuban waters.

The criticism fomented a spirit of forgetfulness, too. Forgotten was the unification in Miami that had helped Brothers save so many lives. Forgotten were the risks these young pilots and volunteers had taken; four had lost their lives doing what they believed was the right thing. Forgotten was the fact that the planes were in international waters. Seemingly forgotten, and surprisingly voiceless, were the 4,200 balseros these pilots had saved.

The families of the pilots were in deep mourning, attending what seemed to be weekly memorial masses and community events. Soon street signs and monuments would sprout up all over Miami, giving homage to the four men. A part of SW 72nd Avenue in South Miami, where the Alejandre siblings, parents, and extended family lived, was renamed Armando Alejandre Jr. Avenue. On the road to the Opa-locka Airport, beyond the four-way stop where Luis Martínez had heard Carlos Costa's voice, would be the future home of a small park with four palm trees and a stone marker for each of the men. A monument to the fallen would be erected in front of the City of Hialeah Gardens City Hall, near where Pablo Morales lived. A "Brothers to the Rescue Corner" would be strategically located across from the Mission of the Republic of Cuba to the United Nations in New York City, thanks to Mayor Rudy Giuliani. José Morales, a pilot from Tampa, would build a monument in Tampa, Florida.

The families busied themselves with meetings, memorials, and trips. On April 16, 1996, Armando Alejandre Jr.'s daughter, Marlene Alejandre, went to the Human Rights Convention in Geneva with her aunt Maggie Khuly, Alejandre's sister. Marlene, who had postponed her freshman year in college to grieve with her family, spoke out at the convention. That day, April 16, would have been her father's forty-sixth birthday. Thousands of miles away in New York City, Armando's wife, Marlene, was picketing in front of the Mission to Cuba, also honoring her husband's birthday.

The pilots at the hangar mourned as well.

"We lost four," Arnaldo Iglesias would often repeat. "Each family lost one, but we lost *four*." He understood that Brothers' depth of loss could never compare with the agony of the families of the murdered pilots, of a mother losing her son, or a wife losing her husband, but the emptiness of the place without Armando, Carlos, Mario, and Pablo overcame Arnaldo on several occasions. He had a silver dog tag like chain necklace made with the names of his four murdered brothers on the tab. Also engraved were their birth dates and the inscription: "Always Remember, February 24, 1996." He would never take it off.

The FAA became a constant source of annoyance for Basulto and the other pilots. It seemed inspectors were at the hangar every week, showing up unannounced to conduct random inspections of the planes, and threatening to cancel their missions for the slightest infractions, like a tear on a seatbelt. So Brothers complied with their every request. They replaced seats, topped off the tanks, emptied the fuel—whatever the FAA wanted, they did. It appeared that the FAA's main objective was to ground them. Legally, they could not do so. They knew it, Basulto knew it, and Sofía Powell-Cosío, Basulto's attorney, most definitely knew it.

"Show me the law that says you have the authority to keep my client on the ground," she continuously countered.

It was when the FBI got involved that Sofía thought things had gone too far. Sofía considered herself the voice of reason on behalf of Brothers to the Rescue. The FBI phoned her almost daily.

"Is Mr. Basulto flying today?"

No, she would say, he's not—because he was not.

One day after one of those phone calls to Sofía, Basulto told her he had seen a lot of "movement" around the hangar. He was certain the FBI was spying on him.

"Let's do a little test," Sofía told Basulto. "Take out your plane, refuel it, and put it on the runway." Basulto followed her instructions. Moments later, the FBI called Sofía.

"I thought you said Basulto wasn't flying today," they told her.

"He isn't," she said, smug in the knowledge that her scheme had worked. She was appalled that the federal government was wasting money spying at the hangar. Brothers to the Rescue had always been such an open organization—so open that it had welcomed people like Juan Pablo Roque. Now they had the FBI watching them from the sidelines, or rather, from just across the tarmac. Quickly, the humor of the little cat-and-mouse game vanished, and Sofía's attitude adjusted.

"What are you looking for?" she demanded on the phone. "Just ask me whatever you want to know, and I'll be happy to tell you," she said, with a trace of cynicism. "Just be honest; that's the way *we* operate." The conversation escalated and the typically controlled Sofía called the man a few names.

"Stop harassing my client!" she added with finality. "And, by the way, you can tell your boss, and the boss of your boss, to go fuck himself!"

It finally took a group of senior White House officials to ground José Basulto. On May 16, 1996, the FAA got the backing of these officials and abruptly clipped his wings. They came to Opa-locka and let him know just minutes before a scheduled mission. FAA officials defended their emergency order of revocation on the basis that Basulto had ignored repeated warnings from the federal government to respect Cuban airspace.

"I can't pilot the plane," thought Basulto, "but they can't keep me from flying."

The months after the shoot-down were grueling for Brothers to the Rescue. The community, the nation, and the world were somewhat divided. While

Brothers mourned for their friends and tried to schedule missions without adequate pilots or planes, Basulto was blasted in the media.

Hundreds of condolence letters arrived, including one from the first- and second-graders of St. John's Academy in Louisville, Kentucky. "We do not like Communism," they wrote, "and we want to help the people who have to float on the water to get away." They sent the money from their Lenten sacrifices to help. Becoming a grandfather had increased Basulto's regard for children, and the tenderness he felt for his grandson Andre was extended to children in general. He found wisdom in their simple declarations and the pureness in their speech. He felt they expressed a yet-unblemished trust in the world, something he had lost long ago.

Closer to home there was another group of children who still believed in Brothers to the Rescue: the rafter children of South Florida. Four months after the shoot-down, two dozen children from Kensington Park Elementary School in Miami invited Basulto to their classroom to remind him of what he had done for them: save their lives.

The children of Kensington Park Elementary danced and sang for him, gave him little love notes, and asked for autographs. They kissed and hugged him. In contrast to the defamations of media, government, and community, they honored José Basulto. You saved our lives! We love you.

Student Pedro Suárez presented Basulto with a life preserver that he and twenty-one other seven- to ten-year-olds had signed. "Please take it with you on the plane in case you need it to save your life, as you saved ours," he said. "We don't want anything to happen to you."

Struggling to control his tears, Basulto sat with them cross-legged on the floor, answering questions and hearing their stories. When they asked him how he felt when his fellow brothers were shot down, Basulto swallowed hard. "It was the worst day of my life. I wish it would have been me."

A few days later, another child came to help Basulto while he was at Opa-locka, slouched over the conference table lost in thought inside the now almost-empty hangar. Looking up he saw a small boy, about nine years old, with blond hair and blue eyes. He was holding a large, round, blue tin container, an old Maxwell House coffee can that had a 1993 racing team scene on it. Without saying a word, the boy placed the heavy can on the table. Quietly, he slid it across the table to Basulto, making a muffled scratchy sound. Basulto looked inside and saw that it was full of pennies.

"He wanted to bring it himself," said the boy's father, who was standing off to the side.

On top of the can was a folded-up note, written in a child's hand:

6-29-96
We are sorry about the planes that got shot down. So, here is some pennise [*sic*] to help buy a new plane.
Best wishes,
Jonathan Aronoff

Basulto got up, tears in his eyes, and unable to speak, nodded his head up and down and embraced the boy and his father.

On August 26, 1996, six months after the shoot-down, Brothers to the Rescue issued a press release stating that their standard search-and-rescue missions would resume. It affirmed that Armando, Carlos, Mario, and Pablo would have wanted it that way. *The struggle is ours.*

33

Backlash

If you're going through Hell—keep going.
Winston Churchill

The exiles were not going to attack Cuba after all, and neither were the U.S. Armed Forces. Alfredo Sánchez, the pilot from West Palm Beach who had been scheduled to fly the day of the shoot-down, had believed a military strike was plausible and justified. "All we got was Madeleine Albright using the word *cojones,* and all Cuba got was a slap on the wrist," he said.

In addition to the wrist slapping, on March 12, 1996, President Clinton signed into law the Helms-Burton Act, also called the Cuban Liberty and Democratic Solidarity Act of 1996. The part about "Cuban liberty and democratic solidarity" may have thrown a lot of people off. Just at the moment when the Clinton administration was on the brink of reestablishing relations with Cuba, after years of meetings with Fidel Castro and his officials, three U.S. citizens and one legal resident were blown out of the sky. The president had to make a 180-degree turn.

Helms-Burton strengthened the embargo against Cuba. One of its many provisions was to penalize foreign companies allegedly trafficking in property formerly owned by U.S. citizens but expropriated by Castro's government after the revolution. It was condemned by the European Union, Britain, Canada, Mexico, and other U.S. allies. Humanitarian groups argued that Helms-Burton would affect only the innocent population.

Helms-Burton had been tabled by Clinton for more than a year, while he was busy flirting with the Cubans. Now only an act of Congress could reverse it. At least it quieted down some of the more conservative Cuban exiles. Presumably, to Clinton, these measures seemed sufficient punishment for shooting down unarmed American citizens in international waters.

Others did not see the need to sign any bills after the shoot-down. Columnists like Pulitzer Prize–winner Mike Royko preferred to ignore the situation and suggested President Clinton use the following words in his next speech on the subject: "I have more urgent stuff to worry about than some Cubans in Miami who insist on flying where they shouldn't be flying and where they have been repeatedly warned not to fly," wrote Royko.

The backlash against Brothers to the Rescue would come in many forms, sometimes catching Basulto off guard, particularly when some of the family members of the murdered pilots began pointing accusatory fingers, blaming him for their sons' demise. Other repercussions would haunt Cubans across the Straits—and not just the rafters still planning their escapes or the dissidents fearing imprisonment (one thousand would eventually be arrested). Eight Havana air traffic controllers were about to lose their jobs.

Ana Miriam Ávila and her group of controllers from Havana ATC had over the years befriended Nick Perdomo of the Miami Center Air Traffic Control office. Nicholas I. Perdomo was born in Washington, D.C., to Cuban parents who had escaped Cuba after the revolution. Opposed to Communism, his grandfather was imprisoned for twelve years. Nick's father was ambushed by Castro's militia and was left with two bullets embedded in his body as a lifelong reminder. Nick grew up in Baltimore, and when his grandfather was released from prison, the Perdomos moved to Miami.

In early March 1996, Nick went to visit his half-sister in Cuba, as well as his friends at Havana ATC. Ana and her team enjoyed Nick's visits to Cuba, and they also welcomed the small gifts he would bring them from the United States, things like bars of soap, shampoo, and powdered milk, of which there were chronic shortages in Cuba.

Ana had worked at Havana ATC for the past six years. She had a steady government job that paid 250 Cuban pesos a month, worth about ten dollars, plus the *jaba* (the bag). The jaba (pronounced ha-ba) was usually filled with extras like shampoo, detergent, and extra food, something very important in the business world of everyday Cubans.

The working class in revolutionary Cuba was divided into two groups: professionals and those "in business." Ana was a professional. To be in business basically meant you woke up every morning and creatively devised a plan for how to make it through the day. If you worked at a restaurant, you could steal some food and exchange it for something someone may have taken from a store, say, a bar of soap. A job in the tourist shops of the luxury hotels on Varadero Beach was good business, because you could always steal a little something, and it would be overlooked. Salaries and government subsidies were never enough to make ends meet, so stealing was an accepted form of survival in Castro's Cuba. Dissidents and anyone who openly disagreed with the government were immediately left without a job—permanently—and subsequently joined the "business sector," unless they were imprisoned.

Ana was thankful to be so well off. Within this professional environment and fairly comfortable existence, Ana and her team had felt that it was OK to befriend Nick Perdomo from Miami, whom they spoke with on average one hundred times a day.

Whenever Nick came into town, they would gather at the home of one of the controllers to eat, drink, and inevitably, discuss politics. "He's a tyrant, a dictator!" Nick would blast, referring to Castro, but no one would respond. One day Nick had been brazen enough to say "Fidel Castro sucks!" over the radio as he was transferring control of a flight from Miami Center to Havana Center. He remembered Ramón, who was on duty the day of the shoot-down, retorting: "Fidel Castro is my god."

Ana's group envied Nick's freedom of expression, how audaciously he ranted against Fidel Castro in their very presence. "I'm an American," he would say, "I can say whatever the hell I want." Then he would spread out whatever wares he had brought as gifts for his friends. One time he planted an American flag in the middle of the gifts. And snapped a picture.

Nick loved taking photos. He would invariably hang an American flag in the background, or ask someone to hold an American flag, then click away. Some of Nick's photographs had him posing in front of revolutionary statues and saluting with a thumbs-down gesture. He snapped photos of his friends and captured images of Cuban life, like the tobacco-rolling factories of Cuba. Nick's father and grandfather had worked at the famous Partagás tobacco company in Cuba. Since 1992, Nick had been trying to revive his family's tobacco business, rolling cigars out of his garage in Little Havana.

Whenever Nick visited Cuba, he stayed at his half-sister's humble home, even though he could well afford the luxury tourist hotels. He refused to leave any money to the Cuban government. But on one particular trip, his sister really wanted a hot shower, something she had never enjoyed. She pleaded with her brother to take her to a hotel. When they got there she was not allowed in—no Cuban nationals could stay in the tourist hotels or eat in the restaurants or swim on the beach.

"Tell me she's your whore and I'll let her in," said the Russian bell captain at the front of the Hotel Nacional.

"I can't do that," Nick said, "she's my sister."

"Then she can't come in, unless she's a prostitute."

Nick battled in his mind with everything his father had ever taught him, but his sister's desperation made him cave in. "OK," he finally resigned himself. "She's my girlfriend."

While Nick's sister was indulging herself with an entire large-size bottle of shampoo to wash her hair, and luxuriating in the first hot shower of her life, Nick remembers going "ape-shit crazy." He emptied out the mini-bar, cleared the shelves of all the hotel amenities, stripped the bed of its sheets, then went downstairs and gave them all to the first taxi driver he saw.

On March 13, 1996, Nick and another American from Miami showed up unannounced at Havana ATC. He was stopped at the front and told he could not come in. He ignored the orders, walked up the stairs, and entered the air traffic control office. And took pictures.

Air traffic control centers around the world are very similar. Havana Center had hosted many representatives from other ATC centers. Since everything that is said or seen is recorded, these centers are usually very hospitable to controllers from other countries. But Nick was from the United States, and his visit came just three weeks after the shoot-down.

After Nick's departure, Ana and seven other controllers would endure two months of debriefing and reprogramming about the events of the shoot-down. They had not worked that day, so they could not understand why so much emphasis was placed on them. After all, they understood the computers had been deactivated to erase any proof of what really happened on February 24, 1996.

The confusion—and fear—escalated when neighbors saw some in Ana's team being picked up by militia and taken to safe houses. They endured hours of interrogation by State Security. They were told that Nick Perdomo was a CIA agent and Security was aware of all conversations they had had with him. After six months of harassment, on August 8, 1996, eight Havana Center air traffic controllers were fired, including Ana. The accusations were many:

- having entertained foreigners in their home without permission, specifically Nic [sic] Perdomo;

- having allowed antirevolutionary declarations in their presence, specifically made by Nic Perdomo;
- having accepted gifts, like powdered milk, from abroad without reporting them to National Security;
- allowing an American of Cuban origin inside the Havana Center office, specifically Nic Perdomo.

As a result of their friendship with an American of Cuban origin who made "antirevolutionary remarks" in their presence, eight professionals from Havana ATC reluctantly entered the "business" sector of Cuban society.

Nick's friends were jobless, spied on by neighbors, and harassed by the government. In the meantime, Nick would launch Tabacalera Perdomo into an award-winning, multi-million-dollar tobacco industry. It would take him eight years, but Nick Perdomo helped the jobless Havana controllers make it to freedom in the United States. Ana would finally arrive on June 9, 2004.

The backlash against anyone associated with the events of February 24 continued. It was also felt by Osvaldo Plá, Tito Fufú, when he visited Cuba in December 1996. He managed to acquire a humanitarian visa to visit his mother, who was dying of cancer. He had not seen his parents for twenty-five years.

"You're crazy for going," Basulto told him. "They'll put you in jail."

He tried to disguise himself by cutting his hair short, and he documented and video-taped everything he put in his bags in case they tried to plant something. Upon arrival, immediately after his face popped up on the screen, Cuban security put him in a room for questioning. He remembers fifteen militia dressed in their drab olive uniforms coming to interrogate him.

"Are you Osvaldo Plá?"

"Yes," he replied. He explained repeatedly over the course of the next few hours that his mother was very sick, in the hospital, dying, and he had a humanitarian visa. After every question, they slapped him, spit on him, and shoved him around.

"How long has it been since you've seen your father?"

"Since 1971," said Tito.

"Well, he's in the next room, we're questioning him, too, and you know what? You'll never see him again."

"Please, chico," pleaded Tito. "I don't know what it is you have against me; we may have different opinions, but we're all Cubans."

"Don't start with that!" They hit him again. "You'll be lucky to make it out alive."

"Listen," he said, facing them squarely. "There comes a time in a man's life when he loses all fear, and when it comes to my mother, I have no fear. Do whatever you want to me, but let me see my mother."

In the meantime, several phone calls were exchanged, and when the militia confirmed he was with Brothers to the Rescue, they were ordered to leave him alone—and put him on the next plane back. That punishment would be worse than the physical abuse.

Still, he begged them to take him to the hospital. "Handcuff me if you want!" he yelled. "But please let me see my mother. I promise that if you need medicines for your mothers, I'll send them to you!" They kicked him once more and put him on the next flight out.

Tito's mother died three months later. He never saw his father again either.

34

Truth and Justice

*Like a lawyer, the human brain wants victory,
not truth; and, like a lawyer, it is sometimes
more admirable for skill than virtue.*

Robert Wright

Mirta Costa needed some answers. She was upset that in the hangar after the shoot-down Basulto had not come to her personally with an explanation of what had happened, a word, an embrace, or a reason. The loss of her son demanded more personal attention, so she summoned Basulto and Arnaldo Iglesias to her home.

Mirta reminded Arnaldo of what she had told him: "I don't want any heroes." Carlos Costa was now not only a hero, but a martyr as well. The only consolation Arnaldo could offer was that the men had died instantly.

Mirta chastised Basulto and Arnaldo for allowing Carlitos to fly that day. The question that would hang forever on Mirta's mind was, "Why didn't Basulto tell Mario and Armando to get out of there?" Her own son, whose plane was the first shot down, did not have a chance, but seven minutes elapsed between the two shootings. Why had Basulto not told Mario to get out of there and go back to Opa-locka, something he himself had done?

After her encounter with Basulto and Arnaldo, she started meeting with the other families. Eva Barbas, Pablo Morales' mother, still had not arrived from Cuba, but the three other families needed to find justice for Carlos, Mario, Armando, and Pablo. Their mutual mourning bonded them, not necessarily as friends, but more in an intimacy of pain. Basulto, Billy Schuss, and other members of the organization joined them. The meetings to help them pinpoint a strategy for arriving at truth and justice even included members of Cuban exile groups like the Democracy Movement with Ramón Saúl Sánchez.

It was at these meetings that Mirta Costa became increasingly disillusioned with Basulto. She knew that Fidel Castro had issued the orders for the shoot-down, and she conceded that her son Carlos was doing what he loved best. But she partially blamed Basulto. "Why did Brothers continue to fly at all when they had been warned not to? Why had Basulto survived and not her precious Carlitos?" She felt that Basulto wanted to manage all aspects of the investigation and that he wanted to control the meetings and events; she felt he would rather be grandstanding on television or on the radio than meeting with the family members. She would bristle whenever he stated that he did not want any help from the U.S. government. *The struggle is ours.*

At one early meeting, she remembers him saying that they would continue their humanitarian missions.

"Then why don't you take your own sons?" she spat back at him.

It was in May, when she went to Washington with Sylvia Iriondo and the Mothers Against Repression, that she first heard any talk about a lawsuit against Cuba, to go after frozen assets held in the United States. When Basulto found out, she remembers that he became annoyed. She heard him say that those frozen assets belonged to the people of Cuba, and that if any money was to be doled out, it should be to replace the planes.

The animosity between Mirta Costa and Basulto escalated as the months went on. In their great loss, some family members sympathized with her in holding Basulto responsible for the loss of their sons, Mario and Carlos, and husband and father, Armando. Mirta Costa would eventually cut off all communication with Basulto. Their last meeting was particularly brutal.

"You know what you should do?" she told Basulto, consumed by the pain of a grieving mother. "You should shoot yourself."

"Madam, why don't you do it for me?" he said.

The words of his friend Janet Ray Weininger came back to haunt Basulto. "They're going to turn the families against you."

In Cuba, Pablo Morales' family was repeatedly interviewed. His mother, Eva Barbas, defiantly called Fidel Castro a murderer, adding a harsh Cuban insult to boot: "Fidel Castro!" she said looking into the camera, "you have no mother."

On May 2, 1996, the ninety-pound, white-haired, 4'10" Eva Barbas was greeted with bouquets of flowers by Miami-Dade County Commissioner Pedro Reboredo, reporters, and Basulto at Miami International Airport.

Eva came from a humble background in Cuba, but her ease and familiarity with the press and radio made her a public darling. Every inch and pound of her small frame was channeled into tireless energy. No matter the occasion or the dress code, Eva Barbas always looked confident. Wherever Basulto went, he took la Viejita (the little old lady): for discussions with Cuban exile groups, for dinner at his house, and for marches in Washington, D.C. Basulto called her daily, and he was awed by the wisdom of this wisp of a woman. Her mantra became "all I want is truth and justice, truth and justice for Pablito." Their affection for each other blossomed, and soon Basulto referred to Eva as his "third mother."

Brothers to the Rescue promised to help the Morales family. After they made a payment on Pablo's Jeep, which was still at the hangar, it was returned to the bank. Radio station WQBA donated a car to the Morales family.

With Eva Barbas in Miami, now all four families could unite in the search for truth and justice, albeit by different routes. The Costa, de la Peña, and Alejandre families employed Miami attorney Frank Angones to file a lawsuit to obtain Cuban government frozen assets held in the United States. Judicial Watch, a conservative watchdog group in Washington, D.C., contacted Basulto and persuaded him to file claims for pain and suffering. Sylvia and Andrés Iriondo and Arnaldo Iglesias did not join him in the civil lawsuit.

While the families prepared themselves for the lawsuit against the government of Cuba, Basulto was busy with his own legal issues. An evidentiary hearing was scheduled on the emergency order of revocation on Basulto's pilot's license. The accusations included violating several sections of the Federal Aviation Regulations when he made two unauthorized flights within the territorial airspace of the Republic of Cuba. Naturally, Sofía Powell-Cosío would be there for him.

Ever since the day back in 1992 when Sofía Powell-Cosío asked José Basulto for a photograph of a rafter for her media campaign in Canada, she had worked as his attorney, for free. Sofía would never charge Brothers to the Rescue one cent for the countless hours she dedicated to them. In addition, she and her husband, Alberto, would raise more than one hundred thousand dollars in two fund-raisers that they sponsored. She was known in the community as *la abogada de Basulto*, Basulto's attorney, and her notoriety soared.

"God sent her to me," Basulto said in an interview. "I would never trust anyone else."

But this time he needed expertise in litigation, so he hired Miami attorney Stuart Goldstein to defend him; Sofía Powell-Cosío would be co-counsel.

"Just keep asking questions," Basulto urged Goldstein. He used the hearing as a means to glean as much information as possible on what happened the day of the shoot-down.

The Honorable William A. Pope II would preside over those eight long days of the evidentiary hearing. No press or court photographers were allowed, only court artists, who drew many colored sketches of the highly publicized hearing. Goldstein would hang one of these portraits in his office, and so would FAA attorney Michael Moulis.

The hearing would reveal a great deal about the true events of the shoot-down. At that time the report of the ICAO, the international committee investigating the shoot-down, was not completed. Basulto would finally hear in their entirety the cockpit recordings of the MiG pilots, their shrill voices celebrating the murders of his friends. Two armed guards paraded in with the recording equipment and the coveted four-track tapes, almost as if they were protecting a national treasure or the relics of a saint. As the tape ran, they stood by protectively, pistols secured but ready, as if at any moment Basulto or his counsel would snatch the evidence and run.

Goldstein brought star witnesses to the stand, particularly Harold Matheison. Matheison was entrusted with reviewing copies of more than one hundred prints that were sent to Goldstein and his group just two days before trial. There was no way Matheison could review all the prints, but those he did, he scrutinized with an unforgiving eye. Basulto nicknamed him "Dr. Watson."

Mike Thomas from the FAA also testified. "I met with him on July 11," he said, "and on July 13, he flies over Havana. That sends out the wrong signal, that Basulto is not a compliant person." Was Thomas aware of his gross understatement?

More than four hundred pages of transcribed testimony was given by Jeffrey Houlihan of March Air Force Base in Riverside, California. He recounted his 911 call to the Southeast Air Defense Sector at Tyndall Air Force Base in Panama City, Florida, and their confirmation to him: "We're handling it, don't worry." He further testified that standard operating procedure was to deploy interceptor jets whenever Cuban MiGs crossed the twelve-mile territorial limit of Cuba. Protocol was not followed.

Judge William A. Pope II asked Houlihan if, based on his extensive log of the flight of February 24, he thought that Basulto was planning on violating Cuban airspace.

"No, your honor, he was not," replied Houlihan. "And in fact . . . he never made any move whatsoever that would have indicated to me that he intended to penetrate Cuban airspace."

Arnaldo Iglesias and Sylvia Iriondo, survivors of the shoot-down, as well as Ramón Saúl Sánchez of the Democracy Movement were also called to testify. Then Goldstein called Orestes Lorenzo to the stand.

Orestes Lorenzo retold his story of escaping the island on a Cuban MiG-23 in 1991 and claiming asylum in the United States. A year and one-half later, he flew a 1961 Cessna into Cuba, swooped down on a road, and picked up his wife and two children. For that, he was on *Larry King Live!*, he wrote a book, he was called a hero. President Bush welcomed him at the White House. Mickey and Goofy hailed him as grand marshal of the Disney World parade. Only in America.

For the thirteen-minute incursion over Havana, Basulto's license was suspended for 150 days. That was not enough for the FAA, so they appealed to the NTSB. What puzzled Basulto was that he had announced that he would be in jurisdictional space on the day of the *Democracia* flotilla. Now, for an unintentional dip into Cuban airspace, followed by a chase by Cuban MiGs that nearly cost him his life after the murder of his four friends, he would ultimately face an emergency revocation.

In the middle of the FAA hearing, the news came in that the four-month ICAO investigation had concluded that the Brothers to the Rescue shoot-down had occurred in international waters. It did not allot Cuba the coveted C-word—a condemnation—but rather proclaimed the action "unjustified." By that time, though, the FAA had already determined their own truth regarding Basulto's incursion into Cuban airspace. Basulto believed unequivocally that it was a politically charged action. The FAA felt justice could only be met by affirming the emergency order of revocation.

The final opinion and order would come down on Basulto, and his license was revoked.

It seemed to him that the only way the FAA could be sure he would not penetrate Cuban airspace again was to take away his right to pilot. But they could not prevent him from flying a mission.

If the attorneys, the FAA, and the NTSB could not find truth and justice, perhaps the U.S. Congress would. Ileana Ros-Lehtinen was the most senior Republican woman in Congress and the first Cuban American woman elected to Congress. She was Basulto's friend, she was the Brothers to the Rescue godmother, and she wanted truth and justice.

With her lobbying, on September 18, 1996, a hearing was held before the Subcommittee on the Western Hemisphere of the Committee on International Relations of the House of Representatives, during the 104th Congress. The hearing was titled: "The Shoot-down of Brothers to the Rescue: What Happened?"

Indiana Republican Dan Burton chaired the hearing. For "national security purposes," Jeffrey Houlihan was not allowed to testify at the hearing, but rather was interviewed in a private closed-door meeting. No one present could understand this move since Houlihan had already testified, under oath, in a federal court of law.

During the proceedings, Ileana Ros-Lehtinen eloquently recounted the events of February 24, 1996, and then posed her questions to the subcommittee:

- Why did the Air Force dismiss the call from the Customs official in California?
- Why did the Air Force not inform Brothers to the Rescue of the presence of MiGs?
- Why was no action taken to intercept the MiGs before the two planes were shot down?
- Why was no action taken to intercept the MiGs that pursued Basulto?

"If the U.S. military officials did not fulfill their duty, then we must step in and examine why their mission was not fulfilled," she concluded.

The government provided what they termed two distinguished witnesses: María Fernández, Deputy Assistant Secretary for Inter-American Affairs for the Department of Defense, and Colonel Michael McMahan, the Deputy J-3 for the Atlantic Command. Neither had any written testimony. Neither Fernández nor McMahan seemed to know anything about the shoot-down.

They defended their positions of ignorance about the events by saying they had both been advised of the hearing only a day and a half prior. Neither could remember who in fact had summoned them to appear before Congress. They were not aware of the MiGs going up and down around Cuba, yet later on in the hearing, McMahan strongly insisted that the MiGs had not gone north of the 24th parallel. Neither knew why Houlihan's 911 call was ignored. Neither could name whomever Houlihan had spoken to. They knew everyone's title, but nobody's name.

After intense grilling, the name of the Senior Southeast District watch officer who had received Houlihan's 911 was produced: Colonel Frank Willy. Colonel Willy was now retired. No reason was ever given as to why he did not attend the proceedings. Colonel Willy was never subpoenaed to testify regarding the events of the shoot-down.

Both Fernández and McMahan were very cordial in promising to come back with answers to all the questions that were being fired at them.

"Let me just say that the Defense Department has done themselves a disservice in the context of who they sent," said ranking Democrat Bob Menéndez of New Jersey, who was visibly frustrated. "This is something I would assume the Defense Department knows all about and it would take a juvenile mind to think about what questions would be asked here today. The Department has affronted our intelligence, whether by design, deception, or just incompetence."

When Ileana Ros-Lehtinen got back to her line of questioning, she honed in on María Fernández.

"You are not here as a token Cuban American?" asked Ros-Lehtinen, tongue-in-cheek, "to represent a good face for the Department?"

"I assure you I am not," said Fernandez.

"Even though you have no information about the shoot-down and you are not able to answer our questions?" Ros-Lehtinen continued.

After Fernández's and McMahan's testimonies, or lack thereof, Basulto presented his carefully worded rendition of everything that had happened, complete with letters, charts, the ICAO report, the FAA and NTSB hearing results, and other evidence.

One of his exhibits was a letter from U.S. Air Force Brigadier General Howard G. DeWolf. DeWolf's review concluded that "at no time was the sovereignty of the United States threatened, and our personnel acted properly at all times." In effect, DeWolf discredited already proven facts: protocol was not followed, a 911 call was not "handled," planes on battle station were told to stand down, and Cuban MiGs were within three minutes of the sovereignty of the United States.

Chairman Burton promised that there would be another hearing, much bigger, with three or four panels, and that he was going to subpoena everyone possible, and "they were going to get to the bottom of it."

Ileana Ros-Lehtinen persevered in her tireless efforts to find truth and justice for the murdered pilots, yet no one was ever subpoenaed, no one ever brought forth the evidence promised, and no further hearing was ever held.

Truth and justice seemed to be beyond the scope of the Congress of the United States of America, so it was doubtful that the federal judges involved in the families' and Basulto's lawsuits would grant it either.

By December 1997, a federal judge ruled in favor of the Alejandre, Costa, and de la Peña families, awarding $187 million in compensatory and punitive damages for the deaths of the three men. It would be three years before the families ever received any monies. Pablo Morales' family was not able to sue because he was not an American citizen at the time of his death.

By mid-2000, the Clinton administration wanted the families to accept a compromise settlement, collecting $50 million in damages for pain and suffering and loss of future wages. Maggie Khuly, Alejandre's sister, argued for the punitive damages, insisting there had to be a deterrent to keep this from ever happening again.

"When Cuba was declared guilty, Cuba didn't care," said Khuly. "They don't care if you call them terrorists, they don't care if you call them murderers, but they do care if you take their money." Armando Alejandre Jr.'s parents and three sisters would not be awarded any monies from the settlement, but Armando's sister fought relentlessly for her sister-in-law and niece.

In the last few days of President Clinton's administration, about half of the $187 million judgment was released to Mrs. Marlene Alejandre and her daughter Marlene Victoria Alejandre, to the estate of Carlos Costa, and to the estate of Mario de la Peña. At that time there were 5,911 U.S. companies and individuals with claims of longer standing against Cuba, so there was hope that frozen assets would eventually be used for those claims. One of those claimants was Janet Ray Weininger. Fidel Castro had kept her father's body in a freezer for seventeen years after the failed Bay of Pigs invasion. It would take Weininger another six years to receive a settlement.

According to *America's Insider* magazine, the families donated $19 million of their award to scholarships for rafters, human rights prizes for journalists and activists, and efforts to indict Fidel Castro for the shoot-down. Ironically, the same FBI that had been paying Juan Pablo Roque to spy on Brothers prepared WANTED posters with the dramatic headline "Murder over International Waters." The families offered a $100,000 reward for "credible information resulting in the indictment of any and all individuals involved in the shoot-down conspiracy."

The families established foundations, including the Armando Alejandre Foundation at the University of Miami Law School. Armando had been pursuing a law degree when he was shot down. Florida International University's College of Law would name its Immigration and Human Rights Clinic after Carlos A. Costa in recognition of a $1 million commitment from the Costa Foundation. Another foundation was C.A.M.P. 4 Justice, the initials representing the first name of each of the murdered men. Its purpose was to promote and defend human rights, particularly in Cuba.

In January 2005, Basulto was awarded a $1.75 million judgment for emotional trauma suffered after the 1996 shoot-down. "This continued fear has affected his daily life activities and ability to enjoy life," wrote U.S. District Judge Kenneth A. Marra.

"I have a MiG on my tail for the rest of my life," Basulto said during the trial. Then he pledged one million dollars of the settlement for his most important project: the indictment of Fidel and Raúl Castro for the murders of Armando, Carlos, Mario, and Pablo.

Basulto never saw a penny of the judgment.

After the Alejandre, Costa, and de la Peña families were awarded their $93 million, the three families wrote to Eva Barbas and offered her $1 million dollars each from the settlement. Eva and her daughter, Nancy, were struggling here in the United States. The initial $300,000 they had been awarded four years earlier had been spent to buy a house, a car, and to pay for all their living expenses. They were definitely in a bind.

La Viejita wrote back to the three families and said no, thank you. All I want is truth and justice.

35

Anniversaries

*There is no greater pain than to remember a happy time when
one is in misery.*

Dante Alighieri

Ever since Hurricane Andrew cut across South Florida on August 22, 1992,
Miami residents had marked time and events as "before Andrew" or "after
Andrew." Following the shoot-down of February 24, 1996, anyone who had
ever flown with, volunteered for, or been involved with Brothers to the Rescue would mark time as "before the shoot-down" or "after the shoot-down."
It would be years before a greater event would mark time for the entire
world: September 11, 2001.

The shoot-down date would not be the only commemorative day that
would be acknowledged to honor the four martyrs. There were birthdays
and anniversaries, family reunions, memorial masses and commemorative
dinners, posthumous degrees, and remembrances—as if one could forget.
For Brothers to the Rescue, the anniversary of the shoot-down was every
day.

Somewhere between the first- and sixth-month anniversary, the Alejandre family booked a cruise on the *Majesty of the Seas*, the cruise ship that
had witnessed the Cuban MiG shooting the planes. The Alejandres had enjoyed many family vacations on cruises, but this particular voyage would
not be for swimming in the pristine Caribbean or visiting the island straw
markets. They yearned to be in the general vicinity of where Armando Alejandre Jr. had died.

"One of the hardest things is having no body, no closure, no tomb," said
Armando's sister Cristina.

The same captain that had been on duty the day of the shoot-down was
sailing on this cruise. He invited the Alejandres to his table the night of the

captain's dinner. He also welcomed them on deck, a privilege rarely conferred. On one afternoon of their cruise, at precisely 3:21 p.m., then again at 3:28 p.m., the captain blew the horn of the *Majesty of the Seas* as the Alejandres threw flowers overboard in the area where the men had been murdered.

On the one-year anniversary of the shoot-down, six planes took off from Opa-locka Airport with a crowd of five hundred wishing them well. When they radioed Havana Center before crossing the 24th parallel they got no answer, so they radioed another plane that was in the area to do a relay for them.

Onboard the other aircraft was Brothers pilot Beverly Brooks. She was main engineer on a freight carrier. On hearing the Brothers pilots asking for a relay to Havana Center, she asked the captain of her flight for permission to do the relay for her friends. Choking back tears, Beverly informed Havana Center that Brothers to the Rescue was crossing the 24th parallel.

After the flight, a memorial mass was held at St. Agatha Catholic Church in southwest Miami. All the families were present, and each member participated. Some sang, some brought up the gifts before Holy Communion, others gave talks after the service was over. José and Rita Basulto were there, along with many of the pilots and volunteers of Brothers to the Rescue.

While the three families of Armando, Carlos, and Mario bonded, the Basultos and Sofía Powell-Cosío's family became close with Eva Barbas, Pablo's mother.

A few months after the first anniversary, Sofía Powell-Cosío found out she was pregnant with her third child. Her husband, Alberto, told her not to share the news with anyone for a while.

"We've had two babies in two years," he said. "People are going to start laughing at us!" A few days later Sofía received a phone call from Eva Barbas that would end the secrecy.

"I had a dream last night that you were pregnant," she said. "You were having a boy, and his name was going to be Pablo."

On June 24, 1997, the same day Sofía turned thirty-two, the Cosíos welcomed Alberto Pablo to their family. The godfather was José Basulto.

Before the third anniversary was commemorated, producer Alex Anton directed a documentary titled *Siempre Presente* (Always With Us), which was shown to a crowd at the Radisson Mart Plaza Hotel on January 22, 1999. It touched on the lives of Armando, Carlos, Mario, and Pablo.

Also for the third anniversary, and for the first time in Cuba, memorial masses would be celebrated in all of the provinces.

Brothers printed more leaflets to float over Havana. A Coast Guard cutter would be there to witness the event, because Basulto had never been able to dispel the rumors that he had flown over Havana in January 1996 to drop the original leaflets. Once again, on one side of the flyers were printed the thirty articles of the Declaration of Human Rights; the other side read: "Armando, Carlos, Mario y Pablo Viven!" (Armando, Carlos, Mario, and Pablo Live!).

From outside Cuban waters, the Brothers' planes succeeded in doing what they had done three years earlier, but on a much smaller scale. Some leaflets made it to the rooftop of the Habana Libre (Free Havana) Hotel. Two flares were dropped at the sites of the shoot-downs, and flowers were tossed from the planes. Basulto sent a message to his brothers on the island, encouraging them to abandon the escapist attitude and realize that organized civil disobedience was in their control.

"Let every Cuban say, I am the change," he said. "The struggle is ours."

Apart from the dates and monuments and memorials, there would be daily reminders of the loss of the four men. Their deaths and the search for truth and justice would be enmeshed in the next three presidential elections. After the shoot-down, any politician vying for Florida's Cuban American vote, which would number more than three hundred thousand by 2008, would have to declare a lot more than the standard *Cuba Sí, Castro No* of the past. This was the litmus test, as important as one's position on Israel for the Jews and one's voting record on discrimination for African Americans. The Cubans would not rest until justice was received.

During the fifth anniversary of the shoot-down, Basulto was involved in yet another legal proceeding. Judge Joan A. Lenard issued a gag order forbidding Basulto from flying on the anniversary to Martyrs' Point, the latitude and longitude where the shoot-downs occurred. The ACLU intervened for him so that Basulto could exercise his "First Amendment right to convey [his] message to the world." They dropped four roses over the shoot-down site.

Just before the eighth anniversary of the shoot-down, Father Francisco Santana from the Virgin of Charity Church died at the age of sixty-two. For years, he had flown with Basulto and prayed at Martyrs' Point. Brothers to the Rescue donated ten thousand dollars to Santana's charity, Faith in Action, which worked to send medicines, first-aid supplies, and other humanitarian gifts to families and churches in Cuba.

Whereas anniversaries for Brothers to the Rescue had previously been happy occasions celebrating the birth date of their organization, with a count of how many rafters had been saved, now they mourned the deaths of their friends.

One rafter family held another kind of anniversary, a "Class of '91" fifteen-year reunion party in 2006, to celebrate their rescue by Basulto and Guille Lares. Nelson Alemán and his family had come over on the *Misladys*. He never got his antique map back, but he had saved the note from Brothers, and he put it on display inside the banquet hall. They spared no expense and rented a party room at Los Violines Banquet Hall, inviting Basulto and Lares.

As a milestone anniversary approached—the tenth year—the Alejandre family set out on the dynamic project of producing a documentary of the shoot-down events. It was Armando Alejandre's niece, Cristina Khuly, who took on this ambitious task. Just as her mother had been the impetus behind the lawsuit, now the daughter was the force behind the camera.

Several events commemorated the tenth anniversary. Panel discussions were held at Miami Dade College, and seven minutes of silence were honored at Florida International University. A commemorative mass was celebrated, once again at St. Agatha Church across the street from the university. Then *Shoot Down*, the first feature-length documentary on the downing of the planes, was played to an invitation-only audience who packed the Gusman Center for the Performing Arts in downtown Miami.

Shoot Down was not well received. Many felt it pandered to the U.S. government, excusing their inaction. The movie was not released to the public.

The Alejandre family would not be dissuaded. Director Cristina Khuly and her husband, Douglas R. Eger, reworked the movie for almost two years, until it won the 2007 Sonoma Valley Film Festival Award for Best Documentary. There were screenings in Washington, D.C., at the Capitol, and at several other film festivals. Then in January 2008, just before the twelfth anniversary, it was released to select theaters in Washington, New York, and Miami. The film ran for several weeks in Miami, quite an accomplishment for a documentary on an event that was twelve years old, long forgotten by most except for Cuban Americans and politicians. It was expertly filmed with spine-tingling graphics portraying what the shoot-down must have appeared like on radar screens across the nation and in Cuba that fateful day. Critics lauded Khuly's work, praising her for her "even-handed" treatment of the events.

Basulto did not agree that he had been treated with an even hand.

Khuly interviewed Richard Nuccio, the special Cuba advisor under President Clinton, who claimed that Basulto had been warned by government agencies not to fly that day. Cristina's mother, Maggie Khuly, gave a professional and even-tempered rendition of what happened, and then added that members of Cuban exile groups had also warned Brothers not to fly.

Nothing of the sort was true, proclaimed Basulto in a detailed letter to the editor that was published in English and Spanish by the *Miami Herald*, as well as several magazines.

> If Cuban exile organizations had warned, asked, pleaded, or even suggested that Brothers to the Rescue not fly the next morning, would it have made sense that both Mr. Alejandre, as a leading member of the Cuban Council's coordinating group, and Mrs. Iriondo, as head of one of the organizations actively supporting the Council, place themselves against their wishes and fly with us? NO . . . the exile groups never asked us to cancel our mission for that day."

He also underscored that at no time had any government agency warned him not to fly that day. "My response [to any warnings] would have been very simple," said Basulto. "Let us take the day off."

Basulto also brought to light something that had not been revealed for twelve years: the note that Armando Alejandre Jr. had penned to him the night before and given to Sylvia Iriondo, stating his heart's desire to be part of the search-and-rescue mission. That note had been given to Armando Alejandre Sr. at the hangar the evening of the shoot-down. It was another testimony of Armando's desire to fly on February 24, 1996, and yet the Alejandre family never made mention of it.

There was no official rebuttal to Basulto's published letter, except for some e-mails that made the rounds, accusing Basulto of not taking responsibility, of being insensitive to the families, and of "putting his tail between his legs and running."

Just when it seemed things could not get worse before the twelfth anniversary commemoration, Luis Martínez, Batman, lost his battle with leukemia. Luis' wife and little daughter were at the hangar on Sunday, February

24, 2008, to say good-bye to the four planes taking flowers to Martyrs' Point. At the ceremony before takeoff, Guille once again led everyone in the prayer circle. When they called out the four men's names to everyone's response of "Presente!" Luis Martínez was added to the roster.

Aurelio Hurtado de Mendoza, Basulto's first U.S. flight instructor, flew the N2506, which also carried Basulto and Arnaldo Iglesias. Mayte piloted her own Cessna 340 with Billy Schuss, Conrad Webber, and a photographer onboard. Piloting his own aircraft was Basulto's friend René Guerra. Guille Lares flew with Jamaican-born Barrington Irving, a pilot and friend he had been mentoring for years. Irving had just been heralded for setting two world records: he was the youngest person and the first black pilot to fly solo around the globe. Barrington was president of Experience Aviation, an organization dedicated to bringing the love, experience, and passion for flying to inner-city children.

To ward off the emotions and jitter, the chatter between the four planes began.

"Who's the stewardess onboard?" asked Conrad, once they were airborne on Mayte's Cessna.

"She stayed on the ground," said Mayte. "So you can have coffee, tea, or Billy."

"When we get to Martyrs' Point, Guille will say a prayer," said Basulto from the N2506. "He's always been our antenna to God." Before crossing the 24th parallel, Basulto called Havana Center and informed them of that day's mission.

"Havana Center received, but you are not authorized to enter our jurisdictional waters," came the reply. "The zone is activated, it's very dangerous, and you don't have any authority to go in. Abandon your mission."

"We're not going to enter the zones of danger," Basulto responded, "and especially not Cuban airspace, but we will be crossing the 24th."

"Abort," they repeated. "The area is activated."

"That means we're hot," said Mayte, a little nervous now. When it came time for her plane to call Havana Center, she told Billy that she would speak in English. She felt that if a woman—an American woman—relayed the message, they would respect it more.

"Havana Center copies," they responded to Mayte in English. "We advise you that the area south of 24th is activated and we recommend you abort your mission."

She turned off her transponder. "Is the Coast Guard down there? Can you see them?" she asked her crew, wanting to make sure the U.S. presence was below. There were other boats in the area, too.

Then the four planes entered an on-air discussion over a "code blue" they heard announced. They could not figure out what it meant or who it came from.

"I think it means 'fuck off,'" said Basulto.

"Don't worry," said Mayte. "I brought my passport, my lipstick, and extra underwear just in case." "Just in case" meant a landing in Cuba, something none of them wanted to do.

When they rallied around Martyrs' Point, the pilots in the Cessnas threw the flowers over the spot where their friends had been murdered twelve years earlier. Guille Lares gave a short eulogy, thanking God for their opportunity to be there and for protecting them.

"Thank you for the assurance that Mario, Carlos, Armando, and Pablo are in your presence, and now, our brother Luis. You know our hearts, Lord; we want justice to be done."

36

Indictment

In the end, Fidel Castro got away with murder.
Matt Lawrence and Thomas Van Hare, in their book, *Betrayal*

Fidel Castro had admitted to *Time* magazine, to Dan Rather on a special edition of the evening news, and to the world that he gave the order for the shoot-down. You can only take so much provocation, he added. However, he would never admit that the "pirate aircraft" of the "terrorist organization Brothers to the Rescue which may have been carrying arms," were shot down in international waters—despite the evidence of radar screens, timing sequences, and the condemnation of the ICAO.

Since Cuba claimed responsibility for the downing, Basulto began a new project: the indictment of Fidel Castro. As head of the military and because of his proven record of drug trafficking, Raúl Castro was included. An audiotape had surfaced with Raúl's voice instructing his military generals that the planes were to be shot down whenever they thought it was prudent, with one stipulation: shoot them over the water. He did not want a ball of fire coming down on the people of Havana.

The rule of law that was to be applied to the Castro brothers was given impetus when a five-year-old rafter was found floating alone in an inner tube on Thanksgiving Day in 1999.

Elián González left Cárdenas, Cuba, with his mother and twelve others several days before Thanksgiving on an aluminum boat that had a faulty engine. His mother and eight others drowned. Elián was found by fishermen, unconscious but unharmed. He would later tell the story of how dolphins protected him during his journey.

Elián received gifts, had birthday parties, played with Diane Sawyer on *60 Minutes*, and went to Disney World. Elián had a great-uncle and cousin in Miami, as well as three hundred thousand Cuban Americans who were going to do their darnedest to make sure he never went back to his hometown of Cárdenas, to a father who had basically abandoned him.

But his uber-Father, Fidel Castro, wanted him home. Under the rule of law and on Attorney General Janet Reno's orders, an eight-member SWAT team made it happen in the wee hours after Good Friday in April 2000. A Border Patrol agent with an MP-5 submachine gun forced Elián out of the closet where he was hiding with the fisherman that had saved his life. While the SWAT team yelled, "Give me the fucking boy or we'll shoot you!" Elián screamed for help. He was whisked away in a white van.

Photographer Alan Díaz (who had sneaked in the house with the SWAT team) won a Pulitzer Prize, Elián's Miami bedroom was turned into a museum, and the boy was reunited with his papi. Father and son spent several months in the United States getting to know each other, on the tab of the American people. America even hosted Elián's class of Junior Pioneers of the Revolution, in uniform, who visited him sans parents, at the Wye Plantation near Andrews Air Force Base. Finally, under the rule of law, Elián went home and Fidel Castro helped blow out the candles at the child's seventh birthday party.

The rule of law, in its most basic form, is the principle that no one is above the law. Thomas Paine stated in his 1776 pamphlet "Common Sense": "For as in absolute governments the king is law, so in free countries the law ought to be king; and there ought to be no other." The rule of law in the United States said that only a parent could rule in an immigration case for their child. The matter was complicated because Elian's mother was dead, the boy was estranged from his father, Cuba was not a free country, and under the Communist dictatorship, Fidel Castro (the king) was law.

In the Brothers to the Rescue case, Fidel Castro had murdered three American citizens and one legal resident, so the rule of law applied in that he could be indicted for murder. The United States had gone after a head of state in the past when they indicted, tried, and convicted Manuel Noriega of Panama. The legal group Judicial Watch in Washington, D.C., and CANF campaigned along with Basulto, who spent two years collecting more than 105,000 signatures for the indictment.

"No congressman, senator, mayor, commissioner, or judge has been able to get as many signatures as Basulto without a political apparatus, or money," wrote *El Nuevo Herald* contributor Soren Triff.

"We can triple that if necessary, but how many signatures do you need to follow the law?" Basulto asked at a news conference early in 2001. In October he would fly to Brussels, Belgium, to pursue the indictment, with Judicial Watch Chairman and General Counsel Larry Klayman.

"If Fidel thinks he's 'off the hook' he is very sadly mistaken," said Klayman. "There's much more to come for this tyrant."

Supporters were vocal. An editorial on July 5, 2000, encouraged President Clinton to charge Castro with murder. "Yes, Mr. Clinton," wrote the editorial board of the *Miami Herald*, "Fidel Castro has no intention of changing stripes and he did murder four South Floridians in cold blood. So why doesn't your Justice Department bring criminal charges against Castro, brother Raúl who leads the military, and all others involved in this atrocious deed?"

Two years later, the Bush administration indicted the Cuban Air Force general that relayed the immediate order to shoot down the planes, as well as the Pérez Pérez brothers who executed the order. The former Clinton policy advisor Richard Nuccio called the indictments "a fairly meaningless gesture that follows in a long string of meaningless gestures . . . and don't do anything to either advance or undermine U.S.-Cuban relations."

Basulto argued that heads of state did not have immunity. "Does the rule of law apply to everyone or is it only used when it's convenient?" asked Basulto. His pledge of $1 million for any information leading to the indictment stood firm. No one came forward and neither did the money.

So he began another project: the preparation of a dossier. For more than a year Basulto gathered, indexed, and photocopied every piece of evidence against the Castro government, and against the U.S. government as well. He and his friend Hank Tester swamped the Department of Justice by enforcing the Freedom of Information Act (FOIA). The average turnaround time was four years. When Basulto or Tester finally received declassified documents, the majority of their contents were blacked out, some pages with only a word or two left to read. Ironically, the lack of information would arrive with a note confirming every citizen's right to request declassified information from the U.S. government.

No grand revelations came about using the FOIA. But nuances in the taped and transcribed conversations among the different government agencies the day of the shoot-down did expose some people's attitudes toward Brothers to the Rescue. The recorders were working in the U.S. Customs offices, and almost every word that was exchanged among the different agencies was made available under the Freedom of Information Act in tomes of documents.

The night before the shoot-down, Hank Tracey, a mission specialist from Miami, had called Mike Durell at the U.S. Customs Service in Riverside, California, asking them to keep the Cudjoe Key balloons up because there was some "intel that they [BTTR] may go down and harass the Cubans."

There was name-calling on the transcribed conversations, too. Brothers was called "a Cuban ancestry type people" that go down and "harass the Cubans" and "inflict havoc over Cuba." When Ron Bechtold, operations officer at the Domestic Air Interdiction Coordination Center confirmed the shoot-down to another officer, the latter replied: "That'll teach them, maybe."

"Yeah!" Bechtold said. "Brothers to the Rescue . . . got themselves heard."

"Maybe we should nuke Cuba," suggested Joe Maxwell at Key West Customs.

The declassified documents also preserved for history the officers' insistence on detaining the survivors on Basulto's plane. "Don't let 'em get away, don't let anybody get to them." The name of the mysterious government official who detained Basulto's attorney outside of Customs the night of the shoot-down was never revealed.

"There's no way we can hold them," said Customs at Opa-locka, "unless the frigging president or the State Department or somebody says do so." Paradoxically, at that moment, agent Joseph A. Tedeschi was on a STU-III secured line with the White House, speaking to "a Helen somebody."

It was all there in black and white, available for the asking to any American who had the time to wait.

Basulto believed there had been a conspiracy in the events of February 24, 1996. The spy within the Brothers organization, Juan Pablo Roque, had been working for the FBI. The FBI knew one of their agents had been exfiltrated and they did not sound the alarms. U.S. government agencies were watching the Brothers to the Rescue flights that Saturday from four different radar stations, and did not warn them. The FAA, which had become a habitual nuisance before takeoff, did not come around that morning. Cuba had never shown any of the proofs they had damning Brothers to the Rescue and their "counterrevolutionary" activities. The interceptors at Homestead were told to stand down battle stations with nary an explanation.

"Tell him we wanted to go," the pilots had pleaded to Janet Ray Wein- inger. Her husband worked at Homestead Air Force Base and had been summoned there the afternoon of the shoot-down. "Please tell Basulto that *we wanted to go.*"

By February 2004, the five-hundred-page dossier was completed and dis- tributed to the local and national media, to Congress, to CANF, and to the attorneys involved in the myriad of cases sprouting from the events of Feb- ruary 24, 1996. Some people refused to accept it, refused to peruse the thick and laborious testimony of Brothers to the Rescue, did not want to touch it, not even some of the family members and their attorney, Frank Angones.

Basulto took a dossier with him everywhere he went, a ten-pound calling card he enthusiastically distributed. He spoke on the radio and on television shows about the dossier, and he delivered copies to lawmakers in Wash- ington. He carried the dossier to every speaking engagement, even to the all-girls high school of Our Lady of Lourdes Academy, which Mayte Greco had attended, and made it the bulk of his talk. Like an evangelical preacher desiring to spread God's message and give out Bibles, Basulto was ready to pound the message of truth and justice and hand out a dossier.

Over more than eight years, Basulto had written repeatedly to the De- partment of Justice, the Office of the Attorney General, and Presidents Clin- ton and Bush. It became his obsession, his every waking moment dedicated to showing the world what really happened on February 24, 1996.

Eight years after the shoot-down, he was unemployed, his savings were wiped out, and his family was struggling to reconnect with him. At every birthday celebration his middle son Felipe would joke about Basulto's final countdown, to age eighty, the number Felipe had calculated would be the nice round estimate of his father's life span. At his sixty-fifth birthday, he would remind him, "You've got fifteen left." A year later, "you've got four- teen left." More than a warning, it was his son's humorous and loving plea for Basulto to live life to the fullest, to enjoy the moment, to get closer to his family, his wife, and his grandchildren.

All Basulto wanted was answers, he wanted truth and justice, and he wanted the rule of law to apply. But the U.S. Justice Department, which had invoked the rule of law to return a little boy to Cuba, did not want to cooper- ate. They would not enforce the same law to bring a murderer to justice.

37

Spies, Wasps, and the Queen of Cuba

*Castro is still there because the world envies the U.S., and all
that hatred for the U.S. has gone to support Fidel Castro.*

Armando Valladares

A stolen laptop computer belonging to Cuban agents in Los Angeles, California, led the FBI to the arrest of ten people in Miami accused of being part of a Cuban government spy ring calling itself the Wasp Network. One of them was Brothers to the Rescue pilot René González. René was the ex–Cuban military pilot who had left Cuba on a crop duster and landed in Boca Chica, in the Florida Keys.

Brothers to the Rescue pilots were incredulous that René had been a spy, like Juan Pablo Roque. René was buena gente, good people.

René had attended the many memorial masses for the downed pilots, murders he knew of in advance. He and Roque had been given orders from Cuba: "Under no circumstances should agents German (Roque) or Castor (René) fly with BTTR or another organization on days 24, 25, 26, and 27 [of February]." Brothers historian Polo Núñez remembered René's comforting hand on his shoulder at one of those masses, giving him a reassuring squeeze, and a nod of sympathy and understanding. How can someone who expressed such emotion be a spy?

Alfredo Sánchez was shocked to hear about René. René was more than buena gente; René was his *friend*. He knew that Alfredo flew every Saturday, the day of the shoot-down. The man had nicknamed Alfredo's grandson "Rum-Rum" (pronounced room-room) because that's what the toddler would say every time he saw a helicopter. The nickname had stuck. How could someone who nicknamed my grandson be a spy?

Basulto and Ramón Saúl Sánchez from the Democracy Movement attended the arraignment of the ten spies. René and the others were brought in shackled. When René's eyes met Basulto's, he smiled. Basulto could never figure out what that smile meant. Was it a hello? Was it a smirk? Was it a grin of victory?

Five of the Wasp Network spies pleaded guilty and were returned to Cuba; the other five were brought before a court of law in Miami. The jury was composed of American citizens of varying backgrounds, none of them Cuban American or of Cuban descent.

Basulto was subpoenaed as a hostile witness and put on the stand for five long days—as if *he* were on trial. During his testimony from March 12 to 16, 2001, Basulto was asked numerous questions about Brothers to the Rescue tax returns and his salary of sixty thousand dollars in 1994. They asked about his previous employment as an engineer, a contractor, and a real estate agent. Basulto had stopped his professional jobs by 1993. It was only after he had depleted his own savings that he asked for a salary in 1994. The attorneys for the spies also questioned Brothers to the Rescue's operating costs of $18,412.00.

"How much was for meals?" they asked.

"I don't know," answered Basulto, "but we ate a lot of pizza."

They attacked him not only for the overflight of Havana on July 13, 1995, but also for the overflight during his trip to Guantánamo, when he flew over Punta Maisí on the eastern end of the island. "Did you do it because you were angry the U.S. authorities had not allowed you to visit the refugees?" they asked him.

"No sir," said Basulto. "I did it because it was *there*." Basulto went on to chastise the court for behaving as if the accused were Brothers to the Rescue and himself, and not "these gentlemen that are here." The court reprimanded him for giving a speech.

The photo Hank Tester had taken on the July 13, 1995, overflight of Havana was subpoenaed from WTVJ. That was the photo showing Basulto and Guille Lares laughing. Although their chuckle was a response to Hank Tester telling them in Spanish that he did not need any more footage, Basulto and Lares were accused of being reckless and of laughing off the severity of their actions.

Another discovery made during the trial was that René González was head of Operation Picada (which means bite), whose objective was to discredit Brothers to the Rescue, possibly by burning down the hangar and making it seem like an accident, negligence, or self-damage. A tale would be spun that the damage was Basulto's scheme for collecting insurance monies and contributions.

The spy trial lasted six months, all paid for by the U.S. government. Sentencing for the spies began December 11, 2001. Apart from his one week of testimony, Basulto was asked by the prosecution not to attend the rest of the trial. The Alejandre family, however, attended every single day for six months.

Judge Joan Lenard reminded René that he had been born in the United States and that when he came back, his citizenship had been honored. "But you came back with the purpose of serving a different country," she said.

"If I had to, I'd do it all over again," René said. He went on to attack the state attorney, the press, and all the exile groups.

René was sentenced to fifteen years in Marianna State Prison in Florida, charged with acting as a foreign agent. Gerardo Hernández, the ringleader, was given two consecutive life sentences for his conspiracy in the murders of Armando, Carlos, Mario, and Pablo. Ramón Labañino was given 216 months for conspiracy to obtain military secrets. Fernando González received twenty-two years for spying. Antonio Guerrero received a life sentence.

Also in the courtroom the day of sentencing were representatives of the International Action Center, a New York– and San Francisco–based antiwar group that was running a campaign called "Free the Five." They referred to the five convicted spies as "U.S.-held Cuban political prisoners."

In Cuba, "Free the Five" campaigns became very popular. They received international attention from countries rallying for the "Five Heroes of the Revolution" to be set free. After all, they argued, their mission had been to infiltrate organizations conducting terrorist activities against Cuba. According to the U.S. National Committee to Free the Cuban Five, their primary target was Brothers to the Rescue.

Apart from the formation of a national committee, there were fund-raising concerts in California, marches on Washington to Free the Cuban Five, and billboards in San Francisco. Free the Five websites allowed the prisoners to communicate with bloggers about the harsh life they endured in U.S. prisons. Petitions and letter-writing campaigns collected 102,000 signatures of people in seventy-eight countries demanding freedom for the convicted spies. Ten Nobel laureates claimed the five had not received a fair trial. The world united in bashing the United States and defending Cuba.

In Hollywood, actor Danny Glover was the force behind the documentary

The Trial: The Untold Story of the Cuban Five. At the premiere he asked his audience to support the work of the National Committee. "Let's get these heroes home to Cuba!" he called out.

Ultimately, the Supreme Court would choose not to hear the final appeal of the Cuban Five.

One week after 9-11, another spy was caught at the Center for Defense Information (CDI). Her name was Ana Belén Montes, the woman who had been directing U.S. policy toward Cuba for more than sixteen years. The group that brought her down included the Defense Intelligence Agency's senior counterintelligence investigator, Scott Carmichael, who wrote a book titled *True Believer* on the events leading up to Montes' arrest. The self-named "Queen of Cuba," Montes told interrogators at the Defense Intelligence Agency that she regretted only two things: getting caught and hurting her mother.

In his book, Carmichael writes that Ana Belén Montes arranged a meeting with representatives from various federal agencies and retired Admiral Eugene Carroll on Friday night, February 23, 1996—the night before the shoot-down—so that everyone could hear about Carroll's recent visit to the island. Carroll was the general to whom the Cubans had posed the question about the ramifications of shooting down the Brothers' planes.

After the shoot-down, as the senior intelligence expert on the Cuban military, Ana Belen Montes was called to the Pentagon. Montes spun the incident to make the Cubans seem like the victims, not the aggressors. She abruptly left the meeting at eight o'clock in the evening for personal reasons, something that simply was never done. But Montes' clout and expertise were seldom questioned. It would later be discovered that at that precise hour she was relaying a message to Cuba detailing the military response the United States was considering.

"The Cubans weren't viewed as the bad guys, after all; the deaths of U.S. citizens were attributed to negligence by the government of the United States," wrote Scott Carmichael in *True Believer.* After all, Carroll had warned them the night before.

According to Carmichael, Montes met with Cuban intelligence officers every two weeks in restaurants in and around Washington, D.C. She never removed classified documents from her office; instead, she memorized them and typed them onto computer disks.

"She gave away all our sources and methods, all our judgments. She participated in every significant policy decision on Cuba for nine years, and she told the Cubans about every single one of them," Carmichael said. "The danger is not that Cuba is going to land troops on Miami Beach," he added. The danger is that the information Montes gave Castro would be passed on to other nations hostile to the United States. "Fidel Castro's greatest strength is his knowledge of us."

The events of 9-11 would hasten the arrest of the Queen of Cuba. She was privy to national security secrets that Cuba could forward to hostile countries.

Montes' name was added to the list of super-spies like Aldrich Ames at the CIA and the FBI's Robert Hanssen. She was one of the longest-running spies in U.S. history. She operated alone, and never received any money from the Cuban government for her spying. She did it because she was a true believer that U.S. policies toward Cuba were wrong.

Montes' admission of guilt softened her sentence to twenty-five years in prison without possibility of parole. Federal Judge Ricardo M. Urbina, of Puerto Rican descent like Montes, pronounced her sentence. "Today is a very sad day for you, your family, your loved ones, and for every American that suffered from your betrayal of the United States," he said. "If you cannot love your country, at least you should do it no wrong."

After the Wasp Network trial, suspicions arose about certain other people who had volunteered for Brothers to the Rescue. Basulto suspected two other pilots, but he had no means of proving anything. Looking back, the organization realized they should have been wary of René and Roque, good friends who were both ex–Cuban military. The two had frequently annoyed the other pilots by conversing in Russian. What had they been talking about all those times?

The suspicions about sabotage of the airplanes that so many Brothers pilots had previously mumbled in muted terms did not seem so far-fetched anymore. The cause of Koki's crippling accident was attributed to a mechanic's error; that never seemed like a good enough explanation. Guille Lares' water crash happened right after the plane had been serviced. Another time, some donated airplane oil had been found to be contaminated with metal dust. A tampered radiator triggered an oil leak in mid-flight, leading to another emergency landing.

The photograph of Roque cutting his fortieth birthday cake in half was now symbolic. The cake was in the shape of a plane.

While the spy trial was taking place in Miami, Fidel Castro was visiting a university in Tehran, where he gave a speech on May 10, 2001. He met with Iranian leaders President Khatami and Ayatollah Khamenei. "Iran and Cuba, in cooperation with each other, can bring America to its knees," Castro told them.

Four months after Castro's visit, when the entire world was sent to its knees after the attacks in the United States on September 11, 2001, Brothers to the Rescue remembered Fidel's comment. They bought a billboard and positioned it on Bird Road in southwest Miami. It showed a picture of Fidel Castro with Sadam Hussein, Osama bin Laden, and Muammar Gaddafi, and quoted Fidel's statement.

> Who said, "Iran and Cuba, in cooperation with each other, can bring America to its knees"?

Commuters drove by, oblivious, or perhaps snickering at those crazy, right-wing Cuban exiles who truly believed that an insignificant island nation a half-hour's flight away could be so dangerous to the United States. They did not ask themselves whether it was possible that Cuban spies were here to gather intel not only for Cuba but also for other rogue nations, terrorist nations. The previous year Cuba had been the only country attending the Ibero-American Summit in Panama that refused to condemn terrorism. "The U.S. regime is very weak," Castro added in his speech at Tehran University, "and we are witnessing this weakness from close up."

Close up indeed, only ninety miles away.

38

Letting Go

*The truth is that our finest moments are most likely to occur
when we are feeling deeply uncomfortable, unhappy, or
unfulfilled. For it is only in such moments, propelled by our
discomfort, that we are likely to step out of our ruts and start
searching for different ways or truer answers.*

M. Scott Peck

On February 4, 2003, Brothers to the Rescue announced that it was discontinuing its search-and-rescue missions over the Florida Straits. By then, the number of people escaping Cuba on rafts had drastically diminished. Brothers to the Rescue had saved 4,200 from the waters of the Florida Straits, and during the 1994 exodus it had helped the Coast Guard to save over thirty thousand more.

The desperation in the Straits was still far from over, however. The Coast Guard was as busy as ever, because a more lucrative method became popular: human trafficking. People on both sides of the Straits were profiting. The price per person was approximately eight to ten thousand dollars, presumably half going to local Cuban authorities on the island bribed to look the other way.

With the proliferation of the trafficking movement, some people accused Brothers to the Rescue of on occasion charging money for looking for people in the Florida Straits. When one of these persons approached Juan González, the pilot and volunteer who had found the first rafter, Juan was livid.

"Brothers to the Rescue?!" he exclaimed. "We have *never* charged a single person for a rescue!" He was incensed. "You bring me the person we ever charged, because if he exists, *then he still owes us the money.*"

Money would have come in handy for Brothers to the Rescue, because there was little support for promoting change from within the island.

After the search-and-rescue flights stopped, the *Coquí,* the Cessna that the Cuban exiles in Puerto Rico had donated to Brothers to the Rescue, was sold for sixty thousand dollars to pay hangar rental space and maintenance for the last remaining plane, the N2506, *Seagull One,* the survivor of the shoot-down. Soon thereafter, the ten-thousand-square-foot Gregorio Pérez Ricardo hangar at Opa-locka retired its nineteen national flags and shut its doors for good.

Now *Seagull One* huddled in a small rented portion of someone else's hangar, among the Lear jets and the weekend island-hoppers of the well-off. She stood in her assigned corner, resting. Anyone opening this hangar, unaware of her past glories, would probably not give her a second look. A casual observer would not know that her body of aluminum, bolts, and rivets had skirted an attack by the longest-living Communist dictator in history. One would never guess that this thirty-foot blue four-seater had outrun a Cuban MiG that was capable of pulverizing her, as it had done to her two sister planes. *Seagull One* did not look like the kind of machinery that had been an instrument of change, floating half a million messages of hope to the Cuban people.

This blue speck in the sky had been the first glimpse of freedom for thousands of people who now walked the streets of Miami. The hum of its motors had awoken many exhausted rafters who thought the end of their life was at hand. The blue bird flying protectively overhead had been their revival. How many arms reached up in hallelujahs to the N2506, how many children had been raised up to her enveloping wings? *Seagull One* was the salvation bird of mariners on a quest for freedom, a holy spirit for rafters. She was the hovering mother that waited until other rescuers—the Coast Guard—would lift, carry, and embrace the souls she had spotted. She may not have looked like the ark that contained heroes, freedom fighters, patriots, fathers, mothers, sons. Her open wings welcomed everyone. Her seats had cradled pilots young and old, all leaving behind the sweat of their labors, the tears of their glories, imprinted forever in her fabric seats worn to a smooth, shiny finish. She had carried water, food, radios, first-aid kits, and life vests—dropping from the heavens the tools that would save a life below.

Like notches carved in the walls of a prison, her body was marked with dates and times and numbers of souls rescued—the stickers her pilots craved, not so much in competition as in compassion: a counting of souls after a successful mission. Was there a tally somewhere of how many na-tionalities of media personnel had sat in the cramped backseat, getting sick in the hundred-degree heat, fighting sleep, capturing shot after shot of the agony below? How many countries had witnessed and recorded the plight of a country just ninety miles away from the freest country on earth? This is happening, they would write. Look at this, it really happened. It will happen again.

Seagull One had completed her threefold mission: save lives, send a message of solidarity, and show the world what was happening. She had declared over and over again: "I am the change. The struggle is ours."

The pilots and volunteers went back to their jobs, their families, their lives. There were weddings, births, baptisms, and funerals, too. The hangar and the offices were shut down, fourteen years of history boxed and stored away.

Rita Basulto continued her real estate business while Basulto unofficially retired. Their savings had been exhausted, so they took advantage of the real estate market before it imploded and sold their beautiful South Miami home. The oversized painting of Manolín Guillot Castellano, the bleeding Cuban, was tenderly shrouded and retired to a new home at A+ Mini Storage.

The Basultos moved a few blocks away into the humble home that had belonged to their eldest son José, nicknamed Peco. The modest two-bedroom, two-bath house was built in the 1950s and had never been remodeled. It was badly in need of repairs, but Rita would have to wait another three years before any remodeling was done. Their new home did not have a proper driveway, so when all the kids came to visit, the street view of the house was blocked by a row of irregularly parked cars. There was a lot of in-and-out traffic of their five children and eight grandchildren. To an outsider, the constant stream of cars and people entering and exiting their rundown home may have raised eyebrows and suspicion about these new neighbors. Bringing levity to their parents' downsized lives, the Basulto children nicknamed their parents' new home "the crack house."

Basulto's hobbies, which had always been guns and planes, had to be downsized, too, since he was no longer flying. His fascination for armaments led him to a new hobby: building cannons. He spent hours sanding, cutting, drilling, and painting his historical replicas of Coastal cannons and Napoleon cannons, each two feet long. He even built the little cannonballs. It was his private therapy after the opus magnum of Brothers to the Rescue.

On the eleventh anniversary of the Brothers to the Rescue shoot-down, he hauled his first cannon to overlook Biscayne Bay behind the Virgin of Charity Church in Coconut Grove. After the memorial mass, he shot off four rounds, one for each man murdered. It was a symbolic wake-up call to people on both sides of the Straits. The blasts from the two-foot replica also set off all the burglar alarms on the cars in the parking lot.

During the same waning years, Billy Schuss retired and began his own project: his memoir on Brothers to the Rescue. Billy, who had never written anything before in his life, spent years penning the day-to-day stories of life with Brothers to the Rescue. He wrote it in Spanish and published it in 2007, titled *Día tras día con los Hermanos al Rescate* (Day after Day with Brothers to the Rescue). Like Basulto's cannon-building, the memoir-writing was therapeutic and healing for Billy, to get down on paper what he could not explain through the spoken word. The day of his book signing, Billy Schuss was all smiles.

Unfortunately for Basulto, that evening marked the death of his closest friend, Guillermo Miranda. Miranda, who had donated more than seven thousand pairs of shoes to the people of Guantánamo, died of a massive, fatal heart attack.

By 2007, the Brothers to the Rescue account had dipped to almost nothing, not even enough to pay for the warehouse space for the boxed files, let alone for *Seagull One* to rest in someone else's hangar. Rita Basulto was reminding her husband about the lack of funds one day as they went to the post office box to pick up the Brothers to the Rescue mail. In the middle of Rita's complaint about finances, Basulto turned around and gave her a letter he had just opened.

"Here, Rita," he said. "Now be quiet." Inside the letter was a ten-thousand-dollar donation from Mr. William B. Iovenko of Kentucky, commending the group for their valiant efforts at saving so many lives. Basulto wrote him back, explaining that Brothers no longer did search and rescue, but merely continued to own and maintain one aircraft that served as a reminder to the community of what they had done. He also said that the Brothers to the Rescue efforts were now concentrated on documenting the history of the organization. Mr. Iovenko never asked for the money back. So the N2506 and the files were housed for another year.

But through 2008, the decimal point in the account kept moving to the left. Once again, someone came to Brothers' rescue. Commercial developer and friend Ralph Sánchez sponsored a cocktail party recognizing Brothers to the Rescue's contribution to the community. Sánchez was well known and respected in the South Florida community, most famous for bringing car racing to South Florida and building the NASCAR racetrack in Homestead.

Sánchez's cocktail party for Brothers to the Rescue raised enough to house the N2506, and the archives, for another year.

"That's how it's always been," said Basulto. "Every time we need something, God finds a person, a way, and we make it. That is the essence of Brothers to the Rescue."

The 2008 hurricane season took out its fury over Cuba. Two Category 4 storms, Gustav and Ike, left Cuba with flooding, death, and billions of dollars worth of destruction. Basulto wanted to do something for his brothers across the Straits.

"Our humanitarian mission has always been to help the people of Cuba," he said. "We've saved lives by rescuing rafters, we've tried to save lives by supporting the internal dissident movement, now we want to save lives by helping the victims of Hurricane Ike."

So he decided to sell the last icon of Brothers to the Rescue: the N2506, his beloved *Seagull One*.

39

Seagull One

Where's the success of Castro's revolution? Look around you,
it's right here, in Miami.

José Basulto

On September 23, 2008, *Seagull One* was shined and polished and rolled under the covered breezeway at Opa-locka Airport in preparation for a press conference. Like paparazzi buzzing around movie stars on the South Beach scene, television and newspaper reporters filmed and photographed her as they interviewed José Basulto and Billy Schuss. Rita Basulto, the Lares brothers, and Mayte Greco-Regan joined the founders of Brothers to the Rescue for one more prayer circle before *Seagull One*'s final mission: to be put on the auction block to raise funds to help the people of Cuba.

The auction was front-page news the next day, and several people expressed interest in purchasing the plane, valued at one hundred thousand dollars. Some balked at Basulto's conditions, though. He stipulated that the N2506 either had to be preserved as is or converted back to its original appearance. If the buyer wished to use the plane for private purposes, the logo of Brothers to the Rescue would have to be stripped and the N2506 registration number retired. The N2506 had saved thousands of rafters, and most important, it had outrun the Cuban MiGs, making it possible to tell the world the true events of February 24, 1996. The agreement specified that Brothers to the Rescue would donate the money from the sale to the Sisters of Charity. The Sisters, in turn, would send the money to hurricane-ravaged Cuba. Once again, Brothers to the Rescue would help their Cuban brothers and sisters.

Basulto's heart's desire was to find someone who would showcase the plane and let it be flown on the anniversaries of the shoot-down. Perhaps that person would donate it to the Smithsonian, the Air and Space Museum, or perhaps the yet-to-be-built Bay of Pigs museum. The plane needed to be sold, but Basulto did not want to let her go. "It's like handing over my daughter; I want to make sure whoever gets her will care for her like I did."

It would be Cuban American success story Benjamín León Jr. that would love and care for the N2506. León, a health-care industry veteran, was owner of the first health maintenance organization (HMO) in Florida, and present founder and chairman of León Medical Centers, a health-care provider serving Miami–Dade County Medicare patients, as well as León Medical Centers Health Plans, an HMO he had recently sold for four hundred million dollars.

León arrived at his Coral Gables home late in the evening of the day the offering was written up in the paper. He went into his bedroom, took off his coat, and threw the day's *Miami Herald* on the bed. The article on the sale of the N2506 stared back at him.

It was almost 11:00 p.m. when he dialed his senior vice president, Charles Núñez, a childhood friend of Basulto's. "Would it be too late to call Basulto?" he asked. He told Charles he wanted the plane, and he wanted to make sure no one got to it before he did. He wanted it right away. "I always listen to God's voice, and I act on it immediately," he would later tell Basulto. "When you go against that intuition, it never works out."

His parents' intuition was what prompted sixteen-year-old Benjamín León Jr. to leave Cuba in 1961, after he was arrested for arguing with a neighborhood Communist about some of Fidel Castro's new policies. León remembers touching down in Miami on January 12, 1961, at 7:25 p.m. on KLM Airlines. He had five dollars in his pocket. Over the next year, he would finish high school and work as a dishwasher at the Shelbourne Hotel on Collins Avenue in South Beach for a salary of $7.50 for a twelve-hour day. He delivered the *Miami Herald* newspaper in the morning and the *Miami News* in the evening. When his parents sent him a one-thousand-dollar bill from Cuba, he hired a private tutor from the Berlitz Academy to teach him English. He later worked in the factories of Hialeah, at grocery stores stocking cans and bagging groceries, and in Cuban bakeries, baking bread and crackers.

His mother, father, and brother arrived in August 1961, and they rented a studio on South Beach for ninety dollars a month. In Cuba, his father had been the accountant for several medical clinics. With León Sr.'s business savvy, his son's administrative and sales talents, the marketing skills of partner Moisés Liber, and the medical skills of recently arrived Cuban doctors—some of whom were not yet licensed to practice in the United States—they opened Clínica Cubana on Flagler Street in 1964. Shortly thereafter, León Sr., León Jr., Liber, and the group of physicians founded Clínica Asociación Cubana (Cuban Clinic Association) in 1970. After much lobbying, the group was awarded the first HMO license in Florida. The small Cuban Clinic Association became a multi-million-dollar health services company and was eventually sold.

At León Medical Centers, the elderly are treated like guests at a five-star hotel: greeted at the door by uniformed doormen and taken personally from doctor to doctor by specially trained staff. All the clinics have a little coffee station, open all day, serving free coffee and pastries to their "guests." The yearly budget for *pastelitos* alone is more than two hundred thousand dollars.

A man of many hobbies, León Jr. became a pilot. He owned a Cessna 182 and a six-passenger Turbo Prop that he called his "Ferrari in the air."

León Jr. had always admired the work of the pilots of Brothers to the Rescue. Basulto and the N2506 had rescued his current director of transportation, Carlos Recino. He wanted the N2506. He needed her to teach his grandchildren another piece of Cuban history. León Jr. had plans to establish a small museum for the N2506, complete with the painting of Cuban patriot Manolín Guillot Castellano. He agreed to all of Basulto's terms.

"I knew God would send me a Cuban pilot with the right financial resources," said Basulto, "and a heart in the right place."

The press conference to finalize the sale on November 18, 2008, was well attended by the local news, print, and radio media. Sister Hilda Alonso of the Sisters of Charity of Miami held the cardboard check for one hundred thousand dollars, while photographers snapped pictures of the five-foot-tall nun surrounded by Benjamín León Jr., José Basulto, and Koki Lares.

Koki Lares' prayer at the press conference sounded more like a eulogy, as if one of his closest friends was moving on to a better place. He was unable to hold back his tears. "José, I felt His presence here today, so strongly," he said as he walked away, steadying himself on his two crutches. "The Lord was here with us today."

The sale of the N2506 seemed like a final parting, a cutting of the umbilical cord connecting the Cubans over here to the Cubans over there. Brothers to the Rescue was without money, planes, pilots, or volunteers. "Yet," said Basulto's friend, Lorenzo De Toro, "I'm convinced the mission of Brothers to the Rescue is not over."

Brothers' rallying cry for change from within Cuba remained steadfast. The only thing Basulto could offer his brothers and sisters across the Straits was the mantra that had spearheaded the organization seventeen years ago: *El cambio soy yo*. I am the change.

40

José Basulto

*The only tyrant I accept in this world is the "still small voice"
within me.*

Mahatma Gandhi

The July Saturday afternoon was typical of a Miami summer: hot and muggy.
Rita and José Basulto were soaking in the beautiful Sunday afternoon with
their eldest son, Peco, and his family, aboard Peco's fifty-foot Viking Sport-
fish named *The Islander*. Sailboats passed them lazily, silently, accepting the
small whiffs of summer wind but in no hurry to get anywhere. *The Islander*
and its twin 820-horsepower engines cut through the ocean waters, creating a much-appreciated breeze for its crew. The aquamarines of the Atlantic
bled up into the blue of the sky. There was nothing to do but spend time
together with family.

Monica, the younger daughter, was visiting from North Carolina with
her husband and their two children, Rogelio and Luca. Felipe, the middle
Basulto son, and Andre, the eldest grandchild, were there, too. The kids
were enjoying cousin time. Absent were Albert, the youngest Basulto, who
was home with his wife and their newborn baby, Sammy. Ana, the elder
daughter, was at home in New Orleans, pregnant with her second son.

The group onboard sailed south from Hallandale, where Peco lived, toward Elliott Key. When they were just east of Miami Beach, one of the kids
pointed to something in the water. Peco slowed down and Basulto went to
the port side of *The Islander*, and scrutinized what was bobbing in the water.
The younger kids scampered to his side, holding on as the boat rocked from
side to side.

He looked up at Peco, standing on the bridge looking back at him seriously, a handsomer and younger version of himself. He saw Andre, now
sixteen years old, and he remembered cradling him in that long-ago photograph taken the day of the inauguration of the hangar at Opa-locka. Andre

had been about two years old then, as old as the organization was at that time; he was now almost a man. Rita was smiling, deep in conversation with Monica, maybe talking about Ana's unborn son, due any day now. Felipe and Rogelio, Monica's husband, were up on deck with Peco, but they were looking out in the opposite direction, laughing at something Basulto was not in on yet. The kids wobbled next to their grandfather as *The Islander* settled down. The children were anxious to arrive at Elliot Key and jump into the water. There was Tina, his only granddaughter, a clever little girl in a sea of boy cousins. Tina, who liked to call him "Googie" and wanted him to build her a cannon of her very own, orange if possible.

The sun blazed down on him as he looked from face to face. It was a moment he wanted to freeze for all time. He had missed so many of these moments.

The old nagging came back, the little voice telling him to do something, to act, the washing machine churning. Spinning around were Gregorio, the first rafter, Billy's call, the Lares brothers—all tumbling around with Armando, Carlos, Mario, Pablo, *Presente!* I am the change. Koki and his crutches, the outstretched hands from the water. The city of rafts. Floating tombstones. *Seagull One.* Truth and justice. *The struggle is ours.*

"What do you want me to do, Dad?" Peco called from the bridge, interrupting the tortuous spinning in Basulto's mind. Basulto looked up at his son and tried to block out the midday sun with his right hand. Serious Peco, successful businessman, responsible son, dutiful father—where had he learned all that? Peco waited, his attention full on his father now. Rogelio and Felipe also put their laughter on hold, pausing for his direction. Everyone seemed to stop for just a moment, waiting for permission to continue with the day, the beautiful day, full of family and fun.

"Let it go, son," Basulto said, louder than necessary, to cover any hesitancy in his voice. He smiled up at Peco, then quickly turned away from everyone and walked alone to the stern of *The Islander* to watch the strong wake of the revved-up motors push away the floating object. It got smaller and smaller, until it seemed like there was an ocean between him and it.

It was an empty raft.

Sources

Unpublished Materials

"Affidavit of Sean Patrick Gearhart," May 20, 1996. Prepared by law firm of Angones et al. In possession of Sofía Powell, Esq.

"Agreement for the use of the Cocoplum Community Club." Contract between Cocoplum Community Club and José Basulto. December 29, 1991. Brothers to the Rescue (hereafter BTTR) Archives. [Contract for use of pool for training exercises.]

"Air drop Elbow Cay, March 10, 1994." Video. BTTR Archives.

Alemán, Nelson to José Basulto, August 7, 2006. BTTR Archives.

Aronoff, Jonathan to José Basulto, June 29, 1996. BTTR. [Note of condolence in Maxwell House coffee can full of pennies.]

Basulto, José. Cockpit in-flight audiotape recording. February 24, 1996. BTTR Archives.

Brothers to the Rescue. Untitled press release. December 25, 1992. BTTR Archives.

———. "Flights of February 24, 1996." Press release. February 22, 1996. BTTR Archives.

———. "Indictment." Press release. February 2, 2001. BTTR Archives.

———. "Operation Martin Luther King Jr." Press release. January 19, 1996. BTTR Archives.

———. "Program for events commemorating February 24, 1998." Press release. February 23, 1998. BTTR Archives.

———. "Resuming of flights." Press release. August 26, 1996. BTTR Archives.

———. "The downing of Brothers to the Rescue aircraft on February 24, 1996: summary of unanswered questions prepared by Brothers to the Rescue." Dossier. BTTR Archives.

———. Letters. Correspondence with Rep. IRL, BTTR Archives. [Various letters to Department of Defense re: mothballed planes.]

———. to President George W. Bush. May 18, 2001. BTTR Archives. [Request for criminal indictment of Fidel Castro for murder of Brothers to the Rescue pilots.]

CBS Evening News. Art Rascon reporting. Video recording of WTVJ broadcast, March 2, 1996, 6:30 P.M. BTTR Video Archives.

Channel 23, WLTV, News. Video recording of June 20, 1996, 6 P.M., broadcast. BTTR Video Archives.

CNN News. Video recording of José Basulto speaking on memorial. March 1, 1996. BTTR Video Archives.

"Cuban Government complaint over flight violation by private aircraft from Guantána-mo." Memorandum from U.S. Interests Section, Havana, to Secretary of State, Washington D.C., Decl. 4-10-02, Nov. 1994. (Declassified April 10, 2002.) BTTR Archives.

"Emergency Order of Revocation." Letter from Keith S. May, FAA, to José Basulto. May 16, 1996. BTTR Archives.

Federal Aviation Administration to José Basulto. September 1, 1995. BTTR Archives.

"Flight of December 19, 1992." June 27, 2000. Raúl U. Martínez, to José Basulto, correspondence. Brothers to the Rescue Archives.

Fox News reports, Channel 7, WSVN. Videotaped excerpts of news broadcasts, February 24–26, 1996. BTTR Video Archives.

Fowler, George J. to James S. Reynolds, U.S. Department of Justice. June 14, 2001. BTTR Archives. [Requesting indictment of Fidel Castro for murder of the Brothers to the Rescue pilots.]

García-Pedrosa, José. Diary of visit to Guantánamo, November 7–8, 1994. BTTR Archives.

International Civil Aviation Organization (ICAO). "Report of the Investigation Regarding the Shooting Down of Two U.S.-Registered Private Civil Aircraft by Cuban Military Aircraft on 24 February 1996," presented by the Secretary General. C-WP/10441 RESTRICTED. June 6, 1996.

"José Monroy Accident." Video footage. August 17, 1993. BTTR Video Archives.

Judicial Watch. "Criminal indictment of Fidel Castro." Mailing. October 6, 2001. BTTR Archives.

———. "Pursuing criminal indictment of Castro." Press release. February 15, 2002. BTTR Archives.

Labor Relations Board. Minutes of meeting with Air Traffic Control (ATC) Administration to investigate Cuban air traffic controllers. September 1, 1996. Rancho Boyeros, Cuba.

"Leaflets over Havana." Video. January 9, 1996. BTTR Archives.

Letter (name withheld) to José Basulto, May 10, 1992. BTTR Archives.

Marshall, Randall C., ACLU official, to José Basulto. August 8, 2001. BTTR Archives.

McCurry, Mike. Press briefing, the White House Office of the Press Secretary, The Briefing Room. February 26, 1996. BTTR Archives.

Memorial mass booklet from St. Agatha Catholic Church. February 24, 1997. BTTR Archives. [Church bulletin from first memorial mass.]

"Memorial Video." March 2, 1996, BTTR Video Archives.

Miami Ahora. Videotape of broadcast featuring Manuel Reboso, July 1995. BTTR Video Archives.

Morales, Pablo. Unpublished manuscripts of various writings and poetry. BTTR Archives.

NBC Evening News. Videotape of April 16, 1996, broadcast on WTVJ. BTTR Video Archives.

Núñez, Leopoldo. "Brothers to the rescue chronology." Unpublished manuscript. BTTR Archives.

Paralelo 24 No. 12 (February–March 1996) and No. 14 (June–July 1996). Publication of Brothers to the Rescue, on file in BTTR Archives.

Rosendahl, Bruce R., Thomas N. Lee, Claes G. H. Rooth; Donald B. Olson, Kevin D. Leaman, and Chris Mooers. "Where have all the rafters gone? Roulette in the Straits of Florida." Draft version 3 of unpublished editorial submitted to the *Miami Herald* and *El Nuevo Herald.* BTTR Archives.

Sánchez, Alfredo J. "21 July 1991: U.S. Military Response to Cuban Threat to Civilian Aircraft." Report prepared for BTTR. BTTR Archives.

"Segundo Borges Ashes over Cuba." Video. March 7, 1995. In possession of Félix I. Rodríguez, viewed by author.

"The Sky's the Limit." Video. 1995. BTTR Archives.

St. John's Academy first and second graders to José Basulto. Condolence card. May 15, 1996. BTTR Archives.

Stone, A. L. "Texaco Lab Test Report." Report prepared for Texaco Corp. February 22, 1994. BTTR Archives. [Re: donation of contaminated oil from Santex Corp.]

Triay, Victor A. "A dark cloud descends." Unpublished manuscript, 2009. Middlesex Community College, Bedford, Mass. Manuscript in the author's possession.

U.S.A. v. G. Hernández et al. Transcript of trial testimony. Docket 98-721-CR-Lenard, March 12–16, 2001. BTTR Archives.

U.S. Coast Guard. "Cuban Military Response to Cuban Brotherhood to the Rescue Aircraft." Transcript of audio communications. July 21, 1991. BTTR Archives.

U.S. Customs Service. "Transcripts of Telephone Calls initiated and Calls Received by the U.S. Customs Service, Domestic Air Interdiction Coordination Center, Riverside, California, on February 24, 1996." U.S. Customs Service Records, copy in BTTR Archives.

U.S. Department of Justice, Executive Office for Immigration Review Board of Immigration Appeals. "Appeal from the Decision of the Immigration Judge in the matter of Bello-Puente, Jose Roberto; Regalado-Ulloa, Adel; and Reyes-Ramirez, Leonardo." A72 560 015, A72 560 016, A74 933 281, Miami District, 132–134. No date. BTTR Archives.

U.S. Department of Justice, Federal Bureau of Investigation. Document H85075, file no. 202A-MM-74253, translated by Ismael Santiago, reviewed by LS Susan A. Salomon. September 24, 2000. BTTR Archives. [Document pertaining to *U.S.A. vs. G. Hernández et al.*]

U.S. Department of Transportation. "Aircraft Accident of N2506, N5485S, N2456S, Opa-locka, Florida, February 24, 1996." Transcript signed by Steve Culbertson, Air Traffic Manager, April 8, 1996. BTTR Archives.

U.S. Department of Transportation. "FAA Emergency Cease & Desist Order and Notice of Enforcement Policy." Memorandum by David R. Hinson, Administrator, February 29, 1996. BTTR Archives.

———. "Miami Automated International Flight Service Station preflight position for the time period from 2-24-96, 1407 UTC to 1434 UTC." Transcript signed by Michael C. Miller, Quality Assurance Specialist. March 15, 1996. BTTR Archives.

———. "Transcript re: aircraft accident, Opa-locka, Florida, February 24, 1996, N2506, N5485S, N2456S, for period 2204 UTC to 2215 UTC." Transcript signed by Steve Culbertson, Air Traffic Manager, April 8, 1996.

US NTSB, Administrator, FAA, Complainant, v. José J. Basulto. Transcript of proceedings. Docket No. SE 14512, July 29, 1996. Brothers to the Rescue Archives.

Wasps & moles: Cuban espionage in the United States. Photocopied English translation by unidentified translator of *Avispas y topos: informe especial sobre el espionaje cubano en los Estados Unidos.* N.p.: Editorial Hispano Cubana, 2004.

Yon, Terry, of Valiant Air Command, Titusville, Fla., e-mails to author, September 15–16, 2008.

Published Materials

"Aircraft Accidents and Incidents: Thursday, December 24, 1992 6:34 A.M. EST MIAMI, FLORIDA 33196." Aircraftone.com website, www.aircraftone.com/aircraft/accidents/20001211X16202.asp (accessed July 13, 2009). [Incident report of Jorge (Koki) Lares' crash.]

Albright, Madeleine. *Madame Secretary: A Memoir.* New York: Hyperion, 2003.

"Alemán Family Processing." *Coast Guard News,* November 19, 1991. BTTR Archives.

Ardila, Norma. "Hundreds of Miamians salute the Democracia." *El Nuevo Herald,* July 16, 1995, 4A.

Attinnger, Joelle, Cathy Booth, and Reginald K. I. Brach. "Fidel's defense." *Time,* March 11, 1996. Available online at www.time.com.

Baker, Christopher P., ed. *Cuba.* 4th ed. Moon Handbooks. Berkeley, Calif.: Avalon Travel, 2006.

Basulto, José. "José Basulto's response to the documentary *Shoot Down.*" *Ideal* 353 (2008): 55.

———. "The plane that foiled Castro's plot." *Wall Street Journal,* March 26, 1996, A18.

"Basulto defies judicial order and honors fallen men." *Girón,* February–March 2001, 4.

Belz, Mindy. "Castro's license to kill?" *World,* August 3–10, 1996, 12–16.

Benedi, Antonio. "No Castro nor his regime." Editorial. *Washington Times,* June 2003.

———. "So the American mothers' sons are not born as slaves." Editorial. *Washington Times,* May 16, 2000. Available on Cubanet, www.cubanet.org/CNews/y00/may00/16e9.htm (accessed July 28, 2009).

Blazquez, Agustín, with the collaboration of Jaums Sutton. "Political correctness: The scourge of our times." NewsMax.com, April 8, 2002. http://archive.newsmax.com/archives/articles/2002/4/4/121115.shtml (accessed March 9, 2009).

"Blue lagoon protest." *El Nuevo Herald,* final edition, October 10, 1994.

Review of Madeleine Albright's *Read My Pins. People,* October 12, 2009, 55.

Branch, Karen. "Gregorio Perez Ricardo, 15 years old." Obituary. *El Nuevo Herald*, February 28, 1990, 2B.

"Brothers to the Rescue sponsors seminar at FIU." *Diario Las Americas,* June 8, 1995, 1B.

Bufill, Dr. José Angel. "Manuel Guillot Castellano: presente! (Bosquejo biográfico de un héroe, de un mártir)." Pamphlet Central America: MRR Secretaría de Información, March 1964.

Calzón, Frank. "Path to freedom paved with Cuban diamonds." *Miami Herald,* July 6, 2000. Available on Center for a Free Cuba website. Archive for 2000. www.cubacenter. org/2000 (accessed May 9, 2007).

Carmichael, Scott. *True believer.* Annapolis: Naval Institute Press, 2007.

Cereijo, Manuel. "Ana Belen Montes." Guaracabuya, official website of Sociedad Económica de Amigos del País, www.amigospais-guaracabuya.org/oagmc202.php (accessed July 14, 2009).

Chardy, Alfonso. "Thirteen minutes over Havana." *Miami Herald*, July 15, 1995.

Chardy, Alfonso, and Michael E. Ruane. "U.S. jets were ready to challenge MiGs." *Miami Herald*, March 1, 1996, 13A.

"Clinton Administration strikes deal on Brothers to the Rescue judgment." *America's Insider,* October 20, 2000.

"Cuba adviser warned attack on exiles possible." Reuters newspaper article. Miami, February 22, 1999. Available on Cubanet. www.cubanet.org/CNews/y99/feb99/22e7.htm (accessed July 14, 2009).

"CUBA: End of the freedom flights." *Time,* September 13, 1971. www.time.com/time/magazine/article/0,9171,903113,00.html (accessed October 1, 2008).

Cuban Democratic Directorate. "Political Prisoner Francisco Chaviano Released in Havana." Directorio Democrático Cubano, Press Releases, www.directorio.org/press releases/note.php?note_id=1674 (accessed July 13, 2009).

"Cuban exiles mourn fliers." *Sarasota Herald-Tribune*, February 25, 1997.

"Cubans warned they might shoot down exile planes." Broadcast interview with Eugene Carroll, U.S. Navy Rear Admiral (Retired), by Catherine Callaway. CNN News, February 25, 1996.

"Cuba's historic role in human rights." Editorial. *Miami Herald,* final edition, May 10, 2008.

"Decomposed body." Editorial. *El Nuevo Herald,* November 5, 1994.

D'Entremont, Jeremy. "Cay Sal Bank Lighthouse: A stately ruin." *Lighthouse Digest,* April 2004.

De Valle, Elaine. "From above, pilots pay homage to fallen fliers." *Miami Herald*, March 3, 1996, 22A.

———. "Rafter children honor Basulto." Editorial. *Miami Herald,* final edition, May 25, 1996, 2B.

De Vise, Daniel, and Elaine De Valle. "Rafters' desperate journeys reshaped the exile experience." Editorial. *Miami Herald,* final edition, August 22, 2004.

Dorschner, John. "A clear and present danger." *Miami Herald*, Tropic Magazine, February 16, 1997.

———. "Swept away." *Miami Herald*, Tropic Magazine, July 3, 1993.

Dye, Joe. "11 cutters, 6 helicopters, 1 C-130 escort memorial flotilla ensure safety." *Coastline*, April 1996, 1.

Epstein, Gail. "Cuban Spies' Sentencing to Begin." *Miami Herald*, December 11, 2001, Local, 3B.

"Exile describes Cuba shelling: 'We used up all ammunition.'" *Miami Herald*, August 26, 1962.

Fedarko, Kevin. "The cold war is back." *Time*, March 11, 1996.

Fernández, Enrique. "What is exile?" Editorial. *Miami Herald*, May 18, 2008, final edition, 1L.

Florida International University, Cuban Council Support Group. "Afro-Cuban dissident nominated for the Nobel Peace Prize." Press release. July 1, 1996, www.fiu.edu/~fcf/concilio.newsi.html (accessed May 26, 2009).

———. "FIU to name law clinic after pilot killed by Cuban fighter jets." Press release. October 25, 2004.

Fonzi, Gaeton. "Jorge who?" Original manuscript on Jorge Mas Canosa, 1993. Cuban Information Archives, Document 0063. http://cuban-exile.com/doc_051-075/doc0063.html (accessed March 6, 2007).

Foundation Marypages. "Our Lady of Caridad del Cobre." www.marypages.com/LadyCaridadDelCobre.htm.

"Founder's Bio." Climadata Corporation website www.climadata.com/eng/fbio.html. [Biography of John Toohey Morales]

"Freedom steals the show." Editorial. *Miami Herald*, December 22, 1993.

Gertz, Bill. "Castro's Mole in the Pentagon." Chapter 8 of *Enemies: How America's foes steal our vital secrets and how we let it happen*. New York: Crown Forum, 2006.

Goldberg, Walter M. "Cay Sal Bank, Bahamas: A biologically impoverished, physically controlled environment." *Atoll Research Bulletin* 271 (September 1983). www.botany.hawaii.edu/faculty/duffy/arb/260-272/271.pdf (accessed November 3, 2009).

Greenhill, Kelly M. "Engineered Migration as a Coercive Instrument: The 1994 Cuban *Balseros* Crisis," Working Paper #12, February 2002. MIT website, web.mit.edu/CIS/www/migration/pubs/rrwp/12_engineered.html (accessed March 9, 2007).

Gugliotta, Guy, and Thomas W. Lippman. "U.S. data forced Cuba to retreat on shooting: Basulto bragged of buzzing Havana previously." *Washington Post*, March 16, 1996.

International Civil Aviation Organization (ICAO). *International Standards, Rules of the Air*. Annex 2 to the Convention on International Civil Aviation, November 14, 1991. Montreal: ICAO.

Kaye, Ken. "Pilots aim to locate refugees: Rescue group formed to save Cuban rafters." *Fort Lauderdale Sun Sentinel*, Local, August 24, 1991, 1B.

Key Biscayne, Florida, island paradise. www.key-biscayne.com.

King, Martin Luther, Jr. "The drum major instinct." Sermon delivered February 4, 1968. Martin Luther King Jr. Research and Education Institute, Stanford University. http://mlk-kpp01.stanford.edu/index.php/encyclopedia/documentsentry/doc_the_drum_major_instinct (accessed October 29, 2009).

Laidlaw, Keith. "Welcome to the countries that cancelled Christmas." *Independent on Sunday*, December 18, 2005.

Landau, Saúl. "Torn families and shot down planes: A Cuba story." *Progreso Weekly*, November 3, 2005. www.tni.org//archives/act/2047.

Lantigua, John. "Castro: U.S. had vowed no more flyovers." *Miami Herald*, May 1, 1996, 10A.

La Riva, Gloria. "'The Trial' premieres in Hollywood." December 7, 2007. Available online at www.freethefive.org/updates/Communiques/CoTheTrialLA120707.htm.

Lawrence, David Jr. "To the rescue: Rafters from the sea." *Miami Herald*, Viewpoints, July 19, 1992, 3C.

Lawrence, Matt, and Thomas Van Hare, *Betrayal: Clinton, Castro and The Cuban Five*. Bloomington, Ind.: iUniverse, 2009.

Lazo, Mario. *Dagger in the heart: American policy failures in Cuba*. Santa Monica, Calif.: Fidelis, 1968.

Letter to the editor [name withheld]. *Florida Keys Keynoter*, Opinion, March 13, 1996.

Long, Toni. "Brothers in the air help their own on the sea." *Coastline*, November–December 1991, 7.

López-Mason, Charisse. "The Armando Alejandre Foundation." University of Miami Campaign, Donor Profiles www6.miami.edu/campaign/donors/priorities_law_donors. html (accessed July 14, 2009).

"Madeline Albright." CNN.com. All Politics CNN Time. www.cnn.com/ALLPOLITICS/1997/gen/resources/players/albright (accessed March 27, 2007).

Martínez, Ana M., with Diana Montané. *Estrecho de traición*. Miami: Ediciones Universal, 1999.

Martínez García, Julio San Francisco. "Octavillas sobre La Habana." January 21, 2002. Cubanet, www.cubanet.org/octavillas.htm (accessed July 13, 2009).

McDonough, Mike. "Tico Belle goes to Guantánamo–Mission to Gitmo." Valiant Air Command, February 1995. Publication provided to the author by VAC.

Menéndez, Ana. "Immigration being unfair to Haitians." *Miami Herald*, May 4, 2008.

———. "Smugglers." Editorial. *Miami Herald*, final edition, March 16, 2008.

Menéndez, Ana, Martin Merzer, and Jack Retjman. "U.S. repatriation policy stirs stoppage," *Miami Herald*, May 17, 1995, 1A.

Miller, John J. "In Castro's service: The undertold story of Cuba's spying and terror." *National Review*, November 5, 2001, 45–47.

Moss, Cedric. "Fox Hill Prison Bahamas . . . Again." Bahamas Issues. www.bahamasissues. com/showthread.php?t=1053 (accessed July 26, 2009).

Murphy, M. E. "The history of Guantánamo Bay 1494–1964." U.S. Navy, Commander Navy Installations Command. https://www.cnic.navy.mil/Guantanamo (accessed July 13, 2009).

Nagin, Carl. "Backfire." *New Yorker*, January 26, 1998, 30–35.

Navarro, Mireya. "Pilots' group, firm foe of Castro, ignored risks." *New York Times*, February 26, 1996.

———. "U.S. judge assesses Cuba $187 million in deaths of 4 pilots." *New York Times*,

December 18, 1997, www.nytimes.com/1997/12/18/us/us-judge-assesses-cuba-187-million-in-deaths-of-4-pilots.html (accessed July 14, 2009).

———. "U.S. policy a betrayal, Cuban exiles protest." *New York Times*, May 8, 1995.

Nicaragua Solidarity Network of Greater New York. "Weekly News Update on the Americas," No. 317, February 25, 1996.

Nielsen, Kirk. "Bird of Paradox." *Miami New Times* 16, no. 3 (2001).

Nuccio, Richard A. Letter to the editor. *Miami Herald*, Opinion, March 3, 1999, 22A.

O'Grady, Mary Anastasia. "The lives of Cubans." Editorial, *Wall Street Journal*, April 2, 2007, A16.

———. "Twenty-two years in Castro's Gulag." *Wall Street Journal*, Opinion, August 16–17, 2008, A9.

Orestes, Lorenzo. *Wings of the morning*. New York: St. Martin's Press, 1994.

Osorio, Sonia. "Ramón Saúl Sánchez: el Gandhi del exilio cubano." Movimiento Democracia–Democracy Movement. www.democracia.org/HungerStrike.html (accessed June 1, 2009).

Pear, Robert. "Cuba arrests top general on corruption charges." *New York Times*, June 16, 1989.

"Perdomo Family History." Perdomo Cigars website, About Perdomo. http://fujipub.com/perdomocigars/aboutperdomo.html (accessed May 31, 2008).

Pérez, Louis A. Jr. "Cuba's Special Period, an Excerpt from *Cuba: Between Reform and Revolution*." History of Cuba.com, written and compiled by J. A. Sierra. Chapter 12—Socialist Cuba, Section XII, pp. 381–387. www.historyofcuba.com/history/havana/lperez2.htm (accessed September 20, 2008).

Pérez, Miguel. "Latino-American History, Chapter 5: Even on HBO, 'The Black Legend' Lives." Creators Syndicate, Opinion. www.creators.com/opinion/miguel-perez/latino-american-history-chapter-5-even-on-hbo-the-black-legend-lives.html (accessed July 13, 2009).

Port of Miami Tunnel Project. www.portofmiamitunnel.com (accessed July 29, 2008).

Remos, Ana B. "José Basulto: un guerrero incansable, un alma generosa." *¡EXITO!* May 24, 1994, 24–26.

"Rescatados 32 balseros." *El Nuevo Herald,* August 22, 1991.

"Response to Roberto Robaina: officers but not gentlemen." February 28, 1996. Florida International University. www.fiu.edu/~fcf/cojones.html (accessed August 11, 2009).

Rodríguez, Aurora. "Calle Ocho: Let's get this party started." www.miami.com/calle-ocho-lets-get-this-party-started-article (accessed September 1, 2008).

Rodriguez, Felix I., and John Weisman. *Shadow warrior: The CIA hero of a hundred unknown battles*. New York: Simon and Schuster, 1989.

Román, Iván. "Exiles mourn teen who died fleeing Cuba." *Miami Herald*, March 2, 1990, 1B.

Roque, Juan Pablo. *Desertor*. Miami: Cuban American National Foundation, 1995.

Rosenberg, Carol. "Troubled cause: Exile fliers seek relevance in face of U.S. policy change, fading support." *Miami Herald*, February 21, 1999, 1A.

Rosin, Hanna. "Little Havana's El Milagro." *Washington Post*, January 22, 2000.

Royko, Mike. "What Clinton should say after next Cuba incident." Editorial. *Chicago Tribune*, March 1, 1996.

Russo, Carolyn. "A day of sorrow." *Air and Space*, November 1996, 14–15.

Santiago, Ana E. "Double triumph for Brothers to the Rescue." *El Nuevo Herald*, final edition, June 23, 1991, 1B.

Savold, David. "100 minutes to freedom." Florida International University. www.fiu.edu/~fcf/orestes.102297.html (accessed September 13, 2008).

Schuss, William. *Día tras día con los Hermanos al Rescate*. Miami: Rodes Printing, 2007.

Scott, Gates L. "Shot down." *PilotMag*, July/August 2008, 31–36.

"Sea Fever & Cay Sal Bank, Bahamas: Trip Report," Gregory Gulick's home page. www.gagme.com/greg/vacation/2001/bahamas.

Shoot down. DVD. New York: Rogues Harbor Studios, 2007.

Shoot Down Victims.org. Bios. "Pablo Morales." www.shootdownvictims.org/bios-PM.html (accessed September 2, 2008).

———. Foundations. "CAMP 4 Justice Foundation." www.shootdownvictims.org.

———. Justice. Honoring Our Loved Ones. Downloadable FBI wanted poster. www.shootdownvictims.org./img/WantedAdSpanish2.jpg (accessed July 14, 2009).

Silver, Vernon. "Rescue plane crashes off Key West." *Key West Citizen*, May 3, 1992, 1.

"So . . . charge Castro for murder." Editorial. *Miami Herald,* July 5, 2000, 10B.

Taylor, Guy. "Daughter of executed pilot wins big suit against Cuba." *Washington Times*, November 20, 2004. Reprinted on Latin American Studies website. www.latinamericanstudies.org/bay-of-pigs/suit.htm (accessed July 14, 2009).

"Tethered Aerostat Radar System." Federation of American Scientists (FAS) website. www.fas.org/nuke/guide/usa/airdef/tars.htm.

"The Twenty-five Most Intriguing People of the Year." *People*, December 24, 1994–January 2, 1995.

Thomas, John F. "Cuban refugees in the United States." *International Migration Review* 1, No. 2 (1967): 46.

Triay, Victor A. *Bay of pigs*. Gainesville: University Press of Florida, 2001.

"Universal Declaration of Human Rights." United Nations General Assembly. www.un.org/Overview/rights.html (accessed January 8, 2007).

U.S. Coast Guard, U.S. Department of Homeland Security. "Alien Migrant Interdiction." U.S. Coast Guard, Office of Law Enforcement. www.uscg.mil/hq/cg5/cg531/amio.asp (accessed June 9, 2008).

———. "The 'other' boatlift: Camarioca, Cuba, 1965." U.S. Coast Guard, Historian's Office. www.uscg.mil/History/uscghist/camarioca1965.asp (accessed March 2, 2009)

U.S. Department of Transportation. "Statement of Captain Anthony S. Tangeman on Coast Guard migrant interdiction operations, before the Subcommittee on Immigration and Claims Committee on the Judiciary, May 18, 1999." Department of Transportation website. http://testimony.ost.dot.gov/test/pasttest/99test/Tangeman1.htm (accessed June 9, 2008).

Viglucci, Andrés. "From guns to leaflets over Cuba." *Miami Herald*, January 20, 1996, sec. A.

Waller, Douglas. "Clinton's Cuban road to Florida." *Time*, October 28, 1996, 45–46.

Walsh, Monsignor Bryan O. "The history of Pedro Pan." March 1, 2001. Official Site of Operation Pedro Pan. www.pedropan.org/history.html (accessed October 1, 2008).

Watson, Julia. "The pig in my Chinese box." *Washington Post*, July 14, 2004, F-1.

Weaver, Jay, and Alfonso Chardy. "High court rejects 'Cuban Five.'" *Miami Herald*, June 16, 2009, 3B.

Werlau, Maria C. "Cuba: The tugboat massacre of July 13, 1994." Cuba Archive/Free Society Project, Cuba Archive website, March 2007, www.cubaarchive.org/downloads/13_DE_MARZO_TUGBOAT_MASSACRE.pdf (accessed July 12, 2009).

"Who are the Sandinistas?" *Time*, July 2, 1979. www.time.com/time/magazine/article/0,9171,96829,00.html (accessed October 29, 2009).

Wilson, Mike. "Daring act of love focuses public's eye on Cuba." *Miami Herald*, January 2, 1993, 1A.

Interviews

Roque, Juan Pablo. Transcript of interview by Lucila Newman. Havana. February 27, 1996. Transcript in BTTR Archives.

———. Television interview with Fabiola López. Originally broadcast, Havana, February 27, 1996. Rebroadcast on CNN International Desk, February 28, 1996. Videotape in BTTR Video Archives.

Yon, Colonel Terry, USA (Ret). E-mails to author, September 15–16, 2008. [Re: C-47 used to deliver toys to Cuban detainees at Guantánamo Naval Base in January 1995.]

Personal Interviews

All interviews conducted by Lily Prellezo, in Miami unless otherwise noted.

Ackerman, Holly. July 16, 2007.

Alejandre, Cristina. April 14, 2008.

Alejandre, Margarita (Mrs. Armando Alejandre Sr.). April 14, 2008.

Alemán, Nelson. February 17, 2007.

Ávila, Ana Miriam. April 19, 2008.

Barbas, Eva. November 30, 2006. Ft. Pierce, Fla.

Basulto, Albert. April 24, 2007.

Basulto, Alberto. April 17, 2008. West Palm Beach, Fla.

Basulto, Felipe. April 25, 2007.

Basulto, José Sr. Series of interviews, 2006–2009.

Basulto, José Jr. April 18, 2007. Hallandale, Fla.

Basulto, Rita. Series of interviews, 2006–2009.

Brooks, Beverly. April 14, 2008.

Buchete Puperoux, Virginie. September 28, 2006.

Campo, Domingo. September 15, 2008.

Carmona, Luis. October 21, 2006.

Castellanos, Mario. March 5, 2008.

Cobo, Arturo. March 5, 2008.

Costa, Mirta and Osvaldo. June 13, 2007.

Cruz, Louis. September 4, 2007.

de la Peña, Mario and Miriam. August 29, 2007.

De Toro, Lorenzo. April 2007.

Díaz, Elio. September 21, 2006. Opa-locka, Fla.

Díaz, Guarione. November 6, 2009.

Díaz, Luis. October 19, 2006.

Domanievicz, Ivan. April 14, 2008.

Domínguez, Luis. April 13, 2007.

García, Alexis. June 26, 2007. Miami Lakes, Fla.

Gartner, Carlos. October 18, 2006. Pembroke Pines, Fla.

Goldstein, Stuart. June 24, 2008.

González, Juan. September 5, 2007.

González, Rubén. May 5, 2007.

Greco-Regan, Mayte. September 29, 2006, February 24, 2008.

Gutiérrez-Boronat, Orlando. July 11, 2007.

Hurtado de Mendoza, Aurelio. April 20, 2007.

Iglesias, Arnaldo. September 19, 2006.

Iriondo, Andrés. October 17, 2007. Key Biscayne, Fla.

Iriondo, Sylvia. September 27, 2007. Key Biscayne, Fla.

Lares, Adalberto "Beto." September 21, 2006. Opa-locka, Fla.

Lares, Guillermo. October 27, 2006. Opa-locka, Fla.

Lares, Jorge "Koki." September 21, 2006. Opa-locka, Fla.

Lawrence, David Jr. April 1, 2009.

León, Benjamín, May 27, 2009.

Martínez, Ana Margarita. July 28, 2007.

Martínez, Luis. October 9, 2007.

Matzinger, Stan. November 30, 2007.

Morales, John Toohey. November 16, 2006. Miramar, Fla.

Murciano, Mike. May 3, 2007.

Núñez, Leopoldo. September 25, 2006.

Pascual, Sylvia. November 30, 2006. Ft. Pierce, Fla.

Perdomo, Nicholas. May 6, 2008.

Plá, Osvaldo. September 5, 2006. Chula Vista, Calif.

Powell-Cosío, Sofía. May 2, 2008.

Prellezo, Jorge. June 26, 2008.

Rodríguez, Félix. April 25, 2007.

Rodríguez Sosa, José Antonio. August 9, 2007.

Rodríguez Tejera, Roberto. March 5, 2007.

Ros-Lehtinen, Ileana. September 18, 2006.

Sánchez, Alfredo. November 15, 2006. West Palm Beach, Fla.

Sánchez, Ramón Saúl. August 2, 2007.

Schuss, Maggie. September 10, 2008.

Schuss, William "Billy." September 26, 2006

Simmons, Chris. June 30, 2008.

Tabernilla, Carlos. November 15, 2006. Wellington, Fla.

Tester, Hank. June 9, 2007.

Triana, Arturo. March 5, 2007.

Triay, Victor A. February 20, 2009. Middletown, Conn.

Van Hare, Thomas. August 15, 2007. Ft. Lauderdale Airport, Fla.

Walton, Steve. August 18, 2007. Opa-locka, Fla.

Webber, Conrad. October 3, 2006.

Weininger, Janet Ray. November 6–7, 2006.

Zayas-Bazan, Eduardo January 30, 2009.

Telephone Interviews

All interviews conducted by Lily Prellezo.

Blalock, Matt. September 18, 2007.

Irving, Barrington. November 3, 2008.

León, Abilio. June 22, 2009.

López Álvarez, Reinaldo. June 18, 2009.

Morejón Almagro, Leonel. July 9, 2009.

Reboredo, Pedro. July 16, 2009.

Rivero, Carlos. March 18, 2008.

Simmons, Chris. April 21, 2008.

Tangeman, Captain Anthony "Tony." March 24, 2007.

Williams, David. March 26, 2008.

Acknowledgments

Thank you, Marta and René Guerra, for seeing in me what I did not see in myself. Thank you, José Basulto, for the greatest of gifts, your trust. Thank you, Rita Basulto, for teaching me patience. My encourager, my husband, my love—thank you, Steve, for believing in me. Thank you, Mami, for being proud of me, and my daughters Lily B. and Lauri for cheering me on. To my writers' group: Deborah, Ellen, and Orlando—this book would not have been possible without your weekly guidance. For María, I hope that I can be the kind of friend that you have been to me. Thanks to all the pilots, rafters, activists, and Brothers volunteers who shared your stories with me. My deep appreciation to the Alejandre, Costa, de la Peña families, and to Eva Barbas, for sharing with me the lives of your martyred loved ones. Thank you, Kristin, Gaby, and Tere, for transcribing my tapes. Thank you Gastón Arellano for being my personal IT guy. Thanks to Roberto Koltun and Lorenzo De Toro for your fabulous photographs. Thank you, Les Standiford, for teaching and encouraging me; thanks to Sterling Watson and Writers in Paradise. So much appreciation to Janell Walden Agyeman for recommending a university press. To authors Victor A. Triay and Eduardo Zayas-Bazán: I am so grateful for your wonderful critiques and support. Special thanks to my copy editor, Kirsteen Anderson, for her sharp eye and thoughtful suggestions. For believing in this project, my deepest appreciation to Amy Gorelick and the University Press of Florida.

Index

Page numbers in *italics* refer to photographs.

ACU (Agrupación Católica Universitaria), 10, 24

Aerostat balloons: during shoot-down, 223; as watchdogs over the Straits, "Fat Albert," 45

Albright, Madeleine: remarks after shoot-down, 243; shoot-down memorial, 250–51

Alejandre, Armando, Jr.: background, *134*, 201; commemorative street signs, 254; and Cuban Council, 200–201; and detainees in Bahamas, 206; events surrounding shoot-down, 210–29; note to JB re flying with BTTR, 210, 278; shoot-down memorial, 251

Alejandre, Armando, Sr., Mr. and Mrs: foundation at University of Miami, 273; lawsuit, 272; post–shoot-down, 235; shoot-down anniversary, 274

Alejandre, Marlene (daughter), *137*, 255

Alejandre, Marlene (wife), 255

Alemán, Nelson (rafter): crossing of Florida Straits, 59–63; 15th anniversary of rescue, 277; rescue of parents, 156

Angones, Frank, attorney for families of murdered men, 267, 285

Anniversaries of BTTR shoot-down, 274–86, 294

Araujo, Jorge, *125*

Aronoff, Jonathan, 258

Ávila, Ana Miriam: Havana ATC, 225, 250; repercussions after shoot-down, 260–63

AVME (Association of Veterans of Special Missions), 19–20

Azqueta, Pilo, 57, 92, 104

Balseros. *See* Rafters

Barbas, Eva (mother of Pablo Morales): arrival in Miami, 265–67; defiance of Fidel Castro, 213; and quest for truth and justice, 267, 273; and Sofia Powell-Coscio, 275; shoot-down anniversary flight, *137*

Basulto, Alberto (Al, brother), 9, 13, 15, 236

Basulto, Alberto (Albert, son), 236

Basulto, Felipe (son), 251, 285, 301–2

Basulto, José, *119, 120, 122, 124, 125, 126, 131, 132, 136, 137, 138, 139*; and attempts to liberate Cuba, 11–14; and Bay of Pigs, 11–12; childhood and youth, 8–10, 45; confrontations with FAA, 255, 256; and Cuban Council, 199–204, 210; dichotomy of, 17, 197; and FBI, 256, 284; and flotillas (*see* Flotillas); and hamburger runs, 6, 7, 15; hobbies, 9, 294; and leaflet drop, 190–98; and license suspensions and hearings, 189, 197, 267–70; marriage to Angélica, 14; marriage to Rita, 5, 15; and Nicaraguan Contras, 15–17; political views, 144; and *Seagull One*, 57, 297–300 (*see also Seagull One*); and shoot-down, chronology, 211–29 (*see also* Shoot-down of BTTR planes); and spy trial (Wasp Network), 286–89; *13th of March* flotilla and FAA, 180–81; truth and justice for murdered men, 265, 267, 270–71, 282–83, 285
—career: Apollo Decking, 15; in Bay of Pigs, 11–12; with CIA, 7, 11, 13, 197; developer, 5; unemployed, 285; and U.S. Army, 14
—flyovers of Cuban airspace: accusations of,

Basulto, José—*continued*
198, 269, 276; to drop ashes, 171–72; over Punta de Maisí, 163, 287; *13th of March* flotilla, 185–87
—nonviolence philosophy: civil disobedience, 178–80 (*see also under 13th of March* tugboat); embracing of, 16–17; mandate of "I am the change," 17; spreads message, 168
Basulto, José, Jr. (nickname Peco, son of JB), 301–2
Basulto, José, Sr. (father), 8–9, 13, 15
Basulto, Rita (wife): and Ana Margarita Roque, 200, 265; courtship and marriage to JB, 5, 15; family life, 50, 54, 294; shoot-down, 222; shoot-down anniversary, *136*; volunteer at BTTR, 25
Berger, Samuel "Sandy," 208–9
Blalock, Matt (nickname "Gringo"): background, 106; filming *Ofelia* accident, 104–6; volunteer for BTTR, 94–95
Borges, Jorge Luis, 171–72
Borges, Segundo, 171–72
Bovo Caras, Esteban, *125*
Brooks, Beverly: background, 79; and Ivan Domanievicz, 173; flight instructor for BTTR, 22, 79, *125*; Kamikaze Crew, 140–41; shoot-down anniversary, 275
Brothers to the Rescue: community support, 92–93; development of organization, 19–23; donations to, 82, 168, 295–96; financing of, 32, 50, 100, 168, 295; fund-raising, 80, 168, 295, 267; hangar (*see* Gregorio Pérez Ricardo Hangar); logo, 22, *120*; monuments, *138*, 254–55; naming of organization, 21; perceived politicization of, 167, 254; post–shoot-down, 255; pilots (nationalities), 111–12; pilots resigning, 168; prayer circle, 26, 53, *124*, 297; press and media coverage, 24, 52–53, 98, 166, 196–97; stickers for rescues, 44; trial runs, 34, 40–41; warnings to rafters, 58, 64, 66
—missions: Anguilla Cay, 140; Elbow Cay (black birds), 109–10; Exodus of 1994, 153–55, 159; first mission, 33; first rescue, 35–38; humanitarian mission during Cuban Council meeting, 199; to Martyrs' Point,
249–50, 276, 279; 1,000th mission, 140; resuming of, after shoot-down, 258; solidarity with Armed Forces of Cuba, 143; suspension of missions, 292
Brothers to the Rescue, planes:
—accidents: Carlos Gartner low pass, 104; *Ofelia*, 105–6
—crashes: Cay Sal and crash of *Sound Machine*, 141–42; JB plane, N5416K, 52–56, *123*; Koki Lares Christmas Eve accident, 84–89 (*see also under* Lares, Jorge)
—fleet: *Big Red* (Steve Walton's Apache, also called "Yom Kippur Clipper"), 96, 108–9, *127*; *El Coquí*: 98, 183–87, 293; first plane, N5416K, 32, 55; *Ofelia*, 49; *Habana D.C.*, N5485S, 206, 215, 225–28; *Seagull One*, N2506, 57, 183–87, 206, 228–29, 293–94; *Sound Machine*, N2352S, 141–42, 155–56; *Spirit of Miami*, N2456, 206, 215, 225–28; *El Viejo Pancho*, 106, 108
—petitioning U.S. government for, 47–49
—sabotage of, 290
Brothers to the Rescue, procedures: drops on Elbow Cay, 108–10; drops to rafters, 37, 49, 62, 70–71, 95; monitoring grids, 35; pilot training, 51; removing airplane doors, 140; spotting rafters, 34
Buchete Puperoux, Virginie (nickname "La Francesa"), 26–27, 42, *125*, 237
Burton, Dan, 270, 272. *See also* Congressional hearing on shoot-down

Campo, Domingo (rafter), 150–52
CANF. *See* Cuban American National Foundation
Cantelli, Adelfa, 7
CARIBROC (Caribbean Regional Operations Center), 223
Carmichael, Scott: and spy Ana Belén Montes, 289–90; *True Believer*, 289
Carmona, Luis (FAA): background, 99; FAA investigation of Koki Lares' accident, 87; planning *13th of March* flotilla, 181
Carroll, Admiral Eugene (retired): events surrounding shoot-down, 208, 242–43; meeting with Cuban generals about shooting down planes, 202–3

Castellanos, Mario: and *13th of March* flotilla, 182–85; volunteer for BTTR, 182

Castro, Fidel: and engineered migrations, 18, 148–49, 152, 155, 166, 177; giving order for shoot-down, 246, 247, 259, 281; meeting with U.S. government officials, 202; response to shoot-down, 246; response to *13th of March* tugboat sinking, 147; threat to U.S. while in Iran, 291

Castro, Raúl, 273, 281

Cay Sal Banks, Bahamas: BTTR accident, 140–42; drops over, 108–10; risk of deportation, 70–71

Cessna 337 Skymaster, "push-pull," 57

Chaviano, Francisco, 178

Chirino, Willy, 89, 92, 98, 111

CIA, and shoot-down files, 252

City of rafts. *See under* Exodus of 1994

Civil disobedience: acts of, 177–78; planning for *13th of March* flotilla, 180–81; seminar at FIU, 177

Clinton, President Bill: and change in policy toward Cuba, 155–56, 166, 176, 178, 203; and Helms-Burton Act, 259; and lawsuit for shoot-down victims, 272; and responses and actions taken related to shoot-down, 245–46, 249–50

Coalición Democrática Cubana (Cuban Democratic Coalition), 168

Cobo, Arturo, and Transit Center, 79–80

Cockpit recordings: aboard *Seagull One* during shoot-down, 234, 243; of Cuban MiGs, 223, 229, 243, 268

Code Victor, 43, 52

Comisión Nacional Cubana (National Cuban Commission), 177, 179. *See also* Sánchez, Ramón Saúl

Concilio Cubano. *See* Cuban Council

Congressional hearing on shoot-down: Ileana Ros-Lehtinen, 270–72; inept government witnesses, 270–71; JB exhibits, 271–72. *See also* Subcommittee on the Western Hemisphere of the Committee on International Relations of the House of Representatives

Costa, Carlos (nicknames Carlitos, "good-looking Carlos," El Intenso): background, 76–77; BTTR pilot, 113, *125, 134*; and Cay Sal

drop, 108–10; chief of pilots, 97; and Cuban MiGs, 82; events leading to shoot-down, 206, 211–12; feasibility studies for leaflet drop, 190–91; first mission, 77; leaflet drop, 194; *Ofelia* accident, 104–6; office at hangar, 112–13; political views, 144; shoot-down, 211–29, 242, 252, 265

Costa, Mirta (mother): background, 76–77; BTTR volunteer, 92, 112; events surrounding shoot-down, 235–37; FBI wanted poster demonstration at FIU, *137*; leaflet drop, reaction to, 202; premonition of Carlos' death, 206–7; relationship with JB, straining of, 265–66

Costa, Osvaldó (father), *137*

Costa Méndez, Mirta (sister), *137*

Cruz, Louis, 82, 239

Cruz, Luis, *125*

Cuban Adjustment Act, 150, 176

Cuban American National Foundation (CANF): and indictment of Castro brothers, 282; publication of Roque's book *Desertor*, 175; purchase of *El Coqui*, 183; shoot-down memorial, 247

Cuban Council: donation by BTTR, 201, 204; meeting in Havana, 195–96, 200–201, 204, 208, 210; meetings in Miami, 202, 210; platform, 201; and shoot-down, 230; venue for, in Havana, 199

Cuban Democratic Directory. *See* Gutiérrez-Boronat, Orlando

Cuban Five. *See under* Spy trial

Cuban gunboats: in Florida Straits, 19; intercepting rafters, 81, 100, *128*; *13th of March* sinking and memorial, 145–46, 183–85

Cuban MiGs: during BTTR missions, 44–46, 82; practice flights before shoot-down, 252; protocol when intercepting other aircraft, 217–18; protocol when sighted by BTTR, 46, 83, 269; shoot-down chronology, 211–29, 272; at *13th of March* memorial, 187; U.S. interception of, 46, 82–83

Cuban people: anti-Castro demonstrations, 142, 149; concept of being "in business," 260–61, 263; reactions to leaflet drops, 194–98; sale of *Seagull One* to help hurricane victims, 296–300

de Cárdenas, Rita María (Basulto). *See* Basulto, Rita

de la Peña, Mario: background, 152–53; BTTR pilot, *135*; feasibility studies for leaflet drop, 190–91; interviewed on Cuban Democratic Directory radio program, 188; leaflet drop, 194; and Operation Able Vigil, 157; political views, 144; *13th of March* flotilla and flyover of Havana, 181, 183, 185–87; shoot-down, 206–8, 211–22, 238, 242

de la Peña, Mario [Sr.] (father), events surrounding shoot-down, 207–8, 232, 235; FBI wanted poster demonstration at FIU, *137*; lawsuit, 267; offer of lawsuit money to Eva Barbas, 273; ruling on lawsuit, 272

de la Peña, Miriam (mother): events surrounding shoot-down, 207–8, 214, 232, 235; FBI wanted poster demonstration at FIU, 137; lawsuit, 267; offer of lawsuit money to Eva Barbas, 273; ruling on lawsuit, 272

Democracia: *13th of March* flotilla, 182–88; vessel of National Cuban Commission, 180

Democracy Movement. *See under* Sánchez, Ramón Saúl

De Toro, Lorenzo, *128*, 246, 300

Díaz, Elio, mechanic for BTTR, 212–14

Díaz-Balart, Lincoln, 111

Dieppa, Mabel, and first BTTR plane crash, 52–56

Dissidents in Cuba: and Concilio Cubano, 195–96, 202, 204, 208, 242, 260–61; dissident movement, 16, 161, 168

Domanievicz, Eduardo: 1,000th mission, 140; pilot for BTTR, *125*

Domanievicz, Ivan: background, 79; and Beverly Brooks, 173; and city of rafts, 154; Kamikaze crew, 140–41; mission to pick up dead girl, 111; pilot for BTTR, *125*

Dossier: distribution and rejection of, 285; prepared by JB, 283

El cambio soy yo, 17, 300

Embry-Riddle Aeronautical University: and Carlos Costa, 76–77; and Mario de la Peña, 207, 152; and Steve Walton, 94

Emergency Cease and Desist Order, of President Clinton, 249

Estefan, Gloria: fund-raising, 92; and Koki

Lares, in hospital, 88–89; *Sound Machine* donation (with husband Emilio), 141

Evidentiary hearing for revocation of JB license: FAA ruling, 270; hearing under Honorable William A. Pope II, 268–69; and witnesses, 268–69

Exodus of 1994: change in Cuban migration policy, 156; city of rafts, 153–54, 156; events leading to, 145, 150, 152; lives saved, 292; and Operation Able Vigil, 156–57

FAA: and Carlos Gartner accident, 104; and events leading to shoot-down, 209, 215, 284; and evidentiary hearing for JB license revocation, 268–70; and Koki Lares accident, 99; meeting with JB to plan *13th of March* memorial, 180–81; monitoring BTTR, 99, 192, 255; post–shoot-down, 255; regulations for flying over Florida Straits, 23; revokes JB license, 256, 267; suspends JB license, 189, 197

FACE (Fuerzas Armadas de Cuba en el Exilio—Armed Forces of Cuba in Exile), 36

FBI: and cockpit recording, *Seagull One*, 234; and Sofia Powell-Cosio, 256; and Ana Margarita Roque, 245; and Juan Pablo Roque, 244, 284; truth and justice for murdered men, 137, 273; and Wasp Network, 286

Floating tombstones, 64, 72, 81, 302

Flotillas: of Brotherhood and Solidarity, 19; to commemorate *13th of March* victims, 178–87; shoot-down memorial, 248

Flyovers of Cuban airspace: allegations of, 196–98, 208; ashes of Segundo Borges, 170–72; Punta de Maisí after leaving Gitmo, 163; *13th of March* flotilla, 185–87, 208

Freedom Fighters for Cuba, 10, 13, 17

FOIA (Freedom of Information Act), and recorded conversations of U.S. Customs employees, 283–84

Fung, Dr. K. Y., and feasibility studies of leaflet drop, 190–91. *See also* Leaflets over Havana

Gandhi, Mahatma, effects of teachings on JB, 16–17

García, Alexis (rafter), 64–72, 98

García-Pedrosa, José: attorney for detained Cubans in Guantánamo, 159–62

Gartner, Carlos (nickname "Cholo"): masthead

accident, 104; pilot for BTTR, 28, 42, 44, 113, *122*, 154, 160, 162; throwing "smokes" to rafters, 95
Gianelloni, Giles, 100
Goldstein, Stuart, attorney for JB at evidentiary hearing for license revocation, 268
González, Elián, and rule of law, 281–82
González, Juan: human trafficking accusations, 292; *Ofelia* accident, 104–6; shoot-down, 211; spotting first rescued rafter, 35–38; volunteer for BTTR, *125*
González, René: BTTR pilot and Cuban spy, *125*, *126*; first mission, 33; friendship with Roque, 144; incident with DEA, 47; post-shoot-down, 232; Wasp Network, 286–87
González, Rubén, first rescued rafter, 35–38
Greco, Mayte: background and family, 39–40, 173; BTTR pilot, 20–21, *121*, *124*, *125*; events leading to shoot-down, 205–6; first rescue, 41–43; marriage to Paul Regan, 173; sale of *Seagull One*, 297; shoot-down, 214, 232; shoot-down anniversaries, 279–80; shoot-down memorial, 249; trial runs for BTTR, 23, 34, 40–41
Green, Dr. Barth, as Koki Lares' neurosurgeon, 88
Gregorio Pérez Ricardo Hangar, Opa-locka Airport: inauguration 111–13, *125*; storing of ashes, 169; warning sign, *128*
Guántanamo (Gitmo): BTTR protest of Cuban detainees, 166–68; Christmas toy drive, 163–64; detaining Haitians in, 158; detaining and returning Cubans in, 156–57, 159, 165; deteriorating conditions in, 164; migration accord, 166; safe haven for Basulto, 12; safe haven for Roque, 143, 244; U.S. naval base, history of, 158; and "Wet-Feet/Dry-Feet," 176
Guerra, René, 144, 220, 279
Gugú (nickname of JB), 6–8
Guillot Castellano, Manolín, Cuban patriot: execution, 13; inspiration for BTTR, 20; portrait by Adelfa Cantelli (nicknamed "the bleeding Cuban"), 7, *119*
Gutiérrez-Boronat, Orlando: Cuban Democratic Directory, *131*, 178, 188; interviews Mario de la Peña after Havana flyover, 188; and leaflets over Havana, 191; provides

attorney for Cuban political prisoner Chaviano, 178; shoot-down memorial, 249

Haitians: detained in Guantánamo, 158; Haitian Adjustment Act, concept of, 150
Ham operators, in Cuba, 142–43
Hangar at Opa-locka Airport. *See* Gregorio Pérez Ricardo Hangar
Havana Air Traffic Control: Cuba's monitoring in the Florida Straits, 34, 224; and Miami Center ATC, 260; and Nick Perdomo of Miami Center ATC, 262; protocol when crossing 24th parallel, 46; repercussions after shoot-down, 260–63; shoot-down, 224–26, 234, 243; shoot-down memorial, 250
Havana Press, and leaflets over Havana, 195–96
Helms-Burton Act (Cuban Liberty and Democratic Solidarity Act of 1996), 259
Hermanos al Rescate. See Brothers to the Rescue
Hernández, Ernesto (rafter), 1–3
Homestead Air Force Base: and F-15 pilots at battle stations, 223, 229, 285; interceptors, 46, 214–15
Houlihan, Jeffrey: BTTR flight tracking of shoot-down and 911 call, 209, 215, 221, 223, 226–27; testimony at Congressional hearing, 270–71; witness at JB evidentiary hearing, 268–69
Houssin, Yves, *122*
Human trafficking, 20, 167, 292
Hurricane Andrew, destruction caused by, 74–75, 77
Hurtado de Mendoza, Aurelio, 253–54, 279
Husta, Joe, *125*

ICAO (International Civil Aviation Organization): investigation and condemnation of shoot-down, 243, 269, 281; presented by JB at Congressional hearing, 271
Iglesias, Arnaldo: background, 30–31; BTTR pilot, 31–32, *125*, *132*, *136*, *138*; Cay Sal crash of *Sound Machine*, 141–42; and civil disobedience, 178; leaflets over Havana mission, 192–94; mail campaign for BTTR, 21; and Mirta Costa, 202, 265; and non-participation in lawsuit, 267; *Paralelo 24*, 164; shoot-down, 211–32, 236–37; shoot-down anniversaries, 279; shoot-down, mourning, 255; witness at JB evidentiary hearing, 269

Ileana. *See* Ros-Lehtinen, Ileana

Immigration policy, of U.S. toward Cubans: as émigrés, 148; and Elián González and rule of law, 282; migrants, 156; as political refugees, 149; "Wet-Feet/Dry-Feet," 176

Indictment of Cuban Air Force general, 283

Indictment of Fidel and Raúl Castro: JB pledges $1 million for, 273; signatures, 281–83

Interceptors, U.S.: F-15 pilots at battle stations, 223, 229, 285; from Homestead Air Force base, 46, 214–15; intercepting Cuban MiGs, 46, 82

Iovenko, William B., and donation to BTTR, 295

Iriondo, Andrés, shoot-down survivor, *136*, 211–29

Iriondo, Sylvia: and Cuban Council meeting, 210; and detainees in Bahamas, 206; friendship with Armando Alejandre Jr., 201, 278; president of Mothers Against Repression, 201; shoot-down, 211–29, 236–37; shoot-down memorial, 248; shoot-down survivor, *136*; witness at JB evidentiary hearing, 269

Irving, Barrington, 279

Itkoff, Andrew, and first BTTR plane accident, 52–56

Judicial Watch, 267, 283

Kamikaze Crew, 140–41

Kennedy, President John F.: administration's betrayal in Bay of Pigs invasion, 12; ceremony with Brigade 2506, 14, 248; Kennedy-Khrushchev Accord, 14, 150; Missile Crisis, 13

Kensington Park Elementary School, and rafter children, 257

Khuly, Cristina (niece of Armando Alejandre Jr.), and Douglas R. Eger, 277

Khuly, Maggie (sister of Armando Alejandre Jr.): and lawsuit against frozen assets of Cuba, 272; and *Shoot Down*, the movie, 278; truth and justice for murdered men, *137*, 273

King, Coretta Scott, and José Basulto, *131*

King, Martin Luther, Jr., effect of teachings on JB, 16, 21

Kirkpatrick, Jean, 209

Koltun, Roberto, photographer for *Miami Herald*, 52

La Casa del Balsero. *See* Transit Center for Cuban Refugees

Lady from Miami Beach (*la señora de Miami Beach*), 92

Lares, Alberto (nickname "Beto"): BTTR pilot, *121*; first mission, 33; and rafters after change in policy, 159; spotting Cuban gunboat, 81. *See also* Lares brothers

Lares, Guillermo (nickname "Guille"): and city of rafts, 153–54; and Cuban MiG, 45; death of rafters in the Florida Straits, 81; first BTTR plane crash, 52–56, *123*; first mission, 33; and media, 52; prayer circle, 26; and Roque, Juan Pablo, 174; shoot-down anniversary, 280; shoot-down memorial, 180; *13th of March* memorial and flyover of Havana, 185–87. *See also* Lares brothers

Lares, Jorge (nickname "Koki"): BTTR pilot, *121, 125, 132*; Christmas Eve plane crash, 84–89; marriage and family, 173–74; rehabilitation, 90, 98; sale of *Seagull One,* 299; shoot-down events, 212, 214, 218, 231, 239. *See also* Lares brothers

Lares brothers: and Cuban MiGs, 82; faith, 24, 52; pilots for BTTR, 24–26, *121, 122, 125, 132*; rescues, 34–38, 42–43; resignation from BTTR, 90; return to flying 98–99; sale of *Seagull One,* 297

Lawrence, Amanda, *122*

Lawrence, David, Jr., 24, *122*

Lawsuit, against frozen assets of Cuba: by JB for emotional trauma, 273; by families of murdered men, 266–67; and Maggie Khuly, 272; and pending claims from U.S. companies, 272; ruling in favor of families, 272; settlement offered to Eva Barbas, 273; settlement proposed by Clinton administration, 272; and Janet Ray Weininger, 272–73

Leaflets over Havana: dubbed Operation Dr. Martin Luther King Jr., 192; FAA intervention, 192; feasibility studies, 190; leaflet drop mission, 190–98; leaflet drop mission in memory of murdered men, 276; reactions in Havana, 194–98; reactions in Miami, 198, 207, 254; and thirty articles of UN Declaration of Human Rights, *133*, 191

Lebwohl, Dr. Nathan, orthopedic surgeon for Koki Lares, 90

Lenard, Judge Joan: and gag order on JB, 276; and Wasp Network spy trial, 288

León, Abilio, 112, *125*

León, Benjamín, Jr., 298–99

Levitán, Aida, 22

Llorente, Amando, S.J., 10

Logo of BTTR. *See under* Brothers to the Rescue

López Alvarez, Reinaldo, 143

López Montenegro, Omar, *131*

Lorenzo, Orestes: flight into Cuba, 82–83, 269; mission of solidarity with Cuban Armed Forces, 143; rescue of Alemán parents, 156; witness at JB evidentiary hearing, 269

Majesty of the Seas cruise ship: during shoot-down, 216, 219–20, 225–28; shoot-down anniversary and Alejandre family, 274–75

March Air Force Base, 209

Mariel Boatlift, 77, 80, 148–49

Martin, Ray, *125*

Martínez, Ana Margarita (Roque): betrayed by husband, 245; events surrounding shoot-down, 204–5, 220, 231; shoot-down memorial, 249; sues for rape, 245, *See also under* Roque, Juan Pablo

Martínez, Luis (pilot), *125*

Martínez, Luis (aka Batman): collecting rafts, 155; death, 278–79; events surrounding shoot-down, 240

Martínez, Raul, 107–8

Martínez García, Julio San Francisco, 195–96

Martyrs' Point, 247, 280

Mas Canosa, Jorge, 75, 142, 202

Matheison, Harold, star witness for JB evidentiary hearing, 268

McNaughton, Bert, 206, 236

Media coverage of BTTR: on leaflet drop, 196–97; on missions, 52–53; plane crashes, 56; on rafter crisis of 1994, 166; support of organization, 24, 98

Menendez, Bob, 271

Miami Air Traffic Control, 223

Migration accords, between U.S. and Cuba: Clinton agreement regarding detainees in Guantánamo, 166; Cuban Adjustment Act, 150; "Wet-feet/Dry-feet," 176–77

Migrations, Cuban: Castro's control of, 155;

Exodus of 1994, 150; history of, 148; Mariel Boatlift, 148–49

Miranda, Guillermo, 82, 100, 295

Molinari, Mike, 234

Monroy, José, and *Ofelia* accident, 104–6

Montes, Ana Belén: meeting with Carroll night before shoot-down, 208, 289; Queen of Cuba, 290; and spy-catcher Scott Carmichael, 289–90; in spy trial, 290

Morales, John Toohey: and leaflets over Havana, 191–92, 194; volunteer for BTTR, *125*, 191; weatherman for Univision, 75, 191

Morales, Nancy, *137*, 273

Morales, Pablo: BTTR volunteer, 115, *135*, 233; events leading to shoot-down, 206; rafter, 115, 154, 206; shoot-down, 211–29. *See also* Barbas, Eva

Morejón Almagro, Leonel: and Cuban Council, 195; donation from BTTR, 201–2; imprisoned, 199; and shoot-down events in Cuba, 230, 241

Mothers Against Repression (M.A.R. por Cuba). *See* Iriondo, Sylvia

Moulis, Michael, FAA attorney, 268

Murciano, Mike: BTTR pilot and background, 81; conflicts of interest between BTTR and his employment, 144–45, 164–65; and spotting Cuban gunboat, 81

Nonviolence philosophy. *See under* Basulto, José: nonviolence philosophy

NORAD (North American Air Defense Command), 215

NTSB (National Transportation Safety Board), and findings in Koki Lares' plane crash, 89, 99

N2506. See *Seagull One*

Nuccio, Richard: premonition of shoot-down, 208–9; in *Shoot Down*, the movie, 278

Nuñez, Charles, 298

Nuñez, Leopoldo (nickname "Polo"): background, 28–29; historian for BTTR, 43, *125*; joins BTTR, 28; post–shoot-down, 232–34

Opa-locka Airport, hangar, 84. *See also* Gregorio Pérez Ricardo Hangar

Operation Able Vigil, 156–57

Operation Dr. Martin Luther King Jr., 192, 199

Orange Bowl stadium, Miami: President Kennedy addresses Brigade 2506, 14; shoot-down memorial, 250–52

Palacios, Major Emilio, Cuban MiG pilot, 225–28
Pantín, Leslie, 247
Paralelo 24, BTTR magazine, 164
Pascual, Sylvia (nickname SSS, *Solo Sylvia Sabe*): joins BTTR, 97–98; mission during Exodus of 1994, 153–54, 156; press release for February 24, 1996, 199
Pekar, Gilberto, *125*
Perdomo, Nick: friendship with Havana ATC, 260–63; repercussions to Havana ATC after shoot-down, 262–63; visit to Havana ATC, 262
Pereda, Lucy, 33
Pérez, Diego, *122*
Pérez, Omar, 1
Pérez Pérez, Francisco (Cuban MiG pilot), 225–28
Pérez Pérez, Lorenzo (Cuban MiG pilot), 225–28
Pérez Ricardo, Gregorio: as catalyst for idea of BTTR, 6–7; death, 3; funeral services, 18–19, *119*; inauguration of hangar named after him, 111–13; journey across the Florida Straits, 1–3
Pilots: nationalities, 111–12; training, 51. *See also* Brothers to the Rescue, procedures
Plá, Osvaldo (nickname "Tito Fufú"): aboard *Democracia* for *13th of March* flotilla, 182, 184–85; background 29–30; ham operator, 70, 143, 239; joins BTTR, 29, *122, 137*; onboard radio transmissions, 142; "Operation Coat Hanger," 93; repeater station, 93; repercussions after shoot-down, 263–64; rescue ideas for BTTR, 30, 70; televised message to Cuba, 142
Powell-Cosío, Sofía: attorney for JB, 267–68; and Eva Barbas, 275; civil disobedience, 177–78; confrontation with FBI, 256; fund-raising for BTTR, 267; meets Basulto, 56; in purchase of *Seagull One*, 57; refers Juan Pablo Roque to BTTR, 143; post–shoot-down, 232–33

Prayer circle. *See under* Brothers to the Rescue
Prellezo, Jorge (NTSB), and findings of Koki Lares' plane crash, 89
Punta de Maisí, flyover, 163, 287
Punto de Mártires. *See* Martyrs' Point
Punto Martí, 19

Radio Martí, 35, 37, 196
Rafters (general): death on the Florida Straits, 81; first U.S.C.G. rescue in history, 18; rafter children of Miami, 257; refusing BTTR help, 159; survival on the Florida Straits, 1, *126, 127, 128, 129*
Rafts, 64, 72, *130*, 155
Ray, Janet (Weininger). *See* Weininger, Janet Ray
Reboredo, Pedro, Miami-Dade County Commissioner: and Barbas, Eva, 266; onboard *Democracia* for *13th of March* memorial, 182, 184; and rumors of shoot-down, 238
Reboso, Manuel, 187
Reno, Janet, 213, 282
Richardson, Bill: meeting in Havana, 202
Robaina, Roberto (Cuban Minister of Foreign Affairs), 243
Rodríguez, Carlos, *125*
Rodríguez, Félix: background ad CIA involvement, 170; dropping ashes of Segundo Borges over Cuba, 171–72
Rodríguez, Mayte. *See* Greco, Mayte
Rodríguez Tejera, Roberto: fund-raising for BTTR, 41; leaflet drop, 194; nonviolence philosophy, 41; post–shoot-down, 231
Román, Agustín (Monsignor), 19
Roque, Ana Margarita. *See* Martínez, Ana Margarita
Roque, Juan Pablo: background, 143–44; book, *Desertor*, 175; courtship and marriage to Ana Margarita Martínez, 174–75; events surrounding shoot-down, 204–5, 238; joins BTTR, 143; and leaflets over Havana, 192–93; misinformation regarding Roque's involvement in shoot-down, 243; pilot for BTTR, *125, 126*; spy for Cuba, 243–44; spy for FBI, 244–45
Ros-Lehtinen, Ileana: Congressional hearing on shoot-down, 270–72; godmother to

BTTR, 47–48, 92, *124*; petitioning President for planes, 48
Rule of law: and indictment of Castro brothers, 281–83, 285; and return of Elián González, 281–82
Russo, Carolyn, 205–6, 214

Sánchez, Alfredo: BTTR pilot, *125*; and Cuban gunboat, 100; events surrounding shoot-down, 206, 235–36, 259; first sighting of Cuban MiGs, 45–46; and René González the spy, 286
Sánchez, Humberto (aka Robin): collector of rafts, 155; Guantánamo protest, 166–67
Sánchez, Ralph, and fund-raiser for BTTR, 295–96
Sánchez, Ramón Saúl: activist, *131*; background, 179–80; civil disobedience, 177; and Comisión Nacional Cubana (National Cuban Commission), 177, 179; and *Democracia*, 180; Democracy Movement, 180, 248, 265, 269, 286; and flotilla to commemorate *13th of March* victims, 179–80; and René González arraignment, 286
Santana, Carlos Rodríguez: and naming of *Seagull One*, N2506, 57; and origins of Brigade 2506, 11
Santana, Father Francisco (priest): blesses *Democracia*, 182; death, 276–77; shoot-down memorial, 247, 249
SEADS (Southeast Air Defense Sector), 223
Seagull One: in hangar, 206, 293–94; naming N2506, 57, *123*, 183–87, 293–94; purchase of, 57; rescues, 61; sale of, 296–300; shoot-down chronology, 206, 211–31, 234; shoot-down memorial, 251; *13th of March* flotilla and flyover of Havana, 183–87
Schuss, Maggie: and Pablo Morales, 114–15, 233, 237; post–shoot-down, 231–33, 237; toys to Guantánamo, 163; work with BTTR, 49, 92, 114
Schuss, William "Billy": BTTR co-founder, 6–7, 20, *120*, *122*, *125*; first mission, 33; first BTTR rescue, 35–38; leaflets over Havana mission, 192–95; operations director, 97; memoir (*Día tras día con los Hermanos al Rescate*), 295; political views, 144; sale of *Seagull One*, 297; shoot-down anniversary,

279; shoot-down events, 231–33, 241; *13th of March* flotilla and flyover of Havana, 181–87; truth and justice for murdered men, 265
Sharp, Gene, of Albert Einstein Institution, 16, 177
Shoot-down of BTTR planes, February 24, 1996: chronology, 211–29; community reactions after, 231–32, 256–58; Cuba denies accusations, 252; events leading to, 202–10, 212; memorial, 247–52; memorial anniversaries, 275–80; New York City meeting with Cuban military, 252; U.S. reaction to, 259–60; world condemnation, 245
Shoot Down, the movie: and JB response to, 278; and Maggie Khuly, 278; released on 10th anniversary, 277–78
Solano, Rafael, 195–96
Sosa, Javier, *125*
Special Period, in Cuba, 64, 145, 149–50
Spy trial: arraignment of spies, 286–87; Basulto as hostile witness, 287; Cuban Five and "Free the Five" campaign, 288–89; René González, 287, 288; of Wasp Network, 286–88. See also González, René
Suarez, Xavier (mayor of Miami): and Koki Lares, 89; visits Guantánamo, 160–61
Subcommittee on the Western Hemisphere of the Committee on International Relations of the House of Representatives, 270–72

Tabernilla, Carlos: background, 106–7; *El Viejo Pancho*, 106; and N5416K plane crash, 54; political views, 144; the Tabernilla Turn, 108, *122*, *125*; visit to Guantánamo, 162
Tamayo, General Arnaldo (Cuban Air Force), and suggestion of shooting down BTTR planes, 203
Tangeman, Captain Anthony "Tony," U.S.C.G., and shoot-down memorial, 248, 250
Tape recording: aboard *Seagull One* regarding shoot-down, 234, 243; United States, of Cuban MiGs, 223, 229, 243, 268
Tester, Hank: and FOIA, 283; reporter for WTVJ, 75–76, *132*, 190; and *13th of March* flotilla and flyover of Havana, 183–89, 287
Tester, Luly (Lourdes González Piñeiro), 187–88

13th of March tugboat: murder of 41 occupants and sinking by Cuban government, 145–49; reaction by Castro, 147; *13th of March* memorial flotilla and flyover of Havana, 185–87; world condemnation of sinking, 146–47, 149, 183–86

Thomas, Mike, of FAA: meeting with JB, 180; testifying at evidentiary hearing, 268

Torrealba, Jennifer, *125*

Transit Center for Cuban Refugees (also called La Casa del Balsero or The Rafter's House): established by Arturo Cobo, 79–80; "Wall of Sorrows," 80, 118

Triana, Arturo (rafter): background, 115–16; journey across the Florida Straits, 116–18; rescue by *Seagull One*, 117

Tri-Liner fishing vessel, during shoot-down, 216, 220, 225, 227–28

Truth and justice, quest for, after shoot-down: by JB, 273, 276, 285; by families of murdered pilots, 265–67, 273; by Ileana Ros-Lehtinen, 270–72. *See also* Indictment of Fidel and Raúl Castro

TV Martí, 142

24th Parallel: description of, 33–34; flying below, 34

Tyndall Air Force Base, 209

United Nations Declaration of Human Rights: Cuba as a signatory, 178, 191; 30 articles printed on leaflets floated over Havana, 191, 198, 276

U.S. Coast Guard: effects of "Wet-feet/Dry-feet" on, 176; Exodus of 1994, 154–55; first meeting with BTTR, 23–24; news coverage, 81; Operation Able Vigil, 156–57; patrol area, Sector 7, 2; rescues, 62, 71, *127*; respect due to, 72–73; search and rescue post–shoot-down, 241

U.S. Customs, recorded conversations during shoot-down, 283–84

U.S. Department of Justice, and rule of law, 285

Valiant Air Command: delivery of toys to Guantánamo, 164; and *Tico Belle*, 164

Valladares, Ernesto (nickname "Ñañy"), crossing of Florida Straits, 66–72. *See also* García, Alexis

Van Hare, Thomas: background, 77–78; Elbow Cay drop (black birds), 109–10; filming *Ofelia* accident, 104–6; inspection of Walton's plane, 94–95; organization for BTTR, 78

Vázquez, Fabio, *125*

Virgin of Charity Church, 18, 54

"Wall of Sorrows," at Transit Center, 80, 118

Walton, Steve: background, 94; and *Big Red*, 96, 108–9, *127*; filming *Ofelia* accident, 104–6; first find, 97; flight with JB, 97; joins BTTR, 94–95, *122*, *125*; Red Cross appliqué on plane, 96; suggestions for rescues, 95–96, 117; and toys to Guantánamo, 163–64

"Washing machine," 6

Wasp Network of spies, and trial, 286–87, 290

Webber, Conrad: background, 24–28; first rescue, 41–43; joins BTTR, 27, *125*; shoot-down anniversary, 279

Weininger, Janet Ray: background, 101–3; and Homestead Air Force Base pilots, 285; joins BTTR, 103; and lawsuits against Cuba's frozen assets, 266, 272–73; letters to Castro for Pete Ray's body, 102; and warnings to JB, 246, 266

"Wet-Feet/Dry-Feet" policy, 176

Willy, Colonel Frank, 271

Lily Prellezo is an author living in Miami with her husband, Steve.

José Basulto is a dreamer, patriot, and family man.